Billy Graham and the Rise of the Republican South

POLITICS AND CULTURE
IN MODERN AMERICA

SERIES EDITORS
Glenda Gilmore, Michael Kazin, and
Thomas J. Sugrue

Volumes in the series narrate and analyze political and
social change in the broadest dimensions from 1865 to
the present, including ideas about the ways people have
sought and wielded power in the public sphere and the
language and institutions of politics at all levels—local,
national, and transnational. The series is motivated by
a desire to reverse the fragmentation of modern U.S.
history and to encourage synthetic perspectives on
social movements and the state, on gender, race, and
labor, and on intellectual history and popular culture.

Billy Graham and the Rise of the Republican South

Steven P. Miller

UNIVERSITY OF PENNSYLVANIA PRESS

PHILADELPHIA

Published by
University of Pennsylvania Press
Philadelphia, Pennsylvania 19104-4112

Printed in the United States of America on acid-free paper
10 9 8 7 6 5 4 3 2 1

Library of Congress Cataloging-in-Publication Data

Miller, Steven P.
    Billy Graham and the rise of the Republican South / Steven P. Miller.
        p.   cm. (Politics and culture in modern America)
    Includes bibliographical references (p.) and index.
    ISBN: 978-0-8122-4151-8 (alk. paper)
        1. Graham, Billy, 1918– —Political and social views.   2. Graham, Billy, 1918– —Influence.
3. Civil rights—Southern States—History—20th century.   4. Religion and politics—Southern
States.   4. Christianity and politics—Southern States.   5. Evangelists—United States—Biography.
6. Southern States—Race relations—History—20th century.   7. Southern States—Social
conditions—20th century.   8. Southern States—Religious life and customs.   I. Title.
BV3785.G69M45   2009
269'.2092—dc22
[B]

2008040924

CONTENTS

Billy Graham's New South

IN JUNE 2005, an elderly Billy Graham returned to New York City, five decades after a foundational moment in his evangelistic career, when he had led a crusade that stretched on for four months in that most secular of American locales. This time, stricken with prostate cancer and symptoms of Parkinson's disease, among other health problems, and reliant on a special lectern that allowed him to sit while preaching, the white-haired Graham held only three services during what was billed as his final domestic crusade. Most of the 230,000-plus attendees knew what to expect from this evangelistic lion in winter. Many elements of Graham's services had remained largely unchanged since the 1950s: the bass-baritone of soloist George Beverley Shea, the volunteer choir and ushers drawn from area churches, the climactic and solemn moment of invitation, and—of course—the presence of celebrities and politicians on the crusade platform. The highest-profile guests in Flushing Meadows were Hillary and Bill Clinton, who feted the evangelist. Standing with Graham at the pulpit, the former president said his admiration for the evangelist had its origins in an integrated Graham rally he had attended as a child in Little Rock, Arkansas. Clinton elaborated on that 1959 service in an interview with the *New Yorker*: "When he gave the call—amid all the civil-rights trouble, to see blacks and whites coming down the aisle together at the football stadium, which is the scene, of course, of our great football rivalries and all that meant to people in Arkansas—it was an amazing, amazing thing. If you weren't there, and if you're not a southerner, and if you didn't live through it, it's hard to explain. It made an enormous impression on me."[1]

As journalists filed datelines that read like obituaries, Graham's status as the grandfather of modern American evangelicalism seemed to set him above the ebb and flow of history. The 2005 New York crusade coverage was a commentary on both the grace of time and the thoroughly mainstream status of Graham's brand of Christianity at the start of the twenty-first century. In the decades following the civil rights movement, Vietnam, and Watergate, Graham had softened his tone and had impressed former critics by embracing nuclear disarmament and criticizing the Christian Right. He also benefited from an irenic demeanor that grew more convincing with age. His refusal to cast stones in the culture wars, as numerous commentators observed, stood in refreshing relief from the rhetorical gauntlets thrown down by Pat Robertson, James Dobson, and even Graham's own son and heir apparent, Franklin. Billy Graham, one writer noted, had "figured out how to triangulate American Protestant Christianity," how to cultivate mainstream appeal without burning conservative bridges. The new consensus saw Graham as "a source of unity" for the nation, left and right alike. He had come to represent the better half of an evangelicalism that again stood as the ascendant religious force in American society. His more controversial days—1971, for example, when two Southern Baptist dissidents branded him a "court prophet" in the Nixon White House, or 1958, when a Deep South governor echoed the sentiments of many segregationists in castigating him as a southerner whose "endorsement of racial mixing has done much harm"—seemed more distant than his first crusade in New York.[2]

The past resurfaced often enough, however, to suggest the fallacy of evaluating Graham solely by the standard of his sanguine final chapters. Three years before the 2005 New York crusade, Graham sloughed off a final round of residue from the Nixon years: the release of a recorded White House conversation in which the evangelist appeared readily to affirm the president's anti-Semitic ranting. With the help of a leading evangelical public relations specialist, Graham responded to the disclosure with swift, if somewhat puzzled, contrition, apologizing to Jewish leaders for words he could not remember uttering.[3] He had long stressed that his flirtation with politics had come to an end. Still, only two years earlier, on the cusp of the 2000 presidential election, Graham offered effusive support for Republican candidate George W. Bush, who credited the evangelist with sparking his journey toward born-again Christianity.[4] And a decade before this second Bush assumed office, Graham had spent a night in the White House with George H. W. and

Barbara Bush watching television coverage of the start of the Persian Gulf War—a fact the president soon recounted at the National Prayer Breakfast.[5] During an era when religion and politics consorted brashly and unapologetically (and when Graham no longer commanded sustained media coverage), these incidents drew merely passing attention.

Clearly, the snapshot of Graham in New York City captured only the twilight of a remarkable career that dated back to the end of World War II. Since the early 1950s, Graham has never relinquished his status as one of the most recognizable and respected of Americans, someone who has mingled comfortably with the powerful, while retaining the common touch. As scholar of religion Joe Barnhart recognized in the early 1970s, the evangelist functioned during his peak years of influence as a kind of conduit through which flowed much of the zeitgeist of the latter half of the twentieth century. Yet Graham was not, as Barnhart went on to contend, merely "an innocent tool of complex dynamics which he may little understand or appreciate."[6]

Rather, Graham was a public actor in his own right—a point this book seeks to demonstrate. In engaging political leaders and the pressing issues of his times, he made important decisions that, while always weighed against his higher priorities as an evangelist, reflected his own values, his own notion of the social and spiritual good. Graham's power, that is, was simultaneously readily visible and more than what met the eye.

Nowhere was Graham's public and private sway more evident than in his native region of the American South, the central (although not the exclusive) purview of this book. Graham's national and international prominence has understandably obscured the southern origins and identity of the Charlotte-born evangelist, who possesses a distinct drawl, whose grandfathers both fought for the Confederacy, and who has made Montreat, North Carolina, his primary residence since 1945. He was a southerner by birth and remained one by choice. Likewise obscured are the keen ways in which Graham paralleled and influenced the course of the post–World War II and post–civil rights era South. Bill Clinton understood this influence, yet voiced only one facet of it on the crusade platform in New York. During the decades after 1950, the South experienced two significant, related shifts away from its status as a "Solid South": the end of legalized Jim Crow and the end of Democratic Party dominance.[7] Through Graham's social ethic, which I term *evangelical universalism*, as well as the political ethic it helped to inspire, which I term the *politics of decency*, the evangelist had a hand in both trends.

A World—and Regional—Figure

This book seeks to reintroduce a familiar figure to the narrative of southern history and, in the process, examine the political and social transitions constitutive of the modern South. It considers the important role Graham played in creating that South, focusing on his behavior and rhetoric regarding the overlapping realms of religion, politics, and race, particularly during the decades after 1950. In these years, the North Carolinian maintained a visible and controversial presence in a region witnessing the civil rights movement and the beginning of political realignment. Alternately a desegregating crusader in Alabama, regional booster in Atlanta, southern apologist in the national press, and southern strategist in the Nixon administration, Graham functioned as a type of regional leader—a product of his times and a player in them, a symbol and an actor. His evangelical Christianity mediated the emergence of a post–civil rights era South simultaneously more open to desegregation and more amenable to Republican Party politics.

Graham's life can tell us much about the modern South in all its ambiguities; viewing him through the lens of southern history can, in turn, enhance our understanding of the evangelist. Like most southerners of his generation, he grew up in a part of the country that was rife with segregation laws, solidly Democratic, and overwhelmingly evangelical. His career coincided with the end of the first two characteristics, although not the third. From the mid-1950s through the mid-1960s, he came to support desegregation, discreetly consulted with Martin Luther King, Jr., and advocated racial tolerance in such national publications as *Life* and *Ebony*. At the same time, Graham remained a member of a Southern Baptist congregation led by the outspoken segregationist W. A. Criswell—and, in the eyes of several conservative moguls, the evangelist was a viable candidate for the 1964 GOP presidential nomination.

Graham held his first intentionally desegregated southern crusade in 1953, before most of the landmark events of the civil rights era. As he began holding desegregated services (that is, services with racially mixed seating patterns) throughout the Upper South, he received public criticism from ardent segregationists. The evangelist largely avoided the Deep South until the mid-1960s, when he visited Alabama and held highly publicized rallies and crusades in the aftermath of racial violence in Birmingham and Selma. The pinnacle of Graham's career coincided with the first term of the Nixon administration and the fitful emergence of what commentators began calling the Sunbelt South.

Starting with President Dwight Eisenhower and continuing through Lyndon Johnson and Richard Nixon, politicians looked to Graham for regional leadership on civil rights matters, particularly among the evangelist's presumed constituency of white southerners. The evangelist consulted with Eisenhower about the Little Rock desegregation crisis and in subsequent years met with a host of regional politicians, including Alabama governor George Wallace. Later, Graham supported the Office of Economic Opportunity (the principal agency for implementing Johnson's War on Poverty) and acceded to a Nixon administration request to record television and radio spots promoting obedience to school integration and busing laws. Yet Graham was more than just a consultant or figurehead. Although nominally a registered Democrat throughout his adult life, he paralleled—and in certain respects, spoke for—those white southerners, many of them with moderate inclinations, who supported Eisenhower, backed Johnson, and then voted Republican again, for Nixon.[8] Through his relationship with Nixon, in particular, Graham functioned as a political strategist and abetted the president's controversial, if not always successful, "southern strategy."

This is a story Graham scholars have inadequately explored and southern historians have largely ignored. As a popular (and popularizing) figure, Graham has always received more attention from journalists than from academics. The earliest scholarly study of Graham, a 1960 biography, casts him as the somewhat atavistic flagship evangelist of a new Great Awakening. During the Nixon era, a generation of scholars offered informed, often lively, polemics about an evangelist they viewed as an agent of civil religion and a spokesperson for the "silent majority."[9] Graham eventually drew more attention from academic historians, who ably treated him in relation to a number of broad trends, such as Cold War religiosity and the emergence of modern American evangelicalism.[10] Several recent studies have focused on aspects of Graham's social ethic.[11] Missing is a comprehensive treatment of Graham's influence on his native South, despite the fact that a committee of prominent historians, journalists, and public intellectuals ranked him as the fourth most influential southerner of the twentieth century, behind only King, William Faulkner, and Elvis Presley.[12]

Two broad interpretations have dominated portraits of the modern South that took shape during Graham's career. Some have cast the South as a dynamic region of economic vitality and demographic relevance (the foil of the Rustbelt North), while others have seen it as the birthplace of a popular conservative ascendancy traversing both faith and politics (the foil of the bicoastal liberal elite).[13] These seemingly contradictory interpretations are evident in the constructed landscape of the region. The banking center of Charlotte, North Carolina, and the fundamentalist bastion of Bob Jones University in Greenville, South Carolina, can be seen to symbolize modernity and reaction, respectively, while Newt Gingrich's booming Cobb County, Georgia, and Pat Robertson's colossal Christian Broadcasting Network (CBN) headquarters in Virginia Beach blend elements of both. Those interpretations are embodied in an equally diverse range of political symbols, including Richard Nixon's and Ronald Reagan's outreach to the white South, Jimmy Carter's and Bill Clinton's New South personas, and George W. Bush's vaunted electoral "base." Significantly for this book, all of these symbols also intersect in some way with the life and career of Billy Graham. The evangelist was born in 1918 in what half a century later became a thriving section of Charlotte, briefly attended Bob Jones College (then located in Cleveland, Tennessee) in 1936, operated an evangelistic office in suburban Atlanta from 1964 to 1976, and dedicated the CBN building in 1979.

Recalled at the close of Graham's remarkable sixty-year run as an evangelist and pastor to kings and commoners alike, such intersections might appear as coincidences or asides in a career that has taken place mostly outside the South. They might also be viewed as mere epiphenomena of the larger historical forces that, through the blessings of time and place, propelled Graham toward fame and influence. After all, the evangelist has not resided in his hometown since the mid-1930s, lasted less than one semester under the thumb of Bob Jones, Sr., maintained his organization's official headquarters in Minneapolis until the present century, and moved comfortably among political figures as liberal as Sargent Shriver and as conservative as Strom Thurmond. For these and other reasons, many Americans, regardless of their theological and political leanings, see Graham as a transcendent icon—and, in an era of culture wars and intense partisanship, as a beacon of stability and graciousness. He has, indeed, become all of these things. However, it would be unfortunate for our understanding of Graham's historical legacy, as well as recent southern history, if his familiarity was to overwhelm his complexity.

Graham, Evangelicalism, and Social Change

Any attempt to interpret how Graham affected his home region of the South requires a step back to consider the influence of modern American evangelicalism on public life. This, in turn, necessitates a historically grounded understanding of evangelicalism that distinguishes it from fundamentalism, its older sibling. Modern evangelicalism has its roots in the pointed doctrinal debates (and periodic divisions) that riled American Protestantism during the early decades of the twentieth century. Fundamentalism, an identity both chosen and ascribed, strongly resisted the influence of theological liberals (eventually termed "modernists") who saw a need to reinterpret their faith amid the challenges posed by biblical higher criticism and Darwinian scientific inquiry. Fundamentalists sought to hold the doctrinal line in what they came to view as a fallen, secularized society. Beginning in the 1940s, evangelicalism in its modern sense emerged as a moderate critique of the fundamentalist hard line. Most of these "neo-evangelicals" had few serious theological qualms with fundamentalism, yet they did desire greater engagement with society at large. By the late 1950s, the divide between fundamentalists and evangelicals had widened to the point of self-conscious differentiation. While fundamentalists initiated the breach, evangelicals like Graham were aware of the public relations benefit of distinguishing themselves from their confrontational (and often controversial) brethren.

Since the 1970s, evangelicalism has boomed both as a badge of identity and as a subject of inquiry for journalists and scholars, in the process stretching the limits of the term's conceptual clarity. At least one prominent historian of American Christianity has recently wished it good riddance as a unit of analysis.[14] As a historian, I appreciate how giving such a term descriptive power risks belying the tensions, fluidity, and general diversity of American Christianity. Yet I also recall my own experiences coming of age in a small Shenandoah Valley community. As a bookish child, I was aware of the theological differences between my rural Mennonite congregation and the Southern Baptist church back in town—especially on matters of military service. Still, despite their overall lack of interaction, the Mennonites and Baptists of Stuarts Draft, Virginia, shared much more than the practice of adult baptism. My own decision to declare my Christian faith came at the young but not preternatural age of ten, and featured elements that might have occurred inside both sanctuaries: the response to an anticipated invitation during the annual revival week, the singing of "Just as I Am, Without One Plea" and "Softly and Tenderly Jesus is Calling," the slow walk forward, the laying on of hands. In worship style and other respects, my fellow congregants drew inspiration not from the prophetic martyrdom of their sixteenth-century Anabaptist forebears but rather from the evangelical instincts of neighboring believers.

Evangelicalism was an avowed, internalized identity for many of the subjects considered here—including, of course, for Graham. Like "liberal" and "conservative," "evangelical" has become a pervasive modifier that, while often frustratingly vague and perpetually contested, has joined the pantheon of American identities. During the years considered here, evangelicalism stood apart from Protestant liberalism and most other forms of mainline denominationalism, as well as from Roman Catholicism and Orthodoxy. Analytically, evangelicalism remains a useful category for interpreting the type of cross-denominational faith Graham and many others upheld—a piety too specific for the label "Protestant" or "conservative," yet obviously much too broad for "Baptist" or "Pentecostal."[15] My intention is not casually to disregard important distinctions among the many traditions that inform modern American evangelicalism, be they theological, denominational, or regional in substance. The very nature of Graham's ministry, however, has lent itself to an elision of such categories. Evangelicalism has worked most influentially on a large and small scale, as a sweeping social force and as a discrete movement within individual souls. The same is true of the expression of evangelicalism most identified with Graham: revivalism.[16]

This book employs an expansive understanding of evangelicalism as operating simultaneously on theological, sociological, and temperamental levels. Evangelicalism holds to doctrinal orthodoxy and biblicism, while emphasizing the born-again moment, a personal relationship with God, and the importance of sharing the good news of salvation. It also features self-conscious, cross-denominational networks of like-minded believers. Finally, evangelicalism can be seen as an attitudinal posture with several leanings. It tends toward individuation and a pietistic emphasis on the correspondence between personal conversion and the transformation of character. Also, during the years considered here, it evinced a habitual wariness toward nonreligious social institutions, along with a more forthright skepticism about religious and political liberalism—stances rooted in ambivalence about the status of evangelicalism in American society.

The above characteristics have applied to evangelicalism in both the South and the nation at large, even though the southern variety has tended to maintain distinctive institutions and communities of discourse. Within the South, even into the present century, evangelicalism has often functioned much more as a general faith.[17] It has served as a kind of informal establishment or point of reference in keeping with the broader American tradition of church-state separation and denominational pluralism. Significantly, Graham bridged both the national and the more particularly southern varieties of evangelicalism.[18]

Delineating the sociopolitical space Graham occupied as a postwar white evangelical requires understanding the nature of his social ethic, here termed *evangelical universalism*. This social ethic, which subsequent chapters explore in detail, featured three coexistent (if not always complementary) tenets: that the individual soul is the primary theological and political unit in society; that relational solutions greatly surpass legislative ones in resolving social problems; and that Christians should, in most cases, acquiesce to ordained governmental authority. This ethic was the product of a self-conscious evangelical pedigree that extended back to the transatlantic revivalism of the eighteenth and nineteenth centuries. Yet evangelical universalism held particular implications for postwar America. In the case of Graham, it is the key to appreciating the depth of his larger impact on the American South.

To a somewhat surprising degree, historians of recent southern religion have shied away from acknowledging the full range of white evangelicalism's influence on social change.[19] Such reticence reflects the legacy of earlier scholars who offered what might be termed the *crisis motif* of southern religious history, stressing the extent to which the white church in the South had not addressed the full needs of its society, particularly in the area of race relations.[20] This emphasis, despite its obvious applicability to numerous facets of the southern religious landscape, can distract from the diverse ways evangelicalism has influenced the modern South.[21] This is certainly true for Graham. Take a 1965 remark attributed to Graham concerning the role of the church in social issues, to the effect that "the church should not answer questions the people aren't asking." The line, which appeared during a time when the civil rights movement was very much in the headlines, resurfaced in a 1967 *Atlantic* article critical of white southern Christianity. Two decades later, a historian used the same remark to cast Graham as emblematic of a white southern "flight from reality," yet remained unaware of one complicating factor. The words came from the advance text of a sermon given in Dothan, Alabama, where the evangelist was holding desegregated revival services, much to the displeasure of the local Citizens' Council.[22] The moral limitations of white southern evangelicalism during the civil rights era, then, are not the only story worth telling.

The crisis motif tends to obscure how Graham's type of evangelical

Christianity was capable, in its own way, of shaping change in the South.[23] Those influences shifted with time. During the immediate postwar years, as Graham and many other mainstream white southern Christians began to distance themselves from Jim Crow apologetics, evangelical piety dulled as a weapon in the segregationist arsenal. That phenomenon, however, scarcely implied larger shifts toward theological or political liberalism—a reality the 1970s Sunbelt ideal only reinforced. Indeed, the rise of a highly organized Christian Right and the growth of televangelism occurred as the civil rights era came to an end.

The interpretations of Graham and evangelicalism embraced here have a number of implications that extend beyond the purview of southern history. This book treats Graham, first and foremost, as an evangelist but also, at times, as a politician, a spokesperson, and a regional leader. Similarly, evangelicalism is understood primarily as a faith perspective and identity but also as a posture with profound sociopolitical implications—or, put more simply, as the expression of born-again Protestantism in the American public sphere. The book seeks to avoid making either religion or political culture a residual product of the other.[24] Likewise, the intention here is not to reinforce what is sometimes an unfortunate division between how religious history is written by scholars trained in the field of religious studies and those housed in history departments. If political historians risk caricaturing evangelicalism as reflexively otherworldly or as merely a cultural component of economic conservatism, historians of evangelicalism have too often employed a language of insularity, focusing on the minutiae of terminology and social networks. This book aspires instead to model a dynamic middle ground between treating religious language with the sophistication it deserves and situating evangelicalism in relation to larger changes in political culture. It offers a kind of history in which the worlds of faith and politics at times intersect seamlessly, in which religious and secular actors and motivations overlap and blend, sometimes without clear distinctions between them.[25] Hence, the social ethic of evangelical universalism possessed a secular corollary, the *politics of decency*, which invoked "law and order," along with evangelical faith, toward moderate ends.

In the life of Graham, as for the South as a whole, such blending was often an everyday phenomenon. This was true even though many southern evangelicals have historically tended to cast the *seam*less quality of the religious and political spheres as *seem*less, drawing from variations on the venerable Southern Presbyterian doctrine of the "spirituality of the church" (emphasizing the duty of the church to reinforce, rather than impede or challenge, the social order overseen by the state) or the Southern Baptist notion of "soul competency" (stressing the primacy of the individual soul and conscience before God). Both perspectives—or, later, their mid-twentieth-century articulations—were selectively employed to limit the social responsibilities of the church during the civil rights era.[26] Graham knew these traditions intimately. He was baptized into a strict Calvinist denomination (Associate Reformed Presbyterian), was nurtured by a mother with ties to the Plymouth Brethren, was rebaptized as a Southern Baptist during young adulthood, and married into a prominent Southern Presbyterian family a few years later. Thus, although this book seeks to counter the tendency of political histories not to take religion seriously, it also adopts a respectful suspicion toward the many mid-century religious figures, Graham included, who tended to characterize their work as solely conversion centered and, hence, wholly nonpolitical.

By analyzing Graham as a significant historical figure, this book treats him as a serious actor and, at times, as a powerful symbol. Graham's familiarity and seeming consistency can sometimes dull an appreciation for his complexity—not as an intellectual or original thinker but, like many politicians, as a public figure with a telling knack for locating the pulse of sociopolitical change. Certainly, someone who (to cite a few among many achievements) contributed more than any other single person to the renaissance of evangelical Christianity in post–World War II America, once addressed an audience of one million during a crusade service in South Korea and routinely met with the leaders of such nations as India, Ethiopia, and Israel scarcely requires justification as a subject of historical analysis.[27] Yet even these high-profile achievements do not fully capture his roles as a political actor and, importantly for this book, as a regional leader.

Gaining insight into these sides of Graham necessitates analyzing both his private and his public dimensions, weighing the Graham of crusade services and press conferences against the Graham of private correspondence and backroom consultations. These spheres, which sometimes (but by no means always) conflicted with each other, constituted parts of a whole. In his public role, Graham was an effective communicator, more consistent than charismatic, with an ability to think on his feet and a talent for staying on task. In his private role, he was an energetic networker greatly attracted to politics and eager to seek out political leaders, whom he selectively attempted to influence, for whom he sometimes did bidding, and by whom he occasionally let himself be used.

Graham was always more of a political creature than either those who praised or dismissed him would concede. He was more of a political creature than even he could admit. Not unlike a rather different communicator par excellence, Ronald Reagan, Graham offers a profound commentary on the underappreciated synergy between innocence and influence, along with the analytical challenge of untangling the two. In Graham's relationships with public figures, he combined an obvious degree of ingenuousness with a much more subtle dose of savvy. This book, then, emphasizes Graham as an independent actor whose actions were also open to myriad influences and applications.

The central story of the book concerns the birth of the post–civil rights era South—and Graham's contribution thereto. Ultimately, Graham represents an illuminating lens through which to consider the relationship between evangelical Christianity and sociopolitical change in the American South. As such, he suggests American evangelicalism's particular relationship to evolving social and political currents—how revivalism and evangelical public theology, while embracing traditional forms of belief, can also sanction new expressions of those same values. These dynamics have resulted in a mercurial mixture of continuity and discontinuity that has made the post–civil rights era South an intriguing and challenging region to interpret. In his simultaneously influential and circumscribed roles as evangelist, peer of political leaders, and regional spokesperson, Graham was both a nexus for, and driver of, many developments central to the creation of the post–civil rights era South. He supplied an acceptable path upon which white southern moderates could back away from Jim Crow, and his postsegregation rhetoric portended the emergence of "color blind" rhetoric within mainstream conservatism. Through both his involvement in the Eisenhower and Nixon administrations and his deep social ties in the South, the evangelist also created space for the decades-long process of political realignment. In the end, Graham suggests the peculiarly evangelical nature of the South's rapprochement with modernity. Such is Billy Graham's New South.

CHAPTER ONE

"No Segregation at the Altar"

*Growing up in the rural South, I had adopted the attitudes of that
region without much reflection.*
　　—Billy Graham, 1997

The audience may be segregated, but there is no segregation at the altar.
　　—Billy Graham, 1952

BILLY GRAHAM ENTERED the 1950s as a nationally known evangelist who
was also an identifiable southerner and a Christian fundamentalist. The following decade saw a struggle—sometimes public, often unstated—between
his singular position as an evangelist and the other, seemingly more expend-
able, labels. While parting ways with many of his fundamentalist allies, Graham chose to retain his regional identity. This decision meant he would
ultimately have to address the specifically southern problem he and his fellow
moderates politely called the "race question" or the "race problem" (hesitant
as they were to use the more prescriptive term "civil rights"). Graham's
southern identity was evident in many things—his theological sensibilities,
his political and social relationships, and his zealous Cold War apocalyptic-
ism—but expressed itself most strikingly when civil rights reemerged as a
national issue in the early 1950s. As an evangelist, Graham also situated his
response to race within the larger context of his ministerial priorities, which
in many respects transcended matters of region. At some level, he attempted
to square his inherited racial customs with his theology, his southern background with his increasingly inclusive ministry.

Graham's early response to the race issue revealed the elusive nature of his racial moderation. During the post–World War II years preceding the rise of "massive resistance" to desegregation in the South—a time when even parts of the Deep South were not yet a completely "closed society" on matters of race[1]—Graham formulated views and rhetorical postures that lasted him for decades. He evolved from a tacit segregationist to a tepid critic of Jim Crow and, finally, to a practitioner of desegregation in his crusade services. The sources and motivations for his changing stance on racial segregation ranged from the theological to the intellectual and the political. They included his exposure to theological spheres outside southern fundamentalism, his concern about his public image, his desire to evangelize within the black community, and his burgeoning Cold War internationalism.

In his discussion of racial matters, Graham retained a familiar evangelical language buttressed by both his celebrity status and his recognizability as a southerner. He also cultivated public positions reflective of his regional affiliation: defensiveness about the South, denunciation of "extremists on both sides" of the civil rights debate, and prophecy of racial disharmony in the North. Graham's actions were never radical, and he cultivated close ties with southern politicians of all stripes. Still, he implicitly (and, with time, explicitly) acknowledged and accepted the fact that the Jim Crow system was on borrowed time—theologically and, quite possibly, politically. While not playing as visible a role in the South during the first half of the 1950s as he later would, Graham paved the ground for his subsequent regional leadership.

The Making of a Racial Moderate

Graham first entered the national spotlight in the fall of 1949 during his two-month-long Christ for Greater Los Angeles campaign. The Los Angeles revival holds a firm place in the Graham mythology. He came to Southern California as a representative, if quite successful, preacher following the well-traveled fundamentalist revival circuit. By the close of the Los Angeles meeting, held in an elaborate circus tent dubbed the "Canvas Cathedral," Graham stood as the heir apparent of Billy Sunday, the last nationally prominent male evangelist, whose career had peaked in the 1910s.

Graham arrived in Los Angeles toward the start of a well-publicized postwar national religious revival that eventually saw Congress add "one nation under God" to the Pledge of Allegiance. Churches and synagogues boomed along with the birth rate. The Southern Baptist Convention (SBC), Graham's chosen denomination, saw five hundred new churches built between 1946 and 1949, with the denomination growing by around 300,000 members during the same period. "Religion-in-general," in historian Martin E. Marty's famous phrase, gained new credence during the postwar years. "Our government," President Dwight Eisenhower flatly declared, "makes no sense unless it is founded on a deeply felt religious faith—and I don't care what it is." Such reflexive, but not self-reflexive, "faith in faith," as Marty also called it, did not inevitably portend a revival of the old-time gospel.[2] Yet it certainly offered an opening for an evangelist claiming that the faith of the fathers could resolve the conundrums of modern man.

The Christ for Greater Los Angeles campaign took a while to gain steam. The pivotal moment came when newspaper mogul William Randolph Hearst ordered his army of editors to "Puff Graham," words that Graham supporters have happily recounted almost from the moment their effects first registered. Hearst, who was likely drawn to the strident anticommunist message of the dynamic young evangelist, had already "puffed" Youth for Christ (YFC), the evangelistic organization for which Graham then worked. This time, the instructions stuck. Word about the lanky young evangelist quickly spread from the headlines of Los Angeles newspapers to the pages of *Time*, *Life*, and *Newsweek*.[3] Graham became a religious media phenomenon to a degree unseen on North American soil since the eighteenth-century peregrinations of English evangelist George Whitefield. The hoopla thrust Graham into a national mainstream from whose current he has rarely strayed since.

Graham's success in Los Angeles and other areas outside his native South had more to do with his southern background than is initially apparent. In his early career, the evangelist benefited from the continuing migration of white southerners westward and northward in search of industrial jobs. The white southern diaspora, a phenomenon less explored than the related Great Migration of black southerners, left a distinct imprint on twentieth-century American Christianity. The 1949 Los Angeles revival drew strength from the many fundamentalist-inclined "country preachers" who had moved from Arkansas, Texas, and Oklahoma to the "Southland" of California. The list included Methodist fundamentalist "Fighting" Bob Shuler, a Texas transplant. Long Beach radio station KGER, owned by Arkansas fundamentalist entrepreneur John Brown, was the first to broadcast news of the upcoming revival meetings. Radio host and country and western musician Stuart Hamblen, the first of several celebrity converts in Los Angeles, hailed from Texas. Simi-

lar patterns appeared elsewhere. The chair of Graham's 1952 Detroit crusade
was a southern preacher. So was the powerful fundamentalist Baptist minister
William Bell Riley, a Kentucky native who in 1947 appointed Graham to
succeed him as president of Northwestern Schools in Minneapolis.[4]

Unlike the preachers of the southern diaspora, Graham was a "commut-
ing southerner," rather than a migrant.[5] Even though the evangelist built his
reputation in the Midwest, especially through his partnership with Torrey
Johnson—head of the Chicago-based YFC—he remained a southerner in the
eyes of most of the public, as well as in his own. In 1952, Graham struck a
Time writer as a flamboyant product of the country South whose concept of
fashion entailed "a jaunty sky-blue gabardine," along with "a blue and white
tie and square-folded white handkerchief, thick-soled, reddish-brown shoes,
a cowboy belt with a silver buckle and silver tip." Graham also played the
part in his language patterns. He closed his ABC radio broadcast with the
colloquial send-off, "May the Lord bless you real good," and referred to the
daughter of President Harry Truman in personal correspondence as "Miss
Margaret."[6]

Newfound fame both permitted and forced Graham to address a host of
national concerns beyond the purview of altar calls and gaudy garb. On one
such issue, the global threat of communism, Graham never hesitated to voice
his opinion. On another matter, race, he remained strikingly more circumspect. When he did address the race issue, however, he spoke not only as an
evangelist but also as a southerner whose background lent him a certain
amount of the authority on the subject.

Like most white southerners of his generation, Graham grew up as a
de facto segregationist—in his own words, someone who "had adopted the
attitudes of that region without much reflection." In this and other senses,
his southern heritage was impeccable. As the evangelist would proudly note
throughout his lifetime, he was descended from Confederate veterans on
both sides of the family. In Graham's rural home area of Sharon Township,
located just outside Charlotte, his Scotch-Irish, God-fearing, dairy-farming
family was of a demographic type. Like the South as a whole, Graham later
reflected in his autobiography, his section of the North Carolina Piedmont
"had never fully recovered economically from the Civil War and Reconstruction." A successful dairy enterprise, however, put the Grahams comfortably
above the economic mean, even during the Great Depression. The local African Americans whom Graham knew best were thus family employees. Later,
he reminisced with unintended condescension about his childhood admira-

tion for Reese Brown, a black foreman who had "a tremendous capacity for working hard" and whose wife made "fabulous buttermilk biscuits in the tenant house that was their home." Such fond memories reflected an up-bringing in which racial moderation translated as benevolent paternalism. (In 1965, during a ceremony in which Graham received an honor for his work on racial issues, Graham praised Brown and presented the aging man with a watch.)[7]

The Christian faith of Graham's youth did not challenge his racial worldview—nor was there good reason to expect it would. In 1934, as a scrawny, playful teenager, Graham famously responded to the brimstone-laden altar call of Kentucky evangelist Mordecai Ham. The hard-hitting re-vivalist who drew Graham down the sawdust trail was a militant fundamen-talist whom Graham later felt compelled to defend against charges of anti-Semitism and support for the Ku Klux Klan.[8] "Even after my conversion," Graham admitted in 1960, "I felt no guilt in thinking of my dark-skinned brothers in the usual patronizing and paternalistic way."[9] His gradual racial awakening did not commence for another decade and a half, after he had attended such segregated institutions as Bob Jones College, whose tightly regimented environment he endured for a mere semester, and Florida Bible Institute, another unaccredited fundamentalist school, from which he gradu-ated in 1940.

A key component of Graham's racial evolution was his exposure during the early 1940s to a moderate brand of northern Protestant fundamentalism then beginning the protracted but conclusive process of refashioning itself as "evangelicalism." Graham entered this world by way of Wheaton, Illinois, a town thirty miles west of Chicago that served as an incubator for the neo-evangelical project. His 1940 enrollment at Wheaton College represented one of the few times the budding preacher had crossed the Mason-Dixon line. At Wheaton, Graham remembered, "people looked at me curiously, as if my heavily accented drawl were a foreign language."[10] The racial views of south-erners of Graham's generation often evolved in the context of comparatively moderate racial environments.[11] While a city like New York or Austin more classically fitted the bill, Chicagoland fundamentalism provided an impetus for Graham's views on race to evolve.

Graham would most likely never have become the leading spokesperson for postwar American evangelicalism had he not passed through Wheaton, then, as now, a leading institution of higher education within conservative, nonmainline Protestant circles. The history of Wheaton paralleled—and, in many respects, influenced—the trajectory of American evangelicalism itself. The college, as Graham occasionally noted later in his career, had deep roots in antebellum evangelical abolitionism. Under the leadership of President Jonathan Blanchard (who took over the newly renamed Wheaton College in 1860), the school presented itself as an abolitionist, coeducational institution in the best tradition of antebellum evangelical reform. The brother of abolitionist martyr Elijah Lovejoy served as a trustee, and early alums included a nephew of Harriet Beecher Stowe. Blanchard made a point of admitting and granting scholarships to black students. Even though Wheaton's commitment to social reform weakened considerably into the twentieth century, the college would have contained a small number of black students during Graham's matriculation there.[12]

Importantly, Graham majored in anthropology at Wheaton. While he later struggled to explain his decision to study a subject commonly linked with agnosticism, if not outright atheism, he was interested enough in the field momentarily to consider pursuing a master's degree at the University of Chicago. He went so far as to register for classes there; but a hectic ministerial schedule precluded further dalliances in academia.[13] By then, though, his studies had given him some awareness of the cultural relativity of race. In 1950, several years before Graham publicly identified himself as a supporter of desegregation, he noted that as a student he had "practically memorized" a textbook titled *Up from the Ape* and written by the evolutionary anthropologist Earnest Albert Hooton.[14] A Harvard professor, Hooton emphasized the highly relative nature of racial categories and categorically dismissed quasi eugenicists, calling them "ethnomaniacs." Although not denying the significance of racial differences, physical and otherwise, Hooton argued that "a 'pure race' is little more than a philosophical abstraction and that the great cultural achievements of humanity have been produced, almost invariably, by racially mixed peoples." He specifically attacked the simplistic chauvinism of arguments for Negro inferiority. Graham filtered such ideas through the net of his true focus at Wheaton, evangelism. While Hooton wrote from an explicitly secular perspective, his universalistic understanding of humanity reinforced Graham's faith in a Christian gospel open and communicable to all peoples.[15]

At Wheaton, Graham met his future wife, Ruth Bell, a model of piety whose prayerful coyness attracted the aspiring groom. Their marriage actually bolstered his southern identity. Ruth's father was L. Nelson Bell, a surgeon and longtime missionary in Nationalist China but also a native Virginian, graduate of Washington and Lee University, and an influential lay leader in the conservative wing of the Presbyterian Church in the United States (which was also referred to as the Southern Presbyterian church). Bell, whom Graham ranked behind only his parents and wife as a life influence, heavily mediated the way the evangelist applied his theological views on race to the social context of the South.[16] During the latter half of the 1950s, at least, Bell functioned as a conservative brake on the evangelist's opinions concerning racial policy. The well-connected Bell also strengthened the ties between Graham and a host of southern religious leaders. After the Bells moved to the Southern Presbyterian mountain retreat community of Montreat, North Carolina, Billy and Ruth followed them there in 1945.[17]

Wheaton may have planted seeds for Graham's subsequent doubts about the racial norms of his home region, yet their public sprouting was a while in coming. In his subsequent telling, the climax of his years-long struggle to reconcile a tacit acceptance of Jim Crow with a strident promotion of the gospel message came at the start of a March 1953 crusade service in Chattanooga, Tennessee. There, Graham personally removed the ropes separating the black from the white sections of the audience.[18] This was the first time he had not followed the dictates of the local crusade committee regarding segregated seating. The Chattanooga incident served as a key moment in Graham's "racial conversion narrative," to use a literary scholar's term for self-styled accounts in which "products of and willing participants in a harsh, segregated society . . . confess racial wrongdoings and are 'converted,' in varying degrees, from racism to something approaching racial enlightenment." Graham himself spoke of his own "racial conversion" on at least one occasion.[19]

Graham's racial development paralleled his theological and temperamental transition from Protestantism fundamentalism to neo-evangelicalism. During the 1940s, as noted above, an influential group of moderate fundamentalists associated with the National Association of Evangelicals (NAE) and hailing mostly from Reformed backgrounds began embracing the label "evangelical," the source of its most common current American usage. While not departing from core fundamentalist doctrines, these "neo-evangelicals" projected an evangelistic optimism not seen since the irrecoverable era before World War I when Protestants of all stripes could speak of "the evangelization of the world in this generation" (the motto of the Dwight Moody–inspired Student Volunteer Movement for Foreign Missions). They sought to revive the influence of a conservative Protestantism that, at least according to popular perceptions, had retreated from public view in the aftermath of the 1925 Scopes "Monkey Trial." In response to the so-called Second Disestablishment of the 1920s and subsequent decades, fundamentalism (the name given to the sizable minority of Protestants who adamantly rejected liberalizing trends within mainline denominations) became synonymous with theological and cultural separation from secular society. As critics of fundamentalist separatism, neo-evangelicals tended to prioritize evangelistic outreach over defenses of the pure faith.[20]

More than any other figure, Graham came to embody the neo-evangelical posture: a greater willingness to witness to secular society and, by doing so, to offer a relevant conservative alternative to the overt or latent liberalism of mainline Protestantism. The shift toward neo-evangelicalism was a gradual process for Graham. As early as the late 1940s, though, he had sermonized against sectarian proponents of "so-called 'ultra-Fundamentalism' whose object is not to fight the world, the flesh and the devil, but to fight other Christians whose interpretation is not like theirs."[21] Neo-evangelicals hoped to restore their brand of Christianity to its rightful place in American— indeed, Western—culture. They evinced an overarching concern for, in the words of NAE founder Harold Ockenga, the "rescue of western civilization by a . . . revival of evangelical Christianity."[22] The publication *Christianity Today*, founded in 1956 with vital assistance from Graham, reflected this mission.

The line between militant fundamentalists and more culturally engaged neo-evangelicals, to be sure, did not fully harden until the mid- and late 1950s. Even after the 1949 Los Angeles crusade, Graham still moved comfortably within separatist fundamentalist circles. He received numerous accolades from fundamentalist leaders, including an honorary doctorate from his abortive alma mater, Bob Jones University, where he spoke on several occasions.[23] From William Bell Riley, Graham had already netted a more burdensome mantle: the presidency of Northwestern Schools, which the evangelist reluctantly accepted in 1947.[24] Despite maintaining his home in North Carolina, Graham nominally occupied the college presidency until 1952. The school's Minneapolis location explains why the city served as the longtime headquarters of the Billy Graham Evangelistic Association (BGEA), incorporated in 1950.

Whereas Riley's fundamentalism was partly a product of the southern diaspora, early neo-evangelicalism was an overwhelmingly northern phenomenon. Southern Protestants, for the most part, had not experienced the doctrinal splits that tore apart northern denominations, especially Baptists and Presbyterians, after World War I.[25] In this sense, Graham introduced neo-evangelical assumptions to his crusades and social relations in the South. There, departing from the doctrinal dogmatism of fundamentalism potentially also meant departing from its racial assumptions.[26] As a result, Graham faced the prospect of criticism from the many southern fundamentalists who, like the eponymous patriarchs of Bob Jones University, advocated a strict, two-kingdom separation between saving souls and reforming societies, while also avowedly supporting the institution of segregation.[27]

Educational and theological influences aside, an evangelist who sought to witness to all of society had to worry about his public image. In the years following the Los Angeles crusade, Graham's audiences widened beyond the spheres of fundamentalism or even neo-evangelicalism. The new constituencies included a secular press ever conscious of the Elmer Gantry type—of the synergy between hucksterism and soul saving. As early as 1950, Graham faced criticism in New England for tolerating segregation down South. Censure came from within Dixie as well. A letter to the *Atlanta Constitution*, a liberal paper by regional standards, chided the evangelist for holding segregated meetings during his 1950 crusade in that city. "Is he implying that God Almighty has room for segregation and discrimination in His work?" the writer wondered. A columnist for the same paper continued on this theme, asking, "Will you preach, Sir, on the sins of violent sectionalism and hatred, with brother pitted against brother? . . . And will you, in all humility, state your position on the greatest thorn in the brow of Southern clergymen . . . the puzzles of race, white supremacy and segregation?"[28]

Graham also drew fire from African American leaders. Black attendance was extremely low at the Atlanta crusade, even though Graham recalled that black congregations were among those that had officially invited him to the city. In Atlanta, he came under fire from prominent African American ministers, as well as the South's leading black newspaper, the *Daily World*, for offering to hold a special service exclusively for blacks.[29] Morehouse University president Benjamin Mays, a foremost theological critic of Jim Crow and an early mentor to Martin Luther King, Jr., chastised the evangelist publicly and in print.[30] Similar tensions were evident in New Orleans, where a prominent African American Congregational minister took out advertisements urging blacks to shun the 1954 crusade there. (He later learned that those services would, in fact, be desegregated.) Outside the South, at least one black newspaper reported that Graham had held segregated services during his 1953

Dallas crusade. His immediate response to the reports about Dallas—sermonizing, from the relatively safer confines of Detroit, "that there is no [racial] difference in the sight of God"—revealed his caution, but also his sensitivity to criticism.[31] Graham viewed African Americans as part of his broader constituency, although not the core of it.

The Cold War represented a final, if delayed, influence on Graham's development on racial matters. Graham may have been the quintessential Cold War revivalist. From the very beginning of postwar tensions with the Soviet Union, he linked his evangelism to the destiny of the United States and its leaders.[32] His warnings of pending national disaster surpassed the tone of his evangelistic predecessors, including Moody, Sunday, and Charles Finney.[33] When Graham advocated "Christ for This Crisis" (the motto of his 1947 revival in Charlotte), the crisis he spoke of entailed the specter of communism, in addition to moral degeneration. His sermon titles ("The End of the World," "Will God Spare America?") reflected an apocalyptic interpretation of the times.[34] Graham offered an emphatically spiritual interpretation of the Cold War. Communism was "Satan's religion," a "great anti-Christian movement" whose gains had been "masterminded" by that same force.[35] The evangelist viewed communism as a rival faith, complete with its own trinity (to quote the 1952 book *Communism and Christ*, which Graham mailed to every member of Congress, along with President Harry Truman and his cabinet): "Marx the Lawgiver, Lenin the Incarnate Truth, Stalin the Guide and Comforter."[36]

For Graham, though, the fight against communism needed to be won by might as well as by the spirit. His Cold War bellicosity resided well to the right of the emerging liberal anticommunist consensus and, as such, held complex implications for his stance on racial matters. In 1950, he castigated the reds who "stole China" and predicted that communists would bomb the United States within two or three years—"and not five years."[37] That same year, he personally urged President Truman toward "total mobilization to meet the Communist threat." South Korea, the evangelist had earlier informed the president by telegram, contained "[m]ore Christians . . . per capita than any part of world." The situation, he declared, necessitated a "show down with Communism now."[38] Following Truman's dismissal of General Douglas MacArthur for desiring just such a confrontation, Graham praised the general as "a great man and a great Christian."[39] After the U.S. Senate censured another anticommunist icon, Joseph McCarthy, in December 1955, Graham likened the legislative body to a fiddling Emperor Nero.[40]

The preoccupation of Graham with the Korean peninsula pointed to his association with an anticommunist right fixated on the reddening of Asia and, indeed, the United States itself. In early 1953, he introduced friendly congressmen to right-wing Australian activist Fred Schwarz, then in the process of creating the influential Christian Anti-Communism Crusade.[41] Moreover, Graham possessed a number of social ties with the broader "China Lobby," which urged an aggressive policy of "roll back" in Asia. His father-in-law, Nelson Bell, had left his missionary post in China on the cusp of the Maoist ascendancy. Early Graham supporters included publishing mogul Henry Luce, who was born in China to missionary parents, and Minnesota congressman Walter Judd, whose background as a medical missionary in China resembled that of Bell. Other conservative anticommunists who admired Graham from a distance included Alfred Kohlberg, the leading spokesperson for the China Lobby, and Albert Wedemeyer, who as a special representative to China had warned President Truman about the impending collapse of the Nationalist regime.[42] Bell himself corresponded with Madame Chiang Kai-shek, met with the Formosan ambassador to the United States, and warned throughout the 1950s and 1960s of Americans "in high places who consistently helped the Communists" and who exaggerated "the weakness and shortcomings of the Nationalists and General Chiang Kai-shek."[43] For the most part, to be sure, Graham did not associate with the right's hardest edges. Still, none of the above anticommunists was known for taking moderate positions on either foreign policy or domestic issues—nor was Federal Bureau of Investigation director J. Edgar Hoover, a Graham supporter who declared in *Christianity Today* that "an America faithful to God will be an America free and strong."[44]

As Graham expanded his international outreach, though, his interpretation of the Cold War shifted in a more moderate direction. His image abroad, as he surely recognized, was keenly intertwined with that of the United States itself. The success of his overseas work, which blossomed after his 1954 London crusade, depended in no small part on the degree to which the rest of the world saw the United States as a goodwill ambassador. Graham resembled the many foreign missionaries within his Southern Baptist denomination whose experiences abroad led them to reconsider the domestic racial status quo.[45] His early travel to Europe only reinforced his hawkish Cold War sentiments.[46] By the mid-1950s, though, as he began to travel through the non-white majority of the world, Graham came to see his nation's poor reputation in the area of racial relations as a potential propaganda tool for international communism and his numerous critics alike.

Graham thus suggested how the first two decades of conflict between the United States and the Soviet Union simultaneously expanded and limited the national discourse on civil rights. The United States Information Agency and similar governmental outlets sought to advance America's image as the leader of the free world. Such efforts (in the words of one legal historian) made "civil rights reform . . . *in part* a product of the Cold War."[47] Southern conservatives, to be sure, eventually launched a "southern red scare" that readily merged rabid domestic anticommunism with opposition to altering the racial status quo.[48] Graham, though, increasingly viewed the Cold War through an international lens, even while he remained on friendly terms with many southerners who clearly (or conveniently) viewed civil rights activism as a front for communist subversion. By the latter half of the 1950s, Graham routinely linked anticommunism with a critique of segregation. The nation, he declared in 1957, resided "in a fish bowl with the whole world looking in," and "our racial tensions are causing some of the people of the world to turn away from us."[49]

In keeping with his move toward a more nuanced understanding of the Cold War, Graham gradually cultivated a clear, if adaptable, declaration of racial moderation.[50] His status as a religious celebrity who was also a southerner made his decision to address the race issue at some level not entirely surprising. Less predictable was his public position, at a reasonably early date, as a moderate desegregationist. When he occasionally addressed racial matters while speaking in the South during the early years of his ministry, his comments were limited in nature. At a 1950 crusade in Columbia, South Carolina, he flatly declared that "revival will also solve the race question by causing both races to be fair toward each other."[51] Graham team member Grady Wilson explicitly defended the residual nature of this formula. "What's the point of attacking a cause when you're after sinners?" Wilson asked an interviewer that same year. "If a man's a sinner and he's a member of the Ku Klux Klan, we're not going to lose the chance of saving him by attacking the organization he belongs to."[52]

Graham began to use somewhat stronger language during his many appearances at ecclesiastical and denominational gatherings throughout the South and the nation. In 1952, he told members of the NAE that the "Church is on the tail end—to our shame!—of progress along racial li[n]es in America today. The Church should be leading instead of following."[53] In an address delivered that same year at the annual meeting of the Southern Baptist Convention, he advocated opening denominational colleges to academically qualified blacks.[54] Some media outlets took notice. For example, the liberal Protestant magazine *Christian Century* published an editorial titled "Sewanee Says No, Billy Graham Yes," favorably contrasting his early criticism of segregation (for which "many think he will pay dearly") with the resistance to desegregation at a leading southern Episcopal seminary.[55]

By late 1953, Graham had worked out much of the racial reasoning that he would voice in response to countless media questions over the next decade and a half. In October 1953, he wrote a telling letter to *Atlanta Constitution* editor Ralph McGill, who had asked the evangelist to clarify his views on racial segregation after reading an interview Graham had given to the *Michigan Chronicle*, an African American newspaper. The renowned, future Pulitzer Prize–winning editor was in the midst of his own shift, reflective of the broader swath of southern liberals, from tolerance of separate-but-equal segregation to acceptance of, and eventual support for, its legal demise. As a critic of the role of southern Christianity in abetting racial injustices, McGill surely wrote to Graham with some skepticism. (Within a year, though, the editor would praise Graham in print as an effective evangelist and an asset to anticommunist efforts overseas.) "In my study of the Bible," Graham replied, "I can find no verses or chapters to support segregation." He affirmed that "Jesus Christ belongs neither to the colored nor the white races" and repeated a sentiment he had already voiced in Detroit: "In race relations the church has been lagging far behind in certain areas and allowing the sports world and political world to get ahead of it." Graham's chariot of justice slowed at the Mason-Dixon line, however. The South, he wrote to his fellow southerner McGill,

> presents a problem particularly all its own that many times our Northern friends do not understand. It is going to take a long process of education rather than legislation to ultimately bring about better relations between the races. We have extremists in both races who cause 90 percent of the trouble. In many parts of the South it is my observation that the race situation is better than in many parts of the North. For example, the sharp divisions between races, and racial tensions, are very strong here in Detroit. Non-segregation thus cannot be forced or legislated. There must be a process of education and faith in Christ.[56]

Most of these sentiments—a color-blind Christology, defense of his home region, embrace of the South's relational culture, and denunciation of "extremists"—would stay with the evangelist for at least the next quarter of a century. The remaining view—a moralistic but chronologically noncommittal gradualism regarding the ultimate abolition of Jim Crow—would wane, without vanishing altogether, during the late 1950s and early 1960s as Graham grew more appreciative of the need for civil rights legislation.

In the South

In his crusade services in the South, Graham did not initially fulfill his professed desire for the church to catch up with the secular world in the area of race relations. Still, he had plenty of opportunities to demonstrate the racial views he voiced to McGill and others. The growing urban South provided a strong base for many early Graham rallies and crusades, beginning with Charlotte (1947) and including Shreveport (1951) and Houston (1952). During the 1950s, a significant majority of Graham's domestic crusades, as well as a substantial portion of his guest sermons and one-day rallies, took place in southern cities, where the local media treated often him like a visiting head of state.[57] His influence was particularly palpable in the South. Atlanta and Chattanooga were among the few cities to construct special tabernacles in which to hold crusade services.[58] His 1950 address to a joint session of the Georgia legislature inspired one house of the state legislature to pass a prohibition law (which the other chamber quickly let die).[59]

However, Graham hesitated to use his cachet in the South to address racial issues. During his first six years of holding solo revivals, he allowed segregated seating arrangements in his southern crusades. He moved only fitfully toward a policy of desegregated seating, which his organization did not standardize until after the 1954 *Brown v. Board of Education* decision. At the 1951 Greensboro crusade, recalled BGEA staffer Willis Haymaker, blacks sat in "special sections of seats reserved for them as was customary in all Billy Graham crusades [in the South] *at that time.*"[60] The racial separation, presumably, did not extend to the area around the crusade platform where respondents gathered during the invitation. Atlanta city police chief Herbert Jenkins recalled segregated meetings during the 1950 crusade there, with exemptions for a few black ministers whom Graham knew. High-resolution BGEA photographs from the Atlanta crusade (generally, a more trustworthy source for crowd shots than southern newspapers, which tended to conceal the presence of blacks), show only two African Americans, maintenance workers at the crusade stadium. BGEA images from the Columbia crusade, held earlier that year, reveal similar results, despite an official claim that the audience for the final service contained "solid blocks . . . of Negroes."[61]

Jim Crow was thus an expected part of Graham's 1952 crusade in Jackson, Mississippi, capital of a state commonly considered the deepest part of the Deep South. The generally glowing coverage from the city's two daily newspapers—one of which ran a "Billy Graham Boxscore" listing the decision tally from the latest service—captured the routine thrust of his social commentary during that presidential election year. The evangelist lamented President Truman's firing of "star quarterback" Douglas MacArthur (who had just spoken at the Republican National Convention in Chicago) and, in a comment easily interpretable as an endorsement of Dwight Eisenhower for the presidency, urged citizens to vote in the upcoming elections for candidates who possessed moral integrity. "Christians Must Be Devoted to Their Cause to Combat Communists," alliterated a headline recounting a Graham sermon.[62]

Then, in the final days of the crusade, a less typical headline appeared in the *Jackson Daily News*: "Billy Graham Hits State Liquor System, Scores Segregation in Church." The paper ran an interview Graham had given in Jackson to the United Press news syndicate. "There is no scriptural basis for segregation," the evangelist declared, even while he admitted to following local racial customs in his services. "The audience may be segregated," he added, "but there is no segregation at the altar." Likewise, there should be none "in the church." Those who come forward during his services, he stressed, "stand as individuals. And it touches my heart when I see white stand shoulder in shoulder with black at the cross."[63] Graham balked at issuing such bold language from the crusade platform, although he did declare in his nightly sermon that God's love was "unlimited racially." The gesture drew expressions of approval from the black section of his audience.[64]

Graham's United Press interview represented his first definitive public statement about Jim Crow given in a southern setting. His comments were sandwiched between less surprising condemnations of obscene book sales and Mississippi's tax on illegal liquor sales. The following day, most likely after Graham had received a concerned phone call from Mississippi governor Hugh White, an article in the *Jackson Clarion-Ledger* emphasized Graham's opposition to legalized liquor before adding the following clarification concerning "another subject": "I feel that I have been misinterpreted on racial segregation. We follow the existing social customs in whatever part of the country in which we minister. As far as I have been able to find in my study of the Bible, it has nothing to say about segregation or non-segregation." Graham emphasized that he "came to Jackson to preach only the Bible, and not to enter into local issues," a statement that rested uncomfortably within an article detailing his prohibitionist pronouncements. (Two days after this retraction, though, Graham passed along an account of his initial critique of segregation to the head of the Detroit Council of Churches.) Neither of the ultrasegregationist Jackson papers further explored the matter of the United Press interview. Following the crusade, the *Daily News* returned to a more comfortable Cold War theme, arguing that Graham's efforts "might not only prove to be our best, but our only real defense against communism."[65] The Jackson crusade, then, featured only a premature expression of antisegregationist sentiments that had yet to congeal.[66]

In his 1953 crusade in Chattanooga, Graham took a more forthright stand against segregation in religious settings.[67] Before the start of the crusade, he personally removed the ropes separating the black and the white sections of the audience. "Either these ropes stay down," Graham recalled telling two ushers, "or you can go on and have the revival without me."[68] Chattanooga thus became Graham's first strategically desegregated crusade in an unambiguous Jim Crow environment.[69] The seating policy went unreported in Chattanooga's major dailies, which gave more attention to Graham's proficiency on the golf course, although the evangelist later claimed that his action "caused the head usher to resign in anger right on the spot (and raised some other hackles)."[70] A photograph attributed to the Chattanooga crusade and later used in a BGEA promotional booklet shows white and black audience members sitting together. Graham made sure to hedge the ramifications of his move. As an Upper South industrial city, Chattanooga was certain to be more tolerant of a policy change than cities in neighboring Deep South states; it housed one of the more liberal newspapers in the region, the *Chattanooga Times*, owned by the Ochs family of *New York Times* fame. Besides, Graham predicted to the crusade ushers, blacks in the audience would probably continue to sit together. According to an early biographer, the evangelist was correct; moreover, the black attendance was disappointingly low.[71]

While Graham had personally come to oppose segregation in his services, he did not formalize that position until after the 1954 *Brown* decision against public school segregation.[72] Less than two months after the Chattanooga crusade, the BGEA reluctantly acquiesced to a Dallas crusade committee's request for segregated seating. An instruction sheet for Dallas ushers described a section to be set aside for black attendees until the start of the service, after which seating would be open to all comers.[73] The May 17, 1954, *Brown* decision broke while Graham was crusading in Great Britain. The author of the unanimous decision, Chief Justice Earl Warren, had led a public gathering of Washington officials who bade Graham farewell before he crossed the Atlantic.[74] In the aftermath of *Brown*, Graham conducted desegregated crusades in Nashville (1954), New Orleans (1954), Richmond (1956), and Louisville (1956), as well as one Deep South city, New Orleans (1954). With the exception of the New Orleans crusade (which had been scheduled before the *Brown* decision), Graham intentionally avoided the Deep South, turning down most invitations to preach there during the mid- and late 1950s.[75]

In the immediate aftermath of *Brown*, the BGEA's policy on desegregation remained in a formative stage. Ten days after the decision, a BGEA associate informed a New Orleans crusade executive committee that Graham "feels very strongly that we must abandon the idea of segregation in our meetings, especially since secular organizations have taken the lead. I hope this will meet with the Committee's approval there in New Orleans."[76] In July of that year, Graham himself wrote to Southern Baptist pastor James M. Gregg of Nashville recommending that "Negroes be allowed to sit anywhere they like . . . and that nothing be said one way or the other about it." Graham also advised having a black pastor lead prayer at the crusade once a week. He did not link these requests with Christian morality but rather stressed the increasingly "world-wide" nature of his ministry: "The Nashville crusade will be written up quite extensively in the British press, and of course our work in England would suffer tremendously if they thought we were having a segregated meeting. They have no conception of the problem and would blame me for anything that would happen. . . . I have been in prayer on this point almost more than any other point concerning our Nashville and New Orleans meetings. So much is at stake. I personally think the less said the better."[77] The evangelist went on to predict that few blacks would attend the Nashville crusade anyway. Gregg recalled that African American attendees tended to sit apart, while another crusade leader remembered more mixed seating.[78] During one sermon in Nashville, Graham did offer an uncharacteristically direct denunciation of white racialism, although not segregationism per se: "We have become proud as a race—we have been proud and thought we were better than any other race, any other people. Ladies and gentlemen, we are going to stumble into hell because of our pride." These words represented a theological restatement of Hooton's warning in *Up from the Ape* against racial presumptuousness. Despite this forceful, if politically ambiguous, declaration, the crusade received glowing coverage in the strongly segregationist pages of the *Nashville Banner*, which published every sermon delivered during the four weeks of services.[79]

With the Nashville crusade, as well as the New Orleans crusade held later in 1954, desegregated seating became a requirement for crusade hosts. Graham gradually grew more direct in his description of this policy. "Naturally," he wrote to Richmond minister James Appleby in 1955, "I am assuming that the meeting in Richmond would be non-segregated." In Richmond, the Graham team began addressing criticisms that it included black ministers in the crusade planning process only as an "after thought" (as one New Orleans minister saw matters), if at all. Haymaker sought assurances from Appleby that tensions did not exist among the ministers of Richmond, whose integrated Ministers' Association was led by John M. Ellison, president of the historically black Virginia Union College.[80] During the crusade, Graham delivered a well-attended convocation address at Virginia Union, where he said the race problem lay at "the heart of man." However, he received criticism for not addressing racial matters in his Richmond crusade services. Such gestures, or lack thereof, did not strike the *Richmond Times-Dispatch*, a moderate segregationist paper, as particularly radical. Without specifically addressing Graham's racial views, a *Times-Dispatch* columnist favorably contrasted public figures of his stripe with those "ultra-liberals" who promoted such agendas as "compulsory integration." The even more staunchly segregationist *Richmond News Leader* offered similarly favorable coverage, noting Graham's intention to visit the Museum of the Confederacy while in town.[81] In light of the political sensibilities of the two Richmond newspapers, their editors conceivably may not have chosen to highlight moments during the crusade where the race issue did surface. Many readers of the papers might not have known about the desegregation policy.

The 1956 Louisville crusade offered a better indication of how residents of a Jim Crow city perceived an evangelist who was beginning to be identified with desegregation. The *Louisville Courier-Journal*, published by Mark Ethridge, stood as one of the leading white liberal voices in the greater South. The Louisville crusade took place just as Graham published an article in *Life* magazine, titled "Billy Graham Makes Plea for an End to Intolerance," in which he dismissed biblical arguments supporting racial segregation and hierarchy, and called for the church to speak out in favor of racial tolerance. He also declared that all of his services were desegregated.[82] Already Graham had begun to catch flack from hardline segregationists who accused him of selectively quoting scripture on racial equality.[83] The Louisville crusade revealed that his comments about race relations did not resonate as clearly as his altar calls. After the *Courier-Journal* announced that all Graham crusades were desegregated, a member of the local Citizens' Council requested a meeting with the evangelist. "We think we can convince him to change his views on this integration," he said. That avowed segregationists thought of Graham as a possible ally was attributable both to the halting, episodic nature of his public statements on race and to the desire of Jim Crow partisans not to "lose" a renowned figure they may have assumed was either in their camp or at least not an enemy. Graham did not accept the offer to meet the council, and his comments on Jim Crow during the crusade did not parallel the confident tone of his *Life* article. When a caller on a local television show asked him a question about segregation, the evangelist reaffirmed the primacy of the conversion moment. "I believe the heart of the problem of race is in loving our neighbor," he declared. "But man must love God before he can love his neighbor." As for the crusade itself, the *Courier-Journal*'s religion editor expressed surprise that the "completely desegregated" services had attracted so few black attendees. Graham had earlier observed a decline in black attendance contemporaneous with the desegregation policy. In Louisville, this pattern appeared in spite of a thoroughly integrated crusade steering committee.[84] Still, low black attendance had been a reality at many Graham crusades even before the change in seating policy.

While Graham's desegregated services during the mid-1950s represented notable accomplishments within the closed (and still closing) societies of the South, they hardly qualify as landmark events in the civil rights struggle. The gatherings straddled an ambiguous line between church services and public meetings. Only the latter was clearly subject to local segregation laws. As historical phenomena, racially separated churches were initially a product of freedmen leaving white-dominated congregations, and thus preceded the formalization of Jim Crow. Attendance expectations at all-white congregations, to be sure, quickly became intertwined with the rules, rituals, and power structures of that system. Technically, though, the pervasive segregation within southern congregations was more customary than official. Biracial worship was not unheard of even during the height of Jim Crow. Graham himself recalled attending a black church service in Florida during his Bible school days in the late 1930s. At the start of the civil rights era, blacks occasionally attended services at white congregations without incident (although black membership was far rarer); not until the mid-1960s did desegregating whites-only church services emerge as a strategy for civil rights activists.[85] In holding his first intentionally desegregated crusade in 1953, Graham was slightly ahead of his time in comparison with his fellow white evangelists in the South. By the end of the decade, independent mass revivalists in the region had begun integrating their services; earlier in the decade, their meetings were largely biracial, yet segregated.[86]

The overall degree or meaning of interracial fellowship at Graham's early desegregated crusade remains difficult to ascertain. Graham crusades did not approach the countercultural environments common to genuine expressions of southern religious "racial interchange," particularly within the Holiness and Pentecostal traditions.[87] Few locations for his early desegregated crusades—with New Orleans being a possible exception (although that demographically distinctive southern city possessed a certain multiracial Catholic tradition)—had a reputation for intractable segregationism akin to a Birmingham or a Jackson.[88] A Graham aide marveled at the ease of ensuring desegregated seating for the 1956 crusade in Oklahoma City, a Jim Crow city located on the southern rim.[89] Still, while Graham's meetings usually reflected community norms, they could sometimes help to change them. A black newspaper in New Orleans described the opening crusade service there as "the first time in recent times that Negroes have been permitted to attend a huge public Protestant gathering, or otherwise . . . without restrictions."[90] This was unquestionably a notable achievement. According to the evangelist, his desegregation policy extended to the hotel restaurants where he met with local ministers.[91] The relatively low black attendance, however, suggested that the Graham team remained most effective in reaching whites. Over the years, Graham and his supporters recounted a number of stories, usually told in an apocryphal manner, of white attendees who experienced racial conversion moments during crusades.[92] While these stories did not indicate a change of heart regarding the larger legal structures of Jim Crow, they suggest that some southern whites no longer thought those structures needed to apply to at least one staple of southern society, public revival services.

Graham's early southern crusades are best seen as emblems of the many, largely unnoticed forms of public desegregation that occurred in the period immediately preceding and following *Brown*. During the early postwar years, as black voter registration grew in some parts of the urban South, a number of southern cities saw modest amounts of desegregation in such areas as police departments, public parks, libraries, and even city councils.[93] The years before the *Brown* decision also saw the nominal desegregation of three SBC seminaries, as well as several other leading seminaries in the region.[94] Graham's desegregation policy thus drew from the momentum of existing trends.

Moreover, Graham's general unwillingness to discuss the race issue beyond the levels of individual decency and Christian neighborliness limited the impact of his early desegregated crusades. For Graham, desegregation had appropriately expanded from the altar into the audience; but the proper Christian understanding of its status beyond the revival service remained less certain. The question of legalized Jim Crow stood outside the sphere over which Graham consciously exerted influence—the quasi-congregational environment of the crusade service—and, hence, still remained classifiable as a separate "political" or "social" question. In light of the *Brown* decision, Graham appears to have viewed his desegregated crusades as violations only of local customs, not of enforceable laws. The BGEA felt uncomfortable using language that might imply an agenda other than evangelism. Haymaker suggested that crusade committees "use the term 'non-segregated'; we like it much better than using the word 'integrated.' "[95] Graham's simultaneously passive and politic attention to language, combined with a constant reassertion of his evangelistic priorities, no doubt allowed him to retain an audience that an established civil rights crusader would long since have lost. "Our concern since God laid the matter [of racial prejudice] on our hearts some years ago," wrote Graham in 1957, "has not been so much to talk as to act, to set an example which might open new paths and stir the consciences of many."[96] To a prospective crusade host in Charlotte, Graham phrased this logic differently: "We have found that if you say nothing about it and just allow the colored people to sit wherever they like, therewill [*sic*] be no difficulties and no problems."[97] In the comparatively moderate Upper South during the immediate post-*Brown* years, though, actions did not necessarily speak louder than words. There, the line separating leadership through unannounced policies from a kind of moral quietism was thin indeed. In those cities, Graham would have exerted greater influence had he declared his position more openly and, by doing so, encouraged a public response from religious and civic leaders.

Politics at the Altar

As Graham grew more active on the race issue, he began to assume authority not just as a renowned evangelist but also as a southerner with particular knowledge about the region's populace, black and white. However, he was not yet the regional leader he would become later in the 1950s and into the following decade. His most significant southern relationships remained largely private in nature and often did not reflect his emerging views on race. What they did often indicate was the periodic disconnect between Graham as racial commentator and Graham as political intimate.

Many times throughout his career Graham admitted a deep interest in, and attraction to, the world of politics. Were it not for his calling to the ministry, he declared in 1950, he might have chosen a career in public service.[98] In practice, the evangelist never kept these vocations as far apart as his membership in the SBC, a denomination long friendly to the Establishment Clause, might have suggested. Graham evinced an almost magnetic attraction to political power. He placed a high value on access to elected officials and was willing to wield his growing ministerial credentials toward that end. Besides the sheer thrill of such access—a far from negligible factor for a product of a modest North Carolina farm and an obscure Florida Bible college—Graham possessed a desire (common to neo-evangelicals) to reestablish the cultural credentials of conservative Protestantism. He also aspired without shame to enhance the profile of his own evangelism. Graham was deeply convinced of the reciprocity between public faith and revivalism—between the piety of elected leaders and the size of crusade crowds. This conviction led him routinely to propose such Christian-friendly policies as national days of prayer. For his preferred politicians, he went a step further and offered strategic advice.

The coolness of President Harry Truman toward Graham is usually remembered as the one exception to the evangelist's close comfort with the White House. Yet their relationship also revealed how, from an early date, the evangelist combined assertiveness with attempts at diplomacy when approaching political leaders. In 1950, Truman consented to a brief meeting with Graham and several evangelistic associates. Immediately afterward, the young ministers proceeded to recount the details to eager White House journalists, going so far as to stage a reenactment of their closing prayer with Truman.[99] In doing so, they violated the custom of respecting the confidentiality of White House meetings. The breach perturbed Truman, who declined further communication with Graham during the remainder of his term.[100] Seemingly unaware of the flap, Graham followed up the meeting with a letter to the president. Besides urging him to call for a "national day of repentance and prayer," Graham touted his possible value as a confidant. "I believe I talk to more people face to face than any living man," wrote the evangelist. "I know something of the mood, thinking, and trends in American thought. . . . If at any time I can be of service to you personally or to our country, please do not hesitate to call. Also, I follow political trends carefully and would be delighted at any time to advise you on my findings among the people."[101] While Graham's inflated tone revealed his political innocence, his tactlessness did entail an effort, however bungled, to push a politician's button. Graham's self-evaluation was in the process of being fulfilled. After Truman left office, the evangelist no longer needed to pitch his services.

As Graham grew in national stature, he befriended a wide range of political movers and shakers from both parties. His early connections, though, ran deepest among southern Democrats, including Tennessee governor Frank Clement, Mississippi senator John Stennis, South Carolina representative Mendel Rivers, Virginia senator A. Willis Robertson, and Alabama representative Frank Boykin. "I had more friends in the Democratic Party than I did in the Republican Party," Graham recalled; "being a southerner, I knew most of them."[102] The process leading to Graham's 1950 meeting with Truman began with a request from Representative Joseph Bryson of South Carolina.[103] Speaker of the House Sam Rayburn, a Texan, permitted Graham to hold the final service of his 1952 Washington, D.C., crusade on the steps of the Capitol.[104] That crusade strengthened Graham ties with southern politicos, including Boykin, who threw several of his famous House Dining Room lunches for Graham during the 1950s.[105]

Graham's political friends in the South ran the ideological gamut from pious moderates to staunch segregationists. Stennis clearly fell into the latter camp, as did two other friends, South Carolinians Strom Thurmond and James Byrnes. The benefits of associating with a popular figure like Graham easily overrode the complicating factor of his emerging support for desegregation.[106] The evangelist's self-described electoral philosophy actually paralleled that of the many ambivalent southern Democrats who grew increasingly comfortable with the thought of voting for Republican presidential candidates: "Though a registered Democrat (a sort of birthright in the part of the South where I came from), I always voted for the man and not the party."[107]

During the early 1950s, Graham's links with politicians who would soon stoke the political flames of massive resistance were tighter than his relationships with southern moderates. These connections were prominently on display during his 1950 crusade in Columbia, South Carolina, where the Graham team first employed the term "crusade" (rather than "campaign").[108] In addition to staying in Governor Strom Thurmond's mansion, Graham inspired an outbreak of civil religion in the state capital. Thurmond, less than two years removed from his presidential run as a segregationist Dixiecrat and more than a decade away from his trend-setting switch to the Republican Party, officially declared the last day of the crusade "South Carolina Revival Day" and signed a proclamation calling the event the "greatest religious gathering ever held in South Carolina—if not the South." Thurmond and his bitter political rival, U.S. Senator Olin Johnson, posed around a Bible with Graham. In Columbia, the evangelist addressed the state general assembly and befriended conservative *Time* magazine publisher Henry Luce, an encounter one scholar has described as "an important event in the marriage of southern fundamentalism and northern anticommunism." While in South Carolina, Graham found time to spend a weekend at the Spartanburg home of James Byrnes, a former secretary of state under President Truman who soon carried the segregationist banner as Thurmond's gubernatorial successor.[109] At a time when Graham rarely spoke about race in public, he evinced little desire to step on the toes of the southern political establishment.

During the year of the Columbia crusade, in fact, Graham received overtures about potentially joining that establishment. Several Democratic Party officials from North Carolina approached him about challenging the state's sitting senator, former University of North Carolina president Frank Porter Graham, a childhood neighbor and friend of the evangelist's father. Byrnes surely had a hand in the offer.[110] Even though the evangelist did not seriously consider entering the race, the incident offers insight into his perceived political usefulness. His suitors saw him as an alternative to the sitting senator, a prominent and well-respected southern liberal who held racial and others views purportedly out of step with the region.[111] (Senator Graham would go on to lose a primary runoff that featured overt race-baiting.) One year later, in 1951, Louisville lawyer James T. Robertson (who, not coincidentally, represented evangelist Mordecai Ham) wrote to David Lawrence, the conservative editor of *U.S. News and World Report*, proposing the evangelist's service on behalf of an ideologically parallel cause: an effort to nominate conservative Republican Walter Judd for the presidency, with Byrnes as his running mate.[112] Graham did not join that unlikely cause, although either he or an associate was undoubtedly aware of the offer. Later, the right-wing, anti-Semitic magazine *American Mercury*, published by Graham supporter Russell Maguire, suggested the evangelist as an ideal presidential nominee; the magazine's other recommendations included Strom Thurmond and Mississippi senator James O. Eastland.[113] In 1957, an Eisenhower-supporting Democrat from Oklahoma organized a quixotic and short-lived "Graham-for-President club" movement.[114]

Even as Graham moved away from theological fundamentalism and latent segregationism, then, he maintained close ties with many southern conservatives. They included not only politicians but also religious leaders, such as W. A. Criswell, pastor of the mammoth First Baptist Church in Dallas, Texas. Criswell later became known as a leading ministerial proponent of Jim Crow. Before the *Brown* decision, though, the rising SBC star was a much less controversial figure. His downtown church had mushroomed into the largest Southern Baptist congregation in the world. Graham and Criswell's relationship dated back at least as far as 1948, when Graham held meetings at First Baptist, and the two dined together two years later during a Graham revival in Charlotte. In 1953, in the midst of his Dallas crusade, Graham publicly requested membership at First Baptist. The evangelist explained his decision by postulating that Criswell's church would not place the same demands on his time as would a congregation closer to home. (In reality, Graham could have said the same of his previous church, Curtis Baptist in Augusta, Georgia.) Taking membership at First Baptist represented a savvy move for Graham, who admired the swaggering style of Texans and often wore a cowboy hat during the early 1950s.[115] The membership of First Baptist later included oil baron H. L. Hunt, an eccentric multimillionaire and rabid right-wing activist who became a fan of the BGEA, especially team member Grady Wilson. Graham's connections in Texas stretched beyond First Baptist and extended deep into the pockets of, to name a few major supporters, defense and energy magnate Russell Maguire, industrialist and evangelical philanthropist R. G. LeTourneau, and most significantly, Dallas-area oilman Sid Richardson, who introduced the evangelist to two rising politicians, John Connally and Lyndon Johnson. The titles of the BGEA's first two feature films, *Mr. Texas* and *Oiltown, U.S.A.*, drew from the well of this Lone Star prospecting.[116]

Graham's growing embrace of desegregation thus stood in tension not only with his white southern roots but also with a substantial portion of his support base. Accordingly, his moderate comments on race often lacked discernible coordinates on the political spectrum. Throughout the mid-1950s, observers assumed that his politics leaned well to the right. His strong support for President Eisenhower, along with the social ethic he increasingly voiced on behalf of racial tolerance, suggested a somewhat more complex dynamic. By the mid-1950s, Graham had moved toward a type of regional leadership.

CHAPTER TWO

Evangelical Universalism in the Post-*Brown* South

Christ was not so much a reformer as he was a transformer.
　　—Billy Graham, 1963

We must respect the law, but keep in mind that it is powerless to change the human heart.
　　—Billy Graham, 1958

THE BRAND OF REGIONAL LEADERSHIP Graham adopted required that he convincingly differentiate himself from leading figures on the southern right. One such person was W. A. Criswell, his pastor at First Baptist Church in Dallas. In February 1956, the firebrand Criswell delivered a well-publicized address to a joint session of the South Carolina legislature in which he endorsed segregation in both society and the church. Elsewhere in Columbia, Criswell castigated integrationists as "a bunch of infidels, dying from the neck up." Echoing many of his fundamentalist peers, he blasted the "spurious doctrine" of the "universal Fatherhood of God and brotherhood of man." Graham was soon pressed for a response to this rhetorical gauntlet. He averred that Criswell and he had "never seen eye to eye on the race question. My views have been expressed many times and are well known."[1]

In truth, Graham's views were only beginning to enter public consciousness during a time when the 1955–56 Montgomery bus boycott and the contemporaneous school integration crisis grabbed the headlines. Such developments cast a spotlight on his identity as a southerner. National politicians, such as President Dwight Eisenhower, and national publications, such as *Christian Century*, looked to the evangelist to exert regional leadership concerning desegregation and race relations, as did a number of persons inside the South. During the latter half of the 1950s, Graham stopped merely responding to the events occurring around him and started carving out his own space and agenda.

As the decade continued, Graham gradually emerged as a regional leader. He published articles about race relations in national publications, consulted with southern church leaders and national politicians on racial matters, and, finally, held rallies in the aftermath of racial crises in Clinton, Tennessee, and Little Rock, Arkansas. In national venues, although less commonly from the crusade pulpit, he criticized legalized Jim Crow, condemned racial violence, and dismissed biblical justifications for segregation. At the same time, he remained publicly skeptical of legislative or judicial solutions to the civil rights crisis, preferring instead to stress the evangelical themes of neighborly love and the transformation of society through individual conversions. His perspective drew from a social ethic rooted in nineteenth-century evangelicalism, but also reflected the predicaments of racial moderation in the postwar United States.

Talking About Race

As Graham formalized his desegregated seating policy in the aftermath of the 1954 *Brown* decision, which declared de jure segregated public schooling to be unconstitutional, he grew more vocal on the subject of race. Beginning in 1955 and continuing into the early 1960s, he used national media outlets to communicate his views concerning race relations and civil rights. In a March 1955 interview on *Meet the Press*, Graham questioned whether segregation measured up to the standards of either Christianity or the American nation.[2] The timing of the comments, delivered a few days before he departed for a crusade in Scotland, allowed him to avoid direct criticism at home while enhancing his image abroad. Upon his return to the United States, though, Graham made similar remarks during an appearance before the National Press Club.[3]

When speaking to southerners, Graham remained less strident in tone. At a 1956 Southern Baptist Convention (SBC) gathering in Kansas City, he called an earlier resolution in favor of the *Brown* decision a "courageous stand" and argued that the SBC should lead in the area of race relations (just as the denomination had always led in matters of evangelism). In Oklahoma City, the *Black Dispatch* ran a brief article touting these remarks in anticipation of a Graham crusade in that Jim Crow city. In Kansas City, though, the evangelist chose not to use the more prophetic language of a draft speech in he which warned that, should his denomination fail on the race issue, "we may eventually find our spiritual power waning and our thrilling statistics only hollow echoes." He also supported a decision at the convention to table further discussion of racial matters.[4]

The evangelist's first widely disseminated foray into racial issues came with an October 1956 article in *Life* magazine, published by Graham supporter Henry Luce.[5] *Life* writer Hugh Moffett prepared the original draft based on interviews with the evangelist, who offered his final revisions two weeks before publication. Graham published the article with some reluctance and apparently passed along a draft for moderate Tennessee governor Frank Clement to peruse. The essay partially fulfilled a promise Graham had made to President Eisenhower to provide leadership in promoting racial tolerance and moderation.[6]

The *Life* article most likely did not change the minds of Graham's liberal detractors. The "vast majority of the ministers in the South," he wrote of both black and white clerics, were "not extremists on either side" of the race issue. They supported desegregation of such services as public transportation, hotels, and restaurants, while remaining skeptical of the current feasibility of school integration in the Deep South. Observing a decline in race relations since the *Brown* decision, most ministers who had talked with the evangelist "confessed that the church is doing far too little about it." In the article, Graham announced his policy of holding "nonsegregated" services and systematically dismantled two common Old Testament proof texts for segregation: the Hamitic curse and the commandment that Israelites separate themselves from other peoples. In the Hamitic curse, Noah, not God, had cursed Canaan, offspring of Noah's son, Ham (and Noah had done so after awakening from a drunken slumber). The condemned descendants of Canaan, Graham confidently asserted, were white Canaanites, not black Africans. As for the Israelites' purity, their social separatism was along religious, not racial, lines. Moreover, Graham added, Jesus had specifically countered the racialism of his own people by praising gentiles and moving among the outcast Samaritans. For the present day, Graham's solution for improved race relations involved "more than justice: the principle of the Golden Rule, the spirit of neighbor-love, and the experience of redemptive love and forgive-ness."[7]

The backhanded dismissal of mere legal remedies ("more than justice") reflected the slipperiness of Graham's prescriptions, along with the conservative assumptions underlying them. Draft references to Graham crusades as "fully 'integrated'" (rather than "nonsegregated") and to segregation as "both UnAmerican and UnChristian" (terms he had used on at least two previous occasions) did not appear in the printed version, while more politically ambiguous anecdotes survived the final editing.[8] For example, after attacking biblical defenses of Jim Crow, Graham noted that black attendance at his desegregated services had not approached that of his segregated 1952 crusade in Jackson, Mississippi. Negroes, he declared, balked at legalized segregation but often preferred to mingle among themselves. Graham also told of an idealistic, integrationist minister who became a racial moderate after moving to the South. While seeming to endorse basic legal remedies to Jim Crow, Graham voiced a modest version of the strongly held position of his father-in-law, Nelson Bell, that some forms of voluntary segregation were permissible. (Bell participated in a roundtable discussion of prominent southern church leaders, the transcript of which appeared alongside Graham's article. The panelists argued against the existence of biblical sanctions for segregation, yet—like Graham—generally avoided discussing specifics in the area of social policy.) The evangelist also defended his native South. "Prejudice is not just a sectional problem," he wrote, labeling criticism of the South "one of the most popular indoor sports of some northerners these days." He ended with a story suggesting a distinctly regional model for improved race relations:

> Shortly after the close of the Civil War, a Negro entered a fashion-able church in Richmond, Va., on Sunday morning while communion was being served. He walked down the aisle and knelt at the altar. A rustle of shock and anger swept through the congregation. Sensing the situation, a distinguished layman immediately stood up, stepped forward to the altar and knelt beside his colored brother. Captured by his spirit, the congregation followed this magnanimous example. The layman who set the example was Robert E. Lee.[9]

Despite the mixed signals inherent in invoking a Confederate hero on behalf of racial tolerance, Graham clearly called for the church to take a greater role in fostering improved race relations. He did so in explicitly evan-gelical terms. "The church, if it aims to be the true church," he wrote, "dares not segregate the message of good racial relations from the message of regen-eration, for . . . man as sinner is prone to desert God and neighbor alike." The most lasting advances in race relations would thus derive from individual conversions to Christ's message of salvation and love. "Any man who has a genuine conversion experience will find his racial attitudes greatly changed," the evangelist concluded.[10]

Graham published three similar national articles—in *Ebony*, *U.S. News and World Report*, and *Reader's Digest*, respectively. The *Ebony* piece—which appeared in September 1957 with the somewhat exaggerated kicker, "South-ern-born evangelist declares war on bigotry"—contained a more strident tone than the *Life* article. The difference was attributable both to the magazine's primary readership, upwardly mobile blacks, and to the timing of the article, which appeared in the aftermath of a New York City crusade during which the Graham team had made special efforts to appeal to African Americans (including inviting Martin Luther King, Jr., to give the invocation at a ser-vice). That crusade had also finalized Graham's rift with leading fundamen-talists, who were distraught by his willingness to associate with liberal Protestants (as well as, one can assume, King). The official crusade invitation had come from an affiliate of the National Council of Churches. Perhaps the break momentarily freed Graham to speak more candidly about social issues. In the *Ebony* article, he promised a revival "to wipe away racial discrimina-tion" and supremacist sentiments. More important, for the first time to a national audience, Graham overtly came out in favor of antisegregation legis-lation, echoing comments he first made when speaking to a black Baptist congregation in Brooklyn. He did not clarify exactly what such laws would entail, however, and quickly added that, absent Christian love, they would result in "nothing but cold war."[11]

In 1960, Graham contributed his thoughts on race relations to *Reader's Digest* and *U.S. News and World Report*. His words there reflected the signifi-cantly more conservative politics of those venues. He called for Christians to "banish Jim Crow from their midst" and again endorsed basic legal remedies, yet he also warned of excessive "belligerence" among both black and white integrationists. While "convinced that 'Jim Crow' must go," he added that society "cannot make two races love each other and accept each other at the point of bayonets."[12] Although Graham embraced the end of Jim Crow on both moral and political grounds, he endorsed only remedies that he believed would not result in the kind of racial tensions present in Little Rock and other desegregation hotspots. Such friction-free solutions were, of course, difficult to identify.

Graham's public commentaries on racial matters lacked intellectual depth and exposed the evangelist to charges of inconsistency. A glaring dearth of symmetry existed between his passionate calls for ending personal prejudice among Christians and his significantly less enthusiastic support for dismantling the actual legal structures of Jim Crow. Like a candidate running for office, Graham avoided committing himself to all but the most general of prescriptions for combating racist practices. Unlike most politicians, however, Graham claimed spiritual and moral authority as a minister of God; he implicitly asked to be held to a higher standard than other public figures. Despite his tepidness and inconsistency, though, he proffered to his audiences something other than, as critics then charged (and have charged since), a simple belief that "religion, like politics, had a duty to uphold the status quo."[13]

Evangelical Universalism

In explaining his positions on racial and other sociopolitical matters, Graham drew from and updated traditions rooted in nineteenth-century American evangelicalism. He evinced an evangelical social ethic centered on the individual soul and will, and predicated on the universal commonality of divinely created humans. This ethic, here termed evangelical universalism, viewed the individual soul as the primary theological and political unit in society, prioritized relational over legislative solutions to social problems, and it tended to acquiesce to the ultimately inscrutable realm of ordained legal authority. According to this ethic (which should not be confused with the inclusive soteriology, or doctrine of salvation, also called "universalism"), the most effective forms of social change emanated from the conversion of individual souls.

These beliefs, or ones similar to them, contained a rich heritage. Graham voiced them from the assumption that evangelical Christianity held a special relationship with American society that—if protected and nurtured—would permit the nation to fulfill its most fundamental values. Many antebellum evangelicals, for example, had seen themselves as having a unique responsibility to ensure the endurance of the young nation's republican foundations.

Electing "Christian statesmen" to office might help, but so would a strong evangelistic witness.[14] Proponents of this "custodial," or guardianship, ideal continued to assume the inherent good of promoting "Christian Civilization," even while they claimed to uphold the formal separation between church and state.[15] Such sentiments help to explain the close association of antebellum evangelism, in the North and South alike, with notions of social progress.[16] The belief that Protestants had a special role to ensure the nation's morality endured well beyond the remembered heyday of antebellum evangelicalism, but it began to weaken during the so-called Second Disestablishment, the weakening of Protestant hegemony during the 1920s, 1930s, and 1940s. By the close of that period, many liberal Protestants had either accepted or acquiesced to the fact that a growing state was assuming many, if not most, of the church's custodial responsibilities.[17]

Many conservative Protestants, of course, did not view the Second Disestablishment as a necessary or even an unavoidable development. Fundamentalists, as well as their neo-evangelical offspring, never consciously accommodated themselves to the relative decline of Protestantism as a moral influence. Graham and his fellow neo-evangelicals specifically sought to restore that influence.

The ancestors of twentieth-century fundamentalists and evangelicals, of course, had resisted liberalizing trends within Protestantism from the moment they first emerged. Following the Civil War, many conservative Protestants departed from the optimism of the antebellum years. Instead, they embraced a pessimistic premillennialist eschatology (or theology of the end times) that stressed the imminent second coming of Jesus Christ and assumed that a period of social decline would precede it. The trend held long-term implications for the relationship between evangelicalism and social reform movements. The synergy between antebellum revivalism and reform causes is well known. Charles Finney, the leading evangelist of the antebellum Second Great Awakening, had declared slavery "pre-eminently, the *sin of the church*" and did not serve communion to slaveholders at his New York congregation. While Finney frustrated abolitionists by viewing their cause as a secondary "appendage" of evangelism, he did not hesitate to invoke the "higher law" of Christ in the face of unjust legislation, such as the Fugitive Slave Law of 1850.[18] By contrast, post–Civil War evangelist Dwight Moody, the revivalist to whom Graham compared most favorably, said little about the labor and monetary conflicts of the Gilded Age and reluctantly began holding segregated services in the postwar South. "Man, away from God,"

Moody declared in 1876, "is not to be trusted, and there is no reform until God has been found."[19] Saving souls came first—a perspective more than a few Gilded Age barons were happy to second.

Moody portended the early twentieth-century process, sometimes called the Great Reversal, through which conservative Protestants abandoned many spheres of social activism. During the Progressive Era, the growth of the Social Gospel, which seemingly elevated social concerns to salvific status, irredeemably tainted such activism as synonymous with theological liberalism.[20] Revivalist Billy Sunday, Graham's immediate forerunner, vociferously opposed Social Gospel theology, even though he did support some Progressive reforms, such as Prohibition, women's suffrage, and child labor laws. Following World War I, the attention of Sunday and what were becoming known as "fundamentalists" turned increasingly to the specter of Protestant "modernism," which embraced the Social Gospel and attacked biblical literalism.[21]

While Graham preached in the shadow of the Great Reversal, he did not view the Second Disestablishment as an irreversible development. The two impulses stood in some tension. Graham sought to recover the lost social status of evangelicalism, all the while checking the gains of mainline Protestantism. Yet he operated on the other side of a deep rupture in American Protestant history. Graham and his peers could not simply re-create the seeming evangelical consensus of yore. The evangelist idealized the social impact of eighteenth-century Wesleyan revivalism, which he claimed had contributed generations of reformers to Great Britain.[22] His more immediate fundamentalist heritage, however, instilled in him a reflexive skepticism about reform causes. His instinct was to keep evangelism and what he and his peers termed "social concern" in separate and usually unequal categories.

Yet Graham was also a product of his times in a more secular sense. Another influence on his social ethic was the universalist momentum of post–World War II public culture—a perspective that viewed humans as sharing common needs, wants, and problems. In his earlier years, to be sure, Graham was nothing if not an unabashed patriot and a Christian chauvinist. But as befitted a proud citizen of an increasingly confident nation (and an even prouder exponent of the Great Commission to spread the good news of the Gospel), he thought on a global scale—not just in terms of new evangelistic frontiers but also in terms of an overarching human nature. In this sense, Graham struck a notably less parochial stance than Billy Sunday, who had dismissed "this twentieth-century theory of the universal fatherhood of God and the brotherhood of man. . . . You are not a child of God unless you are a Christian." Graham, by contrast, distinguished between regenerated souls (a portion of humanity) and loved ones (all of humankind). He allowed that God's love extended even to the atheistic communist. Salvation was a human concern, not just an American one. Graham shared with postwar neo-orthodox and existentialist theologians a concern for the common human condition of original sin.[23]

The universalism of Graham and many of his evangelical peers derived not from an optimistic reading of human nature but rather from a theological recognition of the common condition of individual souls: created, sinful, and requiring salvation. Thus, the explicit biblicism of evangelical universalism distinguished it from the more secular "liberal universalism" that pervaded the political culture of post–World War II reform movements. The latter, in the words of historian Bruce Schulman, entailed "belief in the fundamental unity and sameness of all mankind," meaning that "every person possessed the same intrinsic worth, deserved the same opportunities, [and] shared the same basic aspirations."[24] In Graham's 1956 address to the Southern Baptist Convention, he spoke of his congregants' "common denominator with the rest of the world. . . . It's not race; it's not language; it's not skin color; it's not culture. It's the fact that we are created in the image of God, and that Christ is the savior of all men."[25] Graham was moving toward a position he would describe a decade later as the "biblical unity of the human race. All men are one in the humanity created by God himself. All men are one in the common need of divine redemption, and all are offered salvation in Jesus Christ."[26] While Graham's emphasis on human universals set him apart from Billy Sunday in the past and W. A. Criswell in the present, his were hardly radical sentiments. Christians of many persuasions nominally professed some version of these principles, and their social implications varied wildly. Among white Christians in the American South, for example, what one scholar has called the "inclusionary impulses of evangelical Christianity" could coexist comfortably with racial hierarchies.[27]

Spurred by motivations both religious and secular, though, Graham began by the 1950s to draw connections between spiritual and social equality. He expressed those implications largely in individuated terms—more specifically, in the language of individual sinfulness and redemption. The individual stood as an exaggerated synecdoche of society—a part that defines a larger whole, rather than being a mere component of it. As Graham argued in the pages of the ultraconservative *American Mercury* magazine, "Society is made up of individuals. So long as you have a man in society who hates and lies and steals and is deceitful, you have the possibility of racial intolerance; you have the possibility of war; you have the possibility of economic injustice."[28] By extension, larger social problems derived from core individual ones. "Our international problems and racial tensions," he stated in 1963, "are only reflections of individual problems and tensions."[29] A year later he told a group of media executives that, before altering social structures, "we must change man first. Our great problem today is not social. . . . Our problem is man himself. We've got to change man."[30] The solution had to begin with individual souls. "Society cannot repent corporately," Graham argued in a separate *American Mercury* article.[31]

For the evangelist, only the individual will—effectively, the intellectual corollary of the soul—could stimulate change in one's life and, by secondary extension, in society as a whole. In Graham's theology, as a student of the evangelist has observed, "the human will represents an autonomous ego."[32] Acceptance of Christ, of course, represented the ultimate willful decision for Graham, a choice from which all lasting social change derived. "Our hope," the evangelist declared in a 1966 address, "is . . . that social reform in areas where it's needed can be done by men who have been converted and who believe the Gospel."[33] Such work made up the realm of "social concern," a term Graham and his evangelical peers employed in reference to those Christian activities in the public, or social, sphere separate from evangelism. The term demonstrates how white American evangelicals tended to place social activism in a mental category separate from, and secondary to, traditional missionary efforts.

The born-again moment, described by leading neo-evangelical theologian Carl F. H. Henry and other evangelicals as "regeneration," thus constituted the most legitimate (perhaps the only wholly legitimate) starting point for transforming a fallen society. That transformation would occur on a soul-by-soul and then a relational basis. The role of the state—the critical agent in liberal social activism—remained less certain. The emphasis on individual salvation as a trigger for social change is an oft-cited characteristic of evangelical social engagement. Henry contrasted the authentic "transformation of society" with educational and legislative efforts aimed at "preserving what is worth preserving in the present social order." Henry and his generation of evangelicals tended to associate the state—and, by extension, the law—solely with coercive power, however necessary that power may be. Transformation through regeneration, by contrast, "rests upon spiritual power," as "evange-

lism and revival remain the original wellsprings of evangelical humanitarianism and social awakening."[34] Regeneration first entailed the divine
forgiveness of individual sins. Its social component likewise would commence
voluntarily at the level of everyday human relations, what Graham and others
called "neighbor-love"—a concept they kept distinct from state justice. At
its extreme, this stress on individual regeneration could effect a type of sociopolitical passivism. It could, in classic pietistic fashion, permit evangelicals
tacitly to bless the political status quo while cultivating their own evangelistic
gardens.

Graham and his generation of post–World War II neo-evangelicals, however, did not believe they were proffering a private faith. This was not how
they envisioned the ideal role of evangelical Christianity in American society.
In practice, then, most postwar evangelicals hoped their values would perme-
ate the realm of state leadership, irrespective of their beliefs concerning the
limits of that sphere for transforming society. The evangelical influence on
temporal authority would commence, appropriately, at the level of individual
conversions. As historian D. G. Hart has argued, a paramount conviction of
evangelical political activism has been the belief that "being born again results
in holy instincts about the way societies should be ordered and governments
run."[35] When this principle is applied to Christian statesmen, the personal
becomes political in a peculiarly evangelical way; godly character yields godly
governance.

The focus of postwar evangelicals on Christian statesmanship partially
grew out of their profound respect for ordained authority and the rule of law.
This final element of evangelical universalism often resided uncomfortably
alongside the regenerational theory of social change. Despite Graham's inability to avoid personal political partisanship, he consistently argued that
believing Christians should support their elected leaders as agents of God's
will, irrespective of party or platform. "The devout man," Henry likewise
wrote, "must respect law, and he is spiritually inclined to obey the positive
law of the State" and not "to condition [his] support of the State upon its
promotion of Christian religious principles."[36] While the government's mission remained ultimately negative (i.e., preservational), in contrast to the
regenerative, transformational effects of individual conversions, the state did
possess a legitimate role to play in upholding and implementing justice. That
role, though, was more corrective than constructive—mere justice, in contrast to regeneration and its by-product of human reconciliation.

The distinction between reconciliation and justice (or between salvation and law) is one of the many facets of neo-evangelical social ethics that gave it a strongly conservative political cast. That distinction sometimes entailed differentiating between spiritual and temporal responsibilities, between individual souls bound for eternity and individual bodies occupying a fallen world.[37] Such a distinction made it difficult to voice one's eschatology without tacitly condemning efforts to change society. "From a Christian point of view," Graham declared in late 1967, "I'm very optimistic about the situation in the world. From [the] point of view of a member of the human race, I'm very pessimistic."[38] Christ would ultimately triumph over human sinfulness, but that triumph would have little to do with human efforts to create the good society. Thus, many evangelicals desired to strengthen their influence over national policy even while their theological inclinations led them to acquiesce to the legitimate powers that be and to assume that a period of social decline would precede the triumphant Second Coming. When political leaders professed a Christianity of the appropriate variety, of course, the dilemma seemed less complicated. Indeed, Graham went so far as to state that qualified Christians had a responsibility to run for office.[39]

Post–Jim Crow Evangelism

Applied to both civil rights and the broader postwar South, Graham's evangelical universalism held conflicting implications. In his rhetoric on civil rights, the evangelical tension between justice and regeneration played out as a conflict between belief in a universal moral law (e.g., the need for the state to maintain moral order) and faith in voluntarism (e.g., individual acts of neighborly love). The latter impulse might assume a libertarian quality in keeping with the anti–New Deal rhetoric of property rights and individual choice pervasive among postwar conservatives. In the context of the American South during the latter half of the 1950s and the first half of the 1960s, however, Graham invoked the values of evangelical universalism to offer a theologically grounded, commonsense critique of racism and racialism. At the same time, he drew from the ethic to defend his region and to question the value of legislative or other procedural routes to social change. Finally, his respect for the rule of law informed his responses to racial violence in Little Rock and elsewhere.

The way Graham applied his social ethic in the South made him a racial moderate. The label "racial moderate" remains a notoriously slippery but historically viable identity subject to a confused array of evaluations—courageous, compromising, reasoned, indecisive. Graham's views resembled those of the South's "middle-of-the-road liberals," regional leaders like Ralph McGill and Hodding Carter, editor of the Greenville, Mississippi, *Delta Democrat-Times,* who "advocated an orderly, locally controlled process of racial change keyed to community conditions and economic growth."[40] Some moderates, wrote cultural critic Calvin Trillin in the 1970s, had simply "valued something more than segregation." Others still hoped to retain white control of the political system. All of them assumed that a sudden, legally enforced shift away from Jim Crow would result in chaos. During the years between the *Brown* decision and the Civil Rights Act of 1964, racial moderation usually meant gradualism. Post-*Brown* racial gradualists believed that Jim Crow—for reasons of morality or feasibility, or both—was living on borrowed time. In light of the dramatic social implications of racial mixing, though, the ideal full maturation date for that loan was neither today nor tomorrow, but somewhere in the indefinite future. Meanwhile, however, certain forms of desegregation might cautiously proceed—preferably on a voluntary basis or, if in response to a clear and present court order, according only to the letter of the law. In negotiating the timetable for desegregation, gradualists tended to prioritize "civility" over conflict, paternalistically assuming that their approach was in the best interest of southern whites and blacks alike. Their preferred, even avowed, mode was to work "behind the scenes."[41] As resistance to the *Brown* decision sharpened during 1956 and 1957, gradualist sentiments gained increasing credibility even among liberals outside the South, resulting in a momentary "vogue of moderation." Graham's concerns about extremists on both sides of the race issue, expressed in *Life* and elsewhere, reflected a common dilemma among southern moderates.[42] Like other moderates in the South, the evangelist asymmetrically equated militant segregationists and strident civil rights activists, while worrying that integrationist legislation or aggressive enforcement of Supreme Court decisions would adversely alter the precarious balance of southern race relations. Like those moderates, Graham spoke much more forthrightly and specifically when criticizing acts of racist violence than when offering constructive proposals for racial progress.

These positions and characteristics also resembled the views of President Dwight Eisenhower, with whom Graham stayed in regular contact throughout the president's two terms.[43] The advice Graham offered to Eisenhower on race relations said much about how the evangelist applied his social ethic.

Eisenhower was quite aware of Graham's influence in the South. So was Representative Frank Boykin, an Alabama Democrat who wrote to the president in March 1956, while Graham was visiting the capital. Significantly, Boykin saw Graham as a mediator rather than a prophet—an agent of gradualism rather than of reform. The race question, Boykin wrote in his patently folksy manner, was important "because, in my judgment, the Communists are taking advantage of it. I believe our own Billy Graham could do more on this than any other human in this nation; *I mean to quiet it down and to go easy and in a Godlike way,* instead of trying to cram it down the throats of our people all in one day, which some of our enemies are trying to do. I thought maybe if you and Billy talked, you could talk about this real, real good" (emphasis mine).[44] Clearly, the segregationist congressman from southern Alabama viewed Graham as a shaper of inevitable changes, not as a force that would drive them.

Eisenhower met with Graham the day after Boykin sent his letter. Although the evangelist had just returned from a visit to India and East Asia, his fifty-minute conversation with the president centered on what role he might play in the American South. According to White House notes, Graham asserted that the strong reaction against the *Brown* decision "had set back the cause of integration, but he thinks it is bound to come eventually." The moral issues at stake were obvious, Graham told Eisenhower, but were complicated by the social traditions of the South. In his upcoming appearances in the region, the evangelist agreed to echo the president's recent call for "moderation" and "decency" regarding the transition toward integration.[45] In affirming and possibly even compounding the gradualist leanings of Eisenhower, Graham offered words similar to the advice the president received from moderate-to-liberal southerners, such as Ralph McGill.[46]

Graham and Eisenhower shared a basic understanding of the race problem. They were gradualists wary of purported extremists and skeptical of efforts to legislate racial morality. While the Eisenhower administration officially accepted the *Brown* decision, the president tacitly criticized the Supreme Court and refused to enforce implementation of the ruling.[47] As the president told Graham in a subsequent letter, he did back the desegregation of southern graduate schools—a position that paralleled the evangelist's support for open admission in Southern Baptist colleges. Moreover, Eisenhower thought white ministers in the South should publicly support greater representation of blacks in local governments and school boards. Graham called these suggestions "excellent."[48] They were in keeping with the kind of adult-centered desegregation that had occurred in the years leading up to *Brown*. As with the open-seating policy for Graham crusades, these alterations of Jim Crow had not necessarily required legislative or judicial action. Both Graham and Eisenhower publicly endorsed this type of localized gradualism, contrasting it by implication with the "extremism" of enforcing *Brown* in the Deep South.

Graham's correspondence with Eisenhower following their March 1956 meeting blended moral concerns with racial gradualism. Affirming the belief of the president that "the Church must take a place of spiritual leadership in this crucial matter," Graham pledged to organize a meeting of southern denominational leaders to discuss Eisenhower's recommendations for enhancing race relations. The evangelist further committed to "do all in my power to urge Southern ministers to call upon the people for moderation, charity, compassion and progress toward compliance with the Supreme Court decision." Although the proposed gathering never occurred, Graham did meet privately with a range of church leaders, black and white, "encouraging them to take a stronger stand in calling for desegregation and yet demonstrating charity and, above all, patience." Two moderate southern governors, Luther Hodges of North Carolina and Frank Clement of Tennessee, received similar advice from Graham.[49] Later in 1956, the evangelist and Vice President Richard Nixon attended Southern Presbyterian, Baptist, and Methodist gatherings in western North Carolina. These discussions and meetings increased Graham's optimism but also affirmed his gradualism. "I believe the Lord is helping us," he wrote to Eisenhower, "and if the Supreme Court will go slowly and the extremists on both sides will quiet down, *we can have peaceful social readjustment over the next ten-year period*" (emphasis mine).[50]

The following year, Eisenhower sought advice from Graham during the most pressing racial crisis of his presidency, the attempted desegregation of Little Rock's Central High School in the fall of 1957. Eisenhower consulted Graham about the possible use of federal troops, and Nixon twice contacted the evangelist during the crisis. Graham agreed that Eisenhower had no choice but to employ the troops.[51] The evangelist also communicated with Little Rock ministers and offered to hold services in the strife-torn city. As part of his *Hour of Decision* radio program, he distributed to stations throughout Arkansas a sermon encouraging love across the color line. Oveta Culp Hobby, a Houston newspaper publisher and former member of the Eisenhower cabinet, suggested the gesture. In other statements, Graham called for

Christians in Little Rock to "obey the law" and averred that "all thinking southerners" were disturbed by the events there.[52]

With Little Rock, Graham began to involve himself with specific racial crises in the South. Basic Christian racial decency and obedience to the law emerged as the two distinctive themes of these interventions. In 1957, around the time of the violence in Little Rock, Graham sent a brief card of support to Dorothy Counts, an African American student who had faced severe harassment upon enrolling at a previously segregated high school in his hometown of Charlotte. The curiously sloganeering note juxtaposed faith and Cold War nationalism, separating them only by sentences:

> Dear Miss Counts,
>
> Democracy demands that you hold fast and carry on. The world of tomorrow is looking for leaders and you have been chosen. Those cowardly whites against you will never prosper because they are un-American and unfit to lead. Be of good faith. God is not dead. He will see you through. This is your one great chance to prove to Russia that democracy still prevails. Billy Graham, D.D.[53]

Graham's involvement in the social ferment of the South was not completely voluntary, however. He traveled to Charlotte the following year for a crusade. Afterward, he planned to hold a one-day rally on the statehouse lawn in nearby Columbia, South Carolina. The event would be his first desegregated service in a Deep South city since his seating policy had become public knowledge. (Earlier that year, Graham canceled plans to hold several services in western South Carolina. He cited health reasons, although racial tensions were likely a factor as well.)[54] The leading newspaper in Columbia connected the lack of segregation at the Charlotte meetings with the low black turnout, estimated at between 1 and 3 percent of the total audience. The scheduled statehouse rally turned controversial following the arrival of a racially mixed attachment of soldiers from the nearby Fort Jackson military base; they apparently had been assigned to set up seats for the service. South Carolina governor George Bell Timmerman, ever willing to play the role of blustering segregationist, seized the moment and argued that to permit the service would be to endorse the evangelist's integrationist position. Timmerman implicitly characterized Graham as a traitor to the region. "As a widely known evangelist and native southerner, his endorsement of racial mixing has done much harm, and his presence here on State House property will be misinterpreted as approval of that endorsement," declared the governor.[55]

Timmerman's brashness reflected the reality that newspapers in the Deep South had started reporting on Graham's racial views, especially those he voiced during the 1957 New York City crusade.[56] In Charlotte, the evangelist continued this theme, branding the bombing of schools and religious buildings by segregationists as "symptomatic of the type of thing that brought Hitler to power."[57] Timmerman soon moved to block the statehouse rally. Legally, he hung his hat on the separation of church and state, an argument typical of segregationists seeking to counter ministerial critics of Jim Crow. Besides, the governor claimed, Graham had likely chosen the statehouse location for "propaganda purposes." Timmerman, whose stand garnered national attention, neglected to add that Graham had spoken at the statehouse eight years earlier—or that, at the governor's own invitation, W. A. Criswell had delivered his 1956 harangue against integration there.[58]

Rather than challenging Timmerman, the Billy Graham Evangelistic Association (BGEA) shifted the rally to Fort Jackson, the nearby military base removed from state jurisdiction. The desegregated Sunday gathering drew an estimated crowd of 60,000, and the platform guests included former governor James Byrnes, an avowed segregationist. Graham avoided personally attacking Timmerman, but he alluded at a press conference to people who "have become so unbalanced by this whole issue of segregation and integration that it has become their only gospel." As if to compensate for even this backhanded form of criticism—which, of course, also took aim at liberal Protestants—Graham praised South Carolina's "warm friendship between the races" in his national radio broadcast that evening. "It is most unfortunate," he added, "that much of the world judges this part of the country by a small, minute, extremist minority and sometimes forget[s] that some of the finest Christian people in the entire nation live in this state."[59] That extremist minority had, of course, managed to elect Timmerman as governor. In Columbia, Graham clearly cast himself as a voice of evangelical decency rather than as a prophet of racial justice.

Graham's role in the South grew even more visible later that fall. In November, he made racial tensions a theme of addresses at the Alabama State Baptist Convention in Birmingham and Stetson University in Florida.[60] More important, he held his first desegregated service in a southern city that had experienced racial violence. In his visits to Clinton, Tennessee, in November and to Little Rock one year later, Graham for the first time directly linked his evangelistic services with the region's racial troubles. These postcrisis visits ultimately numbered four in total, and they sharpened the contrast between his evangelistic priorities and the concerns of civil rights activists. Intervening in the South by way of rallies and crusades allowed Graham still to define himself exclusively as an evangelist. In other words, he could safely fold his racial message into his revival sermons and, when pressed, explicitly prioritize the conversion of souls over the transformation of racial sentiments.

The first such intervention took place in the small East Tennessee city of Clinton, where in October 1958 segregationists had bombed the local high school. The school had already experienced rioting during its integration two years earlier. Along with Little Rock and Mansfield, Texas, Clinton had come to symbolize the violent emergence of grassroots massive resistance to the *Brown* decision.[61] Two months after the bombing, Graham responded to a challenge from nationally syndicated newspaper columnist Drew Pearson and moderate Tennessee senator Estes Kefauver, and held a gathering in a gymnasium near the bombed-out high school. The evangelist also worked with an organization created by Pearson to raise funds to rebuild the high school. Graham put Pearson in touch with possible members of the group, although he declined an invitation to chair it.[62] The Clinton meeting was simultaneously a community rally and a church service. Before Graham's sermon, Pearson and area leaders recounted the bombing story and outlined their fundraising efforts. Pearson praised the local school board for its "unflinching determination to go ahead and rebuild the school as a symbol of law and order."[63]

In his Clinton message, Graham voiced his social ethic in all of its doctrinal straightforwardness and political ambiguity. A racially mixed crowd of 5,000 turned out to hear a sermon drawn from the Good Samaritan story and Christ's commandment to love thy neighbor. Christians, Graham emphasized in a recapitulation of his warning to Timmerman, "must not allow integration or segregation to become our gospel." Either position "minus God equals chaos." Reflecting his evangelical focus on the spirit-filled will, Graham argued that "love and understanding cannot be forced by bayonets. . . . We must respect the law, but keep in mind that it is powerless to change the human heart." His stress on the conversion moment and his dismissal of purely political solutions hardly represented a rousing call to extend neighborly love beyond the sphere of daily interaction. What truly distinguished the Clinton rally from the many other services Graham held that year, though, were the circumstances behind his appearance in this traumatized southern town. His decision to affirm Clinton in its response to segregationist violence conveyed a sociopolitical message evident in a *Knoxville News-Sentinel* headline the following morning: "Evangelist Calls for *Love, Law and Order*" (emphasis mine). While Graham later recalled opposition from the local Citizens' Council to his visit, he spoke at the time of his desire to demonstrate that most Clinton residents were Christians and good citizens.[64]

The following year, the evangelist visited Little Rock, well after his initial pledge to travel there if invited by area ministers. Although a small group of pastors had requested Graham's presence the year before, every segregationist minister and most of the pro-desegregation ministers consulted in Little Rock had objected to the idea.[65] Moreover, Little Rock congressman and SBC president Brooks Hays, a racial moderate whose political future then hung in the balance, cautioned the evangelist against visiting so soon after the violence at Central High School. (After Hays lost his 1958 reelection bid, Graham addressed a banquet given in his honor.)[66] Graham's trip to Little Rock finally occurred in September 1959, when he held two rallies in the city's downtown football stadium. Continued tensions over integration likely contributed to his decision to forgo earlier plans for a multiweek crusade in August. The chair of the rally committee was influential Southern Baptist minister and racial moderate W. O. Vaught, whom Graham had introduced and praised at the Charlotte crusade for his work during the Little Rock crisis.[67]

As in Clinton, Graham attempted to clarify his role as an evangelist and only that, but he could not escape the political implications of his visit. The desegregated nature of the rallies had been well publicized, and questions remained about whether Governor Orval Faubus and the Little Rock police force would provide adequate security for the services. These concerns were pressing because the Little Rock Citizens' Council had launched its own crusade against the evangelist. According to Citizens' Council chaplain Wesley Pruden, who was something of a celebrity among the massive resistance set, the group distributed forty thousand flyers attacking the integrationist agenda of both Graham and the ministers who had invited him. In making the case for Graham (and, by implication, the case against Faubus), the liberal *Arkansas Gazette* emphasized the evangelist's southern identity: "Billy Graham has preached the gospel on every continent and in the isles across the sea, but his heart, as he has said, has remained in his native South." The editorial reflected what two sociologists called the "exaggerated southerner technique," a strategy Graham and other moderate or liberal southern ministers (along with their secular counterparts) employed to accentuate their regional credentials.[68]

Even though Graham downplayed the racial aspect of the Little Rock rallies, he did not avoid commenting on that matter altogether. "I have said many times," he reiterated in a press conference, "that nobody can cite the Bible as a defense for segregation." The two services drew a combined crowd of around 50,000 (including a young William Jefferson Clinton) and featured no racial incidents, although fear of violence likely depressed the overall attendance. A glowing report written for the BGEA emphasized that the rally united people "not as integrationists or segregationists, but as Christians." In one of his sermons, Graham urged the audience to "obey constitutional authority as long as it doesn't interfere with the worship of God." Addressing the generic sinner, Graham implied that regenerated hearts should lead to renewed social consciences as well: "When a moral issue comes up you don't really stand up for what you know is right. You're spiritually dead."[69]

More striking than Graham's occasional comments on race were the ways in which his visit served the interests of city boosters seeking to revive the image of Little Rock. That image had received a further blow only days before the rally, when segregationists dynamited the city school board headquarters. The bombings occurred just as public schools were reopening after a year of forced closure by Governor Faubus.[70] In the case of one recognizable Little Rock citizen and Graham supporter, Jimmy Karam, the rallies helped to resuscitate his personal reputation. To label Karam mercurial would be an understatement. A Little Rock clothier, friend of Faubus, and former associate of the Urban League whom bystanders had identified as a supervisor of the 1957 violence at Central High School, Karam was rough-edged and opportunistic, yet desperate to revise his well-earned notoriety as a thug. Only months before his antics at Central High School, a thoroughly nonreligious Karam had attended Graham's 1957 New York crusade, which he claimed had exerted no effect on him. By early 1959, however, Karam had come under the influence of W. O. Vaught, pastor of the most prominent Baptist church in Little Rock, who guided him into the faith. Karam became a leading sponsor of the Graham visit and continued to support the evangelist in subsequent decades. During the Little Rock rallies, the evangelist and the convert visited four of the school board bombing suspects in jail.[71] Karam's story made the pages of *Time* magazine—as did the fact that, although he had recanted his role as a segregationist rabble rouser, he declined to state whether he personally still supported Jim Crow. His critics noted that he definitely still backed Governor Faubus.[72]

The Little Rock rallies, alas, did not net even an ambiguous racial conversion from Faubus, who had also attended the New York crusade (likely with Karam). During the one Little Rock service the governor attended, he arrived late and momentarily had to sit on the stadium's concrete stairs. A photograph in the strongly anti-Faubus *Arkansas Gazette* shows him searching for a seat while a young black male, sporting sunglasses, sits comfortably in front of the pacing governor. According to one report, Graham and Karam paid a discreet visit to the gubernatorial mansion that day.[73]

To Little Rock boosters, most of whom opposed Faubus, the sociopolitical meaning of the rallies centered on "law and order," a term the editorial page of the *Arkansas Gazette* had readily invoked when arguing for obedience to court desegregation orders. The paper's more conservative counterpart, the *Arkansas Democrat*, invoked the same slogan in a political cartoon published during the week of the rallies. The cartoon shows three banners flying over downtown Little Rock; one advertises the Graham rallies, another announces a contemporaneous meeting of the Shriners, and the third declares the "Triumph of Law and Order."[74] What ultimately swayed many business and civic leaders to support school desegregation was opposition to segregationist mob violence and its debilitating effects on the image of the city. Their solution was to embrace law and order.[75] No less malleable than any other civic virtue, the slogan in Little Rock stood for moderation: obedience to constitutional authority, but not support for any specific reform or protest agenda. This usage of law and order preceded the significantly more familiar—and more consistently conservative—connotations the term assumed beginning in the mid-1960s. Graham tapped into a national, as well as regional, discourse of moderation. Two years earlier, *Life* magazine had described *Arkansas Gazette* editor Harry Ashmore as part of a "fifth column of decency" and opened an editorial praising Eisenhower's decision to employ federal troops with the premature declaration, "Law and Order have returned to Little Rock."[76] The Graham rallies offered evidence that Little Rock had finally achieved a degree of law and order, especially since they had occurred without incident. Graham appeared more than aware that his visit buttressed the interests of those moderates in the South who, as he assured an audience elsewhere, would triumph if only other southerners would cease resorting to "flag waving, inflammatory statements and above all, violence." This politics of decency might also triumph if more people knew of its existence. "The newspapers of America and the world have carried stories of violence and trouble on the front pages about Little Rock," Graham declared during the altar call of the final service. "I would like to challenge them to carry this story."[77]

The Theological Status of Segregationism in Postwar America

As both the Columbia and the Little Rock rallies revealed, Graham's actions and statements in support of improved race relations and desegregation garnered growing criticism from hardline segregationists. Governor Timmerman of South Carolina remained exceptional as an elected official willing to castigate Graham on record, although Frank Boykin privately tried to steer the evangelist away from supporting integration.[78] Most of the public reaction against the evangelist came from grassroots racists, including members of the Ku Klux Klan, from whom Graham said he received "incredibly obscene letters." By 1957, Klan leaders had added Graham to their attention-grubbing list of targets, labeling the evangelist a "nigger lover" and (following a freak injury he suffered after an encounter with an aggressive farm animal) declaring, "God bless the ram that butted him down the hill." Segregationist agitator John Kasper protested Graham's desegregated 1958 Charlotte crusade and similarly referred to the evangelist as a "negro lover."[79]

A smaller amount of opposition came from nominally more respectable white southerners, mostly from the Deep South. Following Graham's statement that he and W. A. Criswell did not always see "eye to eye" on race, the evangelist reportedly received several calls from First Baptist congregants demanding that he relinquish his membership.[80] Independent or nonmainline fundamentalist groups in the South, such as the Carolina Baptist Fellowship and supporters of Bob Jones University, represented a more common source of criticism. They chafed at Graham's increasing willingness to cooperate with nonevangelical groups but also objected to his positions on race.[81] Following Graham's 1956 article in *Life*, prominent segregationist minister Carey Daniel announced his break with an evangelist who now embraced "black supremacy."[82] A New Orleans segregationist who had been excommunicated from the Catholic Church for her activism publicly challenged Graham to debate the merits of integration.[83] Other critics attacked Graham for "betray[ing]" his "homeland" by entering into "racial politics" at the expense of his spiritual duties. "A lot of the good people of the Deep South have been heading for Heaven for a long time," editorialized the *Selma* (Ala.) *Times-*

Journal in 1957, "and they are going to get there whether or not [Graham] likes it." The title of another hostile editorial that year read, "Billy Lost South When He Jumped to Politics."[84]

Yet clearly Graham had not lost the whole of the white South. Even outspoken segregationists remained split in their responses to the evangelist. Criswell blasted Bob Jones, Sr., and his heir at Bob Jones University as "crackpot[s]" for their criticism of Graham.[85] While many fundamentalists, in addition to professional segregationists like John Kasper, felt few restraints in dismissing Graham or challenging him to debates, other Jim Crow partisans approached him with relative humility. The evangelist "is personally a fine young man," wrote a Charlotte resident to Graham's father-in-law, Nelson Bell, despite being "misled on the negro question." Another North Carolina critic wrote to Graham (in a letter copied to each southern governor) not "in a spirit of antagonism, but in the hope it will be taken as constructive criticism, not to be finding fault with the ministry, but to plead with [desegregationist ministers] before it is too late." If only Graham knew of Martin Luther King's communist ties, wrote one professed admirer of the evangelist, he would surely denounce the civil rights leader.[86] Perhaps these correspondents did not view the evangelist as a race mixer at heart. At the very least, they were nonplussed that a southerner who shared so many of their theological leanings could differ with them on this issue. A South Carolina newspaper branded Graham "one of the strongest advocates for total integration," while acknowledging his otherwise "wonderful work" as an evangelist.[87] Most important, though, such hedged criticisms testified to the social and spiritual clout Graham possessed, even though he remained hesitant to employ this leverage in a forceful manner. Critics of his racial views often felt compelled to pay their respects to this overwhelmingly popular minister of God. Many other segregationists never felt compelled to criticize him at all.

Nelson Bell responded to a number of segregationist critics on behalf of his son-in-law. Some of the charges coming from foes of Graham bordered on the absurd (e.g., the "black supremacy" allegation) and were easily countered. Other correspondents simply requested clarification of his opinions on racial matters. In answering these letters, Bell sometimes exceeded his task of defending Graham, to the point where he misrepresented or exaggerated the evangelist's positions and injected his own. As a racial conservative and a public defender of "voluntary segregation," Bell possessed many ties with segregationist activists. His biases surfaced in his letters, as when Bell wrote to one Tennessean that blacks "must *earn* social recognition" and declared himself "dead against" Martin Luther King, Jr., "and the cause for which he stands." In a 1958 letter, dated well after Graham's piece in *Ebony*, Bell declared that "Billy does not believe in integration any more than you and I do." When insisting on Graham's opposition to "forced integration," Bell never once acknowledged the evangelist's support for moderate anti–Jim Crow legislation and obedience to judicial rulings on civil rights.[88]

While Graham could not be mistaken for a civil rights activist, he placed much ideological and theological, if not always spatial, distance between himself and his southern segregationist peers during the latter half of the 1950s. He began criticizing segregation in religious settings and attacking the use of Christianity to justify Jim Crow a decade or more before many of his southern peers publicly arrived at such positions. Criswell, for example, did not openly endorse desegregated church services until 1968.[89] Like Criswell, Graham commanded appeal among grassroots white southerners (as well as politicians) well removed from the more racially progressive spheres of denominational publishing houses and policy committees. This appeal gave the evangelist tangible influence in the region—or, at the very least, inspired deference to his desegregationist policies.

Graham's shift toward racial moderation challenges how some scholars have viewed the religious status of segregationism during the civil rights era—and suggests that segregationism faced theological defeat well before it faced political demise.[90] Graham indicates the fairly early timing of this loss. "When southern ministers of Rev. Graham's influence begin to speak out against the evils of segregation," predicted a black North Carolina newspaper in 1955, "it[']s a sure sign that the day of its departure is near at hand." That forecast, of course, represented wishful thinking about both the end of Jim Crow and the role of white southern ministers in bringing about its closure. By no means did Graham create or drive the argument that segregation lacked a theological defense; generations of black theologians had already tilled that ground.[91] Still, his words had attracted obvious notice. His accessible critique of segregation in Christian practice lent the theological defeat of Jim Crow a quality of common sense, even as its exact relationship to political and grassroots efforts for racial change remained ambiguous. "The church should voluntarily be doing what the courts are doing by compulsion," Graham told a national magazine six months after the *Brown* decision.[92]

To be sure, race had not trumped evangelism on Graham's priority list, and it often played third fiddle to politics. Yet race was an issue Graham could scarcely—and increasingly chose not to—avoid. His moderate style and his friendship with numerous southern leaders gave him unusual access to a range of regional actors. Little Rock civic boosters had recognized the good a Graham visit could do to a town's image. His status also made him attractive as a potential consultant, adviser, or mediator for someone such as President Dwight Eisenhower. In this area, Graham functioned as a different type of regional leader.

CHAPTER THREE

The Politics of Decency

*Later, [Graham] confided to a friend that he felt like a fellow in the
1860s who put on a blue coat and some grey trousers—and got shot at by
both sides.*
    —Journalist Tom McMahan, 1960

*You are America's greatest ambassador and I pray for a continuation of
your great strength in the good that you are doing.*
    —Senator John Stennis (D-Miss.) to Graham, 1955

BY THE CLOSE OF 1957, Graham had positioned himself in the middle
ground between the segregationist right and the integrationist left—that is,
somewhere between his nominal pastor, W. A. Criswell, and another Baptist
and southerner, Martin Luther King, Jr. This middle ground held more than
religious implications. In the context of Little Rock and Clinton, Graham's
calls for good citizenship and racial tolerance, which he cast as fruits of the
conversion moment, dovetailed with the moderate rallying cry of law and
order. On other occasions, his politics of decency played out more explicitly
in the realm of governmental power.

    In engaging the South, Graham functioned not only in his self-described
role as an evangelist but also as a type of politician. He was subject to the
tendency of elected political leaders to vacillate between grandstanding and
caution amid attempts to balance seemingly contradictory constituencies.

Even though his stature in both the South and the nation gave him great leeway to express his views, he typically strove to avoid offending all but the most intransigent defenders of Jim Crow. At the same time, his activities in the South were intimately—at times, inextricably—connected with his service as a supporter of, and adviser to, President Dwight Eisenhower. Their relationship sheds critical light on the origins of the evangelist's seemingly obvious, yet persistently elusive, leanings toward the Republican Party. The enduring bond Graham formed with another rising star on the postwar scene, Richard Nixon, reinforced that tendency. Graham attempted to appear above partisanship even though he routinely made comments that buttressed the policy agenda and political ambitions of Eisenhower and later Nixon. His ability to link his international ministry with Cold War themes suggested his partial success in this area.

Graham's behavior during the latter half of the Eisenhower years shaped the remainder of his engagement with the civil rights movement, as well as the broader political trajectory of the South. His chosen leadership role suggests the complexities of the public and political Graham (which coexisted with the pastoral one). As an evangelist, Graham could stand removed from the fray of both the civil rights era's politics of rage and its politics of protest. Instead, he endorsed and advocated a politics of decency, which invoked evangelical faith, combined with law and order, toward moderate ends. The politics of decency straddled and selectively engaged the polarized racial discourse of the period. Here, as with so many areas of Graham's career, the spheres of religion and politics blended almost beyond distinction.

The Parameters of Justice

Graham's initial public criticisms of desegregation raised expectations about his potential as a regional leader. President Eisenhower was not the only one asking the evangelist to play a more active role in the South. In 1956, an Oregon editorial board urged Graham to return from his travels abroad and "try and convert the Negro baiting Alabama legislators."[1] Additional pleas for Graham to speak more forcefully about racial issues or to intervene more actively in the South came from white intellectuals, such as theologian Reinhold Niebuhr and leading southern liberal James McBride Dabbs, as well as African American clergymen and newspaper editorialists. The evangelist, wrote one black newspaper in 1955, "may lose a few of his friends in his own dear Southland because of his stand on segregation but he won't lose his soul." Two years later, a group of black ministers from the Raleigh-Durham, North Carolina, area asked Graham to come "back to our state to tear down . . . every vestige of segregation and discrimination born of our prejudices"—a request he did not take up.[2] In correspondence that same year, Martin Luther King, Jr., similarly urged the evangelist to "see your way clear to conduct an evangelistic crusade in one of the hard-core states in the deep south, even if it is not on as large a scale as most of your crusades. The impact of such a crusade would be immeasurably great."[3] The letter arrived soon after King had delivered an invocation at Graham's heavily publicized 1957 New York City crusade.

The early contact between Graham and King revealed both the potential and the limits of the evangelist's social ethic. Around the time of the 1955–56 Montgomery bus boycott, King and Graham commenced what evolved into a mostly cordial and, at times, consultative relationship. Their common southern background and shared status as Baptist ministers provided them with important bonds. Moreover, at least by 1957, they stood as the national spokespersons for their respective presumed causes: evangelism and civil rights. During a time when King still sought recognition from moderate whites (such as Nixon) and when Graham had promised Eisenhower to consult with southern ministers about the race issue, their paths inevitably intersected.[4] The evangelist spoke highly of King from an early date, declaring in an April 1957 interview in the *New York Times Magazine* that the civil rights leader was "setting an example of Christian love" in the area of race relations. King soon accepted an invitation to give an invocation during the New York crusade. With characteristic eloquence, he called for liberation from "the dungeons of hate" and "the paralysis of crippling fear" in order to create a "brotherhood that transcends race or color."[5] While in New York, King also held consultations with the Graham team on race relations. In a gesture Graham would long recall, King asked the evangelist to call him "Mike," a birth name used mostly by black intimates.[6] Afterward, King added Graham to the list of southern white moderates and liberals with whom he corresponded. With intentionally flattering prose, King praised him for applying the message of the Gospel to race, since Graham "above any other preacher in America can open the eyes of many persons on this question." Graham's southern background, the civil rights leader suggested, gave his message "additional weight."[7]

The continuing intimacy of Graham with segregationists eventually tested their relationship, however. One such friend of the evangelist was Texas governor Price Daniel, an outspoken Christian. As a U.S. senator, Daniel had signed the 1956 Southern Manifesto opposing school desegregation.[8] Around the time of the Southern Manifesto's release, Graham discussed with Senator Daniel his decision to run for the governorship.[9] Following Daniel's 1956 victory, Graham led an inauguration-day prayer breakfast and attended the inauguration ceremony with John Connally.[10]

King entered the picture in July 1958 during the heart of Governor Daniel's reelection campaign. One day before the Democratic Party primary (then the election of consequence in Texas), Daniel was slated to introduce Graham at a San Antonio evangelistic rally. The suspicious timing drew protests from prominent black ministers in San Antonio. The president of the local Baptist Ministers Union wired an urgent note to King, who soon wrote Graham expressing concern. Either dissociate yourself from Daniel, King told the evangelist, or at least "make crystal clear your position on this burning moral issue." Supporting a segregationist would severely hamper Graham's influence among blacks, he added.[11] In a sharp reply to King, Billy Graham Evangelistic Association (BGEA) associate Grady Wilson disavowed any political motivation on Graham's part. "Even though we do not see eye to eye with [Daniel] on every issue," Wilson snapped, "we still love him in Christ, and frankly, I think that should be your position not only as a Christian but as a minister of the gospel of our risen Lord." Wilson added that Graham had gladly invited King to New York City despite the "scores" of critical responses the BGEA had consequentially received.[12]

For Graham, evangelistic priorities trumped matters of social concern; Daniel's segregationist politics did not by definition undermine his Christian loyalties. The service proceeded as planned in San Antonio, where Graham told a nonsegregated crowd of thirty thousand that God judges individuals by their hearts, not their skin colors. Daniel went on to victory. Interestingly, a primary opponent mocked the governor for bringing in "a certain integrationist evangelist from an outside state" for an "11th hour appearance. . . . Is Billy being deceived and rushed to the Alamo City to try to save the Governor's [s]oul, or save his fast-sinking campaign?" Daniel, however, may actually have benefited from public complaints about the San Antonio service by African American U.S. representative Adam Clayton Powell, who also contacted Graham.[13] The relationship between King and Graham, meanwhile, vacillated between mostly private warmth and occasional public frostiness into the 1960s, when the ideological and theological differences between them widened even further. (Meanwhile, Graham remained close enough to Daniel to stay with him during his final night as governor, in 1963.)[14]

Graham's encounters with liberal Protestants were likewise generally less tense than they became a decade later. Here, the much-publicized criticism he received from theologian Reinhold Niebuhr served as the exception proving the rule. During the run-up to the 1957 New York City crusade, Niebuhr, a renowned professor at Union Theological Seminary and an influential liberal anticommunist, dismissed Graham's social ethic as "pietistic individualism" and "moralism," irresponsible atavisms in light of the complexities of the nuclear age. The "evangelical perfectionism" inherent in Graham's style of revivalism (that is, his focus on the conversion moment as a source for personal regeneration) represented a simplistic and potentially escapist response to the challenges of the twentieth century, argued Niebuhr. Thinking exclusively in terms of saving souls ignored the gravity of "collective evil."[15] Graham responded politely to this criticism, yet yielded no theological ground to Niebuhr.[16]

Niebuhr, however, grew significantly more charitable toward Graham when the topic turned to race, going no further than to urge the evangelist to address the matter more extensively in his sermons. Their views on desegregation at the time were closer than either would likely have wanted to admit. Despite their many theological differences (not to mention their political, cultural, and stylistic ones), they responded with striking similarity to the *Brown* decision, favoring gradual implementation of desegregation rooted in respect for the rule of law. Niebuhr, who took pride in his realist gravitas, was only slightly less skeptical than Graham about legislative solutions. Their gradualist positions, though, derived from differing emphases on the individual: for Graham, a stress on individual conversions and human relationships over policy prescriptions; for Niebuhr, a profound caution regarding the ability of individuals to avoid social evils larger than themselves. Niebuhr's significantly more incisive pessimism about group and individual behavior ironically led him to a place similar to Graham's often reflexive optimism about human regeneration. They both worried about the adverse effects of legally coerced justice and tended toward caution when confronted with the mobs surrounding Central High School in Little Rock.[17] They shared their concerns with many other white intellectuals and Protestant leaders.[18]

Niebuhr's critique of Graham resonated with two leading southern liberals, James McBride Dabbs and Francis Pickens Miller. Dabbs, a South Carolina Presbyterian active in the liberal Southern Regional Council, expressed the hope that Graham would mature as an evangelist and urged him to "step into the breach and make his own the power that lies both in the Negroes' insistence on equality and in the whites' shame at maintaining inequality."[19] Miller, a Virginian and former New Deal official, as well as a leading southern Presbyterian, abandoned hope in the evangelist after drawing initial inspiration from Graham's willingness to address race during the New York City crusade. Soon afterward, however, he observed how the evangelist shied away from offering similar remarks at a Presbyterian laymen's conference in Miami. Had Graham spoken like a "true Christian prophet," Miller later reflected, he would not have been "idolized by the rank and file of Southern Protestants." By saying "what he thought his audiences wanted to hear," Graham squandered an opportunity "to create an atmosphere favorable to compliance with the law of the land."[20] In truth, Graham had never ceased crusading in parts of the South and had addressed race in several speeches in the region. Still, as his critics could not help but observe, the evangelist had exhibited little desire since the *Brown* decision to crusade in the Deep South (a sentiment the 1958 Columbia, South Carolina, rally undoubtedly reinforced).

The Eisenhower Network

Many of Graham's critics also noted the way in which his social ethic operated not just within the framework of his theology but within the parameters of the Eisenhower White House as well. Graham's impulse to compromise derived not only from his evangelistic priorities but also from his political connections, which complemented and occasionally clashed with his racial moderation. Indeed, his private communication with political leaders would have confirmed the suspicions of many of his critics. The highest profile of these political allies, Dwight Eisenhower, revealed Graham to be a Republican at heart, if not in name. The Graham-Eisenhower alliance also suggested the way religion and region blended in the evangelist's analysis of contemporary politics.

The relationship between the evangelist and the war hero took root during the run-up to Eisenhower's successful bid for the 1952 Republican presidential nomination. Graham's faith in President Truman, who remained a threat to seek reelection until March of that year, had waned. After the hoopla surrounding their one and only visit, Truman pointedly made no time for the evangelist, despite repeated attempts by Graham to convince the president to appear at the 1952 Washington, D.C., crusade.[21] By then, Graham had joined a host of powerful GOP officials (along with a few optimistic Democrats) in urging Eisenhower to enter the race. Included in this group were several of Graham's political friends, such as Republicans Frank Carlson, a Kansas senator, and Walter Judd, a Minnesota representative.[22] Graham's contribution came primarily by way of Sid Richardson, a Texas oil baron close to both the general and the evangelist. In the fall of 1951, Richardson gave Eisenhower a letter, written by Graham, in which the evangelist expressed the hope that Richardson would convince Eisenhower to seek the presidency. In a quick response to Graham, Eisenhower (then serving as commander of the North Atlantic Treaty Organization forces in Europe) politely balked at assuming a partisan political identity while still in his post. At the behest of Richardson, Graham responded to Eisenhower with a flurry of theologically tinged hyperbole. "Upon this decision could well rest the destiny of the Western World," the evangelist wrote of Eisenhower's possible run. Graham asked for an audience with the general in order "to share with you some of the information I have picked up" from "your many friends" in the United States. With assistance from Richardson, they met in France during March 1952.[23]

After Eisenhower had taken destiny by the reins and entered the race, Graham's public statements routinely echoed the GOP theme of cleaning up a corrupt Washington, D.C. Graham also criticized the Cold War policies of the Democratic administration. "The Korean War," he told an audience in Houston, "is being fought because the nation's leaders blundered on foreign policy in the Far East. . . . [Accused Soviet spy] Alger Hiss shaped our foreign policy and some of the men who formulate it [now] have never been to the East."[24] As Graham would attempt to do in subsequent presidential campaigns, he carefully avoided an official endorsement of his preferred candidate. His public appeals on behalf of Eisenhower, however, were no more subtle than his altar calls. By emphasizing the importance of personal character when choosing elected officials, Graham played to a perceived strength of Eisenhower, who ran on stature more than platform. Even before the Richardson letter, Graham had declared during his 1951 Greensboro, North Carolina, crusade that the "Christian people of America are going to vote as a bloc for the man with the strongest moral and spiritual platform, regardless of his views on other matters . . . and regardless of political affiliation we are going to vote for the right man." He chuckled when noting that Republican senator Robert Taft, the eventual chief rival of Eisenhower, had "been running for years." A newspaper clipping about the sermon found its way into Eisenhower's files.[25] For his part, Eisenhower was keenly aware of the usefulness of the evangelist. At the behest of Frank Carlson, the candidate sought Graham's advice on injecting a religious tone into campaign speeches. The evangelist talked briefly with Eisenhower at the Republican National Convention in Chicago (to which Graham had received tickets from House Minority Leader Joseph Martin of Massachusetts) and later met with the candidate at campaign headquarters in Denver. In communications with Washington governor Arthur B. Langlie, Eisenhower supported organizing Graham and other sympathetic pastors on an informal basis.[26]

Graham specifically viewed Eisenhower as a viable candidate in the South, someone who could garner the votes of conservative nominal Democrats like himself. In a 1952 letter to Walter Judd, the evangelist praised Eisenhower as "the strongest possible candidate, particularly throughout the South." Graham went on to note that he had "been in close touch with Democratic leaders throughout the South," including the Mississippi delegation to the Democratic National Convention. The annual gathering of the Mississippi Democratic Party that election year had overlapped with his Jackson crusade. The chair of the Jackson crusade, hotelier E. O. Spencer, was a prominent Eisenhower Democrat. City newspapers highlighted Graham's visible presence at the meeting, as well as his eagerness to pitch Eisenhower to a prominent area businessman. To Judd, Graham touted the possibility of state conventions endorsing Eisenhower: "I have strongly encouraged these [southern Democratic] leaders to nominate General Eisenhower if they do not get a platform and a candidate suitable to them. They are going to have their Conventions again when they return from the Democratic Convention, as you know. I believe the General can carry great sections of the South."[27] Graham's increasingly apparent leanings raised concerns among his Democratic friends. Well before Eisenhower officially received the GOP nomination, Virginia Democratic senator A. Willis Robertson sent the evangelist a friendly but pointed letter expressing the sentiment of their mutual friends that Graham was crossing the line into partisan politics. Graham replied that he would heed the warning, although his attempt to do so likely differed from what Robertson had in mind. Graham turned down an invitation from Democratic official Leslie Biffle, a longtime secretary of the Senate and native Arkansan, to serve as honorary assistant sergeant at arms at the Democratic National Convention. The title would have granted Graham access to the convention floor; more important, it would have neutralized his seeming support for Eisenhower. Graham claimed that a number of his Democratic congressional friends had advised him to decline the position. Still, he found time to attend the Democratic convention that year.[28]

The 1952 campaign represented Graham's inaugural contribution to the postwar emergence of the Republican Party in southern presidential politics. His support for Eisenhower, while by no means uncommon among evangelists around the nation, also paralleled larger developments in the South.[29] Political scientists Earl Black and Merle Black have described Eisenhower as "the human triggering mechanism for the first Republican breakthrough in the South." In 1952, the GOP candidate departed from party tradition and actively sought votes from the region's many conservative Democrats, beginning the formal part of his campaign with a train tour of the South. Eisenhower captured the peripheral southern states of Tennessee, Virginia, Texas, and Florida, attracting half of all southern white votes. The "partial realignment" of southern whites toward Republican presidential candidates had commenced.[30]

Eisenhower appealed to white southerners for a number of reasons other than the attention he gave them. Obviously, many white southerners were dissatisfied with the national Democratic Party. Most remained loyal, if only for reasons of patronage and tradition. The unsuccessful Dixiecrat rebellion of 1948, when a group of largely Deep South Democrats broke with incumbent Harry Truman, stood as a lesson that the national Democratic majority could withstand southern defections. All of this served to make Eisenhower more attractive. Eisenhower's military stature and Cold War bona fides also helped. Finally, the growing economy of the post–World War II South led some southerners to identify more with the business wing of the GOP. In both the 1952 and 1956 elections, Eisenhower received particularly strong support from affluent white residents of large and small southern metropolitan areas, the very types of growing southern cities—the Greensboros and the Charlottes—that Graham frequented throughout the decade.[31]

Graham worked to bolster this new line of support. During the reelection campaign, he pledged to Eisenhower to "do all in my power during the coming campaign to gain friends and supporters for your cause."[32] At the time, Graham had more social ties with southern politicians than with any other political group (although his congressional friends were by no means limited to his home region). His own words and behavior reveal his deep admiration for those southerners whom he considered the region's "better sort" of leaders. This group included moderates, such as Tennessee governor Frank Clement and Oklahoma senator Robert Kerr—but also strong conservatives like Mississippi senator Stennis and South Carolina governor and former secretary of state James Byrnes. On this list were many persons who backed Eisenhower in 1952, including Byrnes, South Carolina congressman Mendel Rivers, and Alabama congressman Frank Boykin. As a friend and occasional confidant of numerous southern politicians who were supportive of Eisenhower, Graham could serve as an informal conduit between these Democrats and a Republican Party now seeking votes in Dixie. Graham team member Grady Wilson claimed to have also done his part to aid Eisenhower's cause in North Carolina during the 1952 election, but complained to Rivers about "those thick-headed Tarheels [who] would vote Democratic straight down the line even if the Devil himself were running."[33]

Strategic interests aside, Graham held a deep personal attraction to Eisenhower as a national leader. The evangelist clearly delighted in his role as a spiritual influence on the president, having suggested that the denominationally unaffiliated Eisenhower join a Presbyterian church. On inauguration day in 1953, Eisenhower attended a private prayer service at the church Graham had recommended, National Presbyterian. (Soon afterward, Eisenhower was baptized there.)[34] The election of Eisenhower raised Graham's hopes that evangelical Christianity had returned to national prominence. Days after the 1952 election, the evangelist told an audience that he had "sensed a dependence upon God" during two previous conversations with the president-elect.[35] Graham desired to perpetuate the new status quo. The BGEA soon announced a new "permanent national headquarters" in Washington, D.C., for what Graham called the "non-political" purpose of "bring[ing] what influence I can, from a spiritual standpoint, to our national leaders."[36]

Still, the evangelist was conscious of the precarious status of Eisenhower's gains in the South. Along with his father-in-law, Nelson Bell, Graham saw the need for more GOP outreach in the region.[37] In 1956, Graham urged the president to wait until after the campaign to enact specific policies on desegregation. "I hope particularly before November you are able to stay out of this bitter racial situation that is developing," wrote Graham. Meanwhile, he advised, "it might be well to let the Democratic Party bear the brunt of the debate." Two months later, Graham expressed concern that the GOP's efforts to attract northern black voters might hinder its southern ambitions: "I am somewhat disturbed by rumors that Republican strategy will be to go all out in winning the Negro vote in the North regardless of the South's feelings. Again[,] I would like to caution you about getting involved in this particular problem. At the moment, to an amazing degree, you have the confidence of white and Negro leaders. I would hate to see it jeopardized by even those in the Republican Party with a political ax to grind." Eisenhower took notice of the recommendation, although his campaign garnered many African American votes, including that of Martin Luther King, Jr.[38]

Even as Graham supported Eisenhower, he remained a registered Democrat. At the time, he rarely mentioned this status. The correspondence between Graham and Eisenhower revealed the evangelist as someone who, at least in the area of political strategy, thought like a national Republican during the 1950s. In 1954, Graham heard his friend Walter Judd speak at a Lincoln Day dinner in Asheville, an area of North Carolina with a traditional GOP presence. Graham recalled telling Judd afterward that if only his address could be delivered on national television, "*we* wouldn't have to worry about Congress remaining GOP controlled this fall" (emphasis mine).[39]

Graham and Nixon: Act 1

The Eisenhower years inaugurated what would become by far Graham's most significant political relationship, his decades-long alliance with Richard Nixon. Graham and Nixon first met each other, most likely in 1952, by way of North Carolina senator Clyde Hoey, although the evangelist knew Nixon's parents from his evangelistic work in Southern California.[40] The future president inherited from his mother a western brand of Quakerism that was, in the words of one Nixon critic, "more akin to free-church fundamentalists than to the quiet pacifists of the East." Despite the many differences between the Quaker and Reformed theologies of their respective upbringings, Nixon was no less familiar than Graham with the culture of revival tents and altar calls.[41] This underappreciated, overlapping zone of comfort goes a long way toward explaining why Graham felt a sense of intimacy and candidness with a politician whom so many others perceived as guarded, at best, and manipulative, at worst. Nixon did not share Graham's faith commitment, but he was generally comfortable with it. The politician thus differed from many of Graham's high-profile peers who concealed their unease with the salesmanship and panache of evangelism. Moreover, Nixon readily drew a connection between fishing for souls and campaigning for votes.

In critical respects, the early careers of Nixon and Graham paralleled each other. They both rose to fame during the late 1940s, fueled in part by the emerging Cold War culture of southern California (Nixon's home region and the site of Graham's landmark 1949 Los Angeles crusade), and their profiles similarly benefited from close proximity to Eisenhower. Graham surely delighted in the placement of a strong anticommunist on the 1952 Republican ticket (even though his first choice was probably Walter Judd, a finalist for the position).[42] By then, Nixon and Graham had already commenced a long-running tradition of golf outings.[43]

By 1955, Graham and Nixon were regularly corresponding. The evangelist grew increasingly forward in offering political advice and proposing speaking engagements. His letters reflected the flattery he routinely lobbed at political authorities of all stripes. Nixon was the "greatest Vice President in history" and momentarily warranted the title "Mr. President" during one of President Eisenhower's health scares. To a Nixon biographer, Graham labeled him a "Christian gentleman" who had "added luster to the office of Vice President."[44]

Graham stuck with Nixon during a 1956 election year rife with speculation about whether Eisenhower would return Nixon to the ballot. Yet the evangelist also hedged his bets. Following the 1956 Democratic National Convention, Graham made sure Nixon knew he did not approve of the sermonlike keynote address Tennessee governor Frank Clement had delivered there against the Eisenhower administration. Graham felt particularly compelled to distance himself from Clement, who had entered the convention as a vice presidential candidate, because of his friendship with the governor. In fact, rumors had circulated that Graham had ghostwritten a portion not only of Clement's speech but also of Arthur Langlie's GOP address. "I did write a brief note to each of them suggesting that they inject a moral and spiritual note," Graham later admitted, although he denied any ghostwriting. This was likely the case for Langlie. To Clement, though, Graham offered at least two rounds of recommendations on matters ranging from the Suez Canal crisis to South Korea, including advice not "to attack Eisenhower or Nixon personally." Clement, whose political rallies in Tennessee borrowed notes from revival services, had some reason to believe that the evangelist was in his corner.[45]

Graham tended to address the vice president (or, by August 1956, "Dick") as the friend he was, in contrast to the more deferential tone the evangelist struck with President Eisenhower. Graham felt comfortable enough with Nixon to mention the relevance of biblical prophecy for Cold

War and Middle East policy. He candidly asked Nixon for assistance with his overseas travel to such places as India and Egypt, where the vice president helped set up meetings with heads of state. Nixon also intervened in the Department of Treasury's evaluation of the tax status of *Christianity Today*, the evangelical magazine Graham had helped to found.[46]

Two related themes surfaced in the communication between Nixon and Graham: the status of Nixon in the South and the desire of Graham for Nixon to appeal to the conservative Protestant electorate. Both concerned Nixon's political prospects—his electoral viability and opportunities for him to gain influence. After Nixon consulted Graham during the September 1957 Little Rock crisis, the evangelist urged him to attend a Presbyterian gathering at which southern racial moderates would be in attendance. These clergymen, Graham stressed, represented "the most powerful influence on public opinion in the South." The following year, Graham asked Nixon to visit his "fully integrated" crusade in Charlotte, where Nixon's presence "would be extremely helpful at this moment of racial tension." Moreover, Graham wanted to chat with the vice president "on this racial situation."[47]

The religious South contained a wealth of political capital, as Graham alternately implied or stated outright in his correspondence with Nixon. Even though Nixon turned down the Miami and Charlotte offers, along with several others, Graham continued pitching opportunities for the vice president to address important Christian gatherings. Protestant leaders had begun to quiz the evangelist about the seemingly conservative yet religiously aloof vice president. "Very frankly," Graham wrote to Nixon in 1956, "you are in need of a boost in Protestant religious circles. . . . I think it is time that you move among some of these men and let them know you." With the permission of Nixon, the evangelist had already advertised the vice president as a possible speaker at denominational meetings in the South. Nixon soon accepted invitations to appear at summer gatherings of the Southern Baptist, Methodist, and Presbyterian denominations. Graham passed along suggestions for the addresses, in which Nixon appealed for the church's assistance in race relations. Since all three gatherings took place in western North Carolina, the retreat capital of southern white Protestantism, Nixon delivered three speeches in one busy day and found time for his first visit to the Graham home in Montreat.[48] The following year, Nixon offered a brief message during the final service of Graham's New York City crusade—a gesture that earned the vice president dozens of (mostly favorable) letters and telegrams from constituents.[49]

Graham proposed such engagements for Nixon because he wanted to enhance the standing of conservative Protestantism in the Eisenhower administration, and also because he saw Nixon as cut from presidential timber. By the time of the 1956 election, the two had already discussed Nixon's presidential ambitions, and by March of the following year Graham considered him "well on the road to being the next President of the United States." Toward the end of 1957, the evangelist wrote the first of several letters analyzing the vice president's electoral prospects. At that early date, he identified Massachusetts Democratic senator John F. Kennedy as a potentially "formidable foe," even though he thought the "religious issue" could work against the Catholic candidate. Thereafter, nearly every substantive letter Graham sent to Nixon contained some commentary on the upcoming presidential contest. "There is no doubt that you will win the Republican nomination," wrote an increasingly sanguine Graham in 1958. Nixon would face a Democratic Party divided by both religion and, as the evangelist had stressed to Eisenhower back in 1956, race. "There is also a growing possibility of a deep split within the Democratic ranks on the race issue," wrote Graham in a letter that demonstrated the strongly political tone of his correspondence with Nixon. "Therefore I think there is every reason for at least mild optimism."[50]

During the election year of 1960, the evangelist offered advice to Nixon in a dozen letters and telegrams, in addition to phone calls and visits to Washington, D.C.[51] One of those trips was for the National Capitol Crusade, where Graham introduced Nixon at a service.[52] Many of Graham's political suggestions concerned the South, where he thought Nixon could continue the Republican advances of 1952 and 1956. Here, the pivotal figure remained Eisenhower. The evangelist encouraged Eisenhower to stump for Nixon in Dixie, where "even you do not realize with what affection you are held." The president, who remained cool toward the transparently ambitious Nixon, replied that he awaited orders from his vice president. Graham cited this letter when making the same point to Nixon, who noted that Eisenhower was already scheduled to appear in Texas.[53]

Graham was not terribly concerned about the political ramifications of the race issue in 1960. He even suggested that Nixon (who, along with most leaders of his party, was not then perceived as a racial conservative) meet with Martin Luther King Jr. and advised the vice president that "in the South and border states," civil rights issues aside, "the more conservative platform of the Republican Party and the religious issue could well put some of these states in your column." Even the presence of Texan Lyndon Johnson on the

Democratic ticket would not put the South beyond reach, Graham argued. Nixon appeared to agree and noted the great reception he had received during summer visits to Greensboro, Birmingham, and Atlanta.[54]

Although Graham saw race as a divisive issue within the Democratic Party, he viewed religion as the main reason why Nixon could succeed in the South. According to information he passed along to Nixon in June, Democratic speaker of the House Sam Rayburn and Senate majority leader Lyndon Johnson (soon the Democratic vice presidential nominee) had confirmed that "the religious issue is *the* paramount issue in the forthcoming campaign."[55] It was, of course, also the paramount issue for Graham. In the context of the 1960 presidential race, the "religious issue" translated largely as the Roman Catholicism of likely Democratic nominee Kennedy.

Graham's concern about the religious issue did not derive solely from his loyalty to Nixon. Although the evangelist had distanced himself from the papacy-bashing world of fundamentalism by 1960, he clearly fretted about the prospect of a Roman Catholic in the White House. He shared these worries with a host of leading Protestants, including theological conservatives, such as his strongly anti-Catholic father-in-law, but also liberal Protestants associated with the *Christian Century* magazine, and less doctrinal divines, such as celebrity minister Norman Vincent Peale.[56] Yet Graham's evangelical identity and southern background added particular intensity to his worries about a Kennedy presidency. Roman Catholicism stood as a prime religious competitor to the custodial ideal of neo-evangelicalism. Avowed evangelicals like Graham distinguished their desire for more Christian influence on American public life from what they viewed as the outright theocratic and undemocratic vision of the Catholic Church. For some residents of the South, where Catholics were a pronounced minority beyond southern Louisiana, Catholicism served as an assumed other against which they could define themselves. "For it is in stern protest against Catholic monkey business that we feel ourselves most ourselves," muses the lapsed Mississippi Episcopalian protagonist of Walker's Percy's 1966 novel, *The Last Gentleman.*[57]

Graham's correspondence suggests that he was more than aware of the political implications of such sentiments. He surely recalled why his own father and many other Charlotte whites had voted against the 1928 Democratic presidential nominee, Al Smith, a Catholic and a foe of prohibition. The evangelist later remembered doing a victory dance with schoolmates in the aftermath of Smith's defeat. Graham understood that a Kennedy candidacy would stir similar anti-Vatican sentiments and expressed no reservations about that prospect. "I think there is a distinct possibility that you can capture several Southern states if Kennedy is your opponent," Graham wrote to Nixon in May 1960. With Kennedy destined to attract the exclusive support of American Catholics, Graham urged Nixon to "concentrate on solidifying the Protestant vote." As evidence, Graham sent Nixon a clipping about a 1960 Southern Baptist Convention (SBC) resolution urging public officials to remain "free from sectarian pressures"—a thinly veiled nod to fears that Kennedy would acquiesce to Rome.[58]

Graham's proposed GOP vice presidential candidate revealed how religious and regional concerns blended in his mind. Responding to a request from Nixon for input on selecting a running mate, Graham proposed Walter Judd. The anticommunist stalwart and former missionary to China would enable Nixon to "present a picture to America that would put much of the South and border states in the Republican column and bring about a dedicated Protestant vote to counteract the Catholic vote." The arguments made some strategic sense, and Judd emerged as a finalist for the number-two spot. Already in town for the Washington, D.C., crusade, Graham made himself available to Nixon to "talk this point over with you or any of your associates."[59] Nixon soon proposed a private meeting with the evangelist, Judd, two political aides, and Kentucky senator Thruston Morton, chair of the Republican National Committee. Graham also passed along the letter to Judd.[60] Later in July, when a Judd nomination appeared unlikely, Graham recommended New York governor Nelson Rockefeller (ideologically, at the opposite end of the party spectrum from Judd). The highest priority was clearly a Nixon victory. Judd went on to deliver a fiery convention speech, about which he consulted Nelson Bell for advice.[61]

The evangelist stoked the religious issue in 1960 more than he was subsequently able to acknowledge. At the start of the election season, Graham and the strongly Republican Peale turned down a request from Kennedy to sign an open statement that criticized opposing a Catholic president along religious lines.[62] During the run-up to the party conventions, according to Bell, "Kennedy called [Graham] on the phone personally. In that conversation, Billy really put him in his place."[63] In early August, Graham wrote to Lyndon Johnson stating his desire "to stay as much out of the political campaign as possible." Likely conscious of the open-ended nature of this promise, Johnson composed a gracious reply on Kennedy's behalf.[64]

Also in August, Graham convened a group of around twenty-five Protestant leaders in Montreux, Switzerland, for the official purpose of discussing world evangelism. Perhaps the most pressing agenda among the strongly anti-Kennedy group, however, was the looming election. Peale, *Christianity Today* editor Carl F. H. Henry, and conservative philanthropist J. Howard Pew were among the participants in discussions that, ironically, resembled the very type of clandestine cabal many of them associated with the Vatican. The attendees sized up Nixon's chances in the South and fretted about the Kennedy team's superior organization. Graham agreed to join Peale in encouraging Nixon to address religion more specifically in his public speeches. Shedding additional light on Kennedy's Catholicism, the Montreux group believed at the time, would only benefit the Nixon campaign.[65]

While Graham remained overseas, the religious issue brewed into a political storm stateside. In early September 1960, Peale served as chair for the National Conference of Citizens for Religious Freedom, held to address Protestant concerns about the election. Graham astutely refrained from lending his name to the Washington, D.C., gathering, which had close ties to the National Association of Evangelicals (NAE). He did, however, encourage Peale, who did not normally move in evangelical circles, to attend the gathering. Journalists promptly levied charges of anti-Catholicism at what they branded the "Peale group." Peale—who, like Graham, prized respectability—quickly dissociated himself from the conference. For understandable reasons, Peale's supporters later alleged that Graham had let Peale take the fall for what could just as accurately have been labeled the "Graham group."[66] To Nixon, who had steered clear of the conference, such developments reinforced his sense, expressed to Graham, "that you just can't win on that issue!"[67]

The Peale flap likewise confirmed Graham's reconsideration of the politics of religion, as he observed how allegations of religious bigotry could work to the advantage of Kennedy. (Lost on Graham and Nixon alike, of course, was the justifiable nature of many of those allegations.) The evangelist had already moved to protect his image. A week after detailing the Montreux meeting to Nixon, Graham released statements to *Newsweek* and *Time* denouncing religious bigotry and declaring he would not raise the religious issue during the campaign. *Time* had quoted his observation that some Protestant voters might be uncomfortable with Kennedy because Roman Catholicism is "also a secular institution, with its own ministers and ambassadors."[68] Graham might also have wanted to diffuse attempts by Democrats, including Frank Clement, to set up a meeting between Kennedy and the evangelist upon the latter's return from Europe.[69] Following the Peale fiasco (and Kennedy's subsequent address to a group of Houston ministers assuring them of his belief in the separation of church and state), Graham advised Nixon to adjust his use of the religious issue. While the candidate should still address "spiritual things" in his speeches (particularly in light of the NAE's efforts to mobilize voters), argued Graham, he needed to recruit surrogate speakers—preferably, respected Republican elders, such as Eisenhower or former presidential candidate Thomas Dewey—to condemn Democratic manipulation of the religious issue. In both cases, the evangelist waited in vain for action.[70]

Unresolved in the aftermath of the Peale fiasco was the question of a public endorsement of Nixon. More than anything, the vagaries of the religious issue contributed to the evangelist's final decision not officially to back his obvious choice for president. It was a close call, however, as Graham ultimately limited his definition of endorse to the word's most declarative sense. An endorsement had earlier appeared likely. "I have taken my stand," Graham wrote to Nixon in late 1959, "and intend to go all the way." After proposing to come out for the vice president during a June 1960 appearance on *Meet the Press*, however, the evangelist began to waffle. Perhaps, he thought, a strategy of leaving "the implication" of support for Nixon, as he had done at the SBC gathering in May, would carry "greater strength than if I came all out for you at the present time." At some point, the idea was floated of a public endorsement slated to occur before the August Democratic convention.[71]

Graham's overseas travels from August to October, when he held services throughout Western Europe, bought him some time, but seemed merely to delay the inevitable. In his correspondence concerning the Montreux meeting, the evangelist reported that he had sent a letter to members of his mailing list urging them to vote in November. The list was numerically strongest in the heavily populated states of California, Pennsylvania, New York, and the Midwest. "I think in these areas plus the South we can be of greatest help," he wrote, noting the likelihood that a majority of recipients were Democrats or independents. "I am on the trans-Atlantic phone constantly with people in various parts of America," he added, "and will be delighted to be of any service I possibly can." He also suggested that Nixon visit him in North Carolina during the fall. Unimpeded by modesty, Graham forecast that such "a dramatic and publicized event . . . might tip the scales in North Carolina and dramatize the religious issue throughout the [n]ation without mentioning it publicly." Nixon did not accept the offer. When he and his wife Pat arrived at the Charlotte airport during an October campaign swing, though, Graham's mother greeted them with a bouquet of flowers.[72] The evangelist's parents sat on the platform during the candidate's address, which Graham associate Grady Wilson urged the ministers of Charlotte to attend.[73]

By this time, Graham had come to believe that, because of "what the [p]ress did to Peale," he could not overtly mention religion even if he did endorse Nixon. Rather, Graham proposed to back Nixon on the presumably unbiased grounds of the candidate's superior leadership experience as vice president, thus making the evangelist "not so much against Kennedy as I am *for you*." In the final days of October, though, Graham publicly declared that he would not endorse a candidate. He chose to remain on the path he had paved in 1952 and 1956. He offered advice, implored Christians (implicitly, Protestant ones) to vote, and utilized opportunities, as he succinctly wrote to Nixon, to "make statements by implication that will be interpreted as favorable to you without getting directly involved."[74]

The final decision to eschew an endorsement, however, occurred after an incident, unpublicized at the time, that captured the precarious nature of Graham's engagement with Nixon. In mid-October, Graham discussed his endorsement conundrum with publishing mogul Henry Luce, a longtime Republican and an enthusiastic booster of the evangelist. Luce invited him to contribute a piece to *Life* magazine explaining why he supported Nixon. Despite some misgivings, the evangelist dashed off an enthusiastic article clearly endorsing Nixon, while avoiding direct criticism of Kennedy. In the article, Graham invoked his "responsibility as a citizen of the United States to let my views be known," something he noted Reinhold Niebuhr and other religious leaders who supported Kennedy had already done. The evangelist praised Nixon's qualifications, as well as his character. "But in my estimation, his outstanding quality is sincerity," wrote Graham.[75]

The piece ultimately found its way into the archives, rather than into *Life* magazine. No sooner did Graham send the article to Luce than he began seriously to reconsider it. With his wife Ruth, he prayed for some type of divine guidance. Seeming answers soon arrived. Two of his conservative friends, journalists David Lawrence and Paul Harvey, strongly advised him against letting the article see print. Concerned phone calls to Montreat arrived from Frank Clement, Florida senator George Smathers, and North Carolina governor Luther Hodges, all southern Democrats and friends of the evangelist. A similar appeal came from *Atlanta Constitution* editor Ralph McGill, who urged the evangelist to avoid endorsing Nixon and to stay away from the religious issue. Clearly, the story had leaked to the Kennedy campaign (which likely had passed it along to the *Boston Globe*). Luce had experienced his own doubts and had mentioned the article to Kennedy, who unsurprisingly thought *Life* should also publish a piece by Niebuhr or another Protestant supporter. The publication delay gave Graham time to compose a substitute article promoting the duty of every citizen to vote. Luce reluctantly agreed to run this decidedly less newsworthy piece, in which Graham still managed to warn the American people against voting as a bloc, reflexively supporting a particular party, or choosing a candidate based on who "is more handsome or charming"—points easily interpretable as unfavorable to the majority Democratic Party and its nominee. Throughout the frantic deliberations over the *Life* article, the evangelist had repeatedly attempted to contact Nixon, whose staff remained conflicted about how the piece would play politically. Nixon himself was unsure. In Graham's telling of the incident, he eventually received "a definite green light" from the Nixon campaign (probably, correspondence from the time suggests, from Nixon campaign manager Robert Finch), but only after the substitute article had already gone to press.[76] These details do not appear in Nixon's published account of the matter two years later, which has the candidate overruling his staff out of sensitivity to the volatile religious issue.[77]

Graham soon offered Nixon a generous consolation prize. On November 3, four days after declaring he would not endorse a candidate and five days before the election itself, the evangelist appeared with the GOP nominee in Columbia, South Carolina, the capital of that tightly contested southern state. Graham initially decided against traveling there, but he changed his mind at the urging of Nixon supporter James Byrnes, the beloved former governor of South Carolina. The appearance complemented the evangelist's desire to assist Nixon in the South. Graham gave an invocation at the start of a televised address during which Nixon, in a manner foreshadowing his more racialized southern strategies of 1968 and 1972, argued that Democrats had abandoned states' rights and other "time-honored beliefs." Graham, Byrnes, and New York Yankees second baseman Bobby Richardson (a South Carolinian) flanked Nixon on the statehouse steps—where, two years earlier, the evangelist had been prevented from holding a desegregated crusade—beneath a banner reading, "Dixie is No Longer in the Bag."[78] The slogan slightly exaggerated the status of the GOP in the greater South. Nixon picked up electoral votes only in Virginia, Florida, Tennessee, Oklahoma, and Kentucky, and ultimately lost by a slim margin.

Two months after the November disappointment, Nixon revisited the *Life* article, calling the original version "probably the best and most effective statement in my behalf in the entire campaign." He soon pitied himself that the piece was not published and still contended decades later that the article might have "made the difference" in the race. "While I did not come out openly for you," Graham replied in 1961, "I believe tens of thousands knew where I stood by my public and private statements—and by appearing with you in Columbia!"[79] Both of them had a point. Any serious inquirer could have surmised the leanings of Graham through the many well-publicized compliments he paid to Nixon. Still, an outright endorsement in such a tight election might have a swayed a few more evangelical voters—especially among Democratic-leaning southerners skeptical of Kennedy but also wary of a candidate long saddled with the nickname "Tricky Dick." In later elections, if Nixon remembered the difference Graham might have made in 1960, he likely took away lessons from the religious issue about how and how not to appeal to the prejudices of possible supporters.

Cold War "Safari for Souls"

Graham's politics of decency influenced him to hedge not only his racial positions (as seen in his disappointment of Martin Luther King, Jr.) but also the political partisanship his intimacy with Eisenhower and Nixon clearly suggested. Indeed, the value that many politicians perceived in Graham drew sustenance from the fact that much of the American public did not, at face value, consider him a political figure (never mind a politi*cized* one). During an era long before political pundits spoke of a red-blue divide, Graham offered an evangelistic message that, much more often than not, cut across partisan lines. It could also extend across national boundaries in ways that held implications for racial change back home. As Graham began carrying his evangelistic message to the third world in the late 1950s, both the racial and electoral facets of his politics of decency were on display.

During the Eisenhower years, Graham assisted the administration's agenda abroad as well as at home. He was well positioned to do so. As an evangelist with global aspirations and a southern fundamentalist background, Graham instinctively understood the balance the Eisenhower branch of the Republican Party tried to find between traditional conservatism and engaged internationalism. Like the U.S. government itself, Graham sought to cultivate his image abroad while guarding his right flank at home. The evangelist viewed himself as a representative of American democracy; to his supporters in the Senate, he stood as "one of the greatest ambassadors ever to represent us abroad." Graham ardently supported efforts to enhance the reputation of America overseas, lending his visage and voice to at least one United States Information Agency propaganda reel in the late 1950s. He explicitly appealed to Cold War sensibilities in seeking support for his foreign crusades. A 1956 tour of India, Graham wrote to his political friends, was "particularly crucial in view of the recent tour of the two Russian leaders. This will be the first time any American has taken this type of tour of India, trying to appeal to India's masses. . . . As you know, India now hangs in the balance between East and West."[80] Before the tour, Secretary of State John Foster Dulles advised Graham on how to convey a message of friendship to Indian prime minister Jawaharlal Nehru.[81]

Like the Cold War itself, the imperatives of evangelistic diplomacy put the race issue in a different light for Graham. At least since his 1957 article in *Ebony*, the evangelist had made explicit connections between anticommunism and America's racial image. "Race prejudice," Graham apocalyptically wrote, "is a cancer eating at the heart and core of American life and, therefore, threatening to eclipse the dawn of peace and justice for all humanity."[82] Racial tensions also threatened his evangelistic work overseas.

The 1960 "Safari for Souls," Graham's extended tour of nearly a dozen African nations and colonies conducted at the start of that election year, provided a particularly keen example of how his Cold War commitments blended with his evangelistic agenda. The Africa visit represented an intriguing cross section of Graham's Cold War, southern, and evangelistic sensibilities. Encountering firsthand the legacy of European colonialism in Africa was an eye-opening experience for the evangelist and his team. In heavily Muslim Nigeria, for example, they returned to using the term "campaign" in place of the historically loaded "crusade." In several areas still under European control or influence, the team encountered racial structures similar to those in the American South. Graham retained his commitment to holding desegregated services, however. In Southern Rhodesia, the BGEA refused to conduct separate services for Europeans and Africans. Graham eventually held racially mixed meetings in both Southern and Northern Rhodesia, while declining to preach in apartheid South Africa until he could do the same there. From Victoria Falls, he declared that "race barriers" in South Africa "will ultimately have to end." The BGEA had made sure to avoid even traveling through the Union of South Africa, since African American team evange-list Howard Jones would not have been able to obtain a transit visa there.[83]

Graham experienced Africa from the perspective of an American missionary-cum-ambassador. He was keenly aware of the changing racial environment across the continent, of the difference between the newly independent nations and those white-controlled cities he pithily termed "as modern as Europe's and as color conscious as Mississippi's."[84] The Africa tour only reinforced his description of America's racial hypocrisy as "one of its greatest black eyes" to a largely nonwhite world.[85] Likewise, wrote Graham, the "embarrassment" of racism threatened to "weaken us to the point where communism will gain the ultimate victory."[86] His observations resembled those of Southern Baptist missionaries who had already realized how the Great Commission could conflict with Jim Crow traditions.[87] On at least one occasion during his Africa tour, Graham spoke as a representative of the Southern Baptist Foreign Mission Board.[88]

The Cold War context of the Safari for Souls thrust Graham into an ambassadorial position. That setting, specifically, was an emerging postcolonial Africa susceptible to the allure of communist alignment. A brochure advertising the tour noted that the crusade occurred during a critical year "when possibly six new independent states will be born."[89] Cold War concerns were a major subtheme of a book-length treatment of the tour, written by Tom McMahan, a journalist with the *Columbia* (S.C.) *State*. "Africa is reaching out for a new faith to believe, a new flag to follow," wrote McMahan. "Will it be Christ or Mohammad? Or Communism which lurks in the shadows?" To be sure, he offered, "anti-Communism is not the motivating reason for spreading the Gospel, but it is a frequent by-product." To Graham, this side effect was especially evident in Liberia, whose leadership possessed close ties to American Protestantism. The chair of the Liberia campaign was Vice President William R. Tolbert, Jr., who would later serve as president of the Baptist World Alliance. Liberia's president, William V. S. Tubman, was a Methodist minister.[90] The *AME Church Review*, the scholarly publication of the African Methodist Episcopal church, ran a photograph of Tubman presenting Graham with an honorary award at the start of the campaign. Alabama native John F. Little, an AME pastor then based in Monrovia, served as secretary for the Liberia campaign.[91] When Graham returned to the United States, he discussed the Africa tour with Eisenhower and Nixon, encouraging the president to attend independence ceremonies in Lagos, Nigeria.[92] Graham thus remained aware of the interrelation of global anticommunism and moderate racial politics with his evangelism.

That numerous public figures in the latter half of the 1950s saw Graham as a racial mediator in the South as well as an ideal Cold War ambassador suggested the important theological, social, and political space the evangelist occupied. It was an alternately interventionist and hamstrung position that reflected Graham's evangelistic priorities, his personal politics, and his wariness of risking public criticism. Graham, in other words, had options. As an evangelist safely removed from the worlds of Senate filibusters against civil rights legislation and picket lines protesting Jim Crow laws, yet possessing access to persons associated with both activities, he could engage the race issue on his own terms. Graham's moderate position gave him leverage, but it also permitted him to feel a sense of persecution and, in turn, to confuse caution with courage. He likened himself (in the words of a sympathetic reporter) to "a fellow in the 1860s who put on a blue coat and some grey trousers—and got shot at by both sides."[93] In the end, Graham's chosen role pleased Eisenhower and Nixon but disappointed civil rights activists and segregationist stalwarts alike.

Any evaluation of Graham's presence in the Eisenhower-era South, then, must come to grips with his political leanings, as well as his evangelical social ethic. At times, those leanings turned into outright partisanship. His public stature and his message of racial decency made him capable of valuable service to the region, especially to regional boosters. During Eisenhower's second term, as the vogue of racial moderation intensified with each Clinton and Little Rock, Graham was particularly well positioned to lend legitimacy to the forces of civil, if ill-defined, caution. His desegregated meetings in the late 1950s served as foils for, and alternatives to, such arch segregationists as Orvall Faubus and George Bell Timmerman, while simultaneously circumventing the thorny details of school desegregation that had spawned massive resistance in the first place. Graham's appeals to evangelical universalism and its secular corollary, the politics of decency, carved out critical space to the left of ardent segregationists and to the right of civil rights backers, and, more ambiguously, assisted efforts to rehabilitate the South's image. In places like Clinton and Little Rock, Graham appealed to neighbor love as well as law and order—messages sadly missing from so much of the public discourse of the white South. At the same time, he never stopped defending his home region, suggesting that racist demagogues did not speak for the true South, which he sought to showcase in his rallies. For the time being, the moderate white South could assert itself merely by proving what it was not: the mob in Little Rock or the bombers in Clinton. Likewise, Graham could easily condemn extremists on the right while responding hardly at all to the supposed radicals on the other end of the political spectrum. He could describe himself as a foe of Jim Crow and as a friend of racial tolerance, an opponent of racial violence and a supporter of obeying the law—and leave it at that, all the while segmenting his racial views from his ambitions for Eisenhower and Nixon in the South. Such was his politics of decency.

This moment of moderation began to fade during the first half of the 1960s, when civil rights activism, rather than resistance to school desegregation, grabbed the headlines and took clearer shape in the realm of partisan politics. Civil rights leaders increasingly recognized that Graham sought to promote the South's moderate Christian whites at least as much as he aspired to further racial tolerance. The divisive issue of civil disobedience moved to the forefront, requiring national and southern figures alike to take clearer positions on the relationship between the law, justice, and—for Graham— faith. With his answers, the implications of the politics of decency grew more loaded. Meanwhile, the existing discordance between appeals to evangelical universalism and exhortations to the beloved community, between the lyrics of "Just as I Am" and those of "We Shall Overcome," grew more strained.

CHAPTER FOUR

"Another Kind of March"

I have been holding demonstrations for fifteen years, but in a stadium where it is legal.
—Billy Graham, 1965

If the law says that I cannot march or I cannot demonstrate, I ought not to march and I ought not to demonstrate. And if the law tells me that I should send my children to a school where there are both races, I should obey that law also. . . . Only by maintaining law and order are we going to keep our democracy and our nation great.
—Billy Graham, 1965

BY 1960, Billy Graham's racial moderation had made him useful, in differing ways, to both Dwight Eisenhower and Martin Luther King, Jr. When the civil rights movement reached a climax during the mid-1960s, President Lyndon Johnson similarly viewed the evangelist as a mediating presence in the South. To King and other civil rights leaders, though, Graham's reputation had by then begun a decline from which the evangelist would never fully recover. The first half of the 1960s widened the gap between Graham and the broader civil rights movement.

That process was only beginning when in 1960 Graham and King flew together from San Juan, Puerto Rico, to Rio de Janeiro, Brazil, to attend the annual meeting of the Baptist World Alliance. In Rio, King told his fellow Baptists that the evangelist's presence in the South had made his own efforts easier. Their work, Graham asserted in later years, was complementary.[1] In reality, their differences grew greater with each passing year of the tumultuous 1960s. At the time of the Rio meeting, King was already identified with boycotts and other nonviolent forms of protest, but not yet with the significantly more controversial tactic of civil disobedience. Later that summer, he participated in his first sit-in, setting off a chain of judicial retribution that led to a stint in a rural Georgia prison and intervention by Robert Kennedy on his behalf (while John F. Kennedy famously telephoned Coretta Scott King in a gesture of sympathy).[2] Graham, trying only somewhat successfully to avoid a public endorsement of Richard Nixon during that election year, sequestered himself in Europe for the remainder of the summer. During the first three years of the 1960s, the evangelist kept a comparatively low domestic profile and largely avoided the South, expanding into South America the outreach he had already cultivated in Europe, Asia, and Africa. At home, he addressed school prayer as much as any other social issue, railing on a Supreme Court decision restricting prayer in public schools before moderating his initial criticism of the judicial branch.[3]

As civil rights activists adopted more direct strategies and subsequently encountered resistance that made Clinton and Little Rock pale in comparison, Graham shifted his attention back to the race problem. His arguments paralleled those he had made during the school desegregation crisis of the late 1950s. Only now Graham more specifically targeted civil rights activists for censure. He publicly questioned the prudence of their tactics, ominously alluded to subversive elements within the civil rights movement, and routinely called for King and others to eschew protests in favor of dialogue and the legislative process (even though he elsewhere doubted the effectiveness of civil rights laws). Focusing his energy on the White House and away from the streets, Graham tacitly aligned himself with the basic civil rights agenda of President Johnson, who in turn influenced the course of Graham's regional leadership. As the strategic relevance of the evangelist decreased in the estimation of King, it grew in the eyes of Johnson, who sought out Graham as a political ally and a racial conciliator. Graham did not fulfill all of Johnson's expectations, yet he did pay three visits to racially tense Alabama amid the passage of landmark civil rights legislation in 1964 and 1965. During these visits, which featured services billed as the largest integrated meetings in either the state or the locality, the evangelist appealed to the rule of law as well as the rule of grace. In the process, he revised the meaning of his own desegregated services, describing them as lawful alternatives not only to racial violence, as was the case in Clinton and Little Rock, but now also to civil rights demonstrations, as seen in Birmingham and Selma.

The mid-1960s represented the high point of Graham's regional influence, when he facilitated the growth of a faith-informed, postsegregation public language and paved ground for the racially moderate Sunbelt ideal. While Graham and his southern booster collaborators worked to convince white southerners to accept the fated demise of legalized Jim Crow—and, through desegregated evangelistic services, modeled one way of doing so—they also steered the course of social change away from the more substantive goals of civil rights activists. The moderate forces of law and order (so distinct and decent when contrasted with a George Wallace or a Bull Connor) grew less civil in the face of demonstrations and downright vigilant when confronted with urban riots. Graham's brand of demonstrations highlighted the better part of the white South, but also foreshadowed the Nixonian politics of the "silent majority."

Different Dreams

Within American popular evangelicalism, a mythology of sorts has emerged equating the work of Graham and King on behalf of racial justice. "Billy Graham Had a Dream," reads the title of one favorable treatment of the evangelist's efforts to combat racism.[4] Such thinking has blurred the significant distinction between those ministers who marched and those who did not. It also has obscured Graham's fundamental discomfort with the civil rights movement. Part of a larger conservative effort to fashion a "limited civil rights movement" by invoking the legacy of America's most revered civil rights leader, the misleading King-Graham equivalency has drawn sustenance from dreams about what an alliance between them might have accomplished.[5] The interpretation first received popular dissemination in 1979 with the publication by Graham's authorized biographer of a letter from Senator Daniel Patrick Moynihan to the evangelist. "You and Rev. King," wrote the Democrat and former adviser to President Richard Nixon, "more than any two men—and, surely, with God's help—brought your own South out of that long night of racial fear and hate." Graham's own description of his relationship with King has also contributed to the mythology.[6]

A closer look at King and Graham exposes the fundamental differences between Graham's evangelical universalism and King's prophetic realism.[7]

By the late 1950s, the two had commenced a mostly cordial, occasionally consultative relationship. King's appearance at the 1957 New York City crusade led to momentary visions among King associates about a joint crusade that might eventually penetrate even the Deep South. Graham's continued willingness to associate with Christian segregationists, such as governor Price Daniel of Texas, soon put an end to such hopes, although King told a Canadian television audience in 1959 that Graham had taken a "very strong stand against segregation." As historian Taylor Branch has shown, moreover, King drew early inspiration from the tightly coordinated, strategically targeted crusades of the Billy Graham Evangelistic Association (BGEA). Most likely with the encouragement of the evangelist, the Graham team shared some of its trade secrets and public relations expertise with representatives from King's Southern Christian Leadership Conference (SCLC). Such cooperation occurred outside the public eye.[8]

The 1960 Rio conference was both the high point of the King-Graham relationship and the point of no return for the differences between them. At the international gathering of Baptist leaders, Graham organized a banquet in honor of King and invited Southern Baptist leaders to attend. Either in Rio or during a layover in Puerto Rico, the two found occasion for extended conversation. Soon afterward, Graham recounted his effort to sell King on Richard Nixon, and he advised the presidential candidate to meet with the civil rights leader.[9] Later, Graham recalled words from King that now stand as exhibit A in the case for their complementarity. The evangelist attributed the following advice to King: "You stay in the stadiums, Billy, because you will have far more impact on the white establishment there than you would if you marched in the streets. Besides that, you have a constituency that will listen to you, especially among white people, who may not listen so much to me. But if a leader gets too far out in front of his people, they will lose sight of him and not follow him any longer."[10] The first two published versions of this directive reverse the flow of those words, with Graham remembering a proposal to King to "let me do my work in the stadiums, Mike, and you do yours in the streets."[11] A subsequent source offers an earlier point of origin for similar language, the 1957 New York City crusade, but attributes the comments to King.[12] The civil rights leader may well have privately affirmed or uttered sentiments to this effect, and his purported advice contained a certain amount of strategic logic. In a more reliable line taken from the Rio banquet and quoted by the BGEA as early as 1965, King praised "the stand Billy Graham has taken in the South against racial segregation," a position without which "my work would have been much more difficult."[13] In the end, Graham likely would not have chosen any course other than the one he recalled King endorsing, and King was surely aware of these parameters.

Regardless of the origins of the remembered advice, it contained different implications in the context of 1960 than during the latter part of the civil rights era. Earlier in his activism, King found use for mainstream American leaders (especially southerners) who could make a basic case for racial fairness. Graham contributed to this task through his crusades, as well as through private meetings with southern religious and political leaders. As the civil rights movement gained momentum and broadened in ambitions, however, King sought support both for his activism and for strong federal civil rights legislation. He found no such backing from the eight white clergymen to whom he famously addressed the 1963 "Letter from Birmingham City Jail"— and none from Graham.

The 1960 Rio gathering signaled the close of any sort of tacit understanding between King and Graham. A mere four months afterward, as the sit-in movement spread to his hometown of Charlotte, Graham issued a statement on the question of civil disobedience: Christians had the right to "use every legal means to protest" injustice, but they also had a duty to obey laws that did not "interfere with our free worship of God." Graham's words, as news outlets noted, followed a nationally broadcast affirmation by King of the right to disobey "unjust laws."[14] At the same time, the evangelist continued to describe King in interviews and press conferences as a friend and to lend organizational and public relations counsel through backdoor channels.[15] Perhaps the last such encounter occurred during Graham's 1962 crusade in Chicago. By apparent coincidence, King and Graham flew there on the same plane from Miami. Their disembarkation together created an opportunity to pose for a well-circulated *Chicago Tribune* photograph.[16]

Nevertheless, by 1963, Graham was publicly criticizing King's strategies and periodically calling for a halt to demonstrations. The primary reason was the evangelist's opposition to civil disobedience as a strategy for achieving social change. Civil disobedience clashed with Graham's obvious preference for transforming society by way of individual conversions and, even more strongly, with his respect for ordained authority. Graham assumed that re-generated hearts led to obeying the law, not challenging it. "I believe in trying to change the law through the system," the evangelist later said during the height of anti–Vietnam War protests, "but when we go out and break one law, that leads to another law . . . until you teach a whole generation that it is all right to break laws."[17] Following this logic, Graham promptly advocated prosecution of the whites who had attacked the 1961 Freedom Riders, who were testing a Supreme Court ruling concerning interstate travel facilities, yet he remained unsupportive when civil rights activists strategically broke existing laws.[18]

Graham's public description of the civil rights movement suggested more than a little personal distance from it. While Graham knew King, he did not begin to empathize with the struggles civil rights activists faced. As the evangelist was the quintessential "prophet with honor" at home and abroad, his respect for the law had rarely been tested. He was decidedly unequipped and unwilling to grasp the toxic psychology of racial terror. When discussing civil rights activism, Graham often employed grandiosely neutral language, labeling the movement (albeit during appearances in the Deep South states of South Carolina and Alabama) a "great social revolution" that had served to "arouse the conscience" of the nation.[19] During the most tense periods of the civil rights movement, these terms of abstraction evolved into discomfort or even outright opposition. With each new landmark campaign—be it Birmingham (1963), Mississippi Freedom Summer (1964), or Selma (1965)—Graham called for a cessation of protests. Despite the deep Christian faith of many civil rights leaders and activists, Graham did not trust the movement to police itself. Under the influence of Federal Bureau of Investigation head J. Edgar Hoover, an obsessive opponent of civil rights who routinely passed along to public figures classified intelligence skewed to prove the presence of communists in King's inner circle, the evangelist voiced concerns about "subversive groups penetrating the civil rights movement."[20]

Graham's concerns spread to King himself. In April 1963, during the height of the Birmingham demonstrations and amid controversies over the city's mayoral election, Graham urged his "good personal friend" King to "put the brakes on a little bit." The evangelist doubted whether most blacks in Birmingham actually supported the protest movement and worried that continued demonstrations would hinder the influence of white southern moderates, including his editor friends Ralph McGill and Harry Golden.[21] This counsel, while pointed, resembled editorial positions taken by such influential publications as *Time* and the *Washington Post.*[22]

The "brakes" statement represented a turning point in press coverage of Graham and also ignited a long-simmering fuse of anti-Graham sentiment among black civil rights activists who had grown weary of his reflexive moderation. In 1960, while some white southern papers criticized the evangelist for his suggestion that racism damaged the image of the nation, a columnist for the *Chicago Defender*, a renowned black newspaper, praised him as "a powerful friend" who was "not a gradualist," and a *Norfolk Journal and Guide* writer urged him to "come home" and witness to the white South.[23] After Graham criticized King, the two groups exchanged editorial perspectives.[24] The "brakes" comment drew additional censure from the SCLC and the Fellowship of Reconciliation, as well as from Birmingham civil rights crusader Reverend Fred Shuttlesworth. "We have had the brakes on too long," declared Shuttlesworth.[25] Even the president of the National Association of Negro Evangelicals, a group with ties to the BGEA, questioned whether Graham grasped the gravity of the civil rights struggle.[26] As it surely occurred to some observers at the time, the evangelist appeared to fit King's stinging description in "Letter from Birmingham City Jail" of "the white moderate who is more_devoted to 'order' than to justice; . . . who paternalistically feels that he can set the timetable for another man's freedom."[27] King composed the letter a mere day before Graham's criticism.

Graham soon confirmed his new reputation as a roadblock to the civil rights movement. He failed to attend or to offer support for the August 28, 1963, March on Washington, which occurred during his second crusade in Los Angeles. While he eventually affirmed the white clergymen who attended the march, his comments at the time vacillated between insensitivity and dismissal.[28] Graham's weekly radio sermon a few days before the march included much of the racially moderate phraseology he had proffered since the mid-1950s. He raised doubts about "forced integration" occurring at the "point of bayonets" and again summoned the image of Robert E. Lee praying beside a Negro freedman.[29] On the same day when King delivered his "I Have a Dream" address, Graham focused his crusade sermon instead on Supreme Court decisions that restricted the public role of Christianity. If such rulings continued, he prophesied, "there may some day be a march on Washington that will dwarf the one held today for civil rights."[30] In a subsequent address to the segregationist-dominated Georgia state legislature, the evangelist said he agreed with King's vision of interracial brotherhood, although legislation itself could not bring about this dream.[31] Elsewhere, he was even more skeptical. "Only when Christ comes again," he was quoted as paraphrasing King, "will the lion lie down with the lamb and the little white children of Alabama walk hand in hand with the little black children."[32] While Graham still called King a friend and claimed to support his general goals, and while King publicly supported a proposed Graham crusade in

Atlanta, the two ministers differed more than ever in their respective interpretations of the relationship between human laws and higher laws, as well as in what they considered to be the responsibilities of ministers in public life.[33] Their differences only widened when the evangelist began attacking King's opposition to the Vietnam War.[34]

In this context, Graham's response in 1968 to the assassination of King was notable only in its overall clumsiness. The evangelist did not fly home from Australia, where he was holding a crusade, to attend the funeral. Even factoring in the burdens of international travel, this was a surprising move for an evangelist who normally went to great lengths to note his good friendship with all manner of public officials. From Australia, Graham produced a tepid statement that revealed his hesitancy to offer unqualified praise for the civil rights leader even in the aftermath of his martyrdom: "Many people who [have] not agreed with Dr. King can admire him for his non-violent policies and in the eyes of the world he has become one of the greatest Americans. He was my friend and I am stunned to hear of his death." Perhaps because Graham did not return home for the funeral, the BGEA took pains to note that the evangelist had asked his crusade audience to stand and pray silently "for peace in Vietnam, for peace on the streets of America and for the bereaved family of Martin Luther King, Jr." To the Australian press, Graham described King's death as leaving a "gigantic vacuum" in America. However, when Graham addressed the assassination during an *Hour of Decision* radio program only three days after the tragic event, he did not fill that vacuum with talk of social justice. He cited King's death to condemn "the Violent Society, where the law of [the] jungle is beginning to reassert itself."[35]

Lyndon Johnson and Regional Leadership

As Graham's relationship with King declined, his ties to President Lyndon Johnson strengthened. The evangelist and the politician had known one another since the early 1950s, when they met through a mutual benefactor, Texas oilman Sid Richardson (who had also connected Graham with Eisenhower). Their relationship did not really mature, however, until after Johnson assumed the presidency in November 1963.[36] Graham was not firmly in the president's camp until after the 1964 election. Even then, despite their very public association with each other, Graham's support for Johnson lacked the unreserved tone of his backing for Eisenhower and Nixon. Before the assassination of John F. Kennedy, Graham still hoped for a Nixon comeback within the GOP. One month after assuming office, Johnson invited Graham for an extended White House evening of swimming, dining, and a bit of prayer. The visit, which came as a surprise to Graham, flattered the evangelist, who made sure to inform Nixon that the president "did not mention politics once during the entire evening."[37]

President Johnson, while not especially pious, was the type of assertive Texan whom Graham admired. Even though the evangelist's politics were decidedly Nixonian, he held great affection for the gregarious, social Johnson. According to Johnson aide Bill Moyers, the North Carolinian and the Texan had "an almost visceral attraction to each other," due in part to their shared upbringing in southern outposts and, as Johnson later admitted, their propensity for stroking each other's ego.[38] Graham saw Johnson as a churchgoer with a Southern Baptist background (if not affiliation), while the president considered the evangelist a well-meaning, if sometimes inconsistent, ally.

With the presidential election of 1964, Graham momentarily halted his support for Republican candidates. In so doing, he paralleled that segment of the white-collar, metropolitan electorate in the South that had voted for Eisenhower and Nixon in previous elections, but returned to southern Democratic loyalties in 1964. In the presidential vote that year, the Republican Party failed to attain a majority of southern metropolitan voters for the first time since 1948—a development attributable to an increase in black voter registration, but also to the distaste many white moderates held for the GOP candidate, Barry Goldwater.[39]

Much to the consternation of Johnson and his staff, however, more than a few Republicans desired to align Graham with their candidate in 1964. Some even longed to make him the GOP nominee. Such hopes were nothing new. As recently as 1960, a scheme to draft Graham as an independent presidential candidate had surfaced among a group of southern fundamentalists.[40] Their vision, however quixotic, spoke to the ambitions and biases of much of Graham's constituency. The 1964 effort to draft Graham revealed the conservative, even reactionary, leanings of some of his most influential supporters. For a loose association of business and evangelical conservatives, visions of an evangelist in the White House became particularly compelling during the early 1960s. As Graham recalled after the 1964 election, he was "approached about running for president" by "some quite prominent people and financiers and people like that . . . over about a period of a year."[41] Few, if any, of these figures had voted for President John F. Kennedy, whose administration they associated with a number of worrisome trends: heightened Cold War tensions, resurgent political liberalism, and a sense (soon bolstered by a series of Supreme Court decisions restricting religious expression in public schools) that the purported religious boom of the Eisenhower years had ebbed. A number of them likewise desired to counter a perceived drift toward the Social Gospel within their Protestant denominations.[42]

The early Graham-for-president momentum came from at least two sources: John Bolten, a wealthy Massachusetts businessman and exile from Nazi Germany who had rededicated his life to Christ during Graham's 1950 Boston crusade; and John Conlan, a young, energetic conservative Republican activist from Arizona whom Graham had first met in 1954. Conlan and Bolten most likely knew each other by this time, but they did not appear to act in concert. In December 1961, while wintering in Palm Beach, Florida, Bolten shared his dream of a Graham presidency with journalist and aspiring Graham biographer Bela Kornitzer, who (after initial doubts) thought the evangelist a viable future candidate and "a lethal weapon against atheistic Communism." Kornitzer, who still considered Kennedy impervious to a re-election challenge, granted Bolten permission to pass along to Graham or an associate a letter describing his sentiments.[43]

Around the same time in nearby Miami, John Conlan met with BGEA associate Grady Wilson (and, quite possibly, with Graham himself) to discuss Conlan's "program for injecting evangelicals into the political leadership of our nation." Beforehand, Conlan had sent Graham a "confidential" brochure detailing his plan to train and mobilize "thinking, conservative American Christians" in time to affect the 1964 election. The ideological tone of the brochure—evident in its title, "Freedom or Slavery: A Message of Urgent Importance"—was thoroughly in tune with the grassroots right wing of the GOP. Conlan, though, initially sought an audience several tax brackets removed from the suburban warriors crowd. He told Wilson that such evangelical luminaries as W. A. Criswell, *Christianity Today* editor Carl F. H. Henry, and Oregon governor Mark Hatfield had encouraged his efforts. Conlan soon made a similar pitch to a who's who of conservative Protestant philanthropists, many of whom were Graham supporters. The list included Bolten, Maxey Jarman (a Nashville businessman and benefactor of *Christianity Today*), George Champion (chairman of Chase Manhattan Bank), Roger Hull (chairman of the Mutual Insurance Company of New York), Jeremiah Milbank (longtime treasurer of Boys and Girls Clubs of America), and Henderson Belk (Charlotte department store magnate).[44]

With assistance from Jarman, Conlan managed to convene an even deeper collection of Protestant pockets for a January 28, 1962, meeting held in New Orleans. The attendees included Jarman, Pew, and Bolten, as well as J. Howard Pew (head of Sun Oil and benefactor of *Christianity Today*), Russell Brothers (a Nashville businessman with ties to Tennessee governor Frank Clement), and Howard Butt (Texas grocer and evangelical philanthropist). These veteran capitalists naturally remained cautious about such an ambitious venture during an era when right-leaning activists were ever vulnerable to association with such "extremist" groups as the John Birch Society. Conlan's vision overlapped strikingly with the efforts of Christian Citizen, a short-lived organization founded in 1961 by Denver real estate developer and Southern Baptist layman Gerri von Frellick. Conlan acknowledged having had contact with von Frellick, but in a letter to Grady Wilson dismissed Christian Citizen as a "rip off" with confrontational tactics that would constitute "political suicide." Unfortunately for Conlan, the first press coverage of Christian Citizen appeared around the time of the New Orleans gathering, raising red flags about his own plan. According to Conlan, though, the New Orleans group grew less wary when the subject turned to Graham. Effectively, Conlan needed Graham to vouch for him. "The men at New Orleans," Conlan wrote to Grady Wilson, "decided to ask Bolten to report to Billy their enthusiasm for our quiet and rapid program, and to indicate to Billy that if he wanted them to go ahead on this program I had developed they would be off and running." The letter implied that Graham could be the flagship Christian statesman in this effort. "The program is ready," wrote Conlan. "It needs [God's] man to catalyze it." Left unstated was whether Conlan and the New Orleans group had specifically discussed the possibility of a Graham presidency. Their chosen conduit, Bolten, certainly was thinking along those lines. What Wilson had in mind remains less clear. "We shall keep our fingers crossed," he wrote to Conlan, "—hope and pray that in God's own good time we may be able to get some specific plans underway. We have several aces up our sleeve."[45]

One of those aces might have been billionaire Texas oilman H. L. Hunt, who came to share Bolten's dream of a Graham presidency. His son, Nelson Bunker Hunt, had attended Conlan's New Orleans meeting.[46] The elder Hunt was an eccentric billionaire with a history of sinking serious money into far-flung right-wing causes in a manner resembling the subsequent giving of philanthropist Richard Mellon Scaife. Like Graham, Hunt was a registered Democrat with close ties to the anticommunist wing of the Republican Party.

He had supported General Douglas MacArthur for the presidency in 1952.. Unlike Graham, Hunt was also a serial philanderer and bigamist with a penchant for gambling. In 1960, though, Hunt had heeded the influence of his new wife and joined First Baptist Church in Dallas, where Graham had held membership since 1953.[47] Hunt held a deep interest in the work of the BGEA, although he apparently was closer to Grady Wilson than to Graham himself. Starting in the fall of 1962, he sponsored the broadcast of his *Life Line* radio program on the BGEA's North Carolina-based station. Conlan had put the program managers in contact with the station.[48]

Starting at least in the spring of 1963, Hunt began touting Graham as a GOP presidential candidate. Hunt may have first pitched his vision to the evangelist during a visit with him that year.[49] The oilman definitely discussed the idea with John Bolten. Hunt wrote to Wilson in May 1963 regarding a possible Graham run against Kennedy: "Mr. John Bolt[e]n of Andover, Massachusetts, called me this morning suggesting the taking of a poll in 10 states to test the demand for Billy Graham to accept the nomination for President." Hunt opposed the poll idea, if only because so few Americans had even pondered the possibility of a Graham candidacy. "The Republican fortunes are looking up," he wrote, "but they truly do not have a logical candidate for President." Graham "would show up favorably in the polls," Hunt suggested, if only the evangelist would insert more "calls for Freedom" (i.e., anticommunism and antistatism) in his sermons and columns. Hunt appears to have viewed Graham as—in the words of an action plan he passed along to Wilson—a "Prospect," a potential GOP candidate whom the party should discreetly cultivate, without even the knowledge of the prospect himself. The action plan listed the South as a region particularly ripe for Republican gains. Other memos written by Hunt touted the political potential of an otherwise unnamed "Pastor Good." Even before his initial letter to Wilson, Hunt had been unable to keep his ambitions for Graham out of a Dallas newspaper. The story soon gravitated to the wire services, *U.S. News and World Report*, and at least one editorial page.[50] By July of that year, Gallup was polling a hypothetical race between Graham and Kennedy. (Kennedy won handily in large part because respondents had trouble fathoming a Graham candidacy, as Hunt had suggested would be the case.)[51] According to a later report, GOP officials, noting Graham's popularity in the South and Midwest, made inquiries to the evangelist during his 1963 Los Angeles crusade, three months after Hunt had written to Wilson. This was also around the time Goldwater and Graham first met each other.[52]

The oilman's machinations resurfaced dramatically in January 1964 when a well-sourced journalist for the *Houston Press* published an article declaring the willingness of Graham to consider accepting a draft for the GOP nomination. According to the article, which quickly traveled over the Scripps Howard newspaper circuit, interest came from at least three separate groups, as well as several evangelicals close to him. The piece referred to an offer Graham had received for "eye-popping [campaign] support running into the millions." As Jarman and other Graham intimates later confirmed, the unsurprising source of that offer was Hunt. The article appeared during the annual gathering of the Layman's Leadership Institute, held that year in Houston. The overlap between the conference participants and the type of Christian businessmen whom Conlan had solicited two years earlier was extensive. Howard Butt—who attended Conlan's New Orleans meeting but apparently had nothing to do with the Hunt proposal—had helped to found the institute. According to Grady Wilson, who arrived in Houston after the story had broken, none of the many BGEA staffers at the conference claimed any advance knowledge of Hunt's scheme. To the consternation of Wilson and others, Graham did not immediately refute the story, and the delay allowed time for television news anchor Walter Cronkite to mention the possible candidacy that evening.[53]

The following day, Graham moved to squelch the rumors. He would not seek the presidency, he announced. Citing intense pressure from intimates, though, he confirmed the basic truth of the *Houston Press* story. In Houston, Graham reasserted his evangelistic priorities as well as his political neutrality, noting that in previous years he had received similar inquiries from Democratic officials.[54] (Those inquiries, he did not say, came from southern Democrats whose political views did not differ greatly from Hunt's.) In early 1964, Graham could plausibly invoke his political neutrality. His party affiliation remained largely unknown, although the *Houston Press* story inspired Senate Minority Leader Everett Dirksen to embrace him as a fellow Republican.[55] Moreover, Graham's budding friendship with Johnson had yet to garner substantial media scrutiny.

While the Graham-for-president flap was a blip on the election-year radar screen, it occurred at a critical moment in the evangelist's relationship to White House figures, past and present. The liberal Protestant *Christian Century* smirked at Graham's need to convene the media to "disavow so improbable a possibility." Although Graham may indeed have forgotten how farcical a possible run would strike many observers, he was wise to announce himself off limits during a year when a desperate GOP eventually embraced a somewhat improbable candidate. By the time of Hunt's dramatic offer, with Johnson in office rather than Kennedy, Graham had likely overcome whatever temptations of temporal power he had momentarily felt.[56]

Graham had not, however, overcome his doubts about the current Democrat occupying the White House. Indeed, he had apparently not ruled out a triumphant late entry in the presidential race by Richard Nixon. In early February, Graham called Nixon to explain what the message taker termed "that Texas thing." The evangelist also noted that his wife, Ruth, was "terribly depressed" about what she saw as Johnson's "complete ignorance on foreign policy." A few months later, Nixon suggested to Graham that they talk after the Oregon presidential primary, when "we should be able to appraise the political situation much more clearly."[57]

The short-lived and understaffed draft-Graham movement accentuated Graham's perceived political utility and surely caught the attention of Johnson. Only four days after the draft-Graham story broke, the evangelist appeared with Johnson at the Presidential Prayer Breakfast.[58] During the election year, the president remained mindful of how Graham might assist his efforts to appeal to pious moderates nationwide. In May, Johnson pondered attending a North Carolina fundraiser for the Kennedy Presidential Library at which Graham was scheduled to deliver the keynote address. Johnson also thought that Jacqueline Kennedy, then still in a period of mourning, might make an appearance. By attending the event, the president argued, he could "circularize the hell out of it, even run it as an ad on what I say." Johnson ultimately decided not to travel to North Carolina, where before a crowd of 10,000 people Graham praised John F. Kennedy for his efforts to foster "racial understanding."[59]

Johnson, a tireless political brooder, probably remained a bit anxious about Graham until election day 1964. Word surfaced during the Republican National Convention of a possible grassroots effort to promote Graham as Goldwater's running mate. According to political gossip columnist Walter Winchell, the ever-persistent H. L. Hunt had promised to make the grass especially green for Goldwater if he could convince Graham to join his team.[60] Years after the election, rumors lingered about secret overtures to the evangelist from Goldwater aides.[61] In late August, on the cusp of the Democratic National Convention, Johnson broke with precedent to announce that he would attend a Graham sermon at National City Christian Church, which belonged to the president's Disciples of Christ denomination.[62] The Grahams stayed over as White House guests, during which time Johnson quizzed the evangelist about possible running mates.[63] In October, a Johnson supporter fretted that Graham "came very close to endorsing Goldwater" in a recent radio sermon. Goldwater, meanwhile, declared that his message and Graham's were complementary—one emphasizing national salvation via the Constitution, the other salvation through God. The evangelist put to rest most worries when he accepted a strategically timed invitation, facilitated by Bill Moyers, to visit the White House one weekend before the election.[64] The visit occurred amid lingering political concerns over the arrest of Johnson aide Walter Jenkins on a "morals charge," a scandal Graham had noted in his radio sermon.[65] Graham had misgivings about Johnson's request for "spiritual counsel," going so far as to call Nixon about the matter. According to notes from their conversation, Nixon "told Billy Graham he felt he would have to go, but to make it clear that if the visit were announced or referenced to in any way for political purpose, Billy Graham would expose [L]yndon."[66] Over breakfast during the visit, Johnson happily advised Graham how to couch his neutral stance in the presidential race.[67]

Some Goldwater supporters still hoped that, in his heart, Graham knew who was right. At the start of the campaign season, at least, they had some reason for optimism. Graham first met Goldwater during the fall of 1963 (before Johnson assumed the presidency), and the evangelist was favorably impressed with the Arizona senator.[68] Many intimates of the evangelist, including Grady Wilson and Nelson Bell, supported the GOP nominee. So did Graham's sixteen-year-old daughter, Anne, who was photographed and quoted days before election day at a Goldwater rally in Greenville, South Carolina. The event—which, Anne later recalled, made her father "so mad that he wasn't reasonable"—quickly led the evangelist to reassert his "strict neutrality" in the race.[69] Around the same time, Graham claimed to have received "over one-million telegrams" (upward of 60,000 on November 2 alone, according to the Associated Press), the vast majority of which urged him to endorse Goldwater. The correspondence crush bore signs of a well-coordinated effort.[70] Although unrealistic, a late endorsement from Graham might have helped legitimate a candidate battling charges of extremism, while also furthering Goldwater's efforts to reach out to conservative Democrats in the South and elsewhere. Goldwater "needed you as much as I did," Johnson later told Graham. The dreams of GOP loyalists aside, Johnson need not have fretted much about retaining the support of Graham, who informed the president after the election that he was "not only the choice of the American people—but of God."[71] At Johnson's request, Graham preached at an inter-faith church service held on inauguration day.[72]

Johnson obviously found Graham a useful political ally—a link to both the angry South and the proverbial Middle America—in addition to being a valued friend and occasional confidant.[73] The role the president perceived for Graham extended beyond that of electoral symbol or pastoral peer, however. Likewise, Graham's support for Johnson, while undoubtedly rooted in their friendship, also reflected the comparatively moderate nature of the evange-list's own politics during the mid-1960s. The two remained for the most part aligned on a number of critical issues, including civil rights and the Vietnam War, and the president could count on Graham to support much of his agenda. This fidelity was particularly important regarding civil rights, by far the most controversial agenda item during the first two years of the Johnson administration. The president needed allies among the few southern moder-ates who still had the ear of mainstream segregationists, but who had repudi-ated the politics of massive resistance. Graham fitted this bill.

Without specifically endorsing either the Civil Rights Act of 1964 or the Voting Rights Act of 1965, Graham went along with the thrust of the administration's civil rights agenda. He appears to have considered the pas-sage of such legislation as inevitable. His general understanding of sociopoliti-cal equality squared with arguments Johnson employed in support of civil rights legislation and the larger programs of the Great Society. "I believe when we speak of equality," Graham wrote to a skeptical inquirer in 1966, "we refer to equal opportunity, equal rights, and equal chance for develop-ment. Although we may never be equal, we all deserve the chance to advance and improve."[74] "It is insult to human dignity," he said elsewhere, "to turn a man away from a public restaurant because of the color of his skin."[75] While the evangelist was on record as a backer of federal civil rights legislation, he spoke of it less than enthusiastically. He almost always paired such statements with an invocation of evangelical universalism. "We need legislation, we need civil rights legislation," he said in a statement released by the BGEA, "but it's got to come from the heart."[76] Not long after passage of the Civil Rights Act of 1964, Graham similarly quoted liberal Senator Hubert Humphrey as saying, "Billy, legislation alone can't do it. It must ultimately come from the heart."[77] During the Selma crisis of early 1965, which gave momentum to the Voting Rights Act, Graham stressed the "right to vote" but questioned the viability of demonstrations.[78] Following Johnson's nationally televised ad-dress in which he invoked the movement motto, "We shall overcome," Graham effusively labeled it the "greatest speech on civil rights of any president since Lincoln" before characteristically calling for a cessation of demonstrations. With equal predictability, Graham emphasized that "a thousand civil rights bills will not ease the racial tension in America unless we have a spiritual renewal that will change our hearts and give us a new love for each other." He did, though, speak favorably of the pending Voting Rights Act.[79]

Endorsing specific legislation, however, was not Johnson's primary aspiration for the evangelist in the area of civil rights. Rather, the president hoped that Graham would assist with efforts to convince level-headed white southerners peacefully to accept desegregation laws. The search for prophetic moderates, in fact, was a vital component of Johnson's civil rights policy and received its most tangible expression in the Community Relations Service (CRS), a federal agency created to oversee the implementation of the Civil Rights Act in the South. Modeled on existing human relations councils, the CRS was intended to mediate between white leaders and black activists. Along those lines, a late 1965 White House strategy memo, which pondered how to persuade white southerners to stop acquitting whites for crimes of racial violence, proposed

> an organized effort by Southern leaders whose integrity and love of the South cannot be questioned but who have the vision to see what can happen unless there are some changes. These include men like Buford Ellington, LeRoy Collins, Luther Hodges, and others who, even though they hold "advanced views" on human relations, still enjoy the confidence of conservative Southerners. These men should plan a careful tour of the trouble spots of the South in which they will contact influential businessmen, professionals, and other community leaders who, when united, actually determine the fate of political leaders.

These figures, all of whom had close ties to Johnson, would inform the "Southern power structure" of the consequences of inaction, while also "persuading communities that murder is murder and must be handled as such."[80]

Graham clearly fell into the category of the southern moderate who could still garner the respect of segregationist officials. For good or ill, the evangelist had the ear of many opponents of Johnson's civil rights policies. While such access allowed him to crusade in Alabama, it also left him open to misappropriation by segregationists pleased to hear that only personal conversions, not civil rights laws, would finally solve the race problem. South Carolina senator Strom Thurmond, for example, selectively cited the evangelist in one of his many fulminations against the Civil Rights Act of 1964.[81] Later that year, in the aftermath of the murder of three civil rights activists in Philadelphia, Mississippi, Graham questioned the methods of the participants in Freedom Summer, the student-infused voter registration campaign in that most segregationist of states, arguing that "you cannot accomplish a social revolution in one year or in one decade."[82] Mississippi senator John Stennis sent urgent notes asking Graham to come out more strongly against the project and to pressure the National Council of Churches to withdraw support for it. The segregationist senator believed that pressure from church organizations had influenced some of his colleagues to back the Civil Rights Act. Graham responded with an evasive fret about the "many extremists and fanatics in this sphere." In his remarks about Freedom Summer, Graham had asked Americans not to reflexively "convict Philadelphia" over the killings. The congressman who represented that benighted town entered Graham's request into the *Congressional Record*.[83]

Graham was apparently Johnson's top choice to chair the National Citizens Committee for Community Relations, a group of "influential citizens" created to assist the CRS "in obtaining compliance with the [Civil Rights] Act and in creating a better spirit of good relations in the country."[84] As a respected minister with cachet among southerners but without serious political baggage, Graham represented a logical choice for the position. Johnson had recently made a special appeal to Southern Baptist ministers to accept the pending 1964 Civil Rights Act. Before making his pitch to the gathering of 150 pastors, the president adroitly cracked a joke about one of Graham's visits to the White House.[85] Graham likely discussed the possible appointment with Johnson before final passage of the civil rights bill, around the same time the president was soliciting other members for the National Citizens Committee. The evangelist ultimately turned him down (as he would several other formal or casual offers from Johnson), thus passing up perhaps his greatest opportunity for regional leadership outside a crusade context. However, Graham did accept a rank-and-file position in the four-hundred-person National Citizens Committee and promised to increase his evangelistic presence in the South. "He simply said that he felt like he could do more good [through his evangelistic work]," Secretary of Commerce and North Carolinian Luther Hodges told Johnson, "and to tell you that he's gonna try to have a crusade in St. Augustine and two or three other places in the South, including Mississippi, before long, and he thought this other [position] might detract from it." "That may be," Johnson replied laconically.[86] Graham, who had most likely explored his options in those Deep South locales, soon wrote to Johnson justifying his decision. The evangelist cited his busy schedule, as well as his belief that he could "contribute far more in the role of a preacher. . . . Certainly, the Civil Rights legislation needs to be undergirded by a moral and spiritual awakening."[87] As if to underscore his point, Graham soon called on the president to declare a national day of prayer regarding the race problem.[88] While Graham rarely mentioned his role in the National Citizens Committee, he soon claimed that "by and large the new Civil Rights law has been accepted by the people of the South."[89]

Still, the evangelist found more than a few other ways to support the president. During a 1965 crusade in Houston, Johnson became the first sitting executive to attend a Graham service. (Graham invited Nixon as well to attend a service there.) Johnson was also the first to host the evangelist as an overnight guest at the White House.[90] Moreover, Graham lobbied in favor of funding for the Organization of Economic Opportunity (OEO) and, more controversially, defended the administration's Vietnam policy. Although the evangelist turned down an invitation to serve on the OEO advisory committee—a group designed to evaluate the centerpiece program of Johnson's War on Poverty—he took the arguably more visible step of producing an antipoverty documentary with OEO director Sargent Shriver. *Beyond These Hills* captured Graham and Shriver's helicopter tour of Avery County, North Carolina, an impoverished part of Appalachia not far from Montreat. In the film and an accompanying pamphlet, Graham offered a moderate conservative's justification for the federal antipoverty efforts, citing relevant biblical passages and arguing that the OEO and its Community Action Program were not "sort of a handout." The evangelist, who earlier had criticized the "materialistic" goals of Shriver's Peace Corps, now declared himself a "convert" to the War on Poverty and testified in favor of antipoverty legislation at a Capitol Hill luncheon and documentary screening attended by congressmen and business leaders. Shriver made sure to invite a number of conservative southern senators to the event, and the film received wide television and radio distribution throughout the South, its target audience and the region politically most resistant to the program. Graham had hoped that Shriver would not release the film until after Congress had voted on OEO funding. Nonetheless, the evangelist agreed to call congressmen in support of the bill. An OEO administrator took pains to inform Southern Baptist publications that

Johnson had not "twisted the arm" of Graham to support the War on Poverty. "I believe this is the first and only time that Dr. Graham has consented to so endorse a domestic program of the United States Government," Shriver crowed in a memo.[91] To the extent this assertion was accurate, it was largely owing to the evangelist's tendency to avoid details.

When push came to shove, Graham readily marshaled his pastoral authority to defend the person of President Johnson. Vouching for the character of a given leader represented the ultimate trump card for the nominally non-partisan and widely respected evangelist. Graham, though, offered Johnson less effusive praise than he earlier had for Eisenhower or later would have for Nixon. To be sure, the evangelist blessed Johnson with two Christmastime tours of Vietnam.[92] Still, Graham publicly criticized many aspects of mid-1960s liberalism, especially anything pertaining to criminal rights or prayer in school.[93] His politics remained more in line with Nixon.

The Politics of Decency in Alabama

President Johnson held Graham to his promise to preach in the Deep South. By the end of 1964, Graham had invitations to conduct crusades in Jackson, Mississippi, Jacksonville, Florida, Atlanta, Memphis, and Birmingham, where he had already conducted an Easter Day rally that year.[94] At the encouragement of Johnson, the evangelist chose to return to Alabama. In sum, Graham's three mid-1960s visits to the state—a 1964 Easter rally in Birmingham, an April 1965 tour of the state, and a crusade in Montgomery two months later—reprised many of the themes evident in Clinton and Little Rock during the late 1950s. In Alabama, though, the stakes were higher and the risks greater. The visits came in the aftermath of civil rights demonstrations in Birmingham and Selma, two watershed moments of the civil rights movement.

As the civil rights movement grew in intensity and breadth, Graham became more willing to exert influence on the nation's domestic affairs. In 1962, he ventured into the Deep South to hold a desegregated (and strikingly unpublicized) rally in Huntsville, Alabama, where a crowd of 35,000 heard him preach at the Redstone Arsenal.[95] The event took place on federal property beyond the jurisdiction of state segregation laws, as had his 1958 service at Fort Jackson, South Carolina. By 1963, the BGEA had decided to dedicate the next two years to domestic crusades, citing "the moral, spiritual and racial problems" of the nation.[96] The following year, Graham uncharacteristically used the term "integrated" when describing requirements for a proposed crusade in Atlanta.[97] Also in 1964, the BGEA opened an office in Atlanta (from which all crusades would be run, even though the BGEA headquarters and publishing operations remained in Minneapolis), in part because most team members resided in the South.[98]

During the Easter season of 1964, Graham traveled to Birmingham, a city disparaged as "Bombingham" and widely recognized as the most intransigently segregated large city in the nation. It stood as a logical, if menacing, target for civil rights activists and, thereafter, for Graham himself. As early as May 1963, amid the civil rights demonstrations that prodded Kennedy to introduce what became the Civil Rights Act of 1964, Graham declared his willingness to visit the city, provided he received the requisite invitation from its evangelical ministers. Within a few weeks, a local radio director publicly requested the evangelist to visit.[99] An official biracial invitation from Birmingham ministers proved difficult to attain and emerged only when the public relations potential of a rally became more evident. In September 1963, after Graham had described Birmingham as a symbol of violence in a crusade sermon telecast from Los Angeles, distraught Birmingham television executive Raymond Hurlbert wrote to the evangelist lamenting this "unkind cut," which only encouraged "misguided negroes" in their criminal demonstrations. "Having so labeled our city and held it up for world censor [sic]," he wrote, "do you not feel that you are somewhat beholden to come and assist us with our problem?"[100] The letter was composed two days before the September 15 bombing of Sixteenth Street Baptist Church. The explosion killed four young teenage girls and decimated Birmingham's remaining pretensions to moderation. Graham accepted an invitation from syndicated columnist Drew Pearson to serve as an honorary chair of an organization dedicated to rebuilding the church. Meanwhile, Catholic bishop Joseph Durick of Alabama asked President Kennedy to encourage the evangelist to hold an interracial revival in Birmingham. Around the same time, the evangelist reiterated his willingness to visit the city.[101] More letters from Birmingham residents arrived, a development Graham attributed to the visible presence of blacks in the televised Los Angeles services.[102] Some writers might also have been responding (in a much more favorable way) to Graham's reference on his radio program to "a growing suspicion that the [Birmingham] bombings may be from professionals outside Alabama who want to keep the racial problem at fever pitch in the South."[103] Episcopal minister John Turner became the driving force behind the effort to secure for Graham a biracial ministerial invitation, which arrived and was accepted by mid-January 1964. A racial moderate whose ties with the Graham team stretched back more than a decade, Turner also helped to lead the local fundraising effort to rebuild Sixteenth Street Baptist.[104]

The rally had to weather a rocky period of planning. In light of Birmingham's well-earned reputation for violence, the event represented a legitimate risk on the part of Graham. One concerned caller to the BGEA feared "a race riot." Raymond Hurlbert, who had pitched the idea of a crusade to Graham, now wrote that an integrated service was simply impossible.[105] Arthur P. Cook, the Birmingham newspaper mogul who chaired the rally executive committee and who puffed the Graham visit in his chain of local papers, was not inclined to disagree. While aware of Graham's seating policy, Cook chose to deny consciousness of the obvious. "At no time," he declared after the rally, "did I ever consider myself personally sponsoring an integrated meeting."[106] The rally executive committee, though, contained at least two African Americans: "Second Vice Chairman" of the rally John Drew, an insurance salesman who had hosted Martin Luther King, Jr., during the Birmingham campaign; and prominent Baptist minister J. L. Ware. Both Drew and Ware were pillars of Birmingham's black establishment and possessed ties to moderate white leaders in the city. The committee also included white barbecue restaurateur Ollie McClung, who headed the rally prayer committee. In a less pious move, McClung soon challenged Title II of the Civil Rights Act, which banned racial discrimination in public establishments; he lost a famous Supreme Court decision in December 1964.[107] Many executive committee members appeared less than enthusiastic about desegregating the service. Graham's motivations were entirely religious, they conceded, yet his seating requirement came with "a good many problems." One such issue was a legal challenge to the rally by the Jefferson County Citizens' Council, which unsuccessfully asked the Birmingham City Council to block the service. In characteristic fashion, the Council preemptively absolved itself of responsibility for any violence to come. The rally committee ultimately rested its case for desegregated seating on legal grounds (the fact that the city had already authorized the integration of the rally site), as well as the equally compelling reality that Graham would not otherwise come to Birmingham.[108]

Protestations aside, the Birmingham rally was by far the most integrated of any Graham services previously held in the South. An estimated 35,000 people, slightly more than half the capacity of the venue, attended the Easter

Day rally at Legion Field, a football stadium situated at the foot of a black neighborhood bearing the telling nickname "Dynamite Hill." A photo spread in the *Birmingham News*, along with photographs taken by the BGEA, revealed an integrated choir and thoroughly mixed seating patterns amid heavy security. Despite threats of violence, no incidents occurred during the security-heavy service. The guests of honor included Mayor Albert Boutwell, a moderate by Birmingham standards, and University of Alabama football coach Paul "Bear" Bryant, then on his way to pigskin sainthood. J. L. Ware delivered the benediction. Ware, who that morning had hosted the white editor of the BGEA's *Decision* magazine at his church, was a rival of Fred Shuttlesworth and had initially opposed King's coming to Birmingham. Graham's Sunday sermon largely eschewed emotive allusions to the race issue. Although a pre-released sermon text specifically addressed Birmingham's history of racial strife, the spoken sermon referred more generally to bombs "thrown in the South against innocent people," as well as to the "heart trouble" and sin that had "blinded our minds, hardened our conscience, and confused our judgment." In a radio address heard later that day, the evangelist discussed the "racial problem" more specifically but classified it as a world issue "not limited to Birmingham . . . or to the southern part of the United States." According to the paternalistic lead of one local paper, at the rally the first respondent during the invitation was a black woman whose "hat was an old black straw," but whose smile "was as new as the Easter Day." Other descriptions of the rally were less dramatic but no less affirming. Ware identified the rally as a "turning point in changing the outlook and image of Birmingham into a city of peace, tranquility and prosperity for all people," while Boutwell contended that Graham had made the city "an improved and better place in which to live."[109]

Not everyone emerged from the rally in good spirits. The total crowd was actually a good 30,000 smaller than Arthur P. Cook had predicted. In a wrap-up meeting of the executive committee, the rally chair blamed the attendance figure on fears of violence and cited plans by a states' rights group to teargas the stadium. In a bizarre rant, he proceeded to castigate critics of the rally, including Fred Shuttlesworth, extreme rightists, and even Black Muslims. The *Birmingham World*, an African American paper whose editor had taken offense when Cook did not personally invite him to a rally news conference, offered a notable reason to remain skeptical about the influence of the rally. An editorial proposed that "twenty-five Negro policemen on duty [at the service] would have been a better indicator of constructive [racial progress] than the seating arrangements."[110]

Yet the Easter rally did benefit a few interests. For starters, it complemented President Johnson's attempted outreach to Southern Baptist leaders in the area of civil rights. According to one report, the president even briefly considered attending the service, much to the horror of his Secret Service agents.[111] The rally also provided theological support and ideological cover for a statement issued by the National Association of Evangelicals effectively endorsing the Civil Rights Act. In a society where "not all men have been . . . transformed," the statement read, evangelical Christians had a duty "to support on all levels of government such ordinances and legislation as will assure all of our people those freedoms guaranteed in our Constitution."[112]

Most strikingly, though, the Easter rally was a momentary boon for Birmingham's image, a fact city and rally leaders did not hesitate to tout. Graham, who received a key to the city at a country club banquet the night before the rally, predicted that the service would "create a new image for Birmingham," making it "a symbol of love and harmony at the foot of the cross of Jesus Christ and at the open tomb of Jesus Christ."[113] A *Birmingham News* editorial reflected less spiritual aspirations. The city had "been commended, widely, in the nation's press," affording an opportunity to achieve a "harmonious condition of respect and mutual regard, one group of citizens for others." Newspapers around the nation described the rally as the largest interracial gathering in Alabama history, and headlines soon carried such messages as "Birmingham Bastion of Segregation Crumbling" and "Birmingham Giving Ground."[114] Morehouse University president Benjamin Mays, a renowned theologian who had criticized Graham during the segregated 1950 Atlanta crusade, called the rally "one of the most important things he has done in his whole career," giving Birmingham a chance "to redeem its bad name."[115] Respected Raleigh newspaper editor and white moderate Jonathan Daniels added another affirming editorial, while *Time* contrasted the "remarkable demonstration" in Birmingham with the Senate's stalemate over the Civil Rights Act.[116] The afterglow from the rally was bright enough for the *Birmingham News* to declare it "the most significant day of 1964" for the city. "From the front pages of newspapers such as New York Times and Washington Post," wrote a publicly chipper Cook, who had invited members of the national press to attend a prerally press conference, "we now have a beachhead established." To the city sheriff he wrote, "This is certainly something that we have all tried to gain for our city for a long time." Riding this momentum, the recently desegregated Ministerial Association of Greater Birmingham petitioned Graham to hold a full crusade in the city.[117]

Although Graham would not return to Birmingham for another eight years, he did visit other parts of Alabama a year later in 1965, holding rallies in Dothan, Auburn, Tuskegee, and Tuscaloosa from April 24 to 27 and then returning in June for a crusade in Montgomery. Graham's decision to spend additional time in Alabama was a direct response to the civil rights movement. The Selma voting rights campaign reached a crisis point in the winter of 1965 while Graham was holding a crusade in far-away Hawaii, where the often-fatigued evangelist experienced a severe bronchial infection. While recovering in a Honolulu hospital bed, he released a statement affirming the "right to vote" of every citizen and issuing a quintessentially moderate, if highly unrealistic, proposal that President Johnson bring both King and Alabama governor George Wallace to the White House for "a face to face discussion." Graham offered to hold an Easter service in Selma and directed two BGEA staffers to investigate that or a similar possibility.[118] The staffers soon visited Selma and went so far as to propose a date for a service. Business leaders in the city responded favorably, only to withdraw their support amid persistent racial tensions.[119]

Graham's return to Alabama also came at the request of Lyndon Johnson. The evangelist, who announced the Alabama tour after a visit to Johnson and later cited the president's encouragement, canceled engagements in Great Britain to make room on his schedule. At the time, Graham faced a barrage of criticism from segregationists for doing the president's bidding.[120] Johnson wrote Graham beforehand praising him for "doing a brave and fine thing for your country in your courageous effort to contribute to the understanding and brotherhood of the Americans in the South."[121] During the Alabama visits, though, Graham and his associates avoided or denied connections between the president and his visit, stressing to Alabamians and BGEA supporters the many invitations from local religious and civic leaders, black and white.[122]

The Alabama visits gave Graham a platform on which to accentuate the differences between his evangelical universalism and liberal or prophetic approaches to civil rights. A week before returning to Alabama, Graham recorded an interview with Florida senator George Smathers for television and radio broadcast throughout the Sunshine State. The evangelist voiced his preference for "law and order" over both civil rights protests and intransigent segregationism: "If the law says that I cannot march or I cannot demonstrate,

I ought not to march and I ought not to demonstrate. And if the law tells me that I should send my children to a school where there are both races, I should obey that law also."[123] Elsewhere, he cast his desegregated services as alternatives to civil rights demonstrations, a theme he had foreshadowed during his 1959 Little Rock rallies. His comments regarding race had grown increasingly uniform as he faced more questions about the civil rights crisis. At a Los Angeles press conference held two weeks before the 1963 March on Washington, the evangelist distributed copies of his *Life, Reader's Digest,* and *U.S. News and World Report* articles on racial tolerance. He later ordered the production of a flyer detailing his contributions in the area of race relations.[124] During the lead-up to his Alabama visits, Graham characterized his habit of visiting southern cities in the aftermath of high-profile racial violence as an actual policy. "We try to get in there a little bit afterward to see if we can't ring the healing message of the Gospel," he told the *New York Times.* He overtly cast himself as a southerner performing a mediating role, someone who "may have a little more influence than a man with a New England accent." For the moment, he said, "I have a voice in the South and I will try to provide the leadership I can." Still, he stressed that he was not traveling to Alabama "as a civil rights worker" but rather "as a preacher of the gospel" for whom the simple act of holding desegregated services "conveys enough on the subject of race." Graham made a conscious effort to distinguish himself from the activists who had marched before him in Alabama. "I have been holding demonstrations for 15 years," he declared when announcing his Montgomery crusade, "but in a stadium where it is legal."[125]

Word of a possible Graham visit to Alabama set off a flurry of requests from across the state. Inquiring towns faced the challenge of simultaneously demonstrating their racial progress and their need for a spiritual renewal. A letter from Phenix City (which had first proposed a Graham revival back in 1954) lamented the city's large unchurched population, yet emphasized plans to desegregate its school system.[126] Ultimately, Graham settled on holding rallies in comparatively calm parts of the state where he possessed social connections and could safely secure biracial invitations. Although Birmingham met the latter two qualifications, Graham declined an offer to preach there at the black Baptist congregation of the Reverend Lamar Jackson.[127] He did accept an invitation from ministers in the university town of Tuscaloosa who believed a revival there would help "necessary social changes . . . come about more peacefully."[128]

By the fastidious standards of the BGEA, which normally spent two years preparing for a given crusade, the Alabama services were rushed operations.[129] In Dothan, a wiregrass town where BGEA team member T. W. Wilson had recently resided and where Graham's brother-in-law Clayton Bell pastored a Presbyterian congregation, the evangelist held two services before interracial audiences of several thousand each. After one service, he met with area black leaders.[130] The local paper asked Dothan residents to welcome the evangelist as a matter of basic hospitality, despite "something less than unanimity of opinion regarding the timing of his visit." The area Board of Revenue and Control endorsed the rallies, citing the necessity of efforts to "avoid the bitter strife recently created in our great state by outside agitators," of which Graham was apparently not one. As in Birmingham, the area Citizens' Council opposed the Dothan rally, although a prominent council leader agreed to a brief meeting with Graham. Afterward, the segregationist referred to Graham as "our kind of man," citing their shared optimism about the future of the South.[131] Only in Tuskegee, which Graham visited as part of the annual meeting of the Andrew Clinical Society (an interracial medical organization), did the evangelist specifically discuss racial matters in a sermon. Speaking to a largely African American audience at the Tuskegee Institute, where he faced opposition from a student group, he encouraged efforts "to solve the [race] problem through understanding, through dialogue, through legislation."[132] In keeping with precedent, though, Graham defended the state of Alabama in his weekly radio broadcast and bluntly prioritized spiritual over social issues. The Associated Press featured a particularly startling declaration from that broadcast: "The church today spends too much time answering questions nobody is asking." The line—which appeared in a pre-released text but apparently not in the delivered sermon—captured the ambiguity and inconsistency of an evangelical supporter of desegregation who was also a critic of the Social Gospel.[133] His target in the Dothan radio address was the latter. By holding desegregated rallies in Deep South Alabama, Graham clearly was not advising the church to remain silent about race relations. Hardly more than a month removed from the shocking violence in Selma, though, the thought tellingly crossed his mind to attack and caricature attempts to prioritize social concerns over saving souls.

In Montgomery that June, Graham held his first desegregated crusade in the Deep South; it was also his first and only full crusade held specifically in response to racial tensions in the South. By the time of the crusade, most of the city's public institutions had commenced the process of desegregation—reluctant and often modest undertakings not to be mistaken for heartfelt acceptance of the Civil Right Act.[134] The Graham team struggled to organize a truly interracial crusade in the original capital of the Confederacy, where less than three months earlier the instantly famous civil rights march from nearby Selma had come to an end. Graham failed to procure his customary invitation from the local minister's conference, and the initial crusade committee was all white.[135] While some segregationist Alabamians did not count Graham among those "outside agitators" who had "tormented" them, others wrote letters to Governor George Wallace linking the crusade with King's earlier presence in the state. Still others defaced three billboards advertising the Montgomery crusade. With what was surely unintended ambiguity, at least one billboard showed an image of Graham silhouetted in black. To protect Graham, the Alabama Department of Public Safety assigned two officers to stay with him during the crusade week. Even Frank Boykin, the former Alabama congressman who had recommended Graham as a racial mediator back in 1956, questioned why the evangelist had chosen Alabama for unique intervention. In private correspondence, Boykin had already pitched a variety of racist conspiracy theories to Graham in an effort to influence the evangelist's perspective on Jim Crow. Now, Boykin sent the evangelist a police report casting aspersions on the background of Viola Liuzzo, a white civil rights marcher recently murdered near Selma. He also copied his correspondence with Graham to a grateful Wallace.[136] Ever cautious in the face of criticism from his right flank, Graham forcefully, if not convincingly, denied that he had singled out Alabama, which he described as an economically growing state containing "more church-going people . . . than anywhere else in the world." He again disavowed any civil rights agenda, noting simply that his services remained "open to those of all races to sit where they please . . . and listen to the gospel of Christ."[137]

Tensions aside, the rain-drenched Montgomery services proceeded without documented incident, attracting crowds of modest size. BGEA photographs show a thoroughly integrated crowd, and newspaper shots reveal a similar dynamic for the crusade choir. The crusade featured an introductory statement by A. W. Wilson, pastor of a leading black Baptist church in Montgomery, and a performance by Ethel Waters, the famous black vocalist who had worked with the Graham team for nearly a decade. In his sermons, Graham only indirectly addressed race, commanding each audience member: "As one southerner to another, go out of your way to continue the spirit of unity and love that you have demonstrated this week." The Graham team apparently invested a great deal of energy in his visit to Montgomery, where it published a daily reflection piece in the two leading newspapers. One of those papers subsequently labeled the crusade a success, while alluding to "some opinions to the contrary."[138] During the crusade, Graham kept Johnson aide Bill Moyers apprised of the good results, having earlier informed the president of this latest visit to Alabama.[139]

The evangelist went so far as to cast the Montgomery crusade as a complete vindication of evangelical universalism, both its theory of social change and its emphasis on civic order. He termed his services there "another kind of march." "There are those who claim that this type of evangelistic effort is not relevant in our times," he said in his weekly radio broadcast. "The Montgomery crusade proves them wrong." In Montgomery, the evangelist had observed "how reverent the people were as I spelled out the universality of man's need for God's forgiveness" and "as they marched, people of both races, not with hatred but in unity in a spirit of love as Christ drew them together at the foot of the cross." Having elsewhere equated his significance with that of civil rights workers, he went one step further and pulled rank as an evangelist. "In my opinion," Graham bluntly declared, "this march in Montgomery is far more significant, more constructive and more revolutionary than the other marches we've read about in our newspapers and watched on our television screens."[140]

In what would become a habit, Graham publicly criticized the national media for not extensively covering the Montgomery crusade. He reiterated his complaints in a personal conversation with Lady Bird Johnson. A journalist noted the irony of such criticism coming from a man who had "been given more publicity by the press, television and radio than any evangelist in history."[141] In truth, the Montgomery crusade attracted only slightly less newspaper coverage than had the earlier visit to Alabama, a fact attributable both to its redundancy and to the general failure of the evangelist to address race in his sermons.

Graham's portrait aside, other aspects of the weeklong crusade suggested a less rosy story. The evangelist turned down a passionate request from black BGEA evangelist Howard Jones to attend the crusade, fearing Jones's presence might aggravate racial tensions.[142] Graham's decision undoubtedly limited his outreach to black Alabamians and thus contradicted the reasoning behind the BGEA's recent hiring of an additional black evangelist, Ralph Bell.[143] Three of the most visible black supporters of the crusade—the "colored section" editor for the local dailies, along with the respective presidents of the state-controlled Selma University and Alabama State College—came from sectors of the black community largely removed from the civil rights movement.[144] As in Dothan, Graham met with black leaders from the city and, as in Birmingham, the crusade executive committee featured co-chairs from both races. The black co-chair was Baptist minister A. W. Wilson, who had played a leadership role in the Montgomery bus boycott. The full chair was J. R. White, the racially moderate pastor of the white First Baptist church.[145] In the run-up to the crusade, White's congregation had revisited its policy on segregation, with the members voting to bar all racial demonstrators (i.e., blacks and integrationist whites) from attending services. Their decision surprised the church's deacons and prompted an emotional, but futile, address from White urging his congregants to cleanse themselves of racial prejudice (while also criticizing Martin Luther King, Jr., and his peers for using "the Negro church as a platform for social and political action").[146]

One of the white co-chairs, the Reverend Robert Strong, harbored no such reservations about his congregation's similar policy. CRS director LeRoy Collins described him as a "strong segregationist."[147] Trinity Presbyterian, Strong's church, was a target for "kneel-ins" by civil rights activists seeking to desegregate services. A northerner by birth, Strong became a momentary celebrity among genteel partisans of Jim Crow because of a published April 1965 sermon in which he castigated King, defended banning civil rights demonstrators from attending services, and likened activists to the money changers whom Jesus had driven from the temple in Jerusalem. Using the tortured logic of polite racism, Strong explained that, in the climate of the times, even the most respectable blacks or sympathetic whites seeking seats in his church qualified as "in actual fact sociological demonstrators."[148] A segregationist opponent of the Graham crusade actually cited Strong's sermon as evidence for his position.[149]

On the final day of the crusade, a racially mixed group of five persons and (in a separate incident) a black serviceman recently called to Vietnam were denied entry to Trinity Presbyterian as they attempted to attend a sermon delivered by Graham associate Leighton Ford, brother-in-law of the evangelist. (Ironically, Ford was one of the more forthright proponents of racial justice in neo-evangelical circles.) Ford later professed ignorance of the backdoor segregation policy (even though the church bulletin on the day of his visit advertised printed copies of the Strong sermon), and he wrote letters to both Strong and the serviceman clarifying his opposition to church segregation.[150] Still, the event was an embarrassment for Graham, who obviously permitted segregationists to serve on his crusade committees. As for Strong,

his interpretation of the Montgomery rally had little to do with racial reconciliation. In a published commentary, he praised Graham's "willingness . . .
to identify himself with our area at such a critical juncture. A southerner
himself, Billy Graham feels for us, for example, in the unfair treatment we
have been given in the national news picture."[151]

Glimpses of the Sunbelt

Rather than galvanizing support for civil rights, Graham's services instead
served as a venue for articulating a politics of decency in Alabama that foreshadowed the subsequent narrative of Sunbelt progress. The elective affinity
between Graham's visits to Alabama and the politics of decency was nowhere
more evident than in the person of Winton Blount, a wealthy contractor who
served on the Montgomery crusade executive committee and ran a prominent
advertisement for his construction company in a newspaper section dedicated
to the crusade.[152] In many ways, Blount represented the quintessential southern moderate whom President Johnson called upon to support the Civil
Rights Act of 1964. Blount was not a racial liberal; he had supported the
segregation policy of Trinity Presbyterian, his home church.[153] Yet he clearly
saw the long-term futility of massive resistance to desegregation. As a member
of the University of Alabama board of directors during the school's 1963
desegregation crisis, Blount had helped to barter the deal allowing Governor
Wallace to make his symbolic stand in front of the schoolhouse door. He
later served as an honorary member of the National Citizens Committee for
Community Relations and hosted a meeting between white city leaders and
Johnson administration officials before the Selma-to-Montgomery march.[154]
During the week of the Montgomery crusade, he held a reception for the
Graham team.[155] Blount's politics resembled those of Graham, although he
lacked the evangelist's common touch. He chaired the Alabama chapter of
Citizens for Eisenhower in 1952 and ran the volunteer wing of Nixon's south-
eastern campaign in 1960, but was cool toward Goldwater in 1964 and openly
critical of Wallace throughout the decade. Blount officially switched to the
Republican Party during the mid-1960s and later served as postmaster general
in the Nixon administration.[156]

Graham's 1965 visits to Alabama occurred against the backdrop of a quasi
revolt by moderate state business interests against reflexive, counterproduc-
tive resistance to the Civil Rights Act. Such exercises in what Joseph Crespino

has called "calculated compliance" also occurred in other parts of the Deep South as Klan extremism mushroomed during the mid-1960s.[157] They resembled the earlier attempts by Little Rock businessmen to distance themselves from Arkansas governor Orval Faubus. In Alabama, Winton Blount was a force behind efforts to create space for whites to accept federal legislation that now stood as a fait accompli. He helped to coordinate a statement of principles released on April 15, 1965, by a group representing the leading Chambers of Commerce in Alabama, as well as the state's banking, industrial, and textile associations. The group placed advertisements in twenty-two Alabama papers, in addition to the *Wall Street Journal* and *U.S. News and World Report*, conservative publications with wide readership in the national business community.[158]

A rare marshaling of candidness from the white center (or what counted for the center) in Alabama, the statement of principles reflected the extent to which white elites there could no longer dictate the terms of the debate over Jim Crow. The federal government had already passed sweeping legislation, and they needed to respond. The published declaration resembled comments Graham had made for more than a decade in magazines, press conferences, and private correspondence: "The vast majority of the people of Alabama, like other responsible citizens throughout our nation, believe in law and order, and in the fair and just treatment of all their fellow citizens. They believe in obedience to the law regardless of their personal feelings about its specific merits. They believe in the basic human dignity of all people of all races." The statement then offered specific proposals in a manner uncommon to southern moderates. Alabamians should obey the Civil Rights Act—with business leaders taking specific responsibility for Title VII, banning employment discrimination—and respect the right of "every eligible citizen" to vote. In keeping with the tradition of southern moderation, the statement denounced vigilantism from the right and unlawful demonstrations from the left with equal force. The Alabama elites, though, emphasized economic and educational progress for Alabama, urging "the establishment of positive new vehicles for communications between the races throughout all the State."[159]

Blount's involvement in the Montgomery crusade exemplified the overlap between moderate southern business interests and Graham's social message. Theologically informed individualism and respect for the rule of law, values clearly evident in Graham's defense of the Montgomery crusade, were the key ingredients of this synergy. One forum for moderate Alabama business interests, the *Birmingham News*, made the connection explicitly. "April

1965," a correspondent wrote about the business leaders' revolt, "may go down in Alabama history as the month the state rejoined the union." The paper welcomed Graham's return to Alabama that same month in an editorial, titled "See the Human Being," which labeled the civil rights crisis "a *human* as well as a 'legal' and a 'social' problem which is before us. To the extent all, white or Negro, can think in terms of individuals being involved, single human beings and their families, mothers, fathers, children, we shall get a little further down the road toward mutual understanding and tolerance as to others' views. . . . For—as we have said—we are *all* human beings, whatever our color."[160] Later, the *Birmingham News* urged politicians to follow the example of the business and civic leaders who had signed the statement of principles. Because they "wish to move ahead in general prosperity and reasonableness," these figures had "come to understand that life is change, and that they must be part of it." Graham grasped this same reality, still another editorial suggested, and in his April visit had "complimented the better efforts in Alabama." He had also complemented them. "We can afford nothing but the highest in public and private life," the paper argued. "This could be the meaning of Billy Graham's messages."[161] Alabama's late-blooming business moderates viewed Graham's arrival in Alabama not as a slap in the face, as had segregationist critics of the evangelist, but as an opportunity to showcase the feasibility of their posited post–Jim Crow South.

The Montgomery crusade became the site of a modest encounter between Graham's boosterish politics of decency and George Wallace's populist "politics of rage."[162] The evangelist was on record as a critic of the Alabama executive, saying at one point that he did not "often agree with Governor Wallace on very many things" and elsewhere citing Wallace's appeal outside the South as evidence that race "isn't a sectional problem." Yet Graham was characteristically quick to declare his desire to meet with Wallace while in Montgomery.[163] The evangelist, who had recently added Wallace to his extensive prayer list, said that if an invitation from the governor was not forthcoming, he "might ask for it."[164] Wallace received a host of correspondence urging him to shun a meeting with Graham. Some writers questioned Graham's motivations for visiting, while one appealed to the governor "on grounds secular affairs not within province [*sic*] of ministers of gospel."[165] Wallace appeared conflicted about how associating with the evangelist might affect his segregationist constituency. According to Birmingham rally chair Arthur P. Cook, the governor had prepared a statement in favor of the 1964 Easter service, yet chose to withhold it for fear of using the evangelist for political gain.[166] A more likely reason was the risk of linking himself with a desegregated event. Frank Boykin, on edge as the Montgomery crusade approached, wrote to Wallace proposing a special dinner for Graham.[167] The governor, though, followed many prominent Montgomery leaders in steering clear of the services.[168] As both he and the *Birmingham News* recognized in their different ways, Graham abetted the agenda of those Alabama business interests who followed in the footsteps of Little Rock moderates by embracing racial tolerance along the lines of law and order. Unlike those moderate elites, though, Graham could reach a part of Alabama society (in some respects, the very source of Wallace's strength) not accessible to economic elites. After several delays, the governor finally consented to a private "social visit" that lasted more than an hour, during which they discussed "some sociological points," in Graham's words. A picture of them together appeared in newspapers around the state.[169]

In the end, Graham's 1965 visits to Alabama accomplished something more complicated than President Johnson's goal of assisting the transition of Alabama whites toward greater tolerance of existing civil right laws. As was also true of Graham's other services in the South, the Alabama meetings projected a positive image of the region that business moderates and Wallace supporters alike could appreciate. A conservative southern editor who had toured Alabama at the behest of the governor invoked Graham's upbeat evaluation of the state as a confirmation of his own views.[170] The booster impulse was ever present throughout the Montgomery crusade. The local Chamber of Commerce produced store window posters welcoming crusade attendees and workers to the city.[171]

The evangelist's public comments during and following the crusade more than justified the investment by the business community. "I am convinced that the moral and spiritual resources are now available in Alabama for a rapid growth in racial understanding," said Graham at a closing press conference. If the Ku Klux Klan would "quiet down," he added, and if civil rights activists would take a breather and politicians would resist the temptation to score points with white voters, Alabamians would have "time to digest the new civil rights laws" and, presumably, obey them.[172] Earlier, he had cautioned against turning the state into a public "whipping boy."[173] A few "more Selmas" might occur, he conceded, yet the deep friendship between southern blacks and whites boded well for the region.[174] A BGEA-produced documentary about the Alabama visits presented an even more optimistic portrait. While the film condemned racial discrimination in no uncertain terms, it dedicated even more space to remarks about the new spirit of inter-racial cooperation in the state.[175]

Similar rhetoric continued during Graham's lone 1966 domestic crusade, held in Greenville, South Carolina. The evangelist spoke of his desire in Greenville to "show the nation, by television," that an integrated service could be held "in the heart of the deep South." By the time of the immensely well-attended Greenville services—for which the main source of tension was a ban that fundamentalist university head Bob Jones, Jr., placed on student involvement in the crusade—Graham's tone had shifted completely from healing the South's wounds to celebrating its virtues.[176] From Greenville, the evangelist wrote to Ralph McGill of the *Atlanta Constitution* expressing optimism about the direction of their region during "its most difficult period since the Civil War." "While we are not out of the woods yet," wrote Graham, "I do feel that the sound of the wind in the mulberry bushes is evident everywhere."[177] That breeze had not reached the ghettos of the North, where he increasingly identified the nation's main racial problems as residing. Otherwise, though, the evangelist thought the United States was "making the greatest attempt that any nation has ever made" on behalf of racial equality.[178] He reasoned that he had done his part.

Graham's contribution spoke mostly to the needs of a certain group of white southerners. In his Alabama visits, Graham helped to facilitate a momentary coalition of those southern whites who recognized the inevitability of (and, in some cases, the need for) change. They viewed his services as conduits and models for achieving an altered social order—but also for controlling or retaining it. Graham's services offered a safe way out of the racially Solid South.[179] By appealing to law and order but also to such seemingly nonpartisan qualities as neighborly love and spiritual piety, Graham supplied a path upon which moderates could back away from segregationism in a manner acceptable to regional mores. In this context, his evangelical universalism contained clear political meanings: acceptance of existing civil rights laws, condemnation of racial violence, and dismissal of the need for further protests or legislation. These values defined the politics of decency in the mid-1960s white South. Not every supporter of the evangelist completely agreed with him, of course; more than a few Graham backers remained outright segregationists, while a much smaller group held views to his left. These basic principles, though, made up the sum impact of Graham's civil rights era interventions in his home region, suggesting his hand in the creation of an alluring yet evasive Sunbelt South.

CHAPTER FIVE

Billy Graham's Southern Strategy

Yes, there is a "quiet revolution" going on, and every one here tonight is a candidate for this revolution.
—Billy Graham, 1967

Charlotte and the changing South are in difficult struggle, much of which has a moral dimension to which people are blinded. Mr. Graham's court in Washington plays it, almost always, as nothing more than a political drama.
—*Charlotte Observer*, 1971

BILLY GRAHAM'S OPTIMISM about the South in the aftermath of landmark civil rights legislation did not extend to the rest of the nation. His concerns about the increasing social and racial chaos in America ultimately dovetailed with the electoral prospects of Richard Nixon. In December 1967, Graham received the Great American Award, given by Atlanta business leaders and radio station WSB, the self-described "Voice of the South." Recovering from a serious bout with pneumonia, the evangelist used the opportunity to deliver the kind of sermon his illness would prevent him from making for another three months. His acceptance speech reprised his preference for avowedly Christian marches as alternatives to more explicitly political demonstrations. Now, however, he distinguished his preferred demonstrations not from civil rights or antiwar protests but rather from the "rioting and rebellion" of the previous summer. In contrast to this turmoil, which had enthralled the media, Graham celebrated those Americans who were responding to the tumultuous times by turning to Christ and, hence, returning to the nation's moral foundations. These persons, whom the evening news ignored, were candidates for what Graham touted as a "quiet revolution." He included the same phrase in a nationally syndicated newspaper commentary released that holiday season.[1]

Graham's sermon foreshadowed a major theme in the presidency of Richard Nixon. In a 1968 campaign commercial, Nixon invoked another body of quiet citizens: "the forgotten Americans, the non-shouters, the non-demonstrators"—and, once in office, he famously labeled them the "silent majority."[2] Nixon strategically tapped the anxieties of those citizens who had sat out the decade's progressive movements and needed reassurance that their version of America remained viable. In differing yet complementary ways, Graham and Nixon honored sociopolitical communities they had spoken into existence.

The thematic overlap between Graham and Nixon was no coincidence, just as the collaboration between Graham and Nixon was far more than episodic. Graham spent the better part of two decades assisting Nixon's political ambitions primarily because he supported Nixon's values and style of leadership. He believed in Nixon the political leader, in addition to Nixon the man. Nothing revealed this fact more than Graham's persistent and public support for the Nixon presidency, which began at a time when the evangelist had reached the height of his national and international stature. Graham supported Nixon well after his evangelistic enterprise stood to benefit substantially from close proximity to power. From the moment the evangelist spoke before bowed heads at the 1969 presidential inauguration, his backing of Nixon became, for many observers, the defining moment of his public career, a period that tarnished his reputation and threatened to damage his ministry. Graham's intimacy with Nixon far surpassed his closeness to other political figures, including Eisenhower and Johnson. With those presidents, Graham had served alternately as a consultant, liaison, or politically useful chum. For Nixon, Graham was all of these things and more. In a public capacity, he served as "White House chaplain" and "court prophet," among the labels his many detractors affixed to him. Behind the scenes, Graham was a strikingly candid, occasionally incisive, and periodically overwrought political adviser, offering the president and his aides insights they valued and selectively applied.

To assume that Nixon simply "used" Graham, then, is to underestimate the political side of an evangelist who during three presidential elections acted as an honorary member of the Nixon campaign team. Emphasizing Graham's naïveté also does not adequately explain why, well before the Watergate scandal, he knowingly risked his reputation on behalf of Nixon. If Nixon politicized Graham, Nixon also provided the forum through which the evangelist played out his political dreams. While Graham perhaps believed that he had gazed into the soul of the famously aloof Nixon, his steadfast support for the politician derived from a perceived political (and, at times, spiritual) synergy between the two. Graham believed that Nixon embodied the Christian statesman ideal, not least because of the politician's willingness to invoke the symbolic politics of postwar neo-evangelicalism. For a two-decade stretch extending through the presidential election of 1972, Nixon stood as Graham's model national leader, a political risk worth taking.

The Graham-Nixon alliance climaxed with the evangelist's important role in the southern and evangelical politics of the Nixon administration. In between lay many moments when evangelistic activities intersected with political priorities. During the 1968 and 1972 campaigns, even more than in 1960, Graham operated not only as a Nixon supporter but also as a kind of GOP partisan, involving himself both implicitly and directly in the Republican "southern strategy," Nixon's attempt to attract white southern voters. Graham was more than just a role player in Nixon's quest for a new political majority. While his connections with Nixon and other participants in the southern strategy clearly assisted that end (and consequently drew sharp criticism), they also reflected Graham's underlying political values, which he sought to extend throughout the South and the nation.

Law and Order Turns Rightward

The endurance of the Graham-Nixon friendship well beyond the 1960 presidential election was in no small part due to their shared diagnosis of the crisis facing postwar American society. After that bitter election, Graham attempted to contact Nixon on several occasions to offer solace and to inform the vice president that he had accepted an invitation, via Florida senator George Smathers and with the approval of former South Carolina governor James Byrnes, to play golf with President-Elect John F. Kennedy.[3] Nixon soon invited the evangelist to visit him in Washington.[4] In January 1961, Nixon sent Graham a gracious letter thanking him for his friendship and offering flattering words about his political instincts. Graham's postelection correspondence with Nixon commenced with an offer of pastoral care, yet quickly returned to the topic of politics, namely, Nixon's future. Graham soon wrote Nixon of his confidence "that you will be the next president of the United States," and he urged Nixon to speak up on matters of foreign policy. Later that year, Nixon asked for Graham's input on a possible run for the California governorship.[5]

During that unsuccessful 1962 campaign, Nixon remained cognizant of Graham's potential assistance. "We have to get these people to go to work," he declared in a campaign memo regarding the evangelist and his supporters. Graham, who wrote that he had been "following with tremendous interest the developments in . . . California," invited Nixon to contribute to *Decision*, the flagship magazine of the Billy Graham Evangelistic Association (BGEA), which Graham noted had a circulation of 100,000 in the Golden State.[6] Nixon's article, titled "A Nation's Faith in God," appeared in the November issue.[7] In July of that year, Nixon's publicist told the evangelist that his candidate, whose campaign was stalling, needed more photographic coverage. A shot of a Nixon-Graham golf outing soon appeared in the *Los Angeles Times*.[8] After the election ended in bitter defeat for Nixon, followed by a seemingly career-ending meltdown during his concession speech, Graham wrote to reaffirm their friendship. With more than a little forwardness, Graham proposed that Nixon host a banquet for journalists and offer a cordial mea culpa. "Strange as it may seem," the evangelist added, "I feel that if you can come through this defeat with flying colors, you will have another major opportunity in the next few years to serve the American people."[9] Graham soon made a similar comment at a press conference.[10]

The two talked and corresponded regularly during the mid-1960s, including amid the run-up to the 1964 election. Nixon made clear his interest in receiving Graham's perspective on public affairs, while Graham asked for copies of Nixon's speeches and writings "so that I can continue to quote you in my addresses during the winter."[11] Indeed, the evangelist continued to speak highly of Nixon in national venues, including *McCall's* magazine. "I've heard people say, 'I don't like Nixon,'" Graham wrote in 1964. "I have never understood this, because he is one of the warmest and most likable men I've ever known." Elsewhere, Graham called Nixon a possible "American Churchill," and his similar comments during the 1964 election year caught the attention of at least one editorial board.[12] The evangelist also kept Nixon, who had moved to New York City to practice law, apprised of his emerging friendship with President Johnson. When Johnson started cuddling up to Graham, Nixon made sure to send the evangelist a flattering letter declaring him "one of the best political minds in the country." In New York, where Graham suggested that Nixon attend Norman Vincent Peale's church, the former vice president participated in efforts to bring Graham there for another crusade.[13]

The mid-1960s saw the beginning of a shift in American political culture that would facilitate Nixon's comeback. The shift affected Graham as well. By the end of 1965, the momentary, if always awkward and qualified, period of overlap between Graham's evangelical universalism and some of the basic goals of the civil rights movement had come to a swift and bitter end. For Graham, the telling moment came with the Watts, Los Angeles, riots of 1965. In August of that year, only two months after the Montgomery crusade, Graham traveled to Watts, where—via helicopter and protected by a bullet-proof vest—he toured the mostly African American neighborhood with the Reverend E. V. Hill and other city leaders. Hill was a prominent black minister and mayoral appointee whom Graham had met two years earlier and who would later join the BGEA board. A founding member of the Southern Christian Leadership Conference, Hill had nominated Martin Luther King Jr. to head the organization, although he had subsequently distanced himself from the group.[14]

The tour of Watts left a distinct impression on observers of Graham, and the headlines concerning the tour differed markedly from those concerning his turn in Alabama earlier that year. Back in 1958, Graham had told a Charlotte crusade audience that white segregationist violence was sowing "the seeds for anarchy and overthrow of the government."[15] Seven years later, he felt similar premonitions about black rioting in Los Angeles. In response to Watts, the evangelist grew little short of apoplectic, speaking, in an impolitic manner reminiscent of his younger days, about a "great racial revolution" of a more pernicious quality than the civil rights struggle he had sometimes similarly labeled. For Graham, Watts was "only the beginning—a dress rehearsal for revolution." He warned ominously of "sinister forces" working to divide the nation, called for appropriate congressional action, and asked Martin Luther King, Jr., to call for a moratorium on further demonstrations.[16] Conservative media outlets immediately capitalized on these and similar comments.[17] Graham's outburst over Watts included an element of catharsis, coming as it did after years of prophesying that racial violence in the North would exceed that of the South—a point he made again following his tour.[18]

Even before Watts, Graham had asserted that early examples of unrest in the urban North meant that nonsoutherners could no longer "point their accusing, self-righteous fingers" at Dixie.[19] The evangelist's reaction to Watts also revealed his strict adherence, even in the face of gross injustices, to a code of civility, a characteristic that distinguished him from King but had previously allowed him to support basic civil rights laws. What the nation now needed was not new legislation, Graham believed, but rather obedience to existing laws.[20]

The contrast between the Watts tour and earlier trips to Alabama highlighted a critical rightward pivot for the sociopolitical implications of appeals to law and order, which in popular discourse became almost the exclusive domain of conservative politics. In mid-1960s Alabama, the triumph of law and order had meant, in part, an end to segregationist violence. Graham's visits there had offered glimpses of the Sunbelt style that would ascend in the 1970s—image-conscious, "color-blind" boosterism combining developmentalist politics and evangelical piety. Watts stood in stark relief to the rising Sunbelt South; it violated the basic tenets of racial decency and law and order. For Graham, Watts was not a southern problem.

The evangelist's public rhetoric during the latter years of the Johnson administration suggested the need for a mainstream political candidate willing to run on a strong law-and-order platform. Graham grew increasingly concerned about the direction of American society, especially the direction of the church. He focused specific attention on the resurgence of Social Gospel–influenced theology within liberal Protestant circles, whether in the form of the trendy "God is Dead" theology or, more pervasively, in the increasing involvement of members of the clergy in opposing the Vietnam War. "There is no doubt that secularism, materialism, and even Marxism not only have invaded the Church but deeply penetrated it," the evangelist warned in a 1968 *Christianity Today* article, pointedly titled "False Prophets in the Church."[21] Although Graham remained supportive of social concern among Christians, he argued that the trend had moved too far in that direction. In response, he reasserted his evangelical universalism. "There is one Gospel and one Gospel only," he wrote, "and that Gospel is the dynamic of God to change the individual and, through the individual, society."[22]

These theological apprehensions dovetailed with the anxieties about lawlessness Graham had voiced in the aftermath of Watts. "There is no doubt that the rioting, looting, and crime in America have reached the point of anarchy," he declared in a 1967 sermon titled "Rioting or Righteousness."

The nation needed "new, tough laws" to deal with "subversive elements that are seeking the overthrow of the American government."[23] The nation also needed a new kind of Supreme Court chief justice, Graham believed. Responding in 1968 to word that Chief Justice Earl Warren might resign, the evangelist wrote to President Johnson urging him to "give serious consideration to balancing the Court with a strong conservative as Chief Justice." Graham was "convinced that many of the problems that have plagued America in the past few years are a direct result of some of the extreme rulings of the Court, especially in the field of criminology." John Connally, whom Graham had supported for Texas governor in 1962 and whom he had subsequently labeled a superlative future presidential candidate, "would make an ideal and popular choice," despite likely opposition from "extreme liberals and radicals."[24] The electoral implications of Graham's priorities were obvious. "With elections coming up next year . . . ," he predicted in the same 1967 sermon, "the American people are going to show their displeasure by the ballots they cast. The majority of the American people want law, order, and security in our society."[25] Richard Nixon, of course, shared this analysis of the electorate with Graham. "I could not agree more with your comments with regard to the current wave of lawlessness which is sweeping the country," Nixon had written to Graham back in 1966.[26]

While Nixon prepared the groundwork for a possible run in 1968, he could count on Graham as both a public and a private cheerleader. Graham continued personally to encourage the political comeback of his friend, telling Nixon as early as 1965 that he would win the GOP presidential nomination "hands down."[27] During a press conference held before his 1967 "Quiet Revolution" address, the evangelist made clear his desire to see Nixon capture the nomination, calling him "the most experienced" possible GOP candidate on the eve of a year when experience should particularly matter.[28] Graham, who was still suffering the aftereffects of pneumonia, soon regretted this seeming endorsement and called Nixon's secretary to explain himself. Later that night, Nixon invited the ailing Graham to visit him in Key Biscayne, Florida. Nixon had not yet officially declared his candidacy and wanted to discuss the matter with the evangelist. On the third day of the visit, Nixon finally put the question of a run to Graham. In Nixon's telling, the evangelist urged him to seek office, noting the providential course of his receiving a second legitimate shot at the presidency.[29] During the 1968 campaign and in later years, Nixon cited the evangelist's encouragement at Key Biscayne as having "a great deal to do" with his final decision to seek the presidency.

Nixon, who had spent the better part of the mid-1960s ingratiating himself with GOP elites around the nation, almost certainly had made up his mind to run by the time of the December 1967 visit.[30] Still, he clearly viewed Graham as a valuable consultant concerning his political future.

From the Quiet Revolution to the Silent Majority

As the 1968 presidential race approached, observers wondered how Graham's sympathy toward Nixon would affect his loyalty to Lyndon Johnson. Before Johnson withdrew from the race, Graham faced the prospect of a challenger whom he had long encouraged to run opposing an incumbent whom he had publicly supported. In early 1968, after the Key Biscayne discussions with Nixon, Graham sent a letter reassuring the Johnson team of his intention to avoid political involvement.[31] By then, though, the evangelist had informed a highly skeptical Nixon of his belief that Johnson would not seek reelection.[32] Around this time, Graham began to publicize his status as a registered Democrat, something he had not done even when right-wing oil mogul H. L. Hunt had tried to draft him as a Republican candidate in 1964. Graham's self-affiliation found a skeptical media audience. The *Arkansas Gazette*, then emerging as one of his harshest critics, labeled him "one of those self-styled 'Southern Democrats'" who voted like a member of the other major party. During the Nixon presidency, a *Parade* article placed him at the top of a list of powerful "behind the scenes" Republicans.[33]

Intrigue about the evangelist's role in the race only intensified after Johnson surprised the nation by bowing out of the campaign. Democrats from Tennessee expressed alarm that Graham was ready to "come out for Nixon," something they knew he had almost done eight years earlier. They asked Johnson how such a development might be avoided. A handwritten note on their letter to him offered one logical possibility: "John Connally?"[34] Probably unbeknownst to anyone on the president's staff, however, Graham was attempting (unsuccessfully, for the moment) to woo his ideal chief justice toward support for Nixon.[35] Meanwhile, on the Republican side, a syndicated newspaper columnist termed Graham the "X Factor" in the upcoming campaign and cited concerns among GOP supporters of rival candidate Ronald Reagan that the evangelist would back Nixon.[36] Graham, when visiting with the California governor during the fall of 1967, had discussed with him complications that might arise with both Nixon and Reagan in the race. A few days after the "X Factor" piece, then, Reagan might have been surprised to read in *Newsweek* that Graham did "not feel well acquainted with" him.[37] A different source had the evangelist pitching Texas representative George Bush as an ideal GOP running mate for Nixon.[38] Still others speculated that Graham himself might wind up with the vice presidential nomination.[39] These rumblings all surfaced in the aftermath of Graham's May 1968 Portland, Oregon, crusade, which had conspicuously (if inadvertently) coincided with the state GOP presidential primary. Graham—who introduced Julie Nixon, daughter of the candidate, and her fiancé, David Eisenhower, during a service in Portland—met with Nixon in his campaign suite at some point that week.[40] Publicly, Graham denied all rumors about his political activities and suggested that he would not endorse a presidential candidate.[41]

Yet Graham did play an important role in the 1968 campaign, one that takes on particular significance when understood in the larger context of Nixon's southern strategy. That strategy, which remains a highly contested topic among historians of the modern South, primarily consisted of Nixon's outreach to the traditionally Democratic southern white electorate.[42] First, though, Nixon needed to woo the many southern delegates to the Republican National Convention who found the strongly conservative Reagan more appealing. Before and during the GOP convention in Miami, South Carolina senator Strom Thurmond, a 1964 convert to the party of Lincoln, kept the South alive for Nixon. With the encouragement of Thurmond aide Harry Dent, Nixon met with southern Republicans and pledged his reliability on a slate of issues ranging from Supreme Court nominations to forced busing and textile policy. Nixon repeated these pledges at the convention, where in backdoor meetings he convinced southern delegates of his trustworthiness on civil rights.[43]

Graham was a conspicuous presence at the 1968 GOP convention, much more so than at the subsequent Democratic gathering in Chicago, where he gave an invocation. In Miami, the evangelist did more than offer a blessing; he put his connections to use for Nixon. According to reports leaked by the Nixon campaign team and indirectly confirmed by Graham, North Carolina GOP gubernatorial candidate Jim Gardner confided to the evangelist his support for Nixon, only to renege and embrace Reagan, whose official entry into the race put Nixon's southern liaisons in crisis mode.[44] The Associated Press, meanwhile, reported that Graham discreetly visited Nixon's convention headquarters to pick up a packet containing information about members of the highly vulnerable Alabama delegation, which eventually voted fourteen to twelve for Nixon over Reagan.[45]

As Graham acknowledged, he took part in early morning high-level discussions between nominee-elect Nixon and party officials concerning the candidate's vice presidential choice. Graham's involvement came at the invitation of Nixon. When, in what was surely a staged move, Nixon asked Graham, the lone nonpolitico present, for his input, the evangelist proposed Oregon senator Mark Hatfield, among the most liberal vice presidential possibilities. Hatfield was a dedicated Baptist whom Graham thought might balance the ticket. Recent newspaper headlines had touted the Oregon senator as anything but a long shot, yet he stood little chance of surviving a veto from Nixon's southern backers.[46] Nixon already knew that Hatfield was Graham's favorite, having quizzed the candidate about vice presidential options during a pre-convention conversation in Nixon's New York apartment.[47] According to earlier reports, the evangelist had played a role in Hatfield's surprising endorsement of Nixon. In Miami, Graham and Hatfield had sat together in a VIP box before the senator delivered his convention speech.[48] In the end, Nixon asked Graham to inform Hatfield that he would not be the running mate.[49] Nixon might have used Graham's disarming presence during the vice presidential discussions to gauge conservative responses to Hatfield. Just as likely, the candidate was repaying Hatfield for his unexpected support. Many of the above details received national dissemination—much, as Nixon could have foreseen, to the benefit of Hatfield's stature. The national press also took note of Graham in Miami. *Newsweek* published a photograph of Graham waiting to see the nominee-elect at the convention. Nevertheless, as Graham assured his constituents in a mass mailing sent after the GOP convention, he would try his best to stay out of politics during the campaign season.[50]

Nixon had rejected Hatfield in part because the nominee harbored hopes of continuing and even expanding the Republican presidential inroads in the South. Nixon desired to engage the region in a manner resembling Dwight Eisenhower's two winning campaigns. The resounding failure of 1964 GOP nominee Barry Goldwater, who had alienated moderates nationwide while sweeping the Deep South, led Nixon toward a strategy by which, in the 1969 words of Republican analyst Kevin Phillips, the GOP "abandoned its revolutionary Deep South scheme and returned to reliance on evolutionary inroads in the Outer South."[51] This "suburban strategy," as one historian has recently termed it, focused on the region's growing Sunbelt metropolises, invoking a rhetoric of racial color-blindness, rather than racial backlash.[52] Yet the southern strategy lite still derived from regional considerations. Even though Nixon aspired to be a national candidate with broad-based appeal, he adopted a more moderate tone in large part because the third-party candidacy of Alabama governor George Wallace appeared irreversible.

Graham, as Nixon later told White House chief of staff H. R. Haldeman, "was enormously helpful to us in the Border South in '68."[53] Although the evangelist publicly denied it, he was particularly useful in Nixon's efforts to minimize the electoral impact of Wallace, who single-handedly kept several Deep South states out of the Republican column. Nixon ultimately responded to Wallace by casting himself as "opposed to segregation but favoring only voluntary integration."[54] Nixon staffers, seeking to contrast their candidate with a fire-breathing Wallace, remained aware of Graham's status as "the second most revered man in the South among adult voters." Campaign aide William Safire went so far as to propose using Graham directly against Wallace, an idea Nixon vetoed. Nixon adman Harry Treleaven, meanwhile, sought to "follow up on the suggestion that we produce a Billy Graham program for use in the South."[55] Advice along these lines contributed to Graham's visible attendance at a staged question and answer session that Nixon taped in Atlanta. During the early October recording, which appeared on television screens throughout the South, Nixon contrasted his style with the oppositional approach of Wallace and cited Graham when discussing a religious revival among American youth.[56] Even Nixon's September appearance at a Graham crusade service in the swing state of Pennsylvania played out against the backdrop of southern politics. The televised service, during which the evangelist glowingly introduced Nixon, was broadcast the week before election day in a number of states—including, as newspapers noted, closely contested South Carolina and Texas. In response, Texas supporters of Wallace's American Independent Party demanded a federal investigation into what they saw as an unregulated advertisement for Nixon. A San Antonio station even granted Wallace "equal time."[57]

In the campaign of 1968, Graham's greatest contribution to the ambitions of Nixon in the South (and elsewhere) may have been the evangelist's role in raising law-and-order issues in a manner beneficial to a mainstream conservative candidate. Graham's presence at the chaotic Democratic convention in Chicago only reinforced his sentiments along these lines; he remembered commiserating with Southern Democrats worried about the future of their nation (and, most likely, their party).[58] Race hovered over all of these concerns, of course, no matter how much Nixon sought to sell himself as a color-blind moderate.[59] Nixon's calculated inattention to civil rights matters made him a respectable alternative to Wallace. With Wallace running well in the Deep South and in the most racially intransigent regions of the Upper South, Nixon sought and largely won over the growing affluent suburban population of the region, picking up several peripheral southern states, as well as Thurmond's South Carolina.[60]

On a larger level, Graham was emblematic of the long-term, if gradual, success of the Republican Party in attracting presidential adherents in the South. The evangelist was an intimate part of a powerful political, social, and religious network of southerners that had gravitated toward Nixon since the Eisenhower era. Some of them officially joined the GOP, while others remained conservative Democrats who supported Republican presidents. Together, they amounted to a kind of Nixon-Graham nexus. The group included John Connally, who eventually served as secretary of the treasury under Nixon; Winton Blount, a key founder of the modern southern GOP who served as Nixon's postmaster general and later headed Connally's unsuccessful 1980 presidential campaign; and William Walton, cofounder of the Memphis-based Holiday Inn hotel chain and an occasional guest at the Nixon White House.[61] More peripheral figures included James Byrnes, who endorsed Nixon in 1960 and 1968; Democratic congressional representatives Mendel Rivers and Frank Boykin, who had supported Eisenhower during the 1950s; Florida Democratic senator George Smathers, who backed his friend Nixon in 1972; and George H. W. Bush, also a friend of Blount's.[62] What these men held in common was a friendship with Billy Graham, which in some cases preceded their support for Nixon. Their closeness to Graham did not by itself impel them toward Nixon, of course; but the connection is difficult to dismiss as merely coincidence or byproduct of the evangelist's general popularity.

In 1968, as in 1960, Graham flirted with an official endorsement of Nixon but settled for something similar. According to Harry Dent, who left Thurmond to become Nixon's point man for the South, the evangelist was "prepared" to endorse the candidate "if necessary."[63] Graham was, of course, helpful in many other capacities. For example, he put his relationship with the sitting executive to use by extending an olive branch to President Johnson on behalf of Nixon. During a mid-September meeting, which Graham had requested concerning a matter of "some importance," he communicated Nixon's respect for the president and added that, if elected, Nixon would consult

Johnson and do nothing to damage his reputation. The evangelist was repeating instructions Nixon had given him during the Pittsburgh crusade. A gracious, if probably wary, Johnson reiterated his loyalty to the Democratic nominee but said he would cooperate with a President Nixon. According to a leading Johnson biographer, the overture worked at least momentarily; the president had little energy for assisting Hubert Humphrey, his own vice president.[64] Later, when Johnson supporters believed President Nixon had broken his pledge not to criticize the ex-president on Vietnam, Graham wrote a letter disputing the charges.[65]

As the 1968 campaign entered the home stretch, the evangelist assisted Nixon in several other, more visible ways. The two appeared together in widely circulated wire service photographs three times during the final two months of the campaign. The Pittsburgh service was the most publicized of these appearances. There, Graham felt compelled to remind the audience of his policy of avoiding political positions (and, for balance, read a telegram message from Hubert Humphrey).[66] Two weeks later, Nixon once again saw Graham's mother during an election year, this time for a publicized tea at her home in Charlotte. The Nixons traveled there from Raleigh with Graham's daughter, Anne, and her husband, Danny Lotz.[67] Along with Graham's brother, Melvin, Lotz belonged to the sixteen-person Nixon campaign committee in North Carolina.[68] While campaigning in Charlotte, Nixon told a television interviewer of his basic agreement with the *Brown* decision but expressed opposition to busing programs or other forms of "forced integration." At a well-attended rally, he invoked the "forgotten Americans."[69] The visit occurred nine days before Billy Graham Appreciation Day, an event sponsored by the city leadership. At the celebration, Graham similarly spoke about "a great unheard from group . . . both black and white, who [is] probably going to be heard from loudly at the polls."[70] The tea with Morrow Graham came amid sagging poll numbers for Nixon and was part of a late effort to emphasize the personal and familial side of a politician not associated with either quality. When a former member of the Johnson administration questioned the integrity of Nixon, the evangelist countered with an October 16 statement describing his "friend" as "a man of high moral principles."[71] Nixon and Graham soon attended a church service together in Manhattan, taking a very public stroll afterward.[72] Around that time, a flu-stricken Graham returned to New York to preview a campaign documentary that showed the candidate as a family man. Nixon thought it "too personal," yet agreed to let it run pending the approval of Graham. The film received national release.[73] Six days before the election, Graham finally confided to a Dallas newspaper that he had cast an absentee ballot for Nixon, a fact southern strategist Harry Dent highlighted in television advertisements that most likely had been in the works well before the evangelist's revelation.[74]

Two days before Graham celebrated his fiftieth birthday, the evangelist received what one correspondent termed a "nice birthday embellishment," a Nixon victory.[75] The evangelist visited Nixon at his campaign headquarters early the morning after election day. With victory assured, Nixon asked Graham to lead a prayer.[76] The presidential transition period left Graham at the height of his influence as a national figure. During the final months of the Johnson administration, he visited South Vietnam on behalf of the sitting president but also found time to ask John Connally to serve in the future administration as secretary of either the treasury or defense.[77] When Nixon assumed office, Graham quite literally remained at his station. He and Ruth spent the final weekend of the administration as the Johnsons' sole guests in the White House, after which Graham led the inauguration prayer.[78] Its references to the social ills of "crime, division, and rebellion" struck some critics as another form of campaign rhetoric.[79]

Nixon's inaugural address incorporated language familiar to the evangelist. The president spoke eloquently of a "crisis of the spirit," which in turn demanded an "answer of the spirit."[80] Such words, although emblematic of the lofty, metaphysical turns of phrase common to speeches of state, revealed a telling similarity between the rhetoric of Nixon and Graham. While the notion of "crisis" permeated the public discourse of postwar America, it also had a strong evangelical pedigree. Nixon, who grew up hearing the sermons of Billy Sunday, Aimee Semple McPherson, "Fighting" Bob Shuler, and other prominent preachers, knew well the tone of evangelistic jeremiads.[81] Since the mid-1950s, Graham had delivered a durable stock sermon on "America's Great Crisis." It outlined four major crisis points in American history: the American Revolution, the Constitutional Convention, the Civil War, and finally, the present predicament. Cold War anxieties aside, the contemporary crisis did not derive from a war or a political impasse, according to Graham. It was rather a crisis of moral decline threatening to sever the nation from its religious heritage.[82]

During the early years of the Nixon administration, Graham readily latched onto the president's similar invocation of a crisis uniquely confined to the realm of character and values. The evangelist quoted the inaugural address at an October prayer breakfast in Washington, where he delivered his own crisis sermon. "I think that Mr. Nixon is right when he says that ours is a spiritual crisis," he told an interviewer on British television.[83] Graham hoped the Nixon presidency would revive the spiritual progress he thought had defined the latter half of the Eisenhower administration.[84] Theologian Reinhold Niebuhr pilloried such talk as the "Nixon-Graham doctrine," which reductively "regards all religion as virtuous in guaranteeing public justice."[85] Nixon's inaugural performance, though, caught the attention of evangelical leaders. Southern Baptist Convention president Herschel Hobbs, a former Johnson supporter, thanked Graham for his role in the service and praised Nixon for his spiritual earnestness. "I have been delighted with the wonderful way that your administration is beginning," Hobbs wrote to the president. "I want it to continue that way not only because I happen[ed] to vote for you, but because I have a deep interest in you personally through our mutual friend Billy Graham."[86]

Enabling the Administration

During and after the fall of President Nixon, Graham often insisted that, contrary to popular perceptions, he had actually spent more time in the Eisenhower and Johnson White Houses. His point, while difficult to believe at the time, technically may have been accurate, particularly in light of his numerous overnight stays at the Johnson White House, which Graham once estimated at twenty-six in all.[87] Nixon was not nearly so social a man as his predecessor. Yet such clock-consciousness on the part of the evangelist elided the depth of his involvement in the Nixon administration. As much as a sanctifying symbol or a link to a vital constituency, the evangelist served as a political adviser who offered himself as such and whom Nixon saw as such. Graham both administered and received political favors, and he delighted in analyzing the president's television coverage and offering media pointers. His periodic conversations with Nixon, who often phoned the evangelist (along with other supporters) after delivering major addresses, revealed the strikingly political nature of their relationship. The president "wants to get Billy Graham in tomorrow to talk about politics," reads one entry in chief of staff H. R. Haldeman's diary.[88]

In addition to their numerous conversations, the evangelist assisted Nixon by supporting, or seeming to support, his policies on such controversial issues as school busing and the Vietnam War. He also appeared with

Nixon at high-profile events intended in part to connect the president with his asserted silent majority. Whether the issue was busing, Vietnam, or a national crisis of the spirit, the evangelist's rhetoric often paralleled what pundits would now call the "talking points" of the administration.

For a president who had courted the moderate-to-conservative white South so assiduously, the school desegregation issue represented a political dilemma (if not a moral one). Following the 1969 *Alexander v. Holmes County* Supreme Court decision mandating immediate integration, Nixon struggled to support obedience of the law without demonstrating enthusiasm for it. On the cusp of the 1970 school year—the first integrated term for many districts in the Deep South—Nixon and aide Leonard Garment asked Graham to record five television and radio spots for broadcast throughout the region. The evangelist did so with the assistance of Charlotte-based media mogul Charles Crutchfield, a Nixon supporter and racial moderate cut in the mold of Winton Blount (that is, a moderate on race, but little else). Graham recorded the segments at a television station in Rochester, Minnesota, where he had traveled for his annual physical at the Mayo Clinic. Wallace Henley, spokesperson for a White House committee designed to oversee desegregation policy, helped to edit the videotapes.[89]

The spots contained a mixture of the evangelist's traditional support for lawfulness and his equally customary defensiveness about the South. Graham reaffirmed his regional identity and argued that most southerners recognized the value of the public education system. While many persons "don't agree with the changes that are taking place" in the schools, he contended, "I really believe the South will set an example of respect for law." In the end, he asserted, "anybody who expects to be able to make the South the butt of their jokes this fall is going to have to look for a new source of amusement." Many southern whites who heard him on donated media time throughout the region undoubtedly found these words more agreeable than an outright endorsement of integration. Nixon later praised Graham for his work, both publicly and behind the scenes, "in developing support in the South for my civil rights policies." In truth, the president sent strategically mixed signals to southern whites and blacks alike on the nature of those policies. Graham's 1970 television spots perpetuated this ambiguity. In one version, he mentioned the "on record" opposition of Nixon to "busing to achieve racial balance."[90] Soon afterward, the evangelist predicted that "blood [would] flow in the streets of northern cities" if the Supreme Court upheld judicially mandated busing programs, which had then commenced in his hometown of Charlotte.[91]

Graham did not record media spots on behalf of Nixon's Vietnam policy, yet he supported it through unmistakable gestures and only slightly less explicit public statements. Characteristically, the evangelist denied any charges that he was an unabashed supporter of the war effort. If his private communication with Johnson and Nixon is any indication, though, he remained a committed, if chastened hawk into the early 1970s. Writing to Johnson weeks before Nixon assumed office, Graham declared himself "enthusiastically optimistic about the prospects of Vietnam becoming a strong free nation in Southeast Asia. I am certain that history is going to vindicate the American commitment if we don't lose the peace [during negotiations] in Paris."[92] Although these words were partly intended to lift the spirits of Johnson, and while Graham followed most Americans in questioning the viability of a long-term American presence in Vietnam, they evinced an unwillingness to question the legitimacy of a war that would last through the administration of Nixon (who could have lost an election at the 1968 Paris talks). Another indication of Graham's views on Vietnam came from reports, based on conversations with missionary friends stationed in Southeast Asia, which the evangelist passed along to Nixon and, on a separate occasion, to Secretary of State Henry Kissinger. The missionaries and, by strong implication, Graham supported the policy of "Vietnamization"; they remained fiercely opposed to North Vietnam but had grown skeptical about the viability of a visible American presence in South Vietnam.[93] Whatever doubts Graham possessed about Vietnam (and they were not the doubts of a dove), they rarely surfaced publicly. When they did, he mentioned that escalation of the war had occurred under Democratic administrations or, more commonly, attempted to differentiate between support for the war and faith in the president. In one conversation, Graham assured Nixon that in an upcoming op-ed piece in the New York Times he was "putting all of the blame of this whole thing on Kennedy."[94] While Graham said he had not "taken any public stand since the beginning on the Vietnam War," he asserted on a television show in 1970 that he was "going to take the president at his word."[95] In the text of a Birmingham crusade service two years later, Graham more bluntly urged his crusade audience to "get behind the president's goal and objectives of getting out of Vietnam."[96] Wary of a land war from an early date, the evangelist appeared to favor a "hit quick and hit hard" war policy, one that would "get it over with," yet "maintain the honor and dignity of America." He had made similar comments as far back as 1964, well before Vietnam became a quagmire.[97] Early in 1973, he called Nixon to reaffirm his support for the president's Vietnam policies. Nixon hardly needed any reassurance; Graham had already assisted his foreign policy in a multitude of other ways.[98]

What would resonate in the memories of many Americans, though, were those moments when Graham services or appearances seemed to double as Nixon rallies. During a time when the evangelist had grown especially comfortable doing the kinds of things celebrities did (e.g., appearing on the late-night *Dick Cavett Show*—after the White House recommended that the show contact Graham—and serving as grand marshal of the Rose Bowl Parade), he and the president made controversial appearances at high-profile events staged in the heart of Nixon country.[99]

The first such event during the Nixon administration occurred in Knoxville in May 1970 amid the midterm congressional campaign. This was the second and more intense run of the southern strategy, when, according to one historian, Nixon "waged a midterm campaign with very few parallels in American history."[100] Seeking to broaden his right flank, the president intervened in a number of congressional campaigns, including Tennessee Republican Bill Brock's senatorial challenge to liberal incumbent Albert Gore, Sr. With encouragement from Winton Blount and others, Nixon also opposed the gubernatorial run of George Wallace, who needed the office as a base for his presidential ambitions. In advance of this more aggressive stage of the southern strategy, the Nixon team had shifted from a nominal 1968 theme of national unity to an outright embrace of the silent majority (or, alternatively, Middle America) and was keen to engage in suitable symbolic politics.[101] Harry Dent suggested inviting country and western musicians to perform at White House functions. Graham had already proposed the services of his new friend, country musician Johnny Cash, who accepted an invitation to perform in Knoxville.[102]

The Knoxville crusade differed from Graham's earlier desegregated services in the South of the 1950s and 1960s in that it seemed wholly to affirm community norms, rather than even modestly prod them.[103] Knoxville indicated the momentary alignment of his domestic crusades with the Nixonian political style. As the crusade approached its end, newspapers reported that the president would participate in a service billed as "Youth Night." Although he had attended other crusade services, Nixon took the unprecedented step of directly addressing the audience in Knoxville, located in a heavily Republican part of Tennessee. The visit was apparently the president's idea, and his presence complicated Graham's earlier promise to "stay away from politics" during the crusade.[104] An overflow crowd of 100,000, twice the size of the average crusade audience in Knoxville, gathered inside and around the University of Tennessee's Neyland Stadium to hear Nixon and the evangelist. Introducing the president, Graham quoted Nixon on the "crisis of the spirit" and highlighted the stature and difficulty of the nation's highest office: "All Americans may not agree with the decisions a President makes—but he is our President," the leader of "the blacks as well as the whites." As the conservative *Knoxville Journal* and many of the letters that poured into both city papers suggested, the service functioned as a performance of the silent majority, complete with a small but vocal group of protesters acting as foils. In his brief address, Nixon echoed Graham's conciliatory tone, although he expressed pleasure that "there seems to be a rather solid majority on one side rather than the other side tonight." The other side consisted of around three hundred demonstrators who intermittently chanted antiwar slogans throughout the service. They might have hooted even louder if they had known that an empty-pocketed Nixon had to borrow money from Graham during the offering. To the delight of most audience members, the protesters struck a nerve in BGEA vocalist Ethel Waters. "If I was over there close enough, I would smack you," she declared. "But I love you, and I'd give you a big hug and kiss."[105]

Nixon's visit to Knoxville received widespread news coverage, not for its theatrics but because it played out amid his ongoing courtship of the white southern electorate and his more recent efforts to improve his standing among American youth. (It was his first public appearance since the Kent State massacre of May 4.)[106] CBS television news reporter Dan Rather linked the visit with Nixon's intervention in the gubernatorial race in Alabama, where George Wallace faced a June 2 runoff in his quest for the Democratic nomination. Georgia Republican gubernatorial candidate Hal Suit asked Graham to appear at a rally in Atlanta—or, perhaps, to let him offer a prayer in Knoxville.[107] Meanwhile, BGEA board member Maxey Jarman was campaigning (unsuccessfully) for the Republican nomination for Tennessee governor.[108] The most obvious political connections, though, were with the Tennessee senatorial race. The delegation traveling with Nixon to Knoxville included Bill Brock, other Tennessee Republicans running for office that year, and a Democrat whose district included East Tennessee. Brock's campaign director claimed that both Graham and Nixon had personally invited the candidate. Despite having an event scheduled near Knoxville that very day, Senator Gore did not receive an invite, ostensibly on the grounds that he did not hail from East Tennessee (even though a Memphis Republican was part of the delegation). Nixon and Brock posed beside each other in group photographs.[109]

As the 1970 election grew nearer, Graham denied any connection to the southern strategy. He did, though, echo a Nixon campaign theme in declaring his preference for "the moderates and the conservatives," whom he believed voters should give "a chance."[110] Whether assisted or not by the Knoxville service, Brock went on to defeat Gore in November. The crusade also reverberated in local politics when a Republican congressional incumbent spuriously accused his Democratic opponent of picketing the Graham service.[111] Overall, though, 1970 was not a propitious year for Nixon, as his rightward shift reprised the Goldwater failure of 1964. The GOP gained two Senate seats but surrendered twelve seats in the House. Also, Wallace regained the Alabama governorship.[112]

Two other events highlighted the Graham-Nixon alliance for millions of Americans. The first, the Honor America Day celebration of July 4, 1970, represented the somewhat anticlimactic fruition of Graham's long-voiced desire for alternative rallies in the face of political protests. With the approval of Nixon, the evangelist helped to plan the nominally bipartisan affair, which featured performances by Bob Hope, Glenn Campbell, and other beacons of Middle America. At the rally, which Graham unsuccessfully encouraged Nixon to attend, the evangelist delivered a rousing defense of American institutions and patriotism. Graham tapped E. V. Hill, whom he viewed as a possible Nixon ally, to emcee the service.[113]

Another controversial event took place the next year in Charlotte, where Charles Crutchfield hosted an extravagant gala in honor of the evangelist. Nixon, Connally, Thurmond, and most of the leading politicians of North Carolina journeyed to Charlotte to celebrate Billy Graham Day. Crutchfield, whose access to the White House came in part through his friendship with Harry Dent, personally pitched the event to Nixon before mentioning it to Graham. White House notes describe the proposed event as a "contrived deal to calm [the] So[uth]" and to bring blacks and whites together amid the implementation of court-ordered desegregation programs. The second celebration in four years of Charlotte's most renowned native son, it was scheduled so as not to coincide with the start of the school year.[114] Nixon followed Eisenhower and Johnson in thinking of Graham as a mediating presence for white southerners. The political benefits of the event struck many observers as much more apparent, though.

Billy Graham Day encapsulated both the blatant and indirect elements of the southern strategy. As one Nixon critic noted, the October 15, 1971, celebration coincided with a major administration announcement on textile policy.[115] The festivities included a parade, a private reception complete with cross-shaped sandwiches, and the initial unveiling of a plaque at Graham's birthplace. In an address delivered in the Charlotte Coliseum, Graham praised his hometown, which had "peacefully" followed "demanding" court rulings. "If all Americans were like the people of the Piedmont section of the Carolinas, we would have little of the problems we have today in the country," the evangelist said. Nixon's brief comments received wide coverage, including (as Graham reminded him) nationwide broadcast on the BGEA's *Hour of Decision* radio show. "And while it was, indeed, Graham's Day, it might as well have been the beginning of President Nixon's campaign," declared the *Charlotte Observer*. In an editorial, the paper sharply criticized Billy Graham Day as an amoral exercise in "political drama," yet another example of how "Mr. Graham's court in Washington" played the South for electoral gain. Subsequently released documents showed somewhat tense consultations among city leaders, White House staffers, and local Republicans in organizing the event. Presidential aide Charles Colson solicited follow-up phone calls to leading Southern Baptists and reported their positive responses to the Charlotte visit. "I'll tell you this, boy," Nixon exclaimed to Colson. "Billy Graham country. . . . They'll go out and pray and work like nothin[g]."[116]

Peaks and Pending Valleys

While Graham's relationship with Nixon was not completely a one-way street, the traffic flow remained imbalanced. Nixon did occasionally attempt to reciprocate Graham's loyalty—albeit in his own unscrupulous way. The president once ordered a report on a *Washington Post* journalist who had written a piece critical of the evangelist.[117] Similarly, a Baton Rouge VISTA director who had criticized Graham during a crusade there soon faced a federal investigation (ordered by Organization of Economic Opportunity head Donald Rumsfeld).[118] After the evangelist complained to John Connally about a possible tax audit of the BGEA, Nixon pledged to ensure that the Internal Revenue Service would instead look into his Jewish critics and the head of the liberal National Council of Churches.[119] For his part, Graham thanked Nixon for the support the BGEA had started receiving from many of the president's friends.[120]

Ultimately, though, the value of those contributions paled in comparison to the price Graham paid for his loyalty to Nixon. The toll continued into the present century with the 2002 release of a White House recording that quickly came to symbolize the nadir of Graham's association with Nixon. Their exchange of February 1, 1972, suggested just how far Graham's treatment of Nixon then stood from any semblance of pastoral care. The heart of their conversation was tinged with anti-Semitism. It began as a typical discussion about the upcoming presidential race, with Graham counseling the president to run on his record and his "integrity," and (perhaps with Knoxville and Charlotte in mind) to use television more effectively by creating "events" at which to appear. The evangelist then mentioned an upcoming meeting with the editors of *Time* magazine, which he claimed had "dropped" him following the death of publisher Henry Luce. Ever ready for a round of media criticism, Nixon launched into a tirade against the Jewish-dominated Fourth Estate. Graham was more concerned with the pornography industry than with mainstream publications. He most likely had in mind the controversial pending postal rate adjustments that threatened to drive up costs for his monthly magazine, *Decision*. In recent testimony before the postal commission, Graham had urged a "social evaluation of the relative merits of various rates." In his conversation with Nixon, though, Graham did agree with the thrust of the president's critique of liberal elites. Graham denounced the Jewish "stranglehold" on the media and, as the president urged him on, declared that even those Jews who "swarm around" him because of his support for Israel did not "know how I really feel about what they're doing to this country." He "would stand up under proper circumstances," he cryptically added.[121]

The conversation revealed the extent to which mainstream evangelicals like Graham distinguished between Jews as a "People" and Jews as people. In response to the latter, noncovenantal sense of Jewry, Graham was willing to indulge Nixon's prejudices and, in this case, voice a few of his own. The evangelist apparently segregated such thoughts from the work that had garnered him no small amount of public support from American Jewish leaders: his closeness with Israeli prime minister Golda Meir; his friendliness toward the Anti-Defamation League and the American Jewish Committee; and, according to the committee's evangelical liaison, his direct lobbying to Nixon in support of F-15 fighter plane shipments to Israel. Graham did not share Nixon's obsession with liberal Jews, but he was not willing to contradict it either.[122]

The conversation eventually turned away from the Jewish media and back to Nixon's intended topic: politics, namely, the status of Treasury Secretary John Connally in the administration. Nixon, who harbored dreams of asking Connally to serve as his second-term vice president, was concerned about the possible resignation of Connally, then suffering from health problems. Nixon often discussed Connally with Graham and in 1970 had considered asking the evangelist to make a second request to Connally to join the administration. Haldeman eventually made the successful pitch. In the February 1972 conversation, Graham averred that Connally was "important politically right now" and agreed to help with what Haldeman called the "Connally problem."[123]

The now infamous Graham-Nixon exchange revealed the depths of Graham's involvement in the 1972 campaign, during which he behaved in a manner further belying his self-proclaimed nonpartisanship. After momentarily considering steering clear of the election—to the point where he had drafted a letter to Nixon saying he would do so—Graham explicitly made himself available for campaign work that day. Still, Graham maintained a stated preference for avoiding overtly endorsement-like statements or actions. He was willing to move in that direction, though, if the race remained tight. According to Haldeman, who apparently did not distinguish between a Graham sermon and a campaign pitch, the evangelist "agreed to hit the key states during the fall, especially Pennsylvania, Ohio, Illinois, maybe New York, and California." Graham, the Nixon chief of staff continued, would "answer attacks on us and that sort of thing whenever he felt he could, if I would direct the request to him."[124] The president assigned Haldeman to handle direct communication with the evangelist and later gave him instructions to call Graham "about once every two weeks to discuss the political situation."[125] Haldeman was to keep in touch with Connally as well. Using Haldeman as an intermediary kept Nixon, who wanted to make sure Graham felt included in the campaign, removed from overt politicking with the evangelist. The arrangement also protected Graham, allowing him to claim in a press conference that he only occasionally talked with Nixon and that the president never sought advice on specific policies.[126] According to talking papers prepared for Haldeman, suggested topics for discussions with Graham and Connally included the candidacy of George Wallace, school busing, and the status of prospective Democratic nominee Edmund Muskie. Thus, while the evangelist undoubtedly remained oblivious to the dirtiest tricks of the Nixon campaign, he offered insights of obvious use for the reelection effort.[127]

As in earlier campaigns, Graham's direct political assistance to Nixon in 1972 fell into two broad categories: a southern strategy and outreach to evangelical voters. Updated and intensified since the 1968 election, both elements complemented the president's search for an enduring electoral majority.[128] Much of Graham's advice to Nixon or his aides held implications for the still largely Democratic South, where the evangelist had ties with figures ranging from President Johnson and George Wallace to Reubin Askew, the moderate governor of Florida. Graham consulted Askew about the status of McGovern in the Sunshine State and reported to Nixon on his election-year conversations with Johnson, whom the evangelist believed to be "secretly in favor of Nixon." With great exaggeration, the former president had earlier told Graham, "I'm still a Democrat" but "I'm not sure how long I'm gonna remain one." In August of the election year, Haldeman asked Graham to advise Johnson on how to handle an upcoming visit with Nixon's campaign chair. Graham did as requested and passed along a suggestion from Johnson (sagacious, in retrospect) that Nixon should try to appear presidential and largely ignore his opponent. Nixon staffers considered leaking to a political columnist Graham's suggestion that Johnson would not stump on behalf of the Democratic ticket. That same month, Graham received a request from Sargent Shriver to offer a prayer during Shriver's nationally televised acceptance of the Democratic vice presidential nomination. Shriver appealed to Graham as a friend, all the while acknowledging that the evangelist would vote for Nixon. While Graham personally viewed such an invocation as an appropriate extension of his ministerial duties, he turned down the invitation at Nixon's urging.[129]

By the spring of 1972, Nixon's only realistic barrier to reelection was another Wallace campaign, which would surely take away southern votes. Graham had helped to effect this comfortable situation. One year earlier, he had expressed concern about the popularity of prospective Democratic candidate Edmund Muskie in the South.[130] On the GOP side, Harry Dent had informed Graham that Oregon senator Mark Hatfield, who loomed as a protest candidate for the presidency, would receive Nixon's full backing for reelection if he stayed out of the presidential primaries.[131]

Nixon made an overt play for former Wallace voters in 1972. Four years earlier, Nixon had cast himself as a moderate vis-à-vis Wallace, and Dent had argued afterward that a "moderate South would help 'bring the nation together' and concurrently help the fortunes of the Nixon Administration as well as Republicans generally." Soon, however, political analysts Ben Wattenberg and Richard Scammon published alluring data from the 1968 election. In the South, 80 percent of Wallace voters would otherwise have backed Nixon. "Only in . . . a two-party context," warned Kevin Phillips, "would the racially-motivated core Wallace vote be available to the President in 1972." Recognizing the obvious benefits of modifying his 1968 strategy and ensuring that Wallace run as a Democrat (where he would not survive the primaries), Nixon put Dent in charge of his "Wallace-watch."[132]

Graham unofficially served on this watch. He was particularly valuable because of his cordial relationship with Wallace, which dated back to their awkward meeting during the 1965 Montgomery crusade. In June 1972, Nixon told Haldeman that the evangelist "has a line to Wallace through Mrs. Wallace [Cornelia, his second wife], who has become a Christian. Billy will talk to Wallace whenever we want him to. [Nixon] feels our strategy must be to keep Wallace in the Democratic Party and Billy can help us on that. . . . Graham should put the pressure on Wallace to decide whether he's going to be used as a spoiler, which would surely help elect [George] McGovern."[133] This exchange occurred one month after an assassination attempt had left the governor paralyzed from the waist down. Still, the possibility lingered of a renewed run with the American Independent Party.[134] Graham talked with Wallace in a pastoral capacity during the week of the shooting, and in July the evangelist agreed to help dissuade the ailing governor from a third-party run.[135] In a conversation with Wallace following a major operation, Graham told him that his candidacy would take away many more votes from Nixon than from McGovern. "Wallace said he would never turn one hand to help McGovern," Haldeman recorded, "and that he's 99 percent sure he won't do it, but he won't close the door completely."[136] The president considered Graham for the task of making a final appeal to Wallace. Nixon chose Connally for the job instead, although Graham again agreed to "get a read" on Wallace in late September.[137]

If Nixon's attempts to sway the Wallace vote stood as the strongest evidence of his decision to embrace racial politics in the white South, then his belated support for the senatorial run of converted Republican Jesse Helms in 1972 offered further confirmation. Here, too, Graham played a role. Helms had admired Graham since his days as a senatorial aide in the early 1950s. In

1968, Helms had written to ABC television suggesting Graham as an ideal speaker to counter "the glorification of Martin Luther King, Jr.," following the assassination of the civil rights leader.[138] Four years later, during a campaign in which Nixon hung out to dry a number of GOP senatorial candidates in the South, including Winton Blount, the president found time to visit North Carolina and publicly endorse Helms days before the election.[139] Nixon, who had discussed the visit with Graham beforehand, joked to the crowd that the evangelist had asked to receive credit in the event of good weather.[140] During the fall campaign season, Helms and his wife paid a well-photographed visit to have breakfast at the Graham home in Montreat. A turn in Montreat was becoming something of a rite of passage for Tarheel politicians.[141] (The Democratic gubernatorial candidate also visited that year, following an ad his GOP opponent had run picturing a golf outing with the evangelist.)[142] Still, a decision on Graham's part to avoid the particularly contentious and controversial Helms campaign, which had drawn national attention, would have been more than understandable. Helms, a former radio and television host, ran on the racially and ethnically loaded slogan, "He's One of Us!"[143]

Graham's involvement by degrees in the Republican southern strategy raises the question of his complicity in the Nixonian politics of race. Little reason exists to believe that the evangelist avowedly endorsed Nixon's shift toward Wallace-inspired strategies and rhetoric, or that he considered the president or even Helms to be a race-baiter.[144] Yet Graham's election advice dating back to 1956 and 1960, as well as his efforts to check Wallace, demonstrated his awareness and apparent acceptance of the fact that the race issue could work to the GOP's advantage in the South. Like any effective politician, moreover, the evangelist recognized the importance of communicating by suggestion rather than by declaration. Graham came to his own dissembling with much more anguish and much less calculation than did Nixon, yet he repeatedly skirted the truth when praising the president while denying any political motivations. In the late 1960s and early 1970s, Graham clearly knew the electoral score in the area of southern racial politics. He knew that the priorities of many southern white voters extended beyond simply supporting the most God-fearing candidate. He knew why southerners in Charlotte and elsewhere felt marginalized. He knew why Haldeman asked him about the politics of busing. He knew why most Wallace supporters would rather back Nixon than McGovern—and, despite previous hopes to the contrary, he eventually confessed to Haldeman his sense that the president stood little chance of attracting new black voters in 1972.[145] Content to believe that further court rulings or strict enforcement of existing civil rights laws would only exacerbate tensions in the South, Graham could reassure himself that a Nixon landslide would benefit other, more important causes.

As long as Wallace remained off the campaign trail, though, Nixon largely had his ducks in a row in Dixie, where his liberal antiwar opponent, George McGovern, had little chance of summoning traditional Democratic loyalties. The evangelical community, however, stood as an enticing source for additional inroads. Following the 1970 midterm elections, Nixon emphasized to Haldeman the need "to remember that our primary source of support will be among the fundamentalist Protestants, and we can probably broaden that base of support."[146] Graham—with his obvious appeal among fellow evangelicals, whether in the South or elsewhere—was a logical choice to assist such an effort. In keeping with Nixon's dreams of a sweeping electoral realignment, Graham hoped to widen the president's support among evangelicals (especially evangelical youth), whom the evangelist somewhat excessively feared might be attracted by McGovern's credentials as a minister's son. As the peak campaign season approached, Graham reminded Nixon of "an emerging evangelical strength in the country that is going to have a strong bearing on social and political matters probably for a generation to come." He also passed along a review of a book that seemed to make this very point.[147]

The 1972 race represented the culmination of Graham's service as both a bridge to evangelicals and a strategist in the larger effort to establish them as a pillar of the new majority. While he had previously acted as a conduit between presidents and conservative Protestants, his work intensified during Nixon's first term, when one presidential supporter proposed him as a "liaison between the Office of the President and the various religious groups in this country."[148] Although Graham knew better than to accept an official position, he helped to organize the unprecedented and controversial Nixon White House church services and prepared a broad-ranging list of possible Protestant participants.[149] The evangelist later complained of an inability to satiate the many evangelicals who expected him to facilitate face time with Nixon.[150] Graham did his best to balance supply and demand, although in most cases the push came from Nixon, much to the delight of the evangelist.

In addition to his assistance with the White House church services, Graham set up numerous meetings between Nixon and clergymen, usually Protestants and quite often of the conservative variety the president preferred.

(Meanwhile, Department of Veterans Affairs administrator and Southern Baptist leader Fred Rhodes kept Charles Colson apprised of Graham's public statements about Nixon.)[151] Some of these meetings concerned specific policy matters, while others were clearly electoral in nature. In 1970, for example, Graham advised Nixon to meet with the moderate Baptist Joint Committee on Public Affairs and made sure to note two Catholic-related policies many Baptists then opposed: funding for parochial education and U.S. relations with the Vatican.[152] The evangelist also facilitated an extended March 1970 meeting between the president and a group of about a dozen black church leaders, including E. V. Hill, who were upset over administration plans to cut social programs. Graham initially proposed the meeting during a low-profile gathering he had called between white and black evangelicals seeking to find common ground.[153]

Of more striking and long-term significance, though, were Graham's efforts to connect Nixon with the conservative white evangelical establishment. Graham had been trying to do so since the mid-1950s, when he invited Nixon to speak at denominational gatherings in western North Carolina. On several occasions during the Nixon administration, the evangelist helped to mollify the periodic tensions between the president's conservative rhetoric and his often moderate policies. In August 1971, the president met with a who's who of evangelical leaders and Graham supporters, including Harold Lindsell of *Christianity Today* and W. A. Criswell. Before meeting the president, they received a briefing from Henry Kissinger about China policy. Afterward, Nixon and Graham chatted in the Oval Office. "Well, they will go back," the president told Graham, "and they influence so many people, you know." Graham voiced the hope that the hawkish Criswell was coming around on engaging mainland China. "That's what we wanted," added the evangelist, who had set up the meeting at the request of the president.[154] Criswell soon held a press conference to declare his support for Nixon's pending visit to China.[155] Later, Graham organized another consultation between Kissinger and several dozen Christian "friends and acquaintances of Billy Graham" to again explain the administration's China policy. The guest list ranged from divines to donors—for example, from televangelist Oral Roberts to Holiday Inn head William Walton.[156] When Nixon undertook his pathbreaking diplomatic visit to China, he found time to call the evangelist from Beijing.[157]

Years removed from the intense electioneering of the Nixon White House, Graham would express incredulity when presented with evidence of his role in such a deeply politicized administration (a role that, of course, liberal critics at the time took for granted). The president "made it clear to Haldeman that he wanted to nurture whatever influence I might have with certain religious leaders," the evangelist wrote in his autobiography. "Needless to say, this was not discussed with me at the time."[158] Here, as with many of Graham's professions of political innocence, the evidence strongly indicates otherwise.

Graham helped to secure the coalition that gave Nixon a triumphant second-term mandate. The election year saw an all-out effort by the Nixon campaign to woo conservative religious groups, be they Catholic or Protestant (or, in a few cases, Jewish). Retaining and expanding the evangelical vote, though, was a paramount priority in a White House that, to its eventual detriment, refused to take victory for granted. Graham had already stressed to Nixon aide Leonard Garment the hunger among many churchgoers for a brand of social involvement more palatable than the liberal activism presumably emanating from so many pulpits.[159] Colson's notes from an apparent talk with Nixon include a blunt proposal for appealing to this population: "Use Graham's organization."[160] Haldeman's records suggest a similar ambition and also reveal the extent to which Graham reciprocated (but not to the point of surrendering the BGEA's mailing list).[161]

In addition to speaking highly of Nixon at nearly every possible moment during press conferences and interviews, Graham continued to serve as a liaison between Nixon and a wealth of conservative Protestant electoral capital. He recommended, for example, that Nixon establish contacts with the pentecostal-charismatic evangelist Oral Roberts, who had expressed to Harry Dent a desire to assist the campaign.[162] That year, Nixon considered accepting an invitation to address the SBC, where Graham was scheduled to appear. He would have been the first president to do so, and even some otherwise sympathetic Southern Baptists opposed such a blatantly political move.[163] Graham also wanted Nixon to attend Explo '72, a well-publicized Dallas festival that the evangelist termed a "Christian Woodstock." Campus Crusade for Christ director Bill Bright, the organizer of the gathering, supported the idea, yet yielded to a veto from his staff members. A talking paper for one of Haldeman's conversations with Graham notes that a survey of Explo '72 participants (conducted by the *Dallas Morning News*) indicated overwhelming backing of the president. "Is it now appropriate . . . to work with [Graham's assistant] T. W. Wilson to bring some staff of the Committee for the Re-Election of the President [CREEP] together with Bright of Campus

Crusade?" Haldeman was to ask Graham, who had referred to the Explo '72 youth as "the 'silenced' majority." Either Haldeman or Graham proposed that Bright and the evangelist remain in the background, while putting the Nixon forces in touch with evangelical youth workers potentially willing to take leave time for campaign work. (More of their constituents, of course, could vote in light of the Twenty-sixth Amendment.) Graham soon passed along "the names of all his Christian youth types." He also facilitated a conversation between Nixon's youth division and a group consisting of BGEA staffers, evangelical youth leaders, or both.[164] After at least one false start, CREEP ultimately chose to eschew the formal mobilization of Nixon-leaning clergy.[165] Still, the BGEA was apparently willing to surrender the services of Harry Williams, the evangelistic equivalent of a precinct whiz.[166] As if to confirm the success of the Nixon campaign's outreach to evangelicals (and his own role in it), Graham sent to Haldeman an election-eve story noting the influence his support for the president exerted on evangelicals. Earlier, when Graham called Haldeman to recommend Bible verses for Nixon to refer to during his acceptance speech at the Republican convention, the evangelist had argued that the president's strongest supporters would be expecting as much.[167]

At a September press conference held in Florida, Graham officially declared his support for Nixon's reelection. A few weeks before the election, he told Nixon he was available to do "anything you can think of you want me to do. . . . I'm not in a position to know all I could do, but you just tell me and I'll do it." With reelection effectively guaranteed, Nixon assured the evangelist that he did not "need any guidance. . . . Your political instincts are very good."[168] In the aftermath of the landslide victory, the evangelist's influence in the Nixon White House appeared as entrenched as ever. In February 1973, Nixon told Haldeman "to use Billy Graham also in the kitchen Cabinet," which Nixon was assembling to discuss his second-term agenda.[169] Graham could take comfort in knowing that the "quiet revolution" was silent no more. Nixon had won an overwhelming victory among evangelicals, southerners, and most Americans.

Within months of the election, though, the growing Watergate crisis began to expose a side of the Nixon White House which Graham may never have known directly but which he could scarcely escape being implicated with in some way. The Nixon years so thoroughly politicized Graham that such complicating details as the evangelist's record of support for racial tolerance and his friendships with certain liberals grew hazy amid the whirl of photo ops, church services, staged appearances, and bull sessions. Graham could not help but sanctify the Nixon way (even the aspects of it that occurred beyond his notice), because he not only offered his services carte blanche but also actively sought opportunities for political work. The evangelist remained blind to the plumbing beneath Nixon's politics, although not to the basic assumptions above it. Nixon, the usual suspect in all things Machiavellian, did not have to manipulate Graham so much as assent to the evangelist's own proposals. Rather than viewing the evangelist as an innocent or a tool, Nixon treated him like the politico he had momentarily become. In this respect, the Watergate crisis would out Graham along with Nixon. Before then, though (while liberal critics, lacking access to such smoking guns as the White House tapes and the Haldeman diaries, slugged away at the standing target of civil religion), the evangelist retained a distinctive voice in many parts of the South, one that resonated with a brighter side of Nixon's southern strategy, the side of John Connally rather than of Jesse Helms. This was the visage of a Sunbelt on the make.

More than a year before the 1954 *Brown v. Board of Education* decision, Graham held a desegregated crusade in Chattanooga, Tennessee. (Courtesy of Billy Graham Evangelistic Association)

Arkansas governor Orval Faubus arrived late for a Graham service in Little Rock and briefly had to sit on the stadium's concrete stairs. Supporters of Graham's desegregated rallies in September 1959 hoped that they would improve the image of a city tarnished by Faubus's resistance to school desegregation. (Courtesy of Time & Life Pictures)

Graham and Martin Luther King, Jr., posed for a photograph at a Chicago airport in 1962. The evangelist and civil rights leader maintained a largely cordial relationship despite their increasingly apparent theological and sociopolitical differences. (Courtesy of *Chicago Tribune*)

In the face of intense opposition from the local Citizens' Council, the 1964 Birmingham Easter
rally featured thoroughly integrated seating and brought the city positive national press.
Birmingham's recently desegregated ministerial committee soon asked Graham to return for a
full crusade. (Courtesy of Billy Graham Evangelistic Association)

In June 1965, Graham returned to Alabama to hold a week-long crusade in Montgomery. The evangelist cast his integrated services as an interracial alternative to civil rights demonstrations. (Courtesy of Billy Graham Evangelistic Association)

During the 1965 Montgomery crusade, Graham met with area African American leaders. The most visible black supporters of the crusade came from sectors of the black community largely removed from civil rights activism. (Courtesy of Billy Graham Evangelistic Association)

Richard Nixon traveled to Charlotte to participate in the 1971 Billy Graham Day extravaganza, which critics of the president linked with the Republican "southern strategy." (Courtesy of Associated Press)

CHAPTER SIX

Crusading for the Sunbelt South

A group of suburban Baptists, with whom I rode a chartered bus to and from the Crusade one night. . . . liked the idea that Atlanta had progressed—taking them along with it—but they didn't like the accompanying threats. They didn't like the fact that blacks were running their school system, that a black was the front runner in the mayor's race. They didn't like the proposal for a housing project in their neighborhood, which would bring down their property value. But they were going to rededicate their lives to Christ.
—Dale S. Russakoff, 1973

But I think we have seen rather overwhelmingly that what the South does become will not be in fulfillment of all those grand expectations that it would develop models for national emulation of new political alignments or new kinds of cities or new economic prodigies or new never-equaled racial harmony.
—Pat Watters, 1969

WHILE GRAHAM ABETTED the southern strategy, the southerners he most identified with attempted to project an altogether different image. That image was never as removed from the region's Jim Crow past, nor as separated from the specter of racial politics, as either Graham or many of his southern crusade supporters preferred to believe. Yet it became more convincing—and salable—during the 1970s. In September 1976, more than two months after the national bicentennial extravaganza, a special issue of *Time* magazine boasted that the "present Southern emotion is a sense of imminent victory—over circumstances, poverty and history." While the seventy-one pages dedicated to "The South Today" contained some glaring misreadings of the magnolia leaves (in the aftermath of Watergate and on the cusp of a Carter victory, *Time* presented the GOP as a paper elephant in the New South), one truism emerged: the South's image had changed for the better. Even Birmingham, Alabama, slightly more than a decade removed from footage of pressure hoses and attack dogs, was "A City Reborn" and "a model of Southern race relations." Further evidence of regional progress included photographs of the "shimmering skyline of Charlotte" and of a Charlotte native, Billy Graham, addressing a gathering of the rapidly growing Southern Baptist Convention.[1]

Those two pictures held more than circumstantial connections. One of the many symbols of Charlotte's growth, a suburban high-rise that housed the regional offices of IBM, contained a plaque, first unveiled by President Richard Nixon in 1971, commemorating Graham as the "world-renowned evangelist, author, and educator and preacher of the gospel of Christ to more people than any other man in history." The memorial was a nod to the building's location: the birthplace of the evangelist. "My father had a red clay farm that he hardly earned a living on when I was a boy," Graham told an interviewer in 1977. "But some of the best part of Charlotte moved on top of it—banks, IBM, Esso headquarters for the Southeast." In 1979, Graham biographer Marshall Frady, himself of Southern Baptist stock, treated the replacement of dairy farm with IBM building as a metaphor for Graham's theology, which remained bound to the pieties of a vanquished Dixie. Frady mistakenly conflated modern change with latent liberalism, as had many students of southern Protestantism. Instead, the visual contrast between farmstead and officeplex in Charlotte concealed a deeper affinity between evangelical faith and the booster ethos of the Sunbelt South. Writing seventeen years later, another journalist offered a corrective. In Charlotte, Peter Applebome wrote, "God and mammon—a desire to do good and a desire to do well—are knitted together . . . like threads in an intricate pattern."[2]

A range of elements—entrepreneurialism, asserted racial progress, and traditional faith—combined to form what commentators during the 1970s began calling the Sunbelt or, more specifically, the Sunbelt South. Coined by political analyst Kevin Phillips and later popularized by journalist Kirkpatrick Sale, the Sunbelt (which Sale usually called the "Southern Rim") was originally defined to include the Southwest and California, in addition to the South proper.[3] Yet, as historian James C. Cobb observed, "the term became increasingly interchangeable with *the South*."[4] It became, in effect, the Seventies version of the ever-persistent, ever-elusive New South. While the notion of a Sunbelt found its most eager audiences on the extremes of debates about the modern South (i.e., among the region's boosters and critics), the term caught on in part because race was declining, however ambiguously, as a distinguishing characteristic of the region. During the postwar decades, corporate leaders and their political allies in the metropolitan South had embraced a "Sunbelt Synthesis" consisting of "a booster vision designed to transcend the burdens of the region's history through the twin pillars of rapid economic development and enforced racial harmony."[5] This image crested during the 1970s, even in the face of race- and class-tinged controversies over school busing and municipal annexation.

At the start of the post–civil rights era, a peculiar blend of flashy modernity and folksy piety began to replace racism as an ingredient in many popular representations of the South. Billy Graham operated at the nexus of this shift, the intersection of soul winning and boosterism. When Kirkpatrick Sale wrote of "the unmistakable and irreversible shift of power . . . away from the Eastern Establishment and toward the Southern Rim," he cited Graham's influence in the Nixon White House as evidence of this shift. Novelist Walker Percy similarly criticized the "Southern Sunbelt," which he saw as "dominated by such figures as Billy Graham and Oral Roberts, John Connally and Richard Nixon." *Time*, Sale, and Percy agreed that Graham was a significant player in the cultivation of the Sunbelt image.[6]

As historians have claimed the mantle of Sunbelt scholarship, now in its second wave, they have kept their work surprisingly divorced from the topic of religion.[7] The example of Graham offers a corrective to this oversight. Two Graham crusades in the 1970s South—Birmingham (1972) and Atlanta (1973)—revealed his role in promoting the Sunbelt ideal. In the case of Birmingham, civic and religious leaders viewed the crusade as a chance to show how far their newly christened "All-America City" had come since Graham held a desegregated rally there in 1964, several months after the bombing of Sixteenth Street Baptist Church. In the flagship New South city of Atlanta, crusade chair Tom Cousins was even more ambitious. Cousins sought to use the crusade to shape a new generation of leaders for a city on the uncertain cusp of electing its first African American mayor. Graham was a willing partner in both projects. To critics of the evangelist, the Birmingham and Atlanta crusades demonstrated the potent superficiality of nominal postsegregationism stamped with a religious mandate. To supporters of the evangelist, the crusades placed a welcomed spotlight on a region once reviled, now revived. Graham's avowedly nonprophetic brand of activism both reflected and impelled the particular combination of traditional evangelicalism and dynamic boosterism that came to characterize the Sunbelt South, an imagined region blending piety, modernity, and—increasingly—Republican politics.

Whither the New South in Nixon's America?

With varying degrees of intentionality, Graham inserted himself into a debate about the direction of the newest New South. Such was the price of his alliance with the electoral strategies of President Nixon. During the Nixon years, Graham exposed himself to an unprecedented degree of criticism, spread equally among secular and religious commentators, mostly of a liberal persuasion. Some saw Graham as pernicious, others saw him as naive, and almost all left-leaning critics linked him with sociopolitical reaction. (Fundamentalist critics, meanwhile, still considered him a sellout to ecumenism.) A less skeptical earlier generation of journalists had, with a few exceptions, judged Graham's presence in the Eisenhower and Johnson White Houses, in addition to his less-remembered presence at President Kennedy's prayer breakfasts, as more ceremonial than political.[8] In contrast, Graham's support for President Nixon became a persistent opening question during his election-year press conferences. For *Life* correspondent Barry Farrell and other elite journalists, when Nixon took office the evangelist shifted from being a source of mere disapproval (an influential simpleton, but little more than a proxy for the underside of Cold War society) to being an "American Rasputin" (a serious threat to the liberal consensus). For a writer in *Harper's*, Graham was the atavistic "voice of old country boys and Middle Americans everywhere." For aging nemesis Reinhold Niebuhr, the evangelist had helped to effect the "unofficial establishment" of religion in the White House.[9]

Other analysts applied sociologist Robert Bellah's influential "civil religion" thesis to Graham. In a famous 1967 essay, Bellah defined civil religion as a set of rituals, beliefs, and symbols that legitimated and lent transcendence to the national mission, broadly conceived and often historically interpreted through the narrative lens of the biblical Israel. Importantly, he distinguished this civil religion from official religions, including Christianity. While Bellah saw civil religion as a potential vehicle for all types of political ends, many more Vietnam-era critics focused on its obvious expression in the God-and-country pageantry of Billy Graham, whether as Honor America Day speaker or Rose Bowl Parade grand marshal. The civil religion thesis left the evangelist vulnerable to charges not only of blind patriotism but of heresy as well. Several Bellah-influenced works appeared denouncing the "Christian Americanism" and "folk religion" of Graham and the Nixon White House.[10]

The criticism also stung at a more popular level. In 1969, Major League Baseball officials tabled a plan for Graham to throw out the first pitch at a World Series game in New York City. They feared an adverse response from the anti-Nixon crowd.[11] Two years later, novelist-cum-White House satirist Philip Roth savaged Graham as "Reverend Billy Cupcake," a Nixon tool with a penchant for invoking anonymous experts and leaders to make politically useful points: "I was in a European country last summer and one of the top young people there told me that the teenagers in his country want leadership more than anything else."[12]

The presence of Graham in the Nixon administration took on particular significance for participants in a larger debate over the direction and fate of the South. Indeed, Nixon had created the ideological space necessary for the possible triumph of the Sunbelt ideal. In Nixon's most successful political appeals to the South, as historian Matthew Lassiter has contended, he proffered a "regional fairness" argument, suggesting that Dixie deserved to be treated as no less American than the rest of the nation.[13] Graham, of course, had long argued for something similar, although he had never intended his comments as a backhanded sop to backlash sentiments. The significance of the regional fair play proposal evolved as federal civil rights legislation became a fait accompli. The next step for Sunbelt boosters was to voice a hitherto improbable thesis: the South was not simply the equal of the rest of the nation but a trendsetter for it. At this critical stage for a region ambiguously on the cusp of the post–civil rights era, Graham provoked strong criticism from such liberal-leaning southerners as prophet-theologian Will D. Campbell and newspaper editor Reese Cleghorn. At earlier junctures—the Little Rock school crisis and the early years of the Johnson administration, for example—the evangelist and many white southern liberals had not stood so far apart on racial matters. The polarizing politics of the southern strategy changed the context significantly.

The most publicized criticism of Graham from the southern left appeared in the form of "An Open Letter to Billy Graham," published in early

1971 by Campbell and Berea (Kentucky) College professor James Y. Holloway in *Katallagete*, the eclectic publication of the Committee of Southern Churchmen. Campbell, the lone white participant in the founding of the Southern Christian Leadership Conference, had risked his career and livelihood on behalf of racial equality. Since the mid-1960s, he had criticized liberals and conservatives alike for failing to address the needs of poor southern whites. Holloway shared these sentiments. The open letter in *Katallagete* read partly as a squabble among southerners, with Campbell and Holloway accusing their "Baptist brother" of becoming a "court prophet" for Nixon. As students at liberal divinity and graduate schools during an earlier era, the authors had defended Graham's evangelism. Now, in Graham's services in Knoxville and in his comments about busing and Vietnam, he blessed the Nixon line. Such concerns with civility and respectability, Campbell and Holloway implied in their letter and elsewhere, served as crutches for existing institutions and sapped Christianity of its prophetic character. In a deliberately eccentric invocation of scripture, they urged Graham to "prophesy to the Pentagon and White House—in the tradition of Micaiah, son of Imlah" (i.e., to declare divine judgment on temporal rulers).[14] The shift of Campbell and Holloway from defending (or tolerating) Graham to criticizing him held significance for larger debates about the South. Their open letter received national coverage and, in a rare direct response to critics, drew a cordial letter from Graham, who offered to meet with the authors. According to Campbell, though, their follow-up inquiries received no response.[15]

One reader of the *Katallagete* piece was *Charlotte Observer* editor Reese Cleghorn, who applied it to the 1971 Billy Graham Day festivities in Charlotte. Cleghorn, who had earlier worked for the *Atlanta Journal* and the liberal Southern Regional Council, was already on record as a critic of Graham. What Cleghorn saw as the evangelist's "abysmally shallow" theology and "often ill-informed" worldviews were prominently on display during Billy Graham Day. An *Observer* editorial, which he is likely to have written, blasted the evangelist for his comfort with "the material things" as well as "the affluent and the powerful." Discreetly alluding to the *Katallagete* piece, the editorial linked the day with the machinations of the southern strategy. "Charlotte and the changing South are in difficult struggle, much of which has a moral dimension to which people are blinded," the editorial read. "Mr. Graham's court in Washington plays it, almost always, as nothing more than a political drama."[16] (The more conservative *Charlotte News*, in contrast, praised Graham as a forward thinker who, especially on racial matters, had "contributed, in his own way, to deepening the social consciousness of conservative Christianity.")[17]

Cleghorn, Campbell, and Holloway saw Graham as a court prophet for a Sunbelt South in which evangelicalism seemed to overlap unselfconsciously with the spheres of politics and business. They knew that, no matter how incisively Phillip Roth satirized Graham, the evangelist's popularity in the region showed no signs of diminishing. The newspapers of the urban South tended to give more favorable coverage to Graham than did their counterparts in other regions. They did so not solely out of deference to his faith and popularity but also because Graham was a booster of their region.

At press conferences and other venues, Graham's eschatological pessimism regarding national and world events almost reflexively vanished when the subject switched to the South. "During the past few years," the South has been undergoing a gigantic economic and social revolution," the evangelist told his weekly radio audience in 1965. "It is one of the most exciting places in the entire world."[18] His advocacy on behalf of his home region—what might be termed his New South discourse—gave prospective boosters hope that a visit from Graham would reflect well on their cities.[19] When Graham announced his first 1965 visit to Alabama, letters poured in from across the state.[20] During the Greenville, South Carolina, crusade of the following year, members of the clergy from Macon, Georgia, and Memphis attended in hopes of attracting the evangelist.[21] While the Memphis crusade, originally scheduled for 1968, never occurred because of Graham's health problems that year, the correspondence surrounding it was telling. Not only the white ministerial elite of Memphis but also the mayor, the head of Holiday Inn, and the presidents of Memphis State and Mississippi State universities implored the evangelist to visit. Even black Methodist minister and civil rights activist James Lawson, one of the leading teachers of Gandhian tactics of civil disobedience, requested Graham's presence. "Prophetic preaching from such a person as you now, [sic] could make a significant impact upon the atmosphere of Memphis," Lawson wrote to the evangelist in 1966, undoubtedly at the behest of the Memphis Ministers Association, whose executive committee he had recently been invited to join.[22]

In the subsequent eras of the southern strategy and Sunbelt hype, Graham's advocacy on behalf of the South grew even more salient. Since the 1950s, Graham had consistently argued that the South would eventually surpass the North in the quality of its race relations, and such rhetoric persisted two decades later. Graham not only defended the South against its detractors;

he cast the region as a potential model for the nation. "To me it is rather hypocritical for people up North to be talking constantly about the problems in the South," he declared during his 1970 crusade in Baton Rouge, when "they've got it right on their doorstep and it's ready to explode."[23] Elsewhere that year, Graham said he was "very proud" of how the South had responded to court-ordered school busing programs—something, he suggested, Boston or New York City would not handle as well.[24] Upon the death of famed southern liberal and longtime *Atlanta Constitution* editor Ralph McGill, whom the evangelist had earlier labeled "Mr. New South," Graham praised him as "a courageous pioneer in race relations and social reform" who had offered critical advice over the years.[25] In the context of the Sunbelt 1970s, though, Graham's comments on the South reflected the interests not of liberal supporters of McGill's Southern Regional Council, but of regional boosters, including many recovering segregationists.

Thus, many Graham crusade supporters clearly sought more from him than just conversions. These benefits included a more unified leadership class and an improved image for the city. The argument here is not that Graham crusade committee members internalized the lessons of Paul Johnson's famous description of Finneyite revivalism in antebellum Rochester—namely, that revivalism can reify a new socioeconomic order.[26] There are few reasons not to grant the sincere faith of most crusade committee members. Yet few of them would have disputed the logic of a representative of *Dixie Business* magazine who, when awarding Graham its 1975 "Man of the South" award, declared religion "the greatest business in the South and in the world."[27] At a basic level, many of them recognized, Graham crusades (like modern political conventions and the Olympics) were an opportunity to showcase new stadiums, highways, and other civic improvements (not to mention improved race relations). The evangelist encouraged such signs of progress. He was keenly aware, for example, of the importance of stadiums and arenas to the image of the urban South. In 1972, Graham chided Charlotte for lacking a large outdoor stadium (which, of course, would benefit his own evangelistic efforts), "because you are moving very rapidly to big city status like Atlanta or Dallas and to be a big city today one of the things you have to have is a stadium." Seventeen years earlier, he had made similar comments when dedicating Charlotte's indoor coliseum.[28] "The South is no longer the old South that we once knew," Graham stated in a 1972 press conference in Atlanta. "It's become probably the most dynamic part of America."[29] His words echoed the thoughts of Nixon, who two months earlier in the same city had praised the South's progress as "probably the greatest of all in the nation."[30]

An "All-America City"

By 1972, the city of Birmingham touted its own advancement as among the greatest in the nation. In less than a decade, the city had progressed from miscreant to model—from "Bombingham" to "All-America City" (so designated in 1970 by the National Municipal League). The 1964 Easter rally figured prominently in this self-styled narrative.[31] City boosters had immediately presented the rally as both a fresh start and a confirmation that Birmingham had never fallen so far, after all. Crusade chair and regional newspaper baron Arthur P. Cook recognized the image-shaping value of the rally in a letter to the Jefferson County sheriff: "On the front pages of . . . major dailies in the nation were glowing, good remarks about Birmingham. This is certainly something that we have all tried to gain for our city for a long time." To Mayor Albert Boutwell, Cook wrote that "we now have a beachhead established."[32]

Understandably, Birmingham's leaders wanted more of a good thing. Efforts to have Graham return for a full crusade commenced almost immediately after the Easter rally and included the requisite invitation from the Ministerial Association of Greater Birmingham (which, by then, contained one black "associate") "to return to Birmingham for a full-length Crusade at the earliest time." The invitation arrived too late to ensure such a possibility.[33] Still, an eventual crusade seemed likely. Graham, who claimed to consider southern invitations with particular regard, had something of a special relationship with Birmingham, the largest southern city in which he had not held a full crusade.[34] His 1964 visit had occurred following comments in which he had described Birmingham as emblematic of racial violence. During his Easter visit, he publicly declared his desire to return to the city, a pledge to which Billy Graham Evangelistic Association (BGEA) staffers felt bound and which persistent crusade advocate Gilbert L. Guffin (dean of religion at an area university) was not inclined to let anyone forget.[35]

As early as May 1965, Birmingham leaders had identified an ideal period for Graham to return: the city's centennial celebration, set to extend through 1972. Crusade promoters pitched the visit as the climax of centennial festivities—a spiritual gut check for a city on the move—and informed Graham of

the city's racial progress. Methodist minister Denson N. Franklin, vice president of the centennial planning committee, remained in frequent contact
with Graham associate Grady Wilson. In a 1967 letter, Franklin stressed that
blacks and whites in the city were "ready to move forward. . . . I have seen
this city change completely in atmosphere during the last three years. As one
of our leading Negroes says, 'Birmingham has made more improvement than
any city in America in human relations.'" Other correspondents reiterated
the pivotal role of the Easter rally. City Council president M. E. Wiggins
echoed these sentiments, but added that "much remains to be accomplished." Crusade boosters made sure to note the primacy of religious motivations for the crusade. Even with the support of business leaders and the
Chamber of Commerce for the crusade, wrote three Birmingham clerics, "the
motivation of everyone seems to be a deep sense of need for a spiritual awakening among us and not as a mere event in the centennial." Indeed, argued
Guffin, centennial plans had "quickened the pace of the city and, of course,
economic growth and expansion are natural consequences. What we need
most of all, and critically, is a great spiritual awakening." What Birmingham
needed, that is, was a crusade to mediate (and perhaps even stimulate) progress. "How has God used Birmingham?" asked a centennial-year promotional
booklet. "The answer is simple. For He is not yet through."[36]

A letter copied to Graham outlined early plans for the centennial festivities in a city facing a historical watershed. In 1960, the author declared,
Birmingham had ranked thirty-sixth in the nation in population, "and if we
sit still and do nothing we'll still be 36th in the nation" a decade later.
Unstated in the letter, but surely understood, was concern over the city's
lingering association with racial violence. The centennial celebration would
do its part to cleanse this stain through four huge bonfires, to be lighted on
Red Mountain, four hundred feet above the city. The fires would "rival, in
height and heat, the famous Pharos light at Alexandria, the mouth of the Nile
River." A final flame would shine during a Billy Graham crusade, proposed as
the climactic event of the centennial year, since "no man in this world can
so ably tie up the present day world with that of Christ as could Billy Graham."[37] In the end, though, the centennial festivities kicked off in December
1971 with the opening of a more worldly emblem of the city's progress, a new
civic center.[38]

The Billy Graham Alabama Crusade finally occurred in May 1972. Birmingham greeted Graham with public sentiments similar to those previously
expressed in private correspondence. City boosters cited the 1964 rally as "the

first integrated public outdoor meeting in the city's history," when, "in a twinkling, racial segregation at public meetings had become obsolete in the city." (No mention was made of the much more significant role of the 1964 Civil Rights Act, as well as the demonstrations that preceded it, in ending public segregation in the city.) According to this glossy narrative, Graham's visit had sparked what crusade executive committee chair Mark Hodo called a "renaissance." Hodo had served on the same committee in 1964, when Birmingham's reputation had reached its nadir. Since then, contended the Presbyterian and head of the City Federal Savings & Loan Corporation with more than a hint of paternalism, "we have had less racial disturbance than any city . . . in proportion to our size. We developed a communication during that period. We brought in the blacks to meet with us and . . . we developed a camaraderie and a communication that has been terrific." Mayor George G. Seibels, Jr., declared the crusade week "Billy Graham Days," when the Graham team would accentuate "the spiritual heritage which has helped to make this an All-America City." The *Birmingham News*, a font of journalistic boosterism whose motto was "Serving a Progressive South," picked up its affirming editorials where it had left off in 1965. Graham's earlier visit had enabled the resolution of problems that now seemed confoundingly simple, although how exactly these problems had been resolved remained unspecified. In a toast to evangelical universalism, the paper welcomed Graham's social message that "only through spiritual revival of the individual will come improvement in the quality of life of the community, and that without the brotherhood of man no city or people can endure."[39]

In terms of social issues, the most significant theme of the crusade was that which was nominally missing: the race problem, a matter crusade boosters viewed as resolved. Relative lack of discussion about race, of course, itself represented a type of racial discourse—a qualified admission of past problems, perhaps, but an even stronger relegation of them to the dustbin of history. This perspective willfully ignored, among other things, the numerous riots Birmingham had experienced since 1964 in response to such issues as police brutality.[40] "In 1964 the races learned they could sit side by side," gushed the *Birmingham News*. "In 1972 they learned they could work side by side." Graham seemed to concur. "There is a rare situation in Birmingham," he declared at a press conference where he sat alongside Hodo and J. L. Ware, a prominent black Baptist minister who had also participated in the Easter rally. "Things have changed greatly," the evangelist added, noting that blacks had greater access to higher education than ever before. Later that week,

Graham referred to a period of southern racial strife a decade or more removed from the present. For the Easter 1964 sermon, the *Birmingham News* wrote, "the problem was racial. *This time, other issues are at hand*—the decaying church institution, the Vietnam War, a generation of youth questioning the very basis on which this country is founded" (emphasis mine).[41] These latter issues, of course, did not leave the South singled out for ridicule. The *Birmingham World*, a Republican-leaning black newspaper that rightly viewed racial inequality as still a substantial problem in the city, offered minimal (although supportive) coverage of the crusade.[42]

Amid appearances at the crusade by Dallas Cowboys coach Tom Landry, Alabama Crimson Tide head man Bear Bryant, and former Tide star Joe Namath, Graham's sermons and statements addressed the lingering dilemma of American involvement in Vietnam, while hinting at soon to be prominent gender and family issues. In his opening press conference, Graham made good on an assurance to Nixon chief of staff H. R. Haldeman that he would affirm Nixon's renewed hard line in Vietnam. The president, Graham said, wanted peace as much as anyone but believed in sticks as well as carrots; in a sermon, the evangelist urged the audience to support Nixon's plan for pulling troops out of Vietnam.[43] Regarding American social issues, Graham suggested the application of "biblical laws" in the face of crime and violence.[44] While backing down from previous support for a constitutional amendment regarding school prayer, he continued his tradition of calling for alternative, faith-based demonstrations by saying he might lead his own "march on Washington" on behalf of that cause. In another sermon, Graham reaffirmed traditional gender roles, as opposed to "masculinizing women and feminizing men." There is "no unisex in the Bible," he declared.[45]

Another event quickly supplanted the crusade in the minds of most Alabamians: the near assassination of Alabama governor George Wallace, then seeking the Democratic Party presidential nomination. On the second day of the crusade, a would-be killer shot Wallace at a campaign rally in Maryland, leaving the governor paralyzed in both legs. Graham and Wallace had held a cordial, semiprivate meeting during the 1965 Montgomery crusade, and since then they had maintained a line of communication that, as Wallace might well have reasoned, ultimately ended at the Nixon White House. The evangelist had talked with Wallace the day before the shooting, and the two kept in touch throughout the recovery process. Wallace had planned to attend services later in the week, when Graham said the governor "probably would have been asked to sit in the audience and not on the stage to avoid any political overtones" (unlike the treatment Nixon had received during the 1970 Knoxville crusade). Upon learning of the Wallace shooting, Graham called it "a terrible shock indicating the sickness of the country," a condition he attributed to Satan. He asked for a moment of silent prayer and adjusted the topic of his sermon to address the "pornography of violence." All Americans, "black and white, conservative and liberal," Graham declared, should pray for recovery, "whether we agree with him or not. . . . He knew we had differences, especially in the matter of race. But he's always warm and friendly."[46] The moment represented an uncomfortable, if not at all uncommon, intersection of Graham's ministerial responsibilities and his political involvement, of his public duties and the partisanship he tried to reveal only selectively. Conscious of Haldeman's assignment "to keep Wallace in the Democratic Party," Graham talked with the governor following an operation two months later and received assurance that a third-party candidacy remained unlikely.[47]

In Birmingham, Graham criticized the national television networks for not covering those who ventured to Legion Field "to demonstrate for God and in peace" as much as they had covered earlier marches in the city.[48] This contention possessed obvious racial overtones that, at the very least, reflected his continued hesitancy to privilege racism as a sin in need of redress. Certainly, the city's leadership class hoped others were taking note of what was happening in this cradle of the silent majority. Total attendance stood at nearly 375,000, or around 47,000 nightly in the 70,000-seat Legion Field—an above-average crowd for an American city in keeping with the high turnouts typical of southern crusades. African Americans made up more than one-third of the crowd on some nights, numbers similar to Graham's 1964–65 services in Alabama.[49] Gilbert Guffin was sure the crusade would go down as the most significant event of the centennial year. Another correspondent, city clerk Jackson B. Bailey, described the crusade as the "mountaintop experience of all our public celebrations." Birmingham's renewed image, he insisted, would not have been possible without the improved race relations that dated back to the 1964 Easter rally.[50]

Graham compensated for the lack of network news coverage by speaking well of Birmingham to other outlets. Likewise, he assured Mayor Seibels, BGEA broadcasts of the services would mean that "millions throughout America and in other parts of the world will be able to see and hear about Birmingham."[51] One of Graham's next stops was Northern Ireland, whose religiously rooted violence Graham contrasted with developments in the All-

America City. On the front page of the *Birmingham News* a week after the crusade, an Associated Press story quoted Graham upholding Birmingham as proof that a "spiritual awakening" could turn around any city, perhaps even Belfast. "I suddenly realized that Birmingham had perhaps the best race relations of any city in the southern part of the United States. . . . It is one of the most progressive cities in America," Graham said.[52] His characteristic hyperbole was consistent with his description of the South as a whole, a perspective *Time* would echo in its 1976 special issue on the region. An editorial in the *Florence* (S.C.) *News* delighted in Graham's use of a southern example. The flagship magazine of the BGEA, *Decision*, reiterated the post-Easter rally narrative of a city that had straightened out its priorities. "We're an All-America city," declared a Birmingham crusade leader, "but we need spiritual renewal."[53] A newspaper headline for the 1964 Easter rally had read, "Graham Calls on City to Lead." Eight years later, according to the *Birmingham News*, Graham "found a changed city" when he returned to Birmingham. A journalist who had covered the 1964 rally for that same paper confirmed Graham's observation with a biblical metaphor: "People across the world feel the warmth of a new light from Birmingham. We have removed it forever from under the bushel of the past."[54] In 1972, despite the overt persistence of racial inequalities and tensions in Birmingham, crusade boosters told themselves and others that they had answered Graham's call and become a model, a Sunbelt city claiming a spiritual stride with every social and economic one.

Tom Cousins Had a Dream

Unlike Birmingham, Atlanta desired to maintain, rather than surmount, its image. Indeed, during the early 1960s, the city had cemented its identity as a New South capital (in the famous words of Mayor William Hartsfield, a city "too busy to hate") in explicit contrast to the violence 150 miles west in Birmingham. While Bull Connor terrorized the black community of Birmingham, Mayor Ivan Allen, Hartsfield's heir, endorsed what became the Civil Rights Act of 1964. In the mid-1960s, Allen even lured a Major League Baseball franchise and its star African American slugger, Henry Aaron, away from Milwaukee, a move that solidified Atlanta's big-city status.[55] Also attracted was the BGEA, which in 1964 opened its Team Office near the city's airport, meaning that all domestic crusades were henceforth coordinated from Atlanta, rather than from the main office in Minneapolis. At the press conference announcing the new office, Graham reassured persons concerned about how Atlanta would receive Aaron; the evangelist's black associates could vouch for the city's racial tolerance.[56]

In the early 1970s, then, it only seemed natural for Atlanta real estate developer Tom Cousins to believe that a Billy Graham crusade could harvest a new generation of leaders for the city. A Nixon administration document (possibly using Graham's own words) identified Cousins as among "the brilliant, rising young business tycoons of the South. Now frequently introduced as 'Mr. Atlanta.'"[57] Cousins had ascended during the 1960s from a model home builder to a sports franchiser and a major force in downtown development. By the middle of the decade, he had joined Atlanta's famed "power structure." Widely assumed to be one of the inspirations for Charlie Croker, the stoically southern protagonist of Tom Wolfe's 1998 novel *A Man in Full*, Cousins conformed to the stereotypes of an ambitious Atlanta mogul, right down to the requisite quail plantation in southwest Georgia. Cousins was involved in many of the projects through which Atlanta had started defining itself as not only an all-America but an "international" city as well. These undertakings included the quintessentially Sunbelt Omni International, a multiuse complex containing a mall, theme park, and sports coliseum. Cousins also owned two other symbols of Atlanta's big-city ways, the Atlanta Hawks of the National Basketball Association and the Atlanta Flames of the National Hockey Association, the primary tenants of his coliseum.[58] In short, Cousins was an Atlanta booster extraordinaire, a predecessor of the more flamboyant Ted Turner.

As a high-profile player within his city's business community, Cousins fitted the bill of previous and future Graham crusade chairs. His counterpart in the 1970 Baton Rouge crusade was prominent businessman and lawyer Rolfe McCollister. George Champion, a high executive at Chase Manhattan Bank, headed the 1957 New York crusade, while Mutual Insurance Company of New York CEO Roger Hull led the 1969 one. Holiday Inn founder William Walton later chaired the 1978 Memphis crusade.[59] Cousins thus stood out only for his frank use of secular language when discussing the Atlanta crusade.

Cousins and Graham first met during the 1965 crusade in Montgomery, where Cousins owned a lakeside home. They kept in contact through the evangelist's brother-in-law, Leighton Ford, and Cousins eventually began pitching the possibility of a crusade in Atlanta.[60] Cousins described himself as a former agnostic (in his words, not a "religious fanatic") who was initially attracted to church work more than worship services.[61] Not unlike Richard Nixon, Cousins evinced a certain reticence about personal expressions of religiosity, possessing what one friendly observer called "a religious faith reflected in deeds not words."[62] This description was in keeping with both his reputation for having a low-key demeanor (as much as was possible for a prominent developer) and his identity as a Presbyterian. He seemed most comfortable when employing the language of a business prospectus, a mixture of salesmanship and the bottom line.

Atlanta during the late 1960s and early 1970s was experiencing a significant transition within its political and economic leadership, and Cousins thought a Graham crusade would help ease the adjustment. For decades, Atlanta politics had revolved around an alliance between moderate, business-oriented whites and African-American leaders. The former clearly held the upper hand. The 1970s in Atlanta, a close observer has written, saw "a major reformulation of the tacit rules of engagement between city government and the business community, as well as the emergence of a new set of players."[63] From the perspective of the white downtown establishment, the most significant change was the inevitability of political power for the city's emerging black majority. In 1969, Atlanta elected its first black vice mayor, Maynard Jackson. While not a radical (Jackson hailed from the "Morehouse man" lineage of elite black leadership), he threatened a closely guarded tradition of racially moderate, yet inescapably paternalistic white control over city politics.[64] Tom Cousins was part of a new group of white leaders who, while not especially attached to the stewardship tradition of Mayors Hartsfield and Allen, was worried about the direction Atlanta would take if black politicians felt no accountability to business leaders.[65] Their concerns reflected scarcely concealed racial and class anxieties. In 1971, a report by the Atlanta Chamber of Commerce pronounced the death of its "marriage" with City Hall. "The 'junior partner' role of the black leadership in the last decade has been rejected by the black leaders," the report stated.[66] Cousins candidly recalled almost identical concerns about a new generation of Atlanta politicians who thought the business establishment had overlooked them. He believed these tensions would hinder the development and economic vitality of the city.[67] To ward off polarization, he proposed "a shock treatment for Christ"—that is, "spiritual and moral growth along with bricks and mortar."[68]

A Graham crusade could provide just this shock treatment, Cousins reasoned. In the process of organizing the crusade, Cousins hoped to identify a biracial group of current and future leaders and to ensure their involvement in the crusade effort. In March 1972, he brought together area ministers to outline his vision for the crusade that was to occur fifteen months later. After clarifying that he neither had gubernatorial ambitions nor merely sought a new client for his coliseum, Cousins described his "particular first personal concern." Atlanta, he declared, could become "the finest city in the world," a place "where people can live together." For the moment, however, the city was "at a cross roads," and its leadership was "either dying out or being pushed out." The leaders who would inevitably emerge during the crusade would get a taste of how they might influence the city in the future.[69] Cousins remained the face of the crusade and retained the full backing of Graham, despite Cousins's own admission that his personal intentions for the Atlanta crusade might not square perfectly with the mission statement of the BGEA. According to Cousins, the BGEA agreed to the Atlanta crusade on the conditions that he chair the executive committee and that the black community of Atlanta support the endeavor.[70] The latter stipulation proved more difficult to satisfy.

Cousins offered bluntly civic justifications for the crusade. "I don't know that you even have to be Christian to appreciate" the value of a Graham crusade, Cousins declared in the Sunday paper. "I think the non-Christian would acknowledge that the true, convicted Christian is an excellent citizen," he added. (He may have aimed his comments at leading Jews in Atlanta who held reservations about endorsing an evangelistic effort.) An Atlanta journalist wrote of Cousins, "He speaks of 'new leadership' in the sense that some present or future leaders may become 'new' men in Christ as a result of Billy Graham's crusade." After all, a godly city would be a better place for everyone, and in Atlanta such a condition seemed distinctly possible—a sentiment Graham reinforced in his press conferences. Cousins thus set about identifying a new generation of leaders to chair the numerous crusade committees. Most of these persons, according to the same journalist, came "straight out of the power structure." Cousins also garnered a crusade invitation from the Chamber of Commerce and a letter from Governor Jimmy Carter urging members of the state General Assembly to attend Graham's services.[71]

A photograph in the Sunday paper featured Graham smiling over the very downtown Atlanta skyline Cousins had helped to shape.[72] Graham's comments regarding the city appeared to support the ambitions of Cousins, even as the evangelist continued his custom of denying any sociopolitical motivations of his own. As much as in Birmingham, however, Graham operated in full booster mode regarding a city he called "one of my home-towns."[73] In press conferences before and after the crusade, the evangelist voiced confidence about Atlanta's race relations and the city's position in the nation. The racial situation in Atlanta "with all your problems is still one of the best in the country," he said. "And I think that Atlanta has been one of the most progressive cities. I think that what happens in Atlanta gives direction to the rest of the South." Compared to other cities, Atlanta was "a little bit of heaven." Again, the city was "an example of good race relations and progressiveness and economic boom"—as well as, most important, "a city of churches."[74] Graham even credited Atlanta's recently retired police chief, Herbert Jenkins, with influencing his own move away from segregation in the early 1950s.[75]

As Graham had done during the 1965 Montgomery crusade, he published daily articles in the city's two largest newspapers, thus adding to his social message a layer of intentionality that was missing a year earlier in Birmingham. The pieces reflected Graham's evangelical universalism and provided a more overtly spiritual component to the boosterism of Cousins. In one article, Graham quoted Martin Luther King, Jr., on the difference between love and race-consciousness before defining prejudice as "the distance between your biased opinions and the real truth." Honesty before God would eliminate this distance. "Where we've missed the mark in handling racial problems," Graham added in a statement representative of his theory of social change, "is simply that we'[v]e legislated new moral and legal standards, (which incidentally I am for) without suggesting the power that could implement them." In another article, fittingly titled "Social Justice a By-Product of God's Love and Mercy," Graham argued that social justice "is never the main part of the Gospel, nor of a crusade effort. We need something deeper and higher than that—the life-changing experience of faith in Christ." He described a nationwide spiritual and moral "crisis"—a theme which he had voiced since the mid-1950s, but which also resonated with the tone of many Nixon speeches—and argued that the Ten Commandments should be read in every school classroom. As if to rein in whatever utopian expectations Cousins might have unleashed, Graham carefully framed his status as an evangelist, clarifying that he was "not a social reformer; I'm not a political leader. I don't ever intend to go into politics."[76] The editor of the *Atlanta Constitution* affirmed these sentiments, advising that the crusade not be "thought of in a political context at all."[77] The *Atlanta Daily World*, an influential black newspaper supportive of both Graham and Nixon, echoed this sentiment.[78]

Such wishes proved naive in light of Atlanta's racial climate, as well as the emerging politics of Watergate. In the Atlanta crusade, unlike in Birmingham, race ultimately surfaced and exposed the one-sidedness of the Sunbelt image of the South. The crusade suffered from pervasive criticism and low attendance by significant portions of the black community. This occurred in spite of what Cousins considered a good-faith effort to ensure the black support Graham desired. Early in the crusade planning process, Cousins involved the Reverend Martin Luther King, Sr., the father of the civil rights martyr and a civic leader cut out of the more conservative "broker" tradition. King became a consistent backer of the crusade. Cousins also secured a biracial executive committee, including black and white co-chairs (in keeping with a tradition dating back to the Birmingham Easter rally), although his subsequent claim that the committee contained nearly equal numbers of whites and blacks was greatly exaggerated. The committee was stacked with city elites.[79]

The Graham team and a number of civic leaders of both races assisted with these efforts. Crusade director Harry Williams suggested that an interview with King would enhance publicity in Atlanta and elsewhere.[80] Crusade supporters produced a detailed list of leading black Atlantans, and the ministers from this list received invitations to a special meeting hosted by Congressman Andrew Young, former executive director of the Southern Christian Leadership Conference (SCLC), at the Butler Street YMCA, a black Atlanta institution. "While a few of us may have had some reservations about the crusade," the invitation read, "we feel that most of these have been resolved" to the point where they could "work toward bringing Black and White Christians together."[81] Young and Carter had already hosted a breakfast meeting with similar intentions.[82] The governor went so far as to grant leave time for a staff member to focus on stimulating black interest in the crusade.[83]

These efforts did not have their intended effects. Black attendance remained conspicuously low throughout the crusade. Graham himself estimated that no more than 5 percent of the average crusade audience was black—a number much lower than in any of his meetings in Alabama, although more in line with his 1950s desegregated crusades in such places as Louisville and Charlotte.[84] While Graham received his customary attacks from the theological right, the most stinging and publicized criticisms came from black activists, thus continuing a tradition of black skepticism toward

Graham that had evolved into outright animosity during the Nixon years. The criticism of Graham made headlines days before the first crusade meeting when Hosea Williams, a civil rights veteran and president of the Atlanta chapter of SCLC, accused the evangelist of practicing a "theology of hypocrisy" and urged blacks, as well as "right-thinking whites," to boycott the crusade. A survivor of the nightsticks and tear gas of Selma, Williams had developed a well-earned reputation as an activist gadfly. Tellingly, Cousins dismissed him as a notorious racist. Williams was joined in his opposition by national SCLC president Ralph Abernathy, who claimed his congregation had not received materials advertising the crusade. Williams, on the other hand, lamented the "high pressure" crusade supporters had exerted on black ministers to back the revival. Protesters from the local SCLC chapter and the League for Black Justice (a Seventh-day Adventist group) picketed the first crusade service with signs reading, "Billy Graham Is a Racist" and "Billy Graham Feed the Hungry."[85]

Hosea Williams offered a thorough list of his problems with Graham. They resembled the complaints of a group of activists who had confronted the evangelist during his 1970 crusade in Baton Rouge. The evangelist had not only "furnished the theology" of Nixon, said Williams; he had failed to oppose the numerous federal cutbacks supported by the Nixon administration. (Unbeknownst to Williams, Graham had invited Nixon to attend a service in Atlanta or at three other crusades later that year.) In addition, Williams charged, the evangelist was on record as a supporter of capital punishment. Although Graham had publicly stated that he was reconsidering the issue of capital punishment, the matter had particular salience in the recent aftermath of his offhand remark at a press conference that rapists should face the penalty of castration. He was responding to news of the recent gang rape of a twelve-year-old girl in South Africa, where (to complicate matters further) Graham was then holding desegregated rallies. While Graham clearly did not recognize the racially loaded nature of his comment, he was roundly denounced in the American black press. In South Africa, Graham had also spoken optimistically about the future of the nation's race relations, drawing an analogy with "the early days of integration in the Southern part of the United States." In response, Abernathy castigated him as someone who "heaps praise on South Africa, a country which is worse than South Louisiana." Lastly, charged Williams, Graham had yet to speak critically about the allegations surrounding the Watergate break-in.[86] Indeed, while Williams ignored Graham's recent op-ed piece in the *New York Times* arguing in favor of prosecuting Watergate-related crimes (which the evangelist did not link to Nixon), the Watergate crisis represented to Graham in Atlanta what the Wallace shooting had in Birmingham: an outside issue the evangelist could not escape no matter how much he selectively circumscribed his role as a public figure. As Graham continually ducked the many questions about Watergate that came his way, his lack of comments made headlines.[87]

A final source of black criticism derived from the very nature of Cousins's ambitions. The crusade quickly became associated with the business elite of Atlanta. "When Billy Graham came to Atlanta, who was his host?" asked Williams. "Mr. Cousins, one of the richest men in the Southeast. When Jesus Christ came into a town, he dwelled among the poor people."[88] The *Washington Post* likewise quoted an SCLC official who wondered why Graham had not reached out more extensively to lower-income residents. Instead, Graham had "established ties with the rich," with "people like Tom Cousins."[89]

Cousins, unsurprisingly, was not inclined to accept this explanation for the low black attendance, about which he and Harry Williams expressed initial perplexity. As possible reasons, they cited the difficulty of communicating with Atlanta's many small-sized black churches and, most important, an unexpected midweek strike by city bus drivers. The latter explanation had credibility, since many Atlanta blacks relied on the bus system. Cousins successfully sought a court injunction against the allegedly wildcat strike, but the ruling did not take effect until after the crusade had ended.[90] Despite the strike, overall attendance remained high, justifying the decision to hold the crusade in the baseball stadium of the Braves, rather than in the Omni Coliseum, as Graham had originally desired.[91] The strike could not explain away the depth of Graham's unpopularity among many African Americans, a trend that had only increased during the months since the Birmingham crusade. In Atlanta, a city with more influential black civic networks than Birmingham, the distrust of Graham was especially acute. This wound, as subsequent crusades in Raleigh and Minneapolis revealed, would not begin to heal until well after Watergate and Nixon had run their course.[92]

The Graham team responded to its race problem with a mixture of denial and adjustment. Having predicted a solid black response to the crusade, the evangelist initially downplayed the criticism, describing Hosea Williams as a long-time friend (albeit a "misinformed" one) and inviting him and his supporters to attend services whether "they come with a picket or not."[93] The evangelist cited the past support of Martin Luther King, Jr., whose grave he had recently visited with the elder King. He also accurately noted that the younger King had played a role in an earlier effort to host a crusade in Atlanta.[94] Graham also gave an interview to the *Atlanta Daily World* (a more friendly venue than its rival black paper, the *Atlanta Inquirer*) in which he again spoke highly of South Africa and argued that blacks had "more freedom today and [a] higher standard of living" as a result of civil rights advances.[95] Graham's sermons in Atlanta addressed the matter of race in a more direct manner than was the case in Birmingham—or any previous southern crusade. *Agape*—or selfless Christian love—the evangelist stressed, remained "the key to the race question in Atlanta or any other city in America." He also declared, as he had to selected audiences since the 1950s, that Jesus had brown, not white, skin. Still, he dedicated more substantive time in his sermons to other social matters, such as marriage, which he claimed faced greater threats than at any time "since Sodom and Gomorrah."[96]

Other responses to the low black turnout were more programmatic. John Wilson, a white former president of the Atlanta Chamber of Commerce, urged members to bring their black friends to the crusade.[97] The Graham team prominently featured at least one black platform guest during each crusade service. Martin Luther King Sr. gave the invocation during one service, as had his son sixteen years earlier in New York City. Another platform guest was Los Angeles minister Edward V. Hill, a strong Graham backer who was introduced as a founding member of SCLC.[98]

The Graham counteroffensive climaxed with a midweek public affirmation of the crusade by seven leading black clerics, including J. A. Wilborn of Union Baptist, co-chair of the executive committee. The ministers' statement urged greater black attendance and declared that black leaders had been included in all aspects of the crusade from the beginning. It bolstered Graham's subsequent claim that a majority of black ministers in the area supported him. A meeting between the black ministers and Cousins had preceded the release of the statement. Cousins remembered the meeting as a critical moment when he let his guard down, blasting the ministers for not countering Hosea Williams. Attempting to pull rank as a member of the Atlanta power elite, Cousins reminded them of the many times they had asked him for help in the past; this relationship, he bluntly stated, was now in jeopardy. According to Cousins, he then left the room, and the ministers voted in favor of a statement.[99] Still, the gesture did little to increase black attendance. Out of an average crowd of thirty-eight thousand per service, black attendance reportedly dipped as low as four hundred one night.[100]

Following the crusade, Graham grew more candid about his frustrations; like Cousins, he struggled to find explanations. Some black ministers had told him that black Atlantans were hesitant to leave their homes at night for fear of robbery. Besides, the total population of metro Atlanta area was only 20 percent black, making the 5 percent turnout appear somewhat less extreme. Graham also suggested that he lacked the appeal of Reverend Ike (Frederick Eikerenkoetter), a black evangelist and wealth gospel advocate.[101] The crusade gave pause to the BGEA, which soon released a booklet documenting Graham's desegregated crusades as far back as Chattanooga in 1953. The booklet included a small photograph of the Atlanta choir.[102]

Cousins was similarly unsure about the upshot of the crusade for his vision of a renewed Atlanta leadership. His ambivalence reflected larger tensions as he and other white elites braced for the inevitable arrival of black political dominance. Because of the biracial crusade planning process, Cousins optimistically insisted four years later, Atlanta's race relations clearly exceeded those of northern cities. Many of the persons he had identified for crusade duties remained involved in civic activities. Cousins and fellow crusade boosters had discussed such matters as crime and poverty, and had even proposed asking area ministers to boycott the city's liberal newspapers. A biracial "What Now?" committee, headed by John Wilson and created for the purpose of implementing Cousins's vision, yielded few substantive results, however. The major reason was the race issue. Because of the crusade's problems, the hitherto theologically restrained Cousins professed a definite belief in Satan, a force Graham often told crusade committees could disrupt even the most bountiful evangelistic harvest.[103] For the bus strike, at least, Cousins could find no other explanation. Like the real estate king in *A Man in Full*, Cousins went on to hit an economic rough patch during the mid-1970s, when his Omni Coliseum failed to fulfill its promise as a downtown magnet. Likewise, white Atlanta business elites struggled to adjust to African American mayor Maynard Jackson, who won office several months after the crusade and possessed majority strength in the very neighborhoods where Graham's crusade had held little sway. Both Cousins and his fellow Atlanta elites, however, saw better times by the subsequent decade, when they continued the city's habit of reinventions on a New South theme.[104] For Cousins, this meant following the flow of capital to the suburbs.[105] When bidding for the 1996 Summer Olympics, Atlanta sold itself as "a city that has managed to shape a technologically-advanced environment without compromising its moral vision or charming quality of life."[106] Perhaps this was what Cousins had originally had in mind.

The Sunbelt Mystique and Color Blindness

In both Birmingham and Atlanta, to be sure, Graham never fully embraced the more civically oriented ambitions of area crusade boosters, reiterating on numerous occasions the primacy of his spiritual motives. BGEA staffers appeared to share this concern. One longtime Graham supporter complained of a trend, noticeable in Charlotte one month before the Birmingham crusade, in which the crusade leadership consisted of visible area leaders who were not necessarily well-known Christians.[107] Another BGEA staffer directly asked an Atlanta crusade leader whether he thought the crusade was primarily an effort to improve the image of the city and ease its racial struggles.[108]

Yet Graham surely believed that his crusades might boost the civic as well as the religious spirits of Birmingham and Atlanta. Like Charles Finney's seminal revival in antebellum Rochester, Graham crusades had always paid special attention to a given city's leadership class, emphasizing high-profile conversions and platform appearances. While this strategy undoubtedly paid deference to the cult of celebrity, it was a corollary to the regenerational theory of social change. If Graham assumed that social transformation would flow outward to society from the regenerated individual heart, then his crusade practices suggested that Christ-filled leaders would yield better citizens. For Atlanta and Birmingham, then, the perceived benefits of a Graham crusade clearly extended beyond the BGEA's stated mission of spreading salvation. These benefits helped to cultivate an emerging Sunbelt mystique that touted material progress alongside buried Jim Crow hatchets.

In Atlanta, Birmingham, and elsewhere in the South, Graham functioned as what political scientist Paul Luebke has called a southern "modernizer." Applied historically, modernizers positioned themselves as proponents of regional change and growth, whether the issue was bringing Jim Crow to a peaceful close, supporting public education, attracting new businesses, increasing interstate highway funding, or constructing civic centers. While obviously critical of reactionary politics in their region, modernizers did not hew to national liberal currents either in their New Deal or in their McGovernite forms. They generally opposed an expanded welfare state and steered clear of cultural liberalism. In Luebke's schema, most modernizers were

Democrats (particularly in North Carolina, the focus of his study).[109] Graham's questionable status as a Democrat aside, he had long carried the banner of modernization in the statements he made, the company he kept, and the image he projected. His crusades gave southern cities another opportunity to sell themselves—as pious, to be sure, but also as progressive and relevant.

As the Birmingham and Atlanta crusades of 1972–73 revealed, Graham supported the interests of white leaders distancing themselves from their segregationist pasts. Every Graham crusade in the 1970s South featured claims of renewed racial harmony, even as they usually garnered a disappointing amount of black support.[110] To cite one example, John Perkins, a black community activist in Jackson, Mississippi, knew very well that white supporters of a 1975 Graham crusade there were eager "to help to paint a new image" of the Deep South state. Aware that he would be pressed to sit on the crusade platform, Perkins pointedly told the crusade steering committee of his hesitancy to help produce more of "the same kind of white Christians that we've had in the past." Perkins ended up backing the crusade, although he never doubted the basis for his reservations.[111] Still, Graham continued to publicize his crusades as sources of racial harmony and to seek out demonstrations thereof. Benjamin Hooks, head of the National Association for the Advancement of Colored People, attended the final service of the 1978 Memphis crusade.[112]

Graham's presence in the Sunbelt South assisted in the creation of a nominally postsegregation South desiring to shake off images of racial oppressiveness. The evangelist's use of New South discourse alongside his altar calls suggested that the region might do so without also shaking off its evangelical loyalties. Even for George Wallace, who spoke of a "second religious conversion" after his brush with assassination, born-again Christianity offered language for the transition away from racial reaction. In 1974, Wallace famously addressed a black Baptist conference at the church Martin Luther King Jr. had pastored in Montgomery (although, contrary to later recollections, he did not apologize for his past).[113] Graham had set the terms of the racial curve that Wallace and many other segregationist leaders would eventually round. On a rhetorical level, at least, the reconsiderations of Wallace and others made the Sunbelt mystique all the more compelling. The upshot, as some of Graham's critics within and outside the region began to realize during the early 1970s, was that the post–civil rights era South would not satisfy liberal hopes for a new class-based politics, nor would it please such civil rights veterans as Hosea Williams and Ralph Abernathy. Visions of the South as a potential model had shifted out of the hands of civil rights activists and into those of Sunbelt boosters.[114] The imagined Sunbelt South had solved its racial problems—had not only rejoined the nation but could now also make that nation better, modeling good faith as well as good politics. According to this viewpoint, the social problems of the nation were no longer racial in nature (or, if they were, they remained limited to the North); only liberals and black activists, absorbed in their own crusades, still considered race a pressing matter.

Ever hesitant to pronounce the white South guilty even during the height of massive resistance, Graham eventually helped a portion of the region to declare itself racially absolved. As early as 1966, before such terms as southern strategy and Sunbelt had surfaced among the pundit class, Walker Percy wrote of a white South that, after so many decades of defeat, had emerged "happy, victorious, Christian, rich, patriotic and Republican."[115] While certainly not meant to be affirming, Percy's modifiers were more prophetic than accurate at the time. They aptly describe the New South of Billy Graham, the Sunbelt image of the region he celebrated. This was a land of newfound "racial innocence," a land (and, in many respects, a nation) where many whites tried to dissociate themselves from the region's racial past.[116]

An important component of the Sunbelt mystique was something that Graham's postsegregation language had portended since the 1950s: a conservative rhetoric of color blindness. Scholars have linked color blindness (or its intellectual corollary, "racial realism") with such things as the antibusing movement, neoconservative and New Right critiques of affirmative action, and even the original vision of the *Brown* court.[117] Yet, as is true of the Sunbelt phenomenon itself, the religious dynamics of color blindness need more attention. The brand of faith and the social ethic Graham voiced in his visits to southern crisis spots—as well as in his numerous articles, books, addresses, and statements on the subject of race—suggested an additional, evangelical route to color blindness. While many white southerners did not follow the path of color blindness away from Jim Crow, those who did could consult directions formulated in a familiar evangelical language. They could hear, in Graham's own words, "that God is color-blind and that prejudice based on skin color is sinful."[118] They could hear that race becomes irrelevant in the lives of truly regenerated humans, and that Christian love—rather than laws, which still require obedience—remains the most effective solution for ending existing racial tensions. This path coexisted with the parallel post–civil rights era narratives of white backlash, black political advances, and ascendant regional confidence. Even another development, the rise of the Christian Right, occurred only after its spokespersons had abandoned (whether willingly or under duress) theologized support for Jim Crow for the kind of commonsense critique of racialism that Graham had already modeled.

In the end, Graham was willing to be employed—indeed, *used*—on behalf of Sunbelt boosterism. He implicitly (and often explicitly) confirmed assertions that the South had somehow solved most of its racial problems. He readily spoke the language of boosterism in newspaper and national publications, and he eagerly connected the Nixon administration with persons such as Tom Cousins. At the same time, Graham affirmed an evangelical faith that, as attendance figures showed, resonated most effectively in the South. At the start of the post–civil rights era and during a decade when evangelicalism entered the White House, such faith became an overall benefit to the region's reputation—a distraction from race and, moreover, a means of presenting the South as worthy of emulation.[119]

The Atlanta crusade, of course, challenged the Sunbelt mystique and exposed the rising color-blind rhetoric of the Sunbelt in part as an attempt to whitewash reality. When feasible, though, lack of discussion about race created space for a new set of social concerns. In the words of the *Birmingham News* in 1972, "other issues" had emerged. Unfortunately for Graham, Watergate soon became one of those issues.

CHAPTER SEVEN

"Before the Water Gate"

And all the people gathered as one man into the square before the Water Gate; and they told Ezra the scribe to bring the book of the law of Moses which the LORD had given to Israel. . . . And he read from it facing the square before the Water Gate from early morning until midday, in the presence of the men and the women and those who could understand; and the ears of all the people were attentive to the book of the law.
—Nehemiah 8:1, 3 (Revised Standard Version)

"Can Billy Graham survive Richard Nixon?"
—Richard V. Pierard, 1974

DESPITE TENSIONS IN ATLANTA and elsewhere, the main domestic issue that dogged Graham by 1973 was not race but the Nixon administration's Watergate crisis. While the Sunbelt image gained appeal, the president who had done so much to facilitate that image eventually resigned and left office in disgrace. Graham finally went public regarding Watergate during the spring of 1973, when he accepted an invitation from *New York Times* publisher Arthur Sulzberger to write an op-ed piece, titled "Watergate and Its Lessons of Morality." The cynicism evident in the transgressions of Watergate, the evangelist wrote, was "but a symptom of the deeper moral crisis that affects the nation." While Graham urged firm but fair punishment for Watergate-related crimes (assuming Nixon had no part in them), he reserved his harshest words for a nation that had "condoned amoral permissiveness that would make Sodom blush." Preaching his standard brand of soft jeremiad, the evangelist appealed for a return to biblical norms. He quoted a coincidental, yet seemingly appropriate, passage from the Old Testament book of Nehemiah in which post-exilic Jews—having returned from the Babylonian captivity, the product of previous unrepentance—gathered "before the Water Gate" in Jerusalem to hear the scribe Ezra read from the law of Moses, a body of covenantal precepts Graham thought no less relevant to the Watergate scandal.[1] Graham's use of scripture exemplified a phenomenon, which anthropologist Susan Friend Harding has observed in fundamentalist preaching (although it applies equally to the evangelical Graham), wherein scripture takes on a "generative quality" and is "at once a closed canon and an open book, still alive, a living Word."[2] Indeed, Graham's sermons frequently absorbed contemporary catch phrases into established biblical concepts, folding newspaper headlines into scriptural timelines. In the case of Watergate and "Water Gate," however, growing numbers of commentators accused Graham of a reverse operation: employing biblical language for the secular end of defending Nixon by any means—or analogy—necessary.

As the ramifications of Watergate intensified throughout 1973, Graham struggled to find a balance between protecting the president and interpreting the crisis for evangelistic purposes. Initially, the tasks complemented one another; Watergate as synecdoche, or "symptom," served to depersonalize the scandal and shift attention away from Nixon. Defending Nixon proved more difficult, though, as investigators and the public increasingly linked the sins of Watergate with the president himself. Ultimately, Graham found himself caught in the fallout from Watergate. His response was to assume the mantle of Ezra, parlaying the political Watergate into the biblical Water Gate by turning the crisis into a call for personal introspection and national renewal. The move befitted an evangelist, yet also reflected his desire to depoliticize himself.

Graham's influence in the public sphere endured long after a presidential crisis from which he did not escape untainted. This happened despite (but also because of) his largely successful, if somewhat misleading, effort to refine his political activity during the Gerald Ford and Jimmy Carter presidencies. Graham's evangelical explanations of Watergate—how he, as well as several former Nixon staffers, described the crisis in terms simultaneously universalistic and relative—partially suggested why this was so.

"There's a Little Bit of Watergate in All of Us"

The Watergate crisis brought about the nadir of Graham's public image, a fact relished by the many commentators who cast him as, at best, a lackey of the Nixon administration or, at worst, a dangerously influential reactionary. His periodic offering of the adage "There's a little bit of Watergate in all of us" did little to dissuade his critics. From September 1973 until Nixon resigned eleven months later, the evangelist uttered these words (or variations on them) on at least five occasions, including once to a national television audience.[3] While the maxim conveyed an obvious amount of evasiveness, it also reflected an evangelical social ethic that Graham continued to express throughout the Watergate crisis, as he reflexively and then awkwardly defended his friend Nixon. In personalizing Watergate, Graham also defined it as part of a more important, if also more general, crisis of individual hearts. He emphasized the sinful proclivities of humanity (made all the more so by a permissive society), as opposed to focusing on the structural flaws of the political system or even individual offences within the Nixon administration. In locating the meaning of Watergate in human sinfulness writ large and writ individual, rather than in the White House, the evangelist, along with a number of Watergate-era converts to evangelicalism, spoke a language of post-Fall universalism that cast the affair itself in relative terms. Graham's prescription for Watergate thus involved a double standard. Spiritually, the crisis necessitated a universal mandate for repentance and revival; politically, it was but another sin, rather than a constitutional crisis.

Graham passed through three stages in his responses to Watergate. These stages, while developmentally discrete, compounded into an awkward and muddled mixture of theology and partisanship. At first, Graham simply denied the significance of the crisis. Later, he employed the scandal for devotional and prophetic purposes before, lastly, directing the language of conversion toward the inevitable embodiment of Watergate, Nixon himself. Like most of the nation, Graham did not anticipate the tumult to come when news of the Watergate burglary and its possible links to the Nixon reelection effort first appeared during the summer and fall of 1972. Days before the presidential election that year, Graham dismissed the alleged crimes as "shenanigans," said he was "convinced that President Nixon knew nothing about it," and criticized Democratic nominee George McGovern for accusing the Nixon administration of immoral practices.[4] Privately, Graham told Nixon that he would emphasize the president's "personal morality and integrity" at an upcoming press conference and complained to White House chief of staff H. R. Haldeman "that people who made a hero of [Daniel] Ellsberg for stealing the Pentagon Papers are so deeply concerned about the alleged escapade at Watergate." The evangelist also volunteered to vouch for the personal character of Haldeman and fellow aide Dwight Chapin, both of whom later saw prison time for Watergate-related crimes.[5] As the crisis intensified during the winter of 1973, Graham attempted to frame his relationship to Nixon—alternately, as a pastor or a friend—so as to minimize his responsibilities regarding the public discussion of Watergate. "When a member of the congregation is hurt or in trouble, the heart of the pastor goes out to him and to his family," Graham said of Nixon in a statement published on May 1, 1973, immediately following the forced resignations of Haldeman and fellow staffer John Ehrlichman, as well as the firing of White House Counsel John Dean.[6] Still, Graham defended Nixon with the passion of a friend and the rationale of a true believer. It was inconceivable to Graham that someone as ethically sound and politically intelligent as Nixon had any previous knowledge of the Watergate shenanigans.

While Graham the political loyalist could not initially conceive of Watergate as anything other than a partisan attack on Nixon, Graham the evangelist eventually identified a certain devotional value in the crisis. The use of Watergate for evangelistic purposes did not, as Nixon initially feared, signify that Graham was "jumping ship."[7] To the contrary, and to the benefit of Nixon, the meaning Graham found in Watergate remained within the framework of evangelical universalism, as Graham went to great lengths to keep the devotional and political elements of Watergate separate. His May 1 statement and *New York Times* op-ed five days later represented the official line of the Graham team regarding Watergate: the bad apples behind the break-in should be punished, yet the proper national response to Watergate was not political retaliation but a renewed effort to redress the nation's spiritual and moral slippage. In the *Times*, Graham employed Watergate to call for a "national and pervasive awakening," even while he urged readers to "put the Watergate affair in proper historical perspective."[8]

Throughout the Watergate crisis, then, Graham turned the affair into a morality tale in which, to cite one example, Nixon apparatchik Jeb Magruder represented a kind of everyman, swept toward lawlessness by the secular gusts of American society. "A nation confused for years by the teaching of situational ethics now finds itself dismayed by those in government who apparently practiced it," Graham declared, alluding to an ethical system Magruder had attributed to his moral lapses. "We have lost our moral compass. We must get it back."[9] Moral reorientation would require spiritual repentance as well as a renewed recognition of biblical authority—hence, the model from Nehemiah of Israelites turning to the law of Moses during their time of trial. Here, Graham found a compromise typology between his self-characterization as a New Testament evangelist and the repeated calls that he imitate the Micahs and Amoses of the Old Testament: John the Baptist, the New Testament's lone prophet. "All I can do," he told a Chicago audience, "is be one voice in the wilderness crying out Warning! Judgment is coming."[10] Graham the qualified prophet spoke to the nation as a whole, not to the Nixon administration in particular. In referring to situation ethics (and, elsewhere, to the ethos of civil disobedience perpetuated by the protest culture of the sixties), the evangelist cited the very type of "moral decadence" Nixon had campaigned against to explain the actions of the president's aides. Perhaps the ultimate example of Graham's desire to extract a meaning from Watergate without also damaging the president was his employment of the word "crisis," the tagline of Nixon's 1969 inaugural address, to describe the moral context of the scandal. The teleology of permissiveness, rather than the machinations of the Nixon White House, lent a certain inevitability to Watergate. Graham's proposed solution was no less inevitable. While even Adam and Eve had tried to "cover up," Graham said, the "greatest cover up of all was Calvary, where our Lord shed his blood to cover our sins and we're all sinners."[11]

Thus, while Graham readily linked Watergate with moral declension, he did not describe this slippage in terms readily translatable into a political or legal solution. As a result of Watergate, he told a sympathetic group of southern newspaper publishers, the media had an opportunity to lead a "moral revolution," an effort Graham did not believe required more investigative journalism.[12] Watergate was but a *"symbol* of political corruption and evil" (italics mine), another expression of human frailty. As he had done with the issue of racial strife during the civil rights movement, Graham comfortably associated the Watergate affair with such international crisis spots as Cyprus and Vietnam. Both moves—distinguishing between moral and political solutions as well as turning Watergate into a symbol—downplayed the singularity of the crisis. Even as Graham put greater public distance between himself and Nixon by the start of 1974, he still characterized Watergate in a way that distracted attention from the specific culpability of the administration. In a well-publicized interview with *Christianity Today* published in January 1974,

Graham described allegations of his own implication in the crisis as McCarthy-style guilt by association. At the same time, he infused Watergate with an element of tragedy. During the 1972 campaign, he argued, the Nixon staffers' "magnificent obsession to change the country and the world" had led them to employ an ends-justifies-the-means ethic—an argument reminiscent of the testimony of John Mitchell, head of the 1972 reelection campaign.[13] Hubris was a part of the human condition, the Watergate in everyone; it transcended party identification. "The nation needs to repent—not just the Republicans, but my own party, the Democrats, as well," Graham told an audience at Duke University.[14] "What caused Watergate?" he asked a group of Southern Baptists two months before Nixon's resignation. "Sin. And there is a little bit of Watergate in all of us. So let's not go around being so self-righteous. I know bad people in both parties and all over the world."[15]

Graham's truncated moralization of Watergate allowed him to call for national repentance while expressing confidence that Nixon would survive in office and, even as late as June 1973, contending that it was "too early to make a moral judgment" on the political crisis.[16] Again, Graham attempted to keep politics and evangelism in separate spheres. This distinction often meant nothing more than the difference between a press conference and a sermon, however. His evangelistic uses of Watergate initially did little to threaten or even qualify his unabashed support for Nixon, whom Graham continued to counsel and praise. In 1973, a month before Graham came out publicly for the punishment of Watergate wrongdoers, he wrote a supportive letter to Nixon likening the president's predicament to the struggles of the Israelite king David, whom he quoted from Psalms 35:11–12: "They accuse me of things I have never even heard about. I do them good but they return me harm."[17] Four days before the May 6 *Times* op-ed appeared, Graham advised Nixon to seek out photo ops with international dignitaries because, as aide Lawrence Higby paraphrased the evangelist, "the American people need to be diverted from Watergate."[18] Graham did his part by nominating inflation as truly the most pressing problem for the nation.[19]

While many of Graham's public and private defenses of Nixon were no doubt arguments of expediency, his overall interpretation of Watergate reflected his evangelical social ethic. In popular memory, this social ethic manifested itself most acutely in the evangelist's public reaction upon reading the initial transcripts of the Nixon White House recordings; Graham fixated on the matter of Nixon's deleted expletives.[20] Unlike Nixon adviser and former

Jesuit priest John McLaughlin (who later hosted a popular public affairs program), Graham could not dismiss swearing—especially taking the Lord's name in vain—as a form of stress release.[21] Yet Graham's focus on profanity in the midst of so many other damning abuses of power, whatever its value as an anecdote, should not distract us from the larger significance of the social ethic of evangelical universalism that informed his overall response to Watergate. As explicated earlier, evangelical universalism viewed the individual soul as the primary theological and political unit in society, prioritized relational over legislative solutions, and tended to acquiesce to the ultimately inscrutable realm of ordained authority. All three elements were evident in Graham's handling of Watergate.

Focusing on the individual soul and proffering relational (i.e., nonlegal or nonpolitical) solutions worked complementarily. Graham characterized Watergate as a call for national repentance, yet he ultimately issued this call in individuated terms. Rather than specifically condemning Nixon or any other administration official, Graham focused on the generic sins of the generic individual, suggesting that the conversion of individuals would have a ripple effect on society. This "regenerational" approach prioritized the devotional value of Watergate over any legal or political meanings the crisis might hold. Appropriately, then, Graham called the Nixon tapes as "just a little foretaste of what is to come for all of us, when we have to sit before the Great Committee in Heaven and hear all of the tapes played of our own lives."[22] Still, Graham did not wholly abstract Watergate from temporal relevance. To the contrary, he unabashedly hoped that the crisis would contribute to the restoration of a national "moral consensus."[23] Graham's description of this moral consensus, however, reflected a quality scholar Dennis P. Hollinger found in his study of evangelical social ethics: "a blurring together of personal and social dimensions of existence," in which "social problems are regularly viewed as magnified personal problems."[24] For Graham, the nation's loss of moral consensus boiled down to a breakdown in individual morality. Indeed, he identified the potential "great illusion" of Watergate as the belief "that you can have public virtue without private morality."[25] Morality flowed outward from the individual.

Whatever the lessons of Watergate, Graham's political defense of Nixon hinged not only on their friendship but also on assumptions of Nixon's inherent legitimacy and the special nature of the presidency.[26] The evangelical focus on social transformation through the individual, which received healthy in-house critiques from Hollinger and a generation of "young evangelicals," coexisted with equally significant appeals for social order and respect for authority.[27] For Graham and other conservative Christians, *legitimate* authority tended to also mean *ordained* authority.[28] In this perspective, which Graham had invoked as a moderate during the civil rights movement, law becomes something to obey, to be subject to, rather than to create or invoke for positive ends. In his interview with *Christianity Today*, Graham stressed Christians' "one primary duty to those in authority: to pray!"[29] More tellingly, in a quote ridiculed by a *Village Voice* cartoonist, the evangelist wondered if "we as Christians failed to pray enough for Richard Nixon."[30] Such advice assigned to individual Christians a strikingly passive role vis-à-vis ordained authority (although Graham, of course, would not have seen prayer as passive). Indeed, for all of his obvious attraction to the wheeling and dealing of politics and for all of his savvy as an adviser to politicians, Graham at a fundamental level remained in willful (and, at times, uncomprehending) awe of the workings of high political office. On a number of occasions during Watergate, Graham wondered if Americans held presidents to unrealistic standards. "The presidency does so much to a man," he said following Nixon's resignation. "The responsibility is almost too much." These lines—which combined a Nixon apologia with a faint echo of the influential "imperial presidency" thesis of historian Arthur Schlesinger, Jr.—also indicated an important dynamic in Graham's posture toward that political authority which he deemed ordained.[31] If one accepts a modified covenantal theology (i.e., that God actively works through nations or peoples), as Graham did, and if one tends to define sin in individual and not structural terms, as Graham also did, then the mechanics of legitimate political power fall into a unique category, difficult to hold accountable to standards of individual morality. Power attains a degree of divine inscrutability, and something as nebulous as job difficulty can become a plausible excuse for excessive use of that power. Graham found transgressions that were clearly individual and conscious in nature, be they swearing or breaking and entering, easier to identify and denounce than the sins of state.

In addition to reflecting an evangelical posture, Graham's support of Nixon was part of a regional phenomenon, an extension of Nixon's appeal in much of the white South. A number of observers at the time noted that the South remained the region seemingly most loyal to Nixon.[32] Southern Republicans, despite paying a political price for their loyalty to Nixon, were among the most strident congressional defenders of the president, who often visited the region when seeking electoral solace. Just after the resignations of

Haldeman and Ehrlichman, Republican North Carolina senator Jesse Helms, whom Nixon had supported during the 1972 campaign, told the president he had "a real friend there" in Graham.[33] The broader southern support for Nixon had much to do with resentment against the purportedly liberal media, a sign that Nixon's southern strategy and invocations of the silent majority had yielded regional dividends. A prominent journalist quoted a South Carolinian as saying, "We support and sympathize with the President because we Southerners have been on the receiving end so long ourselves."[34] Graham's public opinions regarding the media's bias toward showing only the bad side of the South, voiced as recently as his 1972 Birmingham crusade, certainly paralleled these sentiments. On a more intriguing note, his warning against self-righteousness bore resemblance to a much more famous Nixon apologia by the southern rock band Lynyrd Skynyrd, whose anthem of sectional pride, "Sweet Home Alabama," features the lines "Now Watergate does not bother me / Does your conscience bother you?"[35] One historian has argued that these lyrics "captured a wide-spread belief that Nixon was under fire only because liberal arbiters of opinion hewed to a double standard."[36] While Graham certainly echoed this feeling (e.g., in referring to the sinfulness of Democrats as well as Republicans), the evangelist and the rock band had another thing in common: a desire to turn Watergate into something other than a political scandal with a political solution. Through their obviously contrasting mediums, they called for self-reflection—with a goal, for Lynyrd Skynyrd, of northern retreat, and for Graham, of national revival.

The upshot of Graham's evangelical interpretation of Watergate was to present the crisis as a conversion opportunity not only for America but also for the Watergate participants and Nixon himself. As the crisis extended into 1974, the evangelist entered the final stage of his handling of Watergate. He urged Nixon to confess his own need for forgiveness. Graham went so far as privately to propose remarks for Nixon to voice at what turned out to be the president's final prayer breakfast: "I hope I shall not be judged as hiding behind religion when I say that I have . . . been driven to my knees in prayer. . . . We are all in need of God's forgiveness. Not only for mistakes in judgment, but [for] our sins as well. . . . I want to take this opportunity today to re-dedicate myself to the God that I first learned about at my mother's knee." Perhaps aware of the potential domino effect of even a qualified mea culpa, Nixon did not take up Graham's proposal.[37] The suggested remarks reflected the universalization-relativization dynamic, as well as Graham's hope that Nixon would contritely model an evangelical response to Watergate. Graham wanted Nixon to act like the priest Ezra from the book of Nehemiah, to declare publicly his faith in the Lord so that all might understand the true solution to the nation's crisis. In the eyes of an emerging majority of Americans, however, Nixon personified that very crisis.

Following that prayer breakfast, Graham urged Nixon to draw inspiration from Charles Colson.[38] The Nixon hatchet man was one of a number of high-profile converts to evangelical Christianity during and following Watergate. The conversions of convicted Watergate-related perpetrators Colson, Jeb Magruder, and Harry Dent—or, more specifically, how they described their born-again experiences—echoed Graham's simultaneous universalization and relativization of the crisis. As loyalists who suffered legal consequences because of Watergate, they were more willing than Graham to criticize Nixon as both a person and a leader. Still, none of them joined Common Cause as a result of their experiences; they described the lessons of Watergate in spiritual, rather than political, terms. All three moved on to careers in evangelical organizations directly or closely associated with the Billy Graham Evangelistic Association (BGEA).

Magruder, who had overseen the cover-up of the Watergate burglary and who later took a position with the youth evangelism organization Young Life, attributed his willingness to ignore the law during the 1972 campaign to the lax guidelines he had learned from a college ethics professor. Graham echoed Magruder's assertion in his only sermonic reference to Watergate during the 1973 Atlanta crusade.[39] Interestingly, the preconversion (but postconviction) Magruder had contradicted Graham's argument that a moral private life would necessarily lead to a moral public life. "I think that most of us who were involved in Watergate," Magruder wrote in 1974, "had private morality but not a sense of public morality. Instead of applying our private morality to public affairs, we accepted the President's standards of political behavior, and the results were tragic for him and for us."[40]

The conversion of Colson, which occurred while he remained a consultant to Nixon, garnered the most press and, understandably, its fair share of cynicism. The dirty tricks specialist and contributor to the notorious "Enemies List" was led to Christ in the midst of the Watergate crisis by Tom Phillips, head of the defense and electronics firm Raytheon and himself a Graham convert. Colson became an occasional participant in a White House prayer group that included Harry Dent. Colson's postconversion advice to Nixon paralleled that of Graham. Colson proposed that the president declare April 30, 1974 (the anniversary of Lincoln's 1863 National Fast Day) a national day of prayer. Doing so might save Nixon's political skin; but it would also turn Watergate into an ironic good. "I believe that the country has to be lifted out of the doldrums of Watergate," wrote Colson. "Our best hope is to bring about a rebirth of faith and a renewed commitment to God." Nixon did refer to Lincoln's faith in his prayer breakfast remarks, but it was left to Mark Hatfield to win Senate approval for a National Day of Humiliation, Fasting, and Prayer.[41] While Colson, in later reflections, did not gloss over the specific failings of Nixon, he parlayed Watergate into a critique of liberal humanism, the source of the hubris that had infected the White House. "Were Mr. Nixon and his men more evil than any of their predecessors?" asked Colson in language strikingly similar to Graham's interpretation of Watergate.

> That they brought the nation Watergate is a *truth*. But is it not only part of a larger *truth*—that all men have the capacity for both good and evil, and the darker side of man's nature can always prevail in any human being? If people believe that just because one bunch of rascals [is] run out of office all the ills which have beset a nation are over, then the real lesson of this ugly time will have been missed— and that delusion could be the greatest tragedy of all. . . . Having seen through Watergate how vulnerable man can be, I no longer believe I am master of my destiny. I need God.[42]

Harry Dent's path to born-again Christianity was the least dramatic of the three and technically represented a reaffirmation of faith (although he described it in terms of a conversion). During his tenure as Nixon's political coordinator, the architect of the southern strategy received much publicity as a Southern Baptist, a teetotaler, and an organizer of the White House prayer breakfasts.[43] Unlike Colson and Magruder, Dent saw no jail time and suffered minimal political damage for his Watergate-related conviction. Nonetheless, Dent, who during the 1980s served as director of the Billy Graham Lay Center, traced his 1978 spiritual renewal to the fundamental questions Watergate had raised for him about "the nature of man." His devotional-style book, *Cover Up: The Watergate in All of Us*, utilized (whether intentionally or not) Graham's own phraseology and offered perhaps the most extreme version of the Watergate-as-synecdoche trope. "The story of Watergate," wrote Dent, "is a replay, thousands of years later, of the Garden of Eden." He defined a personal Watergate as "a sudden confrontation with an event or experience which contains the potential . . . for destruction of our personal honor, worth, safety or well-being, or that of our family." According to this therapeutic schema, the day of judgment becomes the "ultimate Watergate," and Hitler had succumbed to his own Watergate by committing suicide.[44]

None of the above born-again experiences entailed a clear political upshot. Colson, Magruder, and Dent described their conversions almost wholly in spiritual terms, and all three eventually moved away from official party work.[45] Fleeing the Beltway, though, did not entail a departure from the broader contours of conservative politics. At a 1987 conference on the Nixon presidency, for example, Colson offered an explicitly biblical justification for the occasional lie of state. His critique of liberal humanism would later resound in popular conservatism (and, ironically, resembled Nixon's own campaign language). Best known for his prison ministry work, Colson became associated with the broader Christian Right during the presidency of George W. Bush.[46] Dent, like many Republicans throughout the South, softened his tone on race, yet remained identified with his adopted party.[47] Magruder, meanwhile, questioned the role government programs could play in solving national problems.[48]

In the end, Graham unsuccessfully attempted to fit Nixon into the conversion narrative modeled by Colson and Magruder, and later embraced by Dent. The evangelist's optimism regarding Nixon was, in a word, resilient. Following an early postresignation meeting with Nixon, Graham declared that the former president had turned to religion.[49] The evangelist had expressed similar sentiments following Nixon's final prayer breakfast.[50]

Such disappointments aside, Graham remained nothing less than a true believer in the beleaguered former president—one of Nixon's biggest admirers this side of the 1980s television sitcom character Alex P. Keaton. Graham never wholly departed from his general defensiveness about both Nixon's stature as a national leader and, more strikingly, Nixon's ultimate culpability in the Watergate affair.[51] As Nixon left the White House, Graham privately lobbied leading Republicans in favor of a pardon and publicly contended that attempts "to further hurt [Nixon] would cause great division in the country." President Ford eventually phoned Graham, who told the president about his concern that Nixon might face prison time.[52] Eight days later, when Nixon received a presidential pardon, Graham released a statement in support of Ford's action.[53] In a private letter months after the resignation of Nixon, Graham agreed with a correspondent's assessment that President Nixon had "physiologically or psychologically experienced an episode that affected his behavior—his capacity to carry on normally."[54] In 1979, after biographer Marshall Frady quoted Graham as attributing the president's behavior to demonic forces operating through sleeping pills, the evangelist wrote to Nixon explaining that he was referring to the Watergate crisis itself (not the behavior of the president).[55] During the remainder of Nixon's life, Graham kept in regular touch with the beleaguered former president, on whom the evangelist lavished praise in private and then again in public on the occasion of Nixon's 1994 funeral. The details of their many conversations, most of which touched on foreign affairs, occasionally surfaced in a manner reflecting favorably on Nixon. While Graham did not abandon his desire to convert the former president to a more active brand of Christianity, he did little to counter sentiments among Nixon defenders that the media stood to blame for the Watergate crisis.[56]

Up from Watergate, Still in the White House

Graham, though, had to tread cautiously in his post-Watergate defense of Nixon. In April 1974, four months before Nixon's resignation and another month before the silver anniversary of Graham's watershed Los Angeles crusade, evangelical historian Richard Pierard published an article pointedly titled "Can Billy Graham Survive Richard Nixon?"[57] The question was more than appropriate in light of the public beating Graham had taken over the Watergate scandal. Many newspaper editorial boards focused specifically on the connection Graham drew between Watergate and a decline in national morality. "The business of blaming a permissive society, a decadent people, and a population prone to sinfulness for high crimes and misdemeanors in the White House will get us nowhere," editorialized the *Norfolk Virginian-Pilot* in response to Graham's *New York Times* op-ed piece. His "short-order sermon," another paper snapped, possessed "the texture and appearance of a flat soufflé."[58] Such criticism gained particular credence, first, as documents revealed attempts by H. R. Haldeman to derive political capital from protests at the 1971 Billy Graham Day celebration in Charlotte, and second, as former White House counsel John Dean testified that Nixon had sought to quash Internal Revenue Service inquiries about the tax status of the BGEA.[59] In Christian circles, criticism of Graham's response to Watergate was not confined to predictable circles. The Presbyterian Church in the United States (Southern Presbyterian church), hardly a bastion of theological liberalism, briefly considered a resolution imploring Graham to urge Nixon to come clean regarding the Watergate allegations. The resolution failed, undoubtedly to the relief of the denomination's outgoing moderator, Graham's father-in-law, Nelson Bell.[60] Additional criticism came from the normally friendly pen of conservative commentator and fellow evangelical Paul Harvey, who imagined Graham's response to the White House transcripts: "You are remembering that the President never once talked like that around you. . . . It hurts, Billy, but you asked for it."[61]

Yet Graham did survive Watergate, as Pierard suspected he could. The evangelist gradually sought to distance himself from Nixon. The process began, however tentatively, with a public statement, prepared with the help of his friend and fellow Nixon intimate Charles Crutchfield for release on Thanksgiving Day 1973. Graham said he did "not always agree" with the administration's actions, yet averred that the "tragic events of Watergate will probably make [Nixon] a stronger man and a better President."[62] He put additional public space between himself and Nixon following the presidential prayer breakfast two months later, his last public appearance with the sitting president. Returning from a major evangelism conference in Switzerland on the cusp of the president's August 9 resignation, Graham unsuccessfully placed several phone calls to Nixon. The president may have been seeking to shelter him from the Watergate fallout.[63]

During the intervening months, Graham had tellingly revised his description of their relationship. The evangelist had claimed during the 1972 campaign to "know the President as well as anyone outside his immediate family."[64] Nearly two years later, however, Graham suggested that he was never an intimate of Nixon, "contrary to what people thought."[65] Interviews with Haldeman and Colson unsurprisingly revealed a much different assumption about the evangelist, whom Haldeman classified as "definitely in [Nixon's] inner circle."[66]

Like the evangelical Watergate memoirists, Graham attempted to use Watergate to announce his exit from the political arena. In the years following the crisis, he proclaimed his distance from the world of politics. He even conceded that his White House church services had been a mistake.[67] Any assumption that Watergate led Graham to take a page from the Old Testament prophets Amos or Micah oversimplifies matters greatly, however. In truth, the evangelist never completely forsook the political arena.[68] While steering very clear of the excesses of the Nixon years, he continued to find his way into White House memos and, inevitably, onto the borderlands of campaign politics.

Graham's early dealings with President Gerald Ford suggested that the evangelist initially failed, or chose not, to grasp one apparent lesson of Watergate: that proximity alone can imply partisanship. The evangelist telephoned President Ford during his first day in the office and soon wrote to declare his "total and complete backing and support" and to make himself available as a prayer partner and "someone to talk to who won't quote you." As if to ensure Ford's awareness of the full menu of his services as national pastor, Graham also invited the president to attend a crusade in Norfolk, Virginia. Ford did not accept the offer, but he eventually followed his predecessor to Charlotte, appearing with Graham at the 1975 bicentennial celebration of the Mecklenburg Declaration of Independence.[69]

The two remained in regular contact. Early in the presidential election year of 1976, Graham open-endedly asked Ford to call him "if there is anything that I can do to help in the months ahead." As the election approached, presidential staffers kept on the lookout for ways to connect their candidate with the evangelist. That September, during a phone conversation with Ford (placed by the president), Graham invited him to attend a crusade service in his home state of Michigan. In a subsequent letter, however, Graham stipulated that he would also extend an invitation to Democratic challenger Jimmy Carter (just as the evangelist had invited Hubert Humphrey to the 1968 Pittsburgh crusade, which Nixon had attended). Likewise, Ford would not be permitted to address the audience.[70] Only Republican vice presidential nominee Bob Dole ultimately traveled to Pontiac. Dole's use of a campaign jet to get there caught the attention of reporters.[71] So did Graham's visit to the White House soon thereafter. Accepting an invitation from Ford, who had reason to believe he might still win over evangelical voters from the increasingly vulnerable Carter, Graham rode in the presidential limousine on the occasion of a reception hosted by Liberian president William Tolbert, a Baptist and a friend of the evangelist.[72]

The ambiguity of Graham's relationship with Democratic president Jimmy Carter provides strong evidence that the evangelist remained a Republican in all but registration. "Graham's partisanship," observed a critical biographer back in 1960, "has been camouflaged by a professed apoliticalism."[73] More recent scholars have been hesitant to look past these persistent professions and identify Graham as a Republican partisan, rather than simply as an Eisenhower and Nixon backer or someone who tended to support GOP leaders and policies.[74] On the other hand, journalists during the Nixon era often assumed that Graham was a Republican, or listed his Democratic registration as a non sequitur. In explaining the lack of intimacy between Jimmy Carter and the evangelist, one Graham biographer rightly cited both the evangelist's post-Watergate hesitancy to involve himself in high-profile political activities and, more important, Carter's assumption that Graham might not offer him support. At the time, syndicated columnists Rowland Evans and Robert Novak contended that Carter initially shunned the evangelist for fear of alienating his liberal constituents. Indeed, the Montana delegation to the 1976 Democratic convention introduced a resolution to ban the Nixon-tainted Graham from delivering an invocation there.[75]

Yet legitimate reasons existed to suspect that Graham might have offered at least tacit support for Carter during the 1976 presidential campaign. In the immediate aftermath of Watergate, Graham made every effort to accentuate his status as a registered Democrat. He went so far as to tape a message for a 1975 Democratic Party fundraising telethon encouraging Americans to support the party of their choosing. Graham did so at the urging of Democratic National Committee chair Robert Strauss, a Texan and friend who broached the subject when they were both testifying as character witnesses in the corruption trial of John Connally. Graham agreed to do so in part because former Republican National Committee chair George H. W. Bush had made a similar appeal for an earlier Democratic telethon. While Graham wanted to reaffirm the American political system, he now also hoped to counter his image as a GOP partisan. He had turned down a similar request from the Democratic Party back in 1973. Two years later, newspaper articles about the telethon described him as a registered Democrat.[76]

Moreover, Jimmy Carter was not a McGovern-style liberal but a moderate, avowedly Southern Baptist Democrat. One South Carolina paper specifically cited Carter as the very fulfillment of Graham's prophecy that the South would solve its racial problems ahead of the North.[77] The pious Carter seemingly more than satisfied the office-holding ideals that Graham had been touting for the preceding quarter of a century. Before Carter emerged as a viable candidate, Graham had highlighted a similar politician, Florida governor and outspoken Christian Reubin Askew, as an ideal Democratic presidential nominee.[78] To be sure, the Episcopalian Gerald Ford also possessed a number of evangelical credentials. His son had attended Gordon-Conwell Theological Seminary, on whose board Graham served.[79] Yet Carter and Graham arguably had deeper historical ties. In the mid-1960s, Carter had overseen a desegregated screening of a BGEA film in Americus, Georgia, and as governor he had directly assisted Graham's efforts to attract a larger African American audience for the 1973 Atlanta crusade.[80]

When the 1976 presidential campaign season arrived, however, Graham made several moves that gave little indication he was behind the peanut farmer from Plains. The evangelist had pledged to stay "a million miles away from politics" in 1976.[81] One of his election-season comments traveled nearly that far. In an interview with the religious editor of the *Los Angeles Times*, Graham said he had not yet decided how he would vote; but he offered a big clue: "I would rather have a man in office who is highly qualified to be President who didn't make much of a religious profession than to have a man who had no qualifications but who made a religious profession."[82] The statement, which probably derived in part from a suspicion that Carter's theology was in reality more liberal than evangelical, emphasized the primary vulnerability of the candidate (inexperience) at the expense of his perceived advantage (spirituality). One of Carter's sons retorted that Graham, a holder of multiple honorary doctorates, had purchased his "doctor of religion" degree through the postal system. The Ford team took notice of the quip, which led Rosalynn Carter to phone Graham with an apology.[83] A political cartoon in the *Washington Post* showed the evangelist thumping a bumpkin-looking Carter with a Ten Commandments tablet. The same paper noted that Graham's visit with President Ford during the Tolbert banquet had followed the publication of a controversial interview Carter had given to *Playboy* magazine.[84]

Once in office, though, President Carter did seek out Graham on a number of occasions. Carter invited Graham to his inauguration, although illness prevented the evangelist from attending. Later in 1977, they discussed the financial scandal surrounding Carter official Bert Lance, an affair that seriously blemished the administration's choir-boy reputation. Carter's press secretary vehemently disputed a characterization of the conversation as an SOS on the part of the president. During the remainder of his term, Carter requested Graham's advice on Middle East policy and attempted unsuccessfully to gain his public endorsement of the SALT II treaty and the Equal Rights Amendment. Graham and the president maintained a friendly correspondence, and the evangelist spent at least one night at the Carter White House.[85]

Yet Graham was far from an ally of this avowedly evangelical president, a fact that in large part boiled down to their political differences. In 1977,

Graham saw fit to tell the Southern Baptist Convention members that they need not feel compelled to endorse all of the policies of their fellow congregant.[86] Unsurprisingly, the evangelist was not among the religious leaders Carter invited to a 1979 Camp David summit to address, in part, the national "moral and spiritual crisis" Graham had long cited.[87]

In the end, then, Graham never relinquished his deep interest in politics (as well as his equally deep attraction to politicians); rather, he lowered the profile of his role as a political and a ministerial counselor. It was nearly impossible for a public figure like Graham to depoliticize himself completely. Watergate, to be sure, led him to tone down his rhetoric. While he still made the occasional controversial statement about public affairs, he astutely avoided the kind of awkward parsing to which he frequently resorted during the Nixon era. Still, the legacy of Watergate lingered, as did the legacy of his reactions to it. In coming decades, American political discourse featured many elements present in Graham's evangelical interpretation of Watergate: individuated and spiritualized interpretations of political crises, a selective reticence to fault ordained authority, and converted politicians without converted politics.

Graham's invocation of the biblical Water Gate likewise took on a new resonance. Only a few years after Nixon left office in disgrace, a new conservative Christian movement arose seeking to save American society through the political system. The Christian Right drew momentum from a host of galvanizing social issues, such as abortion and school prayer, which had bubbled beneath the surface of Watergate. It drew strength from the very southern electorate that Nixon had wooed and Graham had long seen as fertile groups for the GOP. Just as Graham began to downgrade his involvement in politics, then, a growing number of conservative evangelicals and fundamentalists moved into that world. Graham was not comfortable with all facets of the Christian Right; but he had helped to set in motion the historical forces leading to its emergence.

Billy Graham and American Conservatism

He is the kind of man Rudyard Kipling had in mind when he wrote,
"You can talk with crowds and keep your virtue, / Or walk with Kings—
nor lose the common touch."
    —John Connally, 1965

Over the course of that weekend, Reverend Graham planted a mustard
seed in my soul, a seed that grew over the next year. . . . It was the
beginning of a new walk where I would recommit my heart to Jesus
Christ.
    —George W. Bush, 1999

BY THE EARLY 1980S, Billy Graham had safely entered his third and final stage as an American public figure. The evangelist had begun his career as a fundamentalist, a phase that lasted only as long as he remained a sociopolitical outsider—a firebrand novelty or a sawdusted throwback. The 1952 election of President Dwight Eisenhower then helped to thrust Graham forward as a spokesperson and symbol for a resurgent public evangelicalism seeking to rescue the United States (and, with it, Western civilization) from atheistic communism abroad and morally acquiescent liberalism at home. Politically, this neo-evangelicalism translated into a heartfelt, if somewhat strategically unfocused conservatism. In his home region of the South, Graham emerged as racial moderate and a type of regional leader. He continued those roles into the presidency of Lyndon Johnson. The subsequent Nixon years led

Graham toward a type of political partisanship that surpassed even his behavior during the Eisenhower administration. Graham's regional leadership thus became intertwined with Nixon's "southern strategy." By the early 1970s, then, the corrupt Nixon presidency seemed to mock the ideal of Christian statesmanship upon which so much of Graham's political ethic rested. In the years following Watergate, the evangelist cultivated a noticeably more moderate image, which has endured ever since. He reconsidered his associations with partisan politics (after partly acknowledging them) and surprised critics with his newfound support for nuclear disarmament. The reformed Graham drew sustenance from his increasingly international and inclusive ministry. He stood as an elder statesman—an icon beyond partisanship and, by the 1990s, above the culture wars, as well.

The now familiar narrative of a postpolitical Graham, however, does justice neither to the full breadth of his legacy nor to his ongoing comfort with the powers that be. The tale of Graham's self-described "pilgrimage" toward moderation has highlighted certain changes at the expense of other telling continuities. Popular portraits of Graham have exaggerated the nature of his depoliticization. Specifically, they have elided his social ties with the emerging Christian Right, underestimated his presence in the Reagan and George H. W. Bush White Houses, exaggerated his defense of Bill Clinton, and not connected the dots between the motif of Christian statesmanship and the faith narrative of George W. Bush. In short, Graham never completely abandoned the world of politics. As he shed the political residue of the Nixon era, he walked an increasingly forgiving line between his reconstructed image and the fundamental endurance not only of his basic theological assumptions but of his political inclinations as well. During this time, the narrative of the Sunbelt South began to overlap with that of an ascendant conservatism. One need not embrace a glib thesis of "southernization" in order to draw a connection between the two developments—and Graham is a case in point. His pilgrimage in the aftermath of Watergate says much about the transformation of American conservatism at the close of the twentieth century.

Christianity *in* Politics—Not *as* Politics

With time, Graham's post-Watergate claim that "everybody knows I've become politically neutral" grew in credibility.[1] His increasingly nonpartisan identity benefited greatly from his public distance from the Christian Right, the new standard by which the media and many Americans measured Christian political involvement.[2] While Graham criticized Jerry Falwell and the larger Christian Right out of principle, he also knew that even a partial association with such a controversial movement could severely hamper his evangelistic outreach. It is perhaps no coincidence that in 1981, after the election of Reagan led the media to train its sights firmly on the Christian Right, Graham hired evangelical public relations whiz Larry Ross.[3] The evangelist's exact relationship to the Christian Right thus remains unclear or oversimplified. Historians have cast Graham as a conscience figure vis-à-vis the movement, while journalists have often written him out of it altogether.[4] They have done so in spite of the fact that the Christian Right came of age in Graham's very backyard—both in a spatial and a spiritual sense—blossoming at the intersection of an ascendant Sunbelt South and a resurgent public evangelicalism.

In key respects, Graham helped to construct the political and religious culture that made the Christian Right possible. He gave public expression to the shift among many post–World War II evangelicals away from separatist fundamentalism and toward greater social and political engagement. During the 1950s, he helped to make evangelicalism a vital component of anticommunist discourse. He was the best-known, if not necessarily the noisiest, postwar exponent of "Christian Americanism," bluntly upholding an "American way of life" that could survive the challenge of atheistic communism only though "an old-fashioned, heaven-sent revival."[5] Even after Graham toned down his Cold War jeremiads, he continued to view patriotism as a normative manifestation of piety. He prominently displayed his feelings during the July 4, 1970, Honor America Day program in Washington, D.C., where he delivered a rousing defense of American pride and patriotism from the steps of the Lincoln Memorial. Paraphrasing British prime minister Winston Churchill, Graham implored his audience to "pursue the vision, reach the goal, fulfill the American dream—and as you move to do it, never give in! Never give in! Never! Never! Never!"[6]

Graham had long urged God-fearing Americans to express their values through political involvement. One year before the 1952 presidential election, he predicted that the "Christian people of America are going to vote as a bloc for the man with the strongest moral and spiritual platform, regardless of his views on other maters."[7] His repeated calls during the 1960s for alternative Christian "demonstrations" also implied openness to forming a Christian-based political movement. Moreover, his evangelistic efforts modeled the type

of conservative ecumenism necessary to create such a bloc. Graham's subsequent advice to President Nixon, and later to President Carter, that they take
notice of conservative Protestants as an electoral group was not the cool-
headed analysis of a political consultant. It derived in no small part from his
long-voiced desire for greater evangelical influence on policy making.

During the 1950s and 1960s, however, Graham and his fellow neo-evangelicals remained most interested in electing and supporting "Christian
statesmen," leaders who shared their faith perspective or who at least heeded
the integral contribution of evangelical Christianity to the national health.
Graham regularly urged Christians to run for office and had pondered doing
so himself. Many postwar evangelicals assumed a link between the number
of believers in office and the quality of political leadership. They saw no
inherent conflict between Christian statesmanship and the Establishment
Clause of the First Amendment. The emphasis was on Christians entering
public life as individual citizens, rather than as representatives of the church
or a particular denomination.[8] Christian principles, they believed, had always
informed the American political tradition, while the true threat to separation
of church and state, as the 1960 presidential election revealed many of them
still suspected, came from Roman Catholicism. "We believe in separation of
Church and State in this land," said Texas governor Price Daniel in 1958
speech published in *Christianity Today*, "but never have we believed in separation of Church and statesmen."[9] (On Daniel's inauguration day a year earlier,
Graham had bestowed the very label "Christian statesman" on the governor.)[10]

Graham never departed from his preference for Christian statesmanship,
and this consistency eventually helped to distinguish him from the more
activist Christian Right. The Watergate affair only reinforced his belief "that
we need more devoted Christians who are living the Christian life in every
area of their lives in the political arena."[11] He likewise hoped his 1975 crusade
in Jackson, Mississippi, would result in "spiritual growth in the political
arena. We want to see the finest of people entering politics at the local, state,
and national level." He continued voicing the Christians-in-politics theme
well into the 1976 election year.[12] Despite his clear overall bias toward Republican politics, though, Graham often hesitated to link Christianity with specific platforms that might commit believers to positions not explicitly
spiritual in nature (or that might give him a public relations headache). He
and many fellow evangelicals continued to draw a distinction between the
unassailable good of Christians in office and the more ambiguous status of

Christianity as a political movement. Doing so, of course, allowed Graham to deny that his spiritual message sometimes had political overtones—a move that became particularly important following the Watergate crisis. Just as Graham was attempting to cleanse himself from the stain of partisan politics, however, a vocal group of conservative evangelicals and fundamentalists began to challenge the distinction between Christian statesmanship and political activism.

The evangelist possessed obvious ties with many founding fathers of the Christian Right. For example, Bill Bright, the influential Campus Crusade for Christ leader who grew increasingly active in politics during the mid-1970s, had worked closely with Graham during the previous two decades. Graham was involved in early discussions about the Christian Embassy, an outreach to Washington, D.C., politicos that Bright helped to found.[13] One of Bright's intimates was Arizona congressman John Conlan, a strongly conservative Republican who had long seen Graham himself as a model Christian statesman. Conlan spoke at Graham's 1975 Jackson crusade.[14] The following year, the evangelist publicly expressed support for Conlan's bid for the GOP Senate nomination during a private gathering in the Phoenix area.[15] Before the primary, which Conlan ended up losing, two of the candidate's most influential backers mailed letters to Arizona ministers noting their past work as Graham crusade chairs.[16] Graham maintained a similarly cordial, although not collaborative, relationship with another congressional liaison to the Right, his home-state senator Jesse Helms, whose political action committee received donations from Graham associate Grady Wilson.[17] Graham's ties also extended to several ministers-cum-evangelists who mobilized their empires in support of the Christian Right in the late 1970s. He gave early encouragement to the television ministry of Fort Worth televangelist James Robison and later spoke at the respective dedications for D. James Kennedy's mammoth Coral Ridge Presbyterian Church in Florida and Pat Robertson's sprawling Christian Broadcasting Network headquarters in Virginia.[18]

Moreover, Graham appeared to sympathize with important facets of the emerging Christian Right agenda. That platform owed much to the growth during the 1970s of a new set of social issues—including sexual education, women's liberation, homosexuality, and, with time, abortion—that galvanized Christian conservatives. Those issues, most of which concerned matters of gender norms and familial authority, differed in subtle but important ways from the law-and-order and antipermissiveness themes of the silent majority era.[19] Among some conservatives in the post–civil rights era South, gender matters supplanted racial ones as politically viable starting points for assailing liberal politics.[20] Graham, though, did not directly link the new social issues with electoral discontentedness (as he had had with the earlier law-and-order themes). He took no formal stance on the Equal Rights Amendment, distanced himself from the pro-life movement by the time abortion became a partisan issue, and even conceded the possibility that a gay person could be a Christian.[21] Yet he concealed his personal stance more effectively than he had his allegiance to President Nixon. Graham politely dismissed women's liberation in an article for *Ladies' Home Journal*, professed admiration for the anti–gay rights work of Anita Bryant, and helped to found a pioneering Protestant antiabortion organization, the Christian Action Council.[22] On a fundamental level, then, Graham shared with the Christian Right a sense of national decline. In a 1974 address to the Southern Newspaper Publishers Association, he theorized a forty-year moral slippage that paralleled forty years of liberal rule (along with, of course, the Israelites' forty years of wandering in the wilderness).[23]

Other than not formally aligning himself with the Christian Right, Graham did little to arrest its germination. Indeed, he was something of an early shadow presence within a movement he would eventually criticize. In 1979, according to James Robison, Graham helped to organize a two-day prayer and strategy session held in Dallas to address the nation's moral decline. The gathering, for which Bill Bright apparently was the main impetus, clearly indicated Graham's displeasure with the Carter administration. The participants included several ministers who would be associated, to varying degrees, with the Christian Right, including Robison, Robertson, and Rex Humbard. They identified Reagan as an ideal presidential candidate. Robison recalled that Graham declared himself in sympathy with the attendees but stressed that his past experiences with politics precluded any public association with their efforts.[24] The following year, Graham offered only faint support for another Christian Right milestone, the "Washington for Jesus" rally.[25] More important, he claimed to have turned down an offer to speak at a more famous gathering in Dallas, the August 1980 National Affairs Briefing, where Republican presidential candidate Ronald Reagan endorsed the Christian Right.[26]

Graham is better remembered, though, for chiding the Christian Right. His first move in this direction actually came in 1976, well before the movement had formally coalesced. Amid the first presidential campaign after Watergate, Graham placed a premium on asserting his political neutrality (although, as noted, he did not always demonstrate it). In September, *Newsweek* quoted Graham criticizing Bright's political work. The evangelist declared himself "opposed to organizing Christians into a political bloc." Graham's comments came only months after he had expressed support for a senatorial candidate, John Conlan, who wanted to do just that. Since then, though, the left-leaning evangelical publication *Sojourners* had published a pointed expose of the political activism of Conlan, Bright, and several of their supporters. The piece served as a major source for the subsequent *Newsweek* article. Graham, who had already distanced himself from Bright's Christian Embassy, also canceled an engagement to appear at the Bright-sponsored National Prayer Congress, deeming the election-eve event too political. Conscious of the shockwaves his *Newsweek* comments had sent through the larger evangelical community, though, the evangelist taped a message for the gathering.[27]

Graham's public censure of the Christian Right proper began immediately after the 1980 election, in which the movement had played a prominent (if not necessarily electorally decisive) role.[28] Jerry Falwell's Moral Majority "is not my cup of tea," Graham told *People* magazine. "I do not intend to use what little moral influence I may have on secular, nonmoral issues like [opposing] the Panama Canal [treaty]," he added, referring to a galvanizing issue for many conservative voters. In a "Dear Jerry" letter, Graham politely but firmly admonished Falwell for failing to address arms control and other social justice issues. Falwell, an avowed fundamentalist with whom the evangelist possessed only minimal social ties, risked "los[ing] sight of the priority of the Gospel."[29] Falwell apparently took notice. At some point, he visited Graham in Montreat and, in the evangelist's telling, told him to "stay out of the Moral Majority. You keep doing what you're doing and I'll stay in what I'm doing." In public, at least, Graham interpreted Falwell's message as an affirmation.[30]

While critiquing the Christian Right was a wise public relations move for Graham, it also represented a consistent application of his theological values as a neo-evangelical. Graham's behavior suggested that he drew a connection between the contemporary Christian Right and the hardline fundamentalism that he had repudiated decades ago. Such an association might appear ironic, since the Christian Right endorsed the very political activism that fundamentalists had earlier castigated liberal Protestants for practicing. The analogy, though, made genealogical sense. Even during Graham's Youth for Christ days in the late 1940s, when he still moved comfortably among

Bob Jones and similar separatists, he had chided "ultra-Fundamentalism" for its obsession with theological purity.[31] As Graham grew in fame during the 1950s and 1960s, fundamentalist organs, including the *Baptist Bible Tribune* (the flagship publication of Jerry Falwell's home denomination), attacked the evangelist for his ecumenism and moderate support for social causes like desegregation. They argued, as Falwell did in his notorious "Ministers and Marches" sermon of 1965, that "preachers are not called to be politicians, but to be soul winners."[32] Graham, of course, would not have disputed this sentiment per se.

In the late 1970s, though, Falwell and a number of other fundamentalists starkly reversed course and embraced political involvement. They brought to their activism the divisive polemics they had previously applied to sectarian squabbles. Accordingly, they conjured up not the kind of nineteenth-century evangelical social concern that Graham admired but rather an aggressive, partisan, and seemingly new form of Christian politics. Graham could have affirmed many of the basic principles of Falwell's Moral Majority. Still, the evangelist could not support an organization led by someone who, as late as 1981, declared himself "a Fundamentalist—big F!" and urged Graham-style evangelicals to "reacknowledge your fundamentalist roots" and cease "trying to accommodate the Gospel to the pitiful philosophies of unregenerate humankind."[33] In response, Graham voiced legitimate skepticism "that the Moral Majority would represent more than 10 percent of the evangelicals in America."[34] The evangelist thus continued a decades-long pattern by chiding this latest group of fundamentalists for prioritizing ideological trees over the evangelistic forest. The Nixon era, Graham told an interviewer in 1978, had taught him the perils of playing God. He now spoke in the past tense about a time when he had "almost identified Americanism with Christianity."[35]

Graham did explicitly depart from the Christian Right in one policy area: arms control. The evangelist had long been an internationalist, if a hawkish one. Starting in 1979 (the year Falwell founded the Moral Majority), however, he surprised observers by announcing his conversion to the causes of disarmament and nuclear abolition. The former anticommunist militant announced this "rather late conviction of mine" in a CBS news interview in which he lamented the creation of the atomic bomb, as well as Harry Truman's decision to employ it.[36] This was a notable change for someone who, as late as 1965, had criticized the Supreme Court for ending restrictions on the mailing of communist literature.[37] Now, in the pages of *Sojourners*, Graham called for "SALT X," by which he meant "total destruction of nuclear arms."[38] He consistently emphasized, however, that he was neither a pacifist nor a unilateralist, and a Billy Graham Evangelistic Association spokesperson stressed that the evangelist had not taken a "definitive" position on the pending SALT II agreement.[39] Still, Graham's comments drew praise from heretofore critics, including peace activist Colman McCarthy and Southern Baptist rebel Will D. Campbell. The new Graham even warranted a favorable profile in *The Progressive* magazine.[40]

By washing his hands of the Christian Right, of course, Graham also protected a personal image in need of redress after Watergate. As always, he sought to conserve his status as an evangelist—in particular, his appeal to broad audiences, his ties to leading public figures, and, more than ever, his access to prospective crusade locations (now including the Eastern Bloc and China). Graham's new perspective on foreign policy cost him support on the right, as had his desegregated seating policy in the South. Graham was never one consciously to court controversy, though. He apparently viewed disarmament as a less contentious matter than abortion and "some of the other issues that evoke so much emotion."[41]

A Pulpit Setter

Graham's opposition to forming a partisan political movement did not preclude his support for Christian-friendly leaders who also happened to share his general political outlook. Two such persons, Richard Nixon and George H. W. Bush, appreciated this distinction, especially since neither of them possessed much of a comfort level with the Christian Right. Nixon advised Graham to steer clear of the movement, while Vice President Bush privately differentiated Graham's brand of Christian conservative from the "flamboyant money-mad, teary temple builders."[42] The enduring attachment of Graham to the Christian statesman trope, though, did not sustain a storyline in the era of the Christian Right. During the Reagan years and into the administration of George W. Bush, Graham's tone differed so notably from the headline-grabbing pronouncements of Falwell and Robertson that few observers stayed attuned to his continued intimacy with the world of politics.

The 1980 election of Ronald Reagan promised Graham the kind of access to the White House he had lacked since the Ford administration. Reagan and Graham first met during the early 1950s, around which time Reagan, then still a liberal Democrat, reportedly received consideration for the lead role in a Hollywood film about the evangelist.[43] They became friends after Reagan won the 1966 California gubernatorial race as a law-and-order Republican. Their relationship, though, never entailed the frankly political tone of the Graham-Nixon one. While neither an especially pious nor a doctrinaire Christian, Reagan did possess an abiding interest in spiritual matters, especially prophesy and eschatology, topics Graham addressed during a 1971 appearance before the California legislature. Reagan candidly raised theological matters in his pre-presidential correspondence with Graham.[44]

Although Graham declined to describe the contents of the absentee ballot he cast in the 1980 election, his candidate of choice was undoubtedly Reagan (especially after two closer friends, John Connally and George H. W. Bush, ended their Republican presidential campaigns).[45] Graham played nothing resembling a direct role in the Reagan campaign, yet he was not exactly a stranger to it. During the height of the primary season, he met with Reagan and campaign director Ed Meese for a publicized breakfast in Indianapolis, where the evangelist was holding a crusade. Graham turned down a casual request from the candidate to put in a good word for him in North Carolina, where he faced a tight primary race. This was not Graham's only brush with campaign politics in Indianapolis. A few days earlier, the evangelist had appeared with Rosalynn Carter at a rally in support of President Carter. Before a mostly black audience, Graham spoke highly of both the first lady and the president. Still, it was footage from the Reagan meeting, including the congratulations Graham offered the candidate on his victory in the Texas primary, that made the national news feed.[46]

On at least one occasion during the campaign, Graham served as a liaison to the Christian Right. Following the 1980 Republican convention—the only party convention Graham attended that year—he spent time with vice presidential nominee Bush in Kennebunkport, Maine. A photograph of the visit appeared in the *Washington Post*.[47] At the time, Bush was seeking to amend his identity as a moderate. According to Falwell, Graham called the Moral Majority head following the convention to gauge reaction to Bush as a running mate. "Billy," Falwell recalled answering. "I'll just pray that God will give Ronald Reagan eight years of wonderful health."[48]

Graham possessed a discernible comfort level with the Reagan White House, where he spent a number of evenings, as well as a few mornings.[49] The evangelist welcomed the prospect of visible demonstrations of faith from the administration, praying at an inauguration-day church service attended by the Reagans.[50] His ears perked up at rumors that Reagan was considering a renewal of Nixon's controversial White House religious services.[51] Through the impetus of presidential counselor Ed Meese and cabinet member Don Hodel, the evangelist hosted a breakfast for White House officials in 1985.[52] Graham corresponded with the president, Nancy Reagan, and staffers on numerous occasions, and felt comfortable leaning on both Reagans for personal favors. In 1987, for example, Reagan asked French president François Mitterand to meet with Graham during an upcoming crusade.[53]

In most cases, Graham's communication with the White House lacked the partisan content of his interactions with the Nixon administration. While Reagan knew he could expect Graham's "support and friendship . . . to make that new beginning we all desire," he did not jump at advice from staffers that appearances at crusade services might boost his status among mainstream evangelicals or even bolster his tax-cut proposals.[54] Those aides knew enough to differentiate between Graham's brand of evangelicalism and the strident conservatism of the Moral Majority.[55]

On several occasions, mostly during Reagan's first term, Graham privately lobbied on behalf of particular political issues. Even in late 1980, before the president took office, Graham put in a good word on behalf of Nixon-era acquaintance Alexander Haig, whom Reagan had nominated as secretary of state.[56] The evangelist was particularly useful in Reagan's continued efforts to retain the support of the Christian Right without acting on its core agenda. One issue of concern involved a proposal to grant full diplomatic status to the Vatican, an issue that had riled conservative Protestants for several decades. In 1982 or 1983, National Security Adviser William Clark asked Graham to gauge the likely response of conservative evangelicals to a policy of recognition. The request reprised one of the evangelist's roles in the Nixon administration. Graham and an aide contacted prominent mainstream evangelicals, including the editor of *Christianity Today*, as well as Christian Right leaders, such as Falwell and Robertson. In a detailed report, Graham hesitated to offer a formal policy recommendation but noted a perceived decline in anti-Catholic sentiments among evangelicals.[57]

The evangelist served a similar liaison function in the area of weapons policy. Graham's support for nuclear abolition seemingly did not entail opposition to the proliferation of antimissile technology. According to Falwell, Graham encouraged several senators to support Reagan's sale of AWAC defense planes to Saudi Arabia, a policy the Moral Majority rejected as a threat to Israel. A Reagan aide actually cited Graham's position when trying to change the mind of the Moral Majority leader.[58] Reagan wrote to Graham that his opposition to unilateral arms control "will be most useful in . . . anything from AWACS [*sic*] to our disarmament talks with the Soviets."[59]

Graham was not always on the same page with the Reagan administration, however. Most prominently, administration officials strongly opposed Graham's involvement in a 1982 Moscow disarmament conference. The evangelist was one of the highest-profile attendees at the conference (the official title of which likely sent shivers through the *Pravda* copy room: World Conference of Religious Workers for Saving the Sacred Gift of Life from Mutual Catastrophe). Members of the Reagan administration feared (correctly) that the Kremlin would use Graham as a propaganda tool. The most intense opposition came from the U.S. ambassador to the Soviet Union, Arthur Hartman, along with National Security Council (NSC) members, who fretted in a memo that "Billy has been had already" by the Soviets.[60] While Graham resisted administration and other appeals to reconsider his travel plans, he had no personal desire to hinder Reagan's foreign policy. The NSC memo appeared after Graham had already sent two aides to discuss the conference with an administration official, who promptly reported the details to Reagan.[61] Vice President Bush eventually assumed authority over the matter and chose to mediate, rather than resist, Graham's plans. After talking to the evangelist on the phone, Bush briefed a Graham assistant on arms control policy and facilitated what turned out to be an awkward meeting between the evangelist and a group of Siberian Pentecostals who had taken asylum in the U. S. Embassy in Moscow. Graham played a quiet role in negotiations for their emigration.[62]

In the end, the evangelist's foray into antinuclear activism hardly piqued his friends in the White House and the political establishment. (It did, though, raise the ire of conservative columnist George Will, who hyperbolically branded him "America's most embarrassing export.")[63] Henry Kissinger offered Graham advice about his address at the Moscow conference, while Reagan eventually wrote Graham an encouraging letter.[64] Graham's next visit to the Soviet Union, a more extensive preaching tour in 1984, received explicit support from Reagan.[65]

As Reagan shifted toward a policy of engagement with the Soviets, Graham encouraged the president's existing eschatological optimism concerning the fate of communism. "There is no doubt in my mind that there is a quiet religious revival on throughout the Soviet Union, and in much of eastern Europe," Graham wrote to Reagan on the cusp of a December 1987 summit with Soviet president Mikhail Gorbachev. "I think this can be kept in the back of your mind at all times in your dealings with them," Graham added.[66] Reagan soon cited and affirmed Graham's diagnosis during a public question-and-answer session.[67]

During the Reagan years, Graham maintained even closer ties to Vice President and 1988 presidential candidate George H. W. Bush, whom the evangelist had known and admired since the late 1960s. In the early and mid-1980s, Graham became a frequent visitor to the Bush family compound in Kennebunkport, and he was an overnight guest of the vice president two weeks into the Reagan administration.[68] Bush clearly had deep respect for Graham, and their spouses were particularly close.[69] Doug Wead, Bush's adviser on all things evangelical, encouraged the vice president to utilize his ties with Graham. Bush introduced Graham at the start of the 1986 Washington, D.C., crusade.[70] During Bush's successful 1988 presidential campaign, the religiously demure candidate harbored sincere reservations about politicizing his friendship with the evangelist—a point Wead ironically highlighted in a campaign biography of Bush. Readers also learned from a prominent evangelical that Graham considered Bush "the best friend he has in the whole world outside his own immediate staff."[71] During the 1988 campaign, Graham prayed at both the Republican and Democratic conventions but attended the entire GOP meeting. He gave the invocation on the night of Reagan's address and accepted an invitation from the Bush family to be with them during the official nomination.[72] After Bush took office, Graham continued in his roles as friend and spiritual adviser. During the run-up to the 1991 Persian Gulf War, Graham privately and publicly blessed military intervention against Saddam Hussein. He watched television footage of the initial air strikes with the president and the first lady.[73] The Grahams had dinner with the Bushes during their last night in the White House. The following day, Graham prayed a new president, Bill Clinton, into the Oval Office—a reprisal of his role in the transition from Lyndon Johnson to Richard Nixon.[74]

Graham's willingness to identify with President Clinton endures as evidence in favor of his bipartisanship, and garnered no small amount of shock and criticism from antiabortion activists and conservative pundits.[75] It reflected Graham's status as an elder minister publicly committed to nonpartisanship. With the exception of the 1976 Carter inauguration, he had been involved in every inaugural day since Johnson's in 1965.[76] Moreover, Graham was reciprocating the dually sincere and politic generosity of Clinton, who had specifically sought an audience with Graham at a National Governors

Convention in 1985. The two remained on good terms throughout the Clinton presidency.[77]

Graham notably did not follow most public evangelicals in railing on the social policies and personal transgressions of Clinton. Appearing on the *Today Show* two months into the 1998–99 Monica Lewinsky scandal, Graham offered pastoral forgiveness to the president. The evangelist cited "the frailty of human nature," along with the apparent fact that women "just go wild over" over the Arkansan. The remarks drew prompt retorts from conservative pundits Cal Thomas and Bill Bennett, who noted that Clinton had yet even to acknowledge having had sexual relations with the former White House intern.[78]

Yet Graham did not grant Clinton a full pass on the matter of character, the issue that drove so many conservative attacks on the president. Immediately following the *Today Show* flap, Graham adopted a significantly more circumspect tone in a *New York Times* op-ed, titled "The Moral Weight of Leadership." He sandwiched the heart of his message between warnings against reflexively judging his "personal friend for many years" for still-alleged transgressions. Yet he did not wholly depoliticize the president's private life. "A leader's moral character . . . influences the way he or she does his or her job," Graham wrote. "There simply is no such thing as an impenetrable fire wall between what we do privately and what we do publicly." Indeed, he added, "The moral meltdown in our country in part results from a failure of leadership."[79] Graham, to be sure, never went further than to say he was "very disappointed" in President Clinton. He even made a point of sitting with Clinton at a banquet celebrating the seventy-fifth anniversary of *Time* magazine.[80] Still, the *New York Times* piece portended how Graham would respond to the 2000 presidential election.

That Weekend in Kennebunkport (and Beyond)

During the 2000 campaign, Graham's name periodically surfaced in the press coverage of leading Republican contender George W. Bush. The Bush team highlighted the candidate's life-changing 1985 encounter with Graham in Kennebunkport, where the evangelist had spent his customary summer weekend with the extended Bush family. During those weekends, Graham would preach and make himself available to the Bushes for questions about faith matters.[81] The first published account of Graham's influence on George W.

Bush appeared in a 1988 campaign biography of the elder Bush. The younger Bush recalled one family session with Graham that had particularly affected him. The following year, Bush remembered, Graham "made it a point to call me aside and ask how things were going. He took a real interest in me individually, and for that I am forever grateful. It's an example of one man's impact on another person's life. And it was a very strong impact."[82] In George W. Bush's 1999 autobiography, the primary source for most subsequent descriptions of the Graham-Bush encounter, the above events occurred during one visit, climaxing with a stroll at Walker's Point. Their conversation, Bush wrote, "planted a mustard seed in my soul. . . . It was the beginning of a new walk where I would commit my heart to Jesus Christ."[83] Graham has since confirmed that the conversation occurred, although he could not recall any details about his talk with Bush.[84] The evangelist surely administered innumerable annual faith checkups with family friends.

The story gained prominence alongside the political ambitions of George W. Bush. A major facet of those designs entailed wooing the conservative Protestant electorate. Bush had served during his father's 1988 campaign as, in the words of an early biographer, "the family spokesman in the intense and often uncomfortable mating ritual between Team Bush and the Christian Right."[85] George W. Bush's political trajectory required him to repeat that ritual, first during the 1994 Texas gubernatorial race and later during his run for the presidency in 1999–2000. After Bush upset incumbent Democrat Ann Richards for the Texas governorship, Graham prayed at his inauguration. As governor, Bush delivered welcoming remarks at a 1997 Graham crusade in San Antonio.[86]

Bush invoked Graham and the Kennebunkport story from the start of his two-year presidential campaign, during which the candidate successfully repackaged his under-whelming, privileged history as an accessible prodigal son narrative.[87] Bush cast himself as a formerly wayward believer whose recommitment to Christ had given him direction and a sense of decency. On the same weekend when Bush launched his campaign exploratory committee, he delivered two identical sermons before a prominent Southern Baptist congregation in Houston. Bush noted how Graham had inspired him "to search my heart and recommit my life to Jesus Christ." The Houston sermons and subsequent addresses employed language that closely echoed Graham's evangelical social ethic—namely, his belief that regenerated hearts, not the imposition of positive law, represented the ultimate answer to myriad social ills. "To truly change the culture, we must have a spiritual renewal in the United

States," Bush declared. "Faith is a powerful tool for change," he also argued, one that could solve problems immune to prescriptive government programs.[88] Bush tapped into the evolving social consciousness of a modern American evangelicalism now undertaking innovative forms of "social concern" in such areas as hunger relief and prisoner rehabilitation. His campaign soon subsumed such efforts, sanitized of their evangelical exclusivity, under the banner of "compassionate conservatism."[89] Compassionate conservatism sought in part to bend the public sector toward a faith-based theory of social change. The electoral usefulness of the slogan, however, lay in its prescriptive repackaging of a familiarly conservative critique of the liberal state, one that Graham had offered (generally in less partisan tones) since the 1950s and 1960s.

Graham received mention in many, if not most, election-year articles concerning Bush's faith journey and outreach to conservative evangelical voters. A Bush intimate informed a campaign biographer that Graham had personally encouraged Bush to seek higher office, "because of where America is today."[90] A campaign mass mailing included a letter in which Bush mentioned his long-standing friendship with Graham.[91] On at least one occasion, Graham publicly vouched for the intellect of the politically inexperienced candidate, as well as his integrity in the face of investigations into his booze-filled young adulthood. "There's a depth to him that I think [journalists] overlook," the *New York Times* quoted Graham as saying. "They think he's a man of little substance, but that's not true. I think that he's a man of tremendous moral character to begin with, and what they have written about his earlier years could be true of nearly all of us."[92]

Two days before the 2000 election, Graham went a step further and declared his support for a Bush victory. The setting for what can only be called Graham's endorsement of Bush was Jacksonville, Florida, located in a state where the evangelist was wrapping up a three-day crusade and where Bush had staked his electoral prospects. On October 25, Doug Wead sent the candidate a strongly worded memo urging him to contact Graham about attending the crusade.[93] The idea took on new meaning a week later, as Bush found himself fending off a late slip in the polls following the disclosure of a previously unacknowledged 1976 arrest for drunk driving. Already, when introducing Florida governor Jeb Bush on the first day of the crusade, Graham had come close to declaring his preference for president. Two days later, on Sunday, November 5, Graham met with George and Laura Bush for a private prayer breakfast. The gathering took place after Bush had attended a

worship service with prominent Florida evangelicals and before he commenced a whirlwind final tour of the state. Jeb Bush made sure to mention
the breakfast on the Sunday morning news show *Face the Nation*. "I'm confident that Dr. Graham will be able to purge all that evilness from my brother's soul," the candidate's brother quipped, referring to the good-versus-evil
rhetoric of Democratic nominee Al Gore. After the prayer meeting, Graham
(accompanied by his son, Franklin) posed with the Bushes for photographs
and talked with reporters. "I don't endorse candidates. But I've come as close
to it, I guess, now as any time in my life, because I think it's extremely
important," said the aging evangelist. "It's comforting to be with a close
friend," Bush noted, before briefly recalling that weekend in Kennebunkport.
Graham further affirmed the character of Bush, who faced accusations of
covering up his drunk-driving arrest. "I believe in the integrity of this man,"
Graham told reporters, insinuating that he had cast an absentee ballot for the
Republican candidate. "I'll just let you guess who I voted for," he added,
making sure (as he had during the Nixon years) to reiterate his status as a
registered Democrat.[94]

Graham's remarks, which would have generated front-page headlines
during the 1950s, 1960s, or 1970s, received only modest coverage from a print
media more attuned to last-minute poll data. The national papers ignored
the portion of his comments that most resembled a traditional endorsement.
"And we believe," Graham had said on behalf of his family, "that there's
going to be a tremendous victory and change by Tuesday night in the direction of the country—putting it in good hands. . . . And if [George and
Laura], by God's will, win, I'm going to do everything in my power to help
make it a successful presidency."[95] The prayer breakfast details (the timing of
the arrest story excepted) later received prominent reprisal in a reelection year
homage to Bush's piety.[96]

At this late stage in Graham's career, he did not play a prominent role
in the Bush administration. Franklin Graham filled in for his ill father at the
first Bush inauguration. The elder Graham retained his role as national pastor, now mostly in an emeritus capacity. Three days after the terrorist attacks
of September 11, 2001, Graham spoke at the National Day of Prayer and
Remembrance at the National Cathedral, where he comforted the audience
and asserted God's love and relevance in the face of the terrorists' "twisted
and diabolical schemes." In January 2005, Graham was healthy enough to
pray at an ecumenical church service following Bush's second inauguration.[97]
The evangelist largely retreated from the public eye following the passing of

his wife Ruth in 2007. Still, his name surfaced during the 2008 presidential campaign, when presumptive Republican nominee John McCain traveled to Montreat for an private but well-publicized meeting with Billy and Franklin Graham. The meeting, which came at the request of McCain, occurred at a time when the candidate was attempting to shore up his standing among conservative evangelical voters while also distancing himself from endorsements by controversial Christian Right ministers.[98]

Remembering Graham

Three decades after Watergate, Graham's legacy stood secure. By altering his stances on some issues and his tone on others, he had accomplished a notable feat: disassociating himself in the popular imagination from his own political leanings. The result was a watershed in how secular observers interpreted Graham. A 1984 analysis of popular evangelicalism dedicated several pages to detailing Graham's self-described "pilgrimage" toward a more international-ist, holistic understanding of the relationship between faith and social ac-tion.[99] Similar portraits continued into the next century. Graham had developed more enlightened views on foreign policy, just as he had earlier embraced desegregation in his southern services. Prodded by Graham, the mainstream American media correctly avoided classifying him with the Christian Right. Indeed, as the Christian Right grew in prominence, the evangelist sometimes hardly looked conservative at all. However, just as Gra-ham's impact on the South was more than the sum total of his desegregated services, so his later significance entailed more than his distance from the Christian Right. His legacy, in part, remains intertwined with that of Ameri-can conservatism.

Graham's intimacy with Reagan and both Bushes begs the question of his perceived status as a counterweight to the Christian Right. To what extent did Graham represent a sustainable alternative to Jerry Falwell, Pat Robert-son, and their peers? Graham was more successful in distinguishing himself from the Christian Right than in checking its growth. The movement, in fact, sprang from Sunbelt soil that Graham had tilled. Indeed, the Christian Right ascended only after its spokespersons had walked a path Graham had modeled: departing from Jim Crow without accepting liberal theology or politics.

In this sense, Graham ultimately reflected and influenced the evolution not only of American evangelicalism but also of American conservatism. His post-Watergate pilgrimage modeled an important yet underappreciated strand of American conservatism that learned to speak a compassionate language of postracialism and international humanitarianism without abandoning a profound wariness of the liberal state. Many American evangelicals have followed Graham toward a greater appreciation for such issues as racial justice, AIDS relief, and environmentalism (and, of course, Graham himself followed the lead of other evangelicals in altering his own perspectives). Programmatically, Graham's legacy has received expression in the work of Samaritan's Purse, an international relief organization led by his son and heir apparent, Franklin, and in the recent willingness of certain theologically conservative evangelicals to address global warming.[100] Because the specter of the Christian Right looms over almost any treatment of recent evangelical faith and politics, it is tempting to remove the above story from the history of American conservatism. Doing so would be a mistake.

The George W. Bush era revealed the ways in which a malleable politics of decency can operate with some comfort under the big tent of modern American conservatism. The hyperpoliticization of conservative Protestantism under Bush undermined the very distinction between fundamentalism and conservative evangelicalism upon which arguments for Graham as a counterpoint to the Christian Right have at some level relied. During the first six years of the Bush administration, issues like terrorism and judicial appointments drove such certified evangelical practitioners of social concern as Charles Colson and Franklin Graham toward an antisecular rhetoric scarcely differing in content from the Christian Right proper.[101] The legacy of Billy Graham, then, looked different from the vantage point of a Bush presidency that had in important ways subsumed the diverse political agendas of conservative Protestants. Graham may have decried the tone of politicized conservative Christianity, yet he had assisted the Christian statesmen who most benefited from that same phenomenon. In this respect, his legacy speaks to the endurance of a broad evangelical conservatism (of which the Christian Right is but one part) without which the full history of the modern American conservative movement cannot be told.

While Graham's political leanings appear somewhat obvious in retrospect, they often came across much less pointedly or controversially to the many Americans who encountered the evangelist primarily through his radio shows, television specials, and newspaper columns. A smaller number had the privilege of attending a crusade service. Through these forums, Graham gained, and rarely lost, the ears of multiple publics. Most of his supporters interpreted him as an evangelist and nothing else, a reality that makes a sensitive consideration of his full political cultural significance something of a challenge. For many Americans, southerners and non-southerners alike, Graham reaffirmed and reinvigorated their basic assumptions about faith, family, and country. His persistent popularity was in no small part the product of his overall flexibility and relative inclusiveness. With several important exceptions, the Nixon years being the most obvious one, Graham largely evaded extended criticism, even from many religious and political liberals. His astounding run of appearances on the Gallup poll's "Most Admired" list (forty-eight times from 1948 to 2004) was the subject of a clue on the television quiz show *Jeopardy.*[102]

This is not to say that Graham made no enemies, as this book has made clear. During the decades of his greatest influence, his best friends and fiercest critics both hailed from his home region of the South. Diehard southern segregationists (and, with them, many fundamentalists) especially disparaged Graham during the years between 1956, when he heeded Dwight Eisenhower's request to play a more direct role in southern race relations, and 1965, when he visited strife-torn Alabama at the urging of Lyndon Johnson. For certain defenders of Jim Crow, Graham stood as a regional traitor, a political prostitute, and even a "nigger lover." Yet the southern Right remained split in its responses to Graham, who kept the attention of many other segregationists. His ability to retain this audience derived from his asserted identity as a southerner, his privileged position as an evangelist, and his social ethic of evangelical universalism, which (unlike liberal or prophetic Christianity) was resistant to charges of secularism or radicalism but also hesitant to single out Jim Crow for unique condemnation. Graham could question certain southern shibboleths by way of affirming other ones. Such was the slippery but significant sociopolitical space that Graham occupied in many facets of his career.

What, finally, does this story—a tale of the intersection of evangelicalism, race, politics, and regional transformation—tell us about Graham and the South? Someone in his position, who possessed both the common touch and the support of kings, was peculiarly well positioned to help shepherd his region, however ambiguously, into a new era. Moving comfortably in many spheres, Graham's role was often indirect and sometimes symbolic. In many cases, though, it was also intentional. His influence derived from his seeming authenticity and his established identity, allowing him gracefully to change particular positions and artfully to avoid specifics about more controversial subjects—all in a manner elected politicians might have envied. Graham was a desegregationist who later criticized Martin Luther King, Jr., a southern strategist who had earlier supported Lyndon Johnson. Yet the evangelist retained a degree of consistency that has proven persistently frustrating to most of his critics and deceptively straightforward to more sympathetic interpreters. Graham's central theme never altered; the evangelist preached Christ crucified and resurrected, with salvation through Him available to all who would invite Him into their hearts. The message remained familiar, even while its context shifted dramatically—even as Graham's childhood homestead evolved into an IBM officeplex.

Yet that conventional image of modernization offers only a partial metaphor for a South that has demonstrated its own forms of continuity amid change. In May 2007, the three living former presidents traveled to Charlotte to dedicate the new Billy Graham Library, which will be the final resting place for Billy and Ruth Graham. Presidents Clinton and Carter touted the influence of Graham's desegregated crusades in the South, while George H. W. Bush spoke of the evangelist's influence behind the Cold War Iron Curtain. Looking over the audience, Clinton jokingly noted that he and Carter stood out as Southern Baptists who were also Democrats. Located on the grounds of the Billy Graham Evangelistic Association, four miles from the dairy farm where Graham came of age, the 40,000-square-foot complex was constructed at a cost of $27 million. The Graham family farmhouse is now the first stop for library visitors. Its previous owner was televangelist Jim Bakker, who had relocated it to his now defunct religious theme park, Heritage USA.[103] In the post–civil rights era South, skyscrapers, sports arenas, megachurches, and many other monuments to prosperity have arisen. Racial traditions have waned and political loyalties have switched. Many faiths, however, have remained steadfast.

NOTES

INTRODUCTION. BILLY GRAHAM'S NEW SOUTH

1. Peter J. Boyer, "The Big Tent: Billy Graham, Franklin Graham, and the Transformation of American Evangelicalism," *New Yorker*, 22 August 2005, 42–55 (Clinton quoted on 42, 44). See also *Atlanta Journal-Constitution*, 24 June 2005; and *New York Times*, 27 June 2005.

2. Boyer, "Big Tent," 44. For other responses to the New York crusade, see *New York Times*, 26 June 2005 and 12 June 2005. John Meacham, "God, the Bushes, and Billy Graham," *Newsweek* online article, 11 April 2006, <http://www.msnbc.msn.com/id/12271894/site/newsweek> (accessed 3 April 2007). See also Meacham, "Pilgrim's Progress," *Newsweek*, 14 August 2006, 37–43. Will D. Campbell and James Y. Holloway, "An Open Letter to Dr. Billy Graham," *Katallagete*, Winter 1971, inside cover–3. *Columbia* (S.C.) *State*, 12 October 1958.

3. White House conversation 662–4, 1 February 1972, National Archives and Records Administration, Nixon Presidential Materials. *New York Times*, 4 April 2002, 17 March 2002, and 12 June 2005. Strawberry Saroyan, "Christianity, the Brand," *New York Times Magazine*, 16 April 2006, 48.

4. *Atlanta Constitution* and *Florida Times-Union*, 6 November 2000.

5. Billy Graham, *Just as I Am: The Autobiography of Billy Graham* (New York: HarperCollins, 1997), 584–587. Jim McGrath, ed., *Heartbeat: George Bush in His Own Words* (New York: Scribner, 2001), 134.

6. Joe E. Barnhart, *The Billy Graham Religion* (Philadelphia: Pilgrim Press, 1972), 62–63.

7. The term *post–civil rights era* comes from political scientist Alexander P. Lamis, *The Two-Party South* (New York: Oxford University Press, 1984), vii. I use the term in reference to the period starting when federal civil rights legislation entered into nominal force and the politics of "massive resistance" had largely run its course (i.e., the late 1960s and early 1970s). This period has seen three striking trends: the growth of African-American involvement in Democratic Party politics, the rise of Republican Party influence in state congressional delegations and legislatures, and the electoral salience of gender-based issues not explicitly (but sometimes implicitly) linked with race.

"Solid South" is employed both in its traditional sense (i.e., in reference to the historic power of the Democratic Party in the region) and in reference to the region's network of Jim Crow laws and enforced racial mores. The latter usage draws inspiration from the title of a classic volume of southern religious historiography: Samuel S. Hill et al., *Religion and the Solid South* (Nashville: Abingdon Press, 1972). On the former usage, see, among many examples, Dewey Grantham, *The Life and Death of the Solid South: A Political History* (Lexington: University Press of Kentucky, 1988). As used here, the persistently contested term "the South" builds on the above understanding of the Solid South. In broad terms, the South includes those states where both exhaustive Jim Crow laws and, in most cases, the segregationist wing of the Democratic Party were dominant until the post–civil rights era. This definition includes large portions of the "border" or "rim" states, such as Texas and Kentucky. The "Upper South" includes Virginia, North Carolina, Tennessee, Arkansas, and parts of the border/rim states. The "Deep South" generally refers to South Carolina, Georgia, Alabama, Mississippi, and Louisiana.

8. On this electoral demographic, see Matthew D. Lassiter, *The Silent Majority: Suburban Politics in the Sunbelt South* (Princeton, N.J.: Princeton University Press, 2006), 229–241.

9. William G. McLoughlin, *Billy Graham: Revivalist in a Secular Age* (New York: The Ronald Press, 1960). See, for example, Barnhart, *Graham Religion*; Lowell D. Streiker and Gerald S. Strober, *Religion and the New Majority: Billy Graham, Middle America, and the Politics of the 70s* (New York: Association Press, 1972); James Morris, *The Preachers* (New York: St. Martin's Press, 1973), 367–387; Charles P. Henderson, *The Nixon Theology* (New York: Harper & Row, 1972); and Marshall Frady, *Billy Graham: A Parable of American Righteousness* (Boston: Little, Brown, 1979). See also the significantly less reliable work, Chuck Ashman, *The Gospel According to Billy* (Secaucus, N.J.: Lyle Stuart, 1977).

10. Stephen J. Whitfield, *The Culture of the Cold War*, 2nd edition (Baltimore: Johns Hopkins University Press, 1996), 77–82. Joel A. Carpenter, *Revive Us Again: The Reawakening of American Fundamentalism* (New York: Oxford University Press, 1997), 211–232.

11. William Martin's 1991 biography, which remains the definitive work on the evangelist's full career, documents many of his activities in the South but focuses more on his progressive movement toward evangelical ecumenism. William Martin, *A Prophet with Honor: The Billy Graham Story* (New York: William Morrow, 1991). Elsewhere, Martin linked Graham with the origins of the modern Christian Right. See Martin, *With God on Our Side: The Rise of the Religious Right in America* (New York: Broadway, 1996). Two dissertations provide valuable insights into Graham's social ethic. See Jerry Berl Hopkins, "Billy Graham and the Race Problem, 1949–1969" (Ph.D. dissertation, University of Kentucky, 1986); and Eric J. Paddon, "Modern Mordecai: Billy Graham in the Political Arena, 1948–1980" (Ph.D. dissertation, Ohio University, 1999).

Three portents of a renaissance of scholarship on Graham are David L. Chappell, *A Stone of Hope: Prophetic Religion and the Death of Jim Crow* (Chapel Hill: University of North Carolina Press, 2004); Andrew Finstuen, "Hearts of Darkness: American Protestants and the Doctrine of Original Sin, 1945–1965" (Ph.D. dissertation, Boston College,

2006); and a forthcoming biography of Graham by historian Grant Wacker. A more critical perspective can be found in Michael G. Long, *Billy Graham and the Beloved Community: America's Evangelist and the Dream of Martin Luther King, Jr.* (New York: Palgrave Macmillan, 2006), 5–7. A recent work by two *Time* magazine journalists is a rich source of information about Graham's relationship with presidents, presented from the vantage point of the close of his evangelistic career. Nancy Gibbs and Michael Duffy, *The Preacher and the Presidents: Billy Graham in the White House* (New York: Center Street, 2007).

12. John Shelton Reed, "The Twenty Most Influential Southerners of the Twentieth Century," *Southern Cultures*, Spring 2001, 96–100.

13. For the former, see "Special Section: The South Today," *Time*, 27 September 1976, 28–99; and Peter Applebome, *Dixie Rising: How the South Is Shaping American Values, Politics, and Culture* (New York: Random House, 1996). For the latter, see Dan T. Carter, *The Politics of Rage: George Wallace, the Origins of the New Conservatism, and the Transformation of American Politics*, 2nd edition (Baton Rouge: Louisiana State University Press, 2000); Kevin M. Kruse, *White Flight: Atlanta and the Making of Modern Conservatism* (Princeton, N.J.: Princeton University Press, 2005); and Joseph Crespino, *In Search of Another Country: Mississippi and the Conservative Counterrevolution* (Princeton, N.J.: Princeton University Press, 2007).

14. D. G. Hart, *Deconstructing Evangelicalism: Conservative Protestantism in the Age of Billy Graham* (Grand Rapids, Mich.: Baker Academic, 2004). Others have criticized the use of evangelicalism in a southern context. See the contribution of Beth Barton Schweiger in "Forum: Southern Religion," *Religion and American Culture* 8, no. 2 (Summer 1998): 161–166; and Donald G. Mathews, " 'Christianizing the South'—Sketching a Synthesis," in *New Directions in American Religious History*, ed. D. G. Hart and Harry S. Stout (New York: Oxford University Press, 1997), 102–107.

15. The understanding of evangelicalism employed here draws inspiration from historian George M. Marsden's description of evangelicalism as a highly informal "denomination" that can be defined in three alternating and overlapping manners: as "a conceptual unity" marked by a commitment to certain Christian principles; as a broad "movement" linked by common histories and directions; and as a "consciously organized community or movement." Marsden, "Introduction: The Evangelical Denomination," in *Evangelicalism and Modern America*, ed. Marsden (Grand Rapids, Mich.: Eerdmans, 1984), vii–xix. For a historical overview of American evangelicalism, see D. G. Hart, *That Old-Time Religion in Modern America: Evangelical Protestantism in the Twentieth Century* (Chicago: Ivan R. Dee, 2002).

16. Michael J. McClymond's definition of revivalism is applied here: " 'Revivalism' is a spiritual movement within Christianity that calls individuals to make a self-conscious decision to repent of sin and believe the gospel, and thereby seeks to bring them an assurance of being in the right or proper relationship with God, and integrate them into a community with other like-minded individuals." See McClymond, "Issues and Explanations in the Study of North American Revivalism," in *Embodying the Spirit: New Perspectives on North American Revivalism*, ed. McClymond (Baltimore: Johns Hopkins

University Press, 2004), 10. In the case of Graham's brand of evangelism, revivalism refers specifically to the organized expression (largely via public services or their broadcasts) of these goals.

17. In the context of southern Christianity, where Southern Baptists in particular have retained a discrete, decidedly nonecumenical identity, such scholars as Samuel S. Hill have identified a general southern evangelicalism focused on conversion and the "regeneration of human hearts." Hill, *Southern Churches in Crisis Revisited* (Tuscaloosa: University of Alabama Press, 1999), 114.

18. Several leading historians of American evangelicalism have, with varying degrees of intentionality, treated its northern expressions as normative. See, for example, Marsden, *Fundamentalism and American Culture: The Shaping of Twentieth-Century Evangelicalism, 1870–1925* (New York: Oxford University Press, 1980). Because Graham often stands as the benchmark for delineating American evangelicalism, some historians have, in effect, presented him as a northern evangelical who happened to have a southern background. Such biases may explain why a major historian of Southern Baptists could scarcely mention Graham in an otherwise comprehensive study of the conservative takeover of the Southern Baptist Convention. See Carpenter, *Revive Us Again*; Hart, *Deconstructing Evangelicalism*; and Barry Hankins, *Uneasy in Babylon: Southern Baptist Conservatives and American Culture* (Tuscaloosa: University of Alabama Press, 2002).

19. On related themes, see Martin E. Marty, "The Revival of Evangelicalism and Southern Religion," in *Varieties of Southern Evangelicalism*, ed. David Edwin Harrell (Macon, Ga.: Mercer University Press, 1981), 7–21. Beth Barton Schweiger, "Max Weber in Mt. Airy, Or, Revivals and Social Theory in the Early South," in *Religion in the American South: Protestants and Others in History and Culture*, ed. Schweiger and Donald G. Mathews (Chapel Hill: University of North Carolina Press, 2004), 31–66. Evangelical Christianity, Marty argued, has served as "the characteristic Protestant (and, eventually and by indirection, Christian) way of relating to modernity" in the United States (9). One might also speak of evangelicalism's capacity to create modern change. What Schweiger writes about the antebellum South applies equally to the times of Billy Graham: "The history of Protestant revivals in the South indicts any understanding that pits religion against modernity" (34). In other words, as most sociologists of religion now believe, modernization does not reflexively equate with secularization. On the decline of secularization theory, see R. Stephen Warner, "Work in Progress Toward a New Paradigm for the Sociological Study of Religion in the United States," *American Journal of Sociology* 98, no. 5 (March 1993): 1044–1093; and William H. Swatos, Jr., and Kevin J. Christiano, "Secularization Theory: The Course of a Concept," *Sociology of Religion* 60, no. 3 (Fall 1999): 209–228. Modernization and modernity are used here very generally in a developmentalist sense (i.e., as the process or result of moving away from "traditional" social and/or economic structures and toward something identified as modern). In the political and industrial history of the twentieth-century South, modernization entailed a language of progress and advancement—a certain comfort with change or, somewhat more complexly, a desire to mediate or control that change. Regarding religion in the South, the point here

is that evangelical Christianity was not a casualty of modernization. On the political language of modernization, see Paul Luebke, *Tar Heel Politics 2000* (Chapel Hill: University of North Carolina Press, 1998).

20. Samuel S. Hill, a path-breaking scholar of southern religion, was the founding father of the crisis motif. See Hill, *Crisis*, esp. 193–211; Hill et al., *Solid South*; Rufus B. Spain, *At Ease in Zion: A Social History of Southern Baptists, 1865–1900* (Nashville: Vanderbilt University Press, 1967); and Andrew Michael Manis, *Southern Civil Religions in Conflict: Civil Rights and the Culture Wars*, 2nd edition (Macon, Ga.: Mercer University Press, 2002). The crisis motif reflected a long and commendable tradition of native southerners using their learned pens to speak truth to the region. The purpose here is not to question the value of such prophetic engagement; it endures because of the still-truncated nature of political discourse in so much of the South outside academia.

21. Schweiger offers a similar critique in "Max Weber," 37–38 and passim.

22. Marshall Frady, "God and Man in the South," *Atlantic Monthly*, January 1967, 40. Original version of quotation in *Charlotte Observer* and other newspapers (AP), 25 April 1965; all in Billy Graham Center Archives, Collection 360, Reel 30. David R. Goldfield, *Black, White, and Southern: Race Relations and Southern Culture, 1940 to Present* (Baton Rouge: Louisiana State University Press, 1990), 85–86.

23. Those changes, to be sure, may not equate with many scholars' idea of progress. As originally put forth by Hill, the crisis motif rested on one inaccurate prediction: that the silence of the southern white church on social issues would eventually lead to its irrelevance in an evolving region. Few would now question that evangelicalism has continued to thrive in the South. This is true in part because its relevance for many southerners remains much more personal than consciously political, but also because many white evangelicals eventually found a middle ground—unsatisfactory to civil rights activists and segregationists alike—on racial matters. Graham helped to create and broadcast this middle ground, which became the public face of much of the modern South. In other words, the faith of white southerners did more than simply abet the conservative status quo. At the very least, it altered the parameters of that status quo.

For an overview of debates about the political cultural influence of white southern Christianity, see Glenn Feldman, "Introduction," in *Politics and Religion in the White South*, ed. Feldman (Lexington: University Press of Kentucky, 2005), 1–10.

24. A helpful definition of political culture comes from political scientist Richard W. Wilson: "a set of values that stabilize institutional forms and hierarchical social relationships in terms of ethical constructs; over time these values reflect developmental changes in individual psychology and in social norms of legitimation; they evolve as a consequence of the interaction between them." Wilson, *Compliance Ideologies: Rethinking Political Culture* (New York: Cambridge University Press, 1992), 6.

25. Influences for this blending model include Henry Goldschmidt, "Introduction: Race, Nation, and Religion," in *Race, Nation, and Religion in the Americas*, ed. Goldschmidt and Elizabeth McAlister (New York: Oxford University Press, 2004), 3–31. The anthropologists Goldschmidt and McAlister seek to "blur the boundaries between religion

and society without reducing either to a pale reflection of the other—to demonstrate the concrete, empirical foundations of religious discourse and experience, as well as the otherworldly, metaphysical foundations of social order and identity" (21). Two works that fruitfully explore the intersection of faith and political culture are Susan Friend Harding, *The Book of Jerry Falwell: Fundamentalist Language and Politics* (Princeton, N.J.: Princeton University Press, 2000); and Lisa McGirr, *Suburban Warriors: The Origins of the New American Right* (Princeton, N.J.: Princeton University Press, 2001), 217–261.

26. On the "spirituality of the church," see Paul Harvey, *Freedom's Coming: Religious Culture and the Shaping of the South from the Civil War Through the Civil Rights Era* (Chapel Hill: University of North Carolina Press, 2005), 24. Scholar Charles Marsh described the extreme conservative interpretation of soul competency as the "piety of the pure soul." See Marsh, *God's Long Summer: Stories of Faith and Civil Rights* (Princeton, N.J.: Princeton University Press, 1997), 106–112.

27. South Korea in Martin, *Prophet*, 414–419.

CHAPTER 1. "NO SEGREGATION AT THE ALTAR"

Note to epigraphs: Billy Graham, *Just as I Am: The Autobiography of Billy Graham* (New York: HarperCollins, 1997), 425. *Jackson* (Miss.) *Daily News* (UP), 9 July 1952.

1. Charles W. Eagles, "The Closing of Mississippi Society: Will Campbell, *The $64,000 Question*, and Religious Emphasis Week at the University of Mississippi," *Journal of Southern History* 67, no. 2 (May 2001): 331. See also James W. Silver, *Mississippi: The Closed Society*, 2nd ed. (New York: Harcourt, Brace and World, 1966).

2. Robert Wuthnow, *The Restructuring of American Religion: Society and Faith Since World War II* (Princeton, N.J.: Princeton University Press, 1988), 36–37. James T. Patterson, *Grand Expectations: The United States, 1945–1974* (New York: Oxford University Press, 1996), 327. Martin E. Marty, *The New Shape of American Religion*. New York: Harper, 1959), 31–32 passim.

3. William Martin, *A Prophet with Honor: The Billy Graham Story* (New York: William Morrow, 1991), 112–120.

4. Darren Dochuk, "From Bible Belt to Sunbelt: Plain Folk Religion and Grassroots Politics in the Conservative Southwest, 1940–1980" (Ph.D. dissertation, Notre Dame University, 2005), 1–5, 12n31, 329–331, 342–346. Martin, *Prophet*, 117. James N. Gregory, *The Southern Diaspora: How the Great Migrations of Black and White Southerners Transformed America* (Chapel Hill: University of North Carolina Press, 2005), 224, 228–229.

5. Gregory, *Southern Diaspora*, 228.

6. "Personality," *Time*, 17 November 1952, 47. Graham to Harry Truman, undated [received 23 December 1951], Billy Graham Center Archives (BGCA), Collection (CN) 74, Box 1, Folder 11 (1–11) [original in Harry S. Truman Presidential Library (HTPL)].

7. Graham, *Just as I Am*, 4–5, 425, 12. Martin, *Prophet*, 61. *Amsterdam News*, 4 July 1964, in BGCA, CN 360, Microfilm Reel 29 (R29).

8. *Oregonian*, 20 August 1950, in BGCA, CN 360, Reel 3 (R3).

9. Graham, "Why Don't Our Churches Practice the Brotherhood They Preach?" *Reader's Digest*, August 1960, 55.

10. Donald E. Hoke, "Knowledge on Fire," *Christian Life*, July 1949, 12, in BGCA, CN 360, R61. Graham, *Just as I Am*, 64.

11. See, for example, Willie Morris, *North Toward Home* (New York: Vintage, 2000 [1967]). Two other writers who fit this category are Robert Penn Warren and William Styron. See Fred Hobson, *But Now I See: The White Southern Racial Conversion Narrative* (Baton Rouge: Louisiana State University Press, 1999), 80–83.

12. Jackson, Mississippi, press conference, 7 May 1975, BGCA, CN 24, 3–34. Paul M. Bechtel, *Wheaton College: A Heritage Remembered, 1860–1984* (Wheaton, Ill.: H. Shaw, 1984), 18–30, 285 and passim.

13. Graham, *Just as I Am*, 64. *Houston Press*, 10 May 1952, in BGCA, CN 360, R5. Curtis Mitchell, *Billy Graham: The Making of a Crusader* (Philadelphia: Chilton Books, 1966), 184, 188. Later, Graham cited a popular visiting professor at Wheaton, as well as "the remote possibility that I might end up on the mission field," as reasons for his major. See Graham, *Just as I Am*, 65.

14. *Boston Post*, 7 January 1950, in BGCA, CN 360, R1. Somewhat ironically, Graham referred to Hooton during his 1950 Boston crusade while criticizing the Harvard anthropologist's defense of euthanasia. Graham called Hooton a "materialist and evolutionist" who did not believe in the Christian God. See *Boston Herald*, 9 January 1950.

15. Earnest Albert Hooton, *Up from the Ape* (New York: Macmillan, 1931), 397, 501, 591–593; and 394–605 passim. Martin, *Prophet*, 84.

16. John C. Pollock, *A Foreign Devil in China: The Story of Dr. L. Nelson Bell, An American Surgeon in China* (Grand Rapids, Mich.: Zondervan, 1971), 9. David L. Chappell, *A Stone of Hope: Prophetic Religion and the Death of Jim Crow* (Chapel Hill: University of North Carolina Press, 2004), 117–121, 140–141.

17. Martin, *Prophet*, 92.

18. Graham, *Just as I Am*, 426.

19. Hobson, *But Now I See*, 2. Billy Graham (with Kurt Singer), "A Southerner Changes His Mind," *Campus Life*, August/September 1970, 54, in BGCA, CN 360, R101.

20. On neo-evangelicalism, see D. G. Hart, *That Old-Time Religion in Modern America: Evangelical Protestantism in the Twentieth Century* (Chicago: Ivan R. Dee, 2002), 115–145; and Joel A. Carpenter, *Revive Us Again: The Reawakening of American Fundamentalism* (New York: Oxford University Press, 1997), 141–232. Mark Silk, "The Rise of the 'New Evangelicalism': Shock and Adjustment," in William R. Hutchinson, ed., *Between the Times: The Travail of the Protestant Establishment in America* (New York: Cambridge University Press, 1989), 285. On the "Second Disestablishment," see Robert T. Handy, *A Christian America: Protestant Hopes and Historical Realities*, 2nd edition (New York: Oxford University Press, 1984), 159–184.

21. Carpenter, ed., *The Early Billy Graham: Sermon and Revival Accounts* (New York: Garland, 1988), 23.

22. Ockenga quoted in Carpenter, *Revive Us Again*, 149.

23. "Billy Graham Speaks at BJU in Greenville," *Little Moby's News*, March–April 1950, in BGCA, CN 360, R1. During the late 1940s, Graham repeatedly flattered Bob Jones in personal correspondence. See Farley P. Butler, "Billy Graham and the End of Evangelical Unity" (Ph.D. dissertation, University of Florida, 1976), 62–63.

24. Carpenter, *Revive Us Again*, 219–220.

25. Barry Hankins: *Uneasy in Babylon: Southern Baptist Conservatives and American Culture* (Tuscaloosa: University of Alabama Press, 2002), 20–21.

26. See Bill J. Leonard, "A Theology for Racism: Southern Fundamentalists and the Civil Rights Movement," in *Southern Landscapes*, ed. Tony Badger et al. (Tübingen, Germany: Stauffenburg Verlag, 1996), 165–181. Barry Hankins has observed how, in the 1970s, a later generation of Southern Baptist conservatives drew inspiration from the neo-evangelical posture of cultural engagement. See Hankins, *Uneasy in Babylon*, 14–40.

27. On Bob Jones Sr., Graham, and race, see Mark Taylor Dalhouse, *An Island in the Lake of Fire: Bob Jones University, Fundamentalism, and the Separatist Movement* (Athens: University of Georgia Press, 1996), 78–84, 155. Jones incorporated race into his theological critique of Graham. See *Greenville* (S.C.) *Piedmont*, 10 September 1957, in BGCA, CN 360, R26.

28. Jerry Berl Hopkins, "Billy Graham and the Race Problem, 1949–1969" (Ph.D. dissertation, University of Kentucky, 1986), 33. *Atlanta Constitution*, 27 November 1950 and 29 November 1950.

29. Martin, *Prophet*, 168–169. Graham, *Just as I Am*, 184.

30. *Pittsburgh Courier*, 18 April 1964, in BGCA, CN 506, 2–10.

31. *New Orleans Weekly*, 9 October 1954, in BGCA, CN 360, R25. Rev. Charles A. Hill to Willis Haymaker, 11 June 1953, BGCA, CN 1, 1–18. Quoted in Hopkins, "Race Problem," 49.

32. Stephen J. Whitfield, *The Culture of the Cold War*, 2nd edition (Baltimore: Johns Hopkins University Press, 1996), 77–82.

33. Silk, *Spiritual Politics: Religion and America Since World War II* (New York: Simon & Schuster, 1988), 66.

34. Promotional poster, November 1947, in BGCA, CN 360, R1. Sermon titles in *Atlanta Constitution*, 7 December 1950, and *Chattanooga Times*, 13 April 1953.

35. Quoted in K. A. Courdileone, *Manhood and American Political Culture in the Cold War* (New York: Routledge, 2005), 82.

36. Charles W. Lowry, *Communism and Christ* (New York: Morehouse-Gorham, 1952), 37. Charles W. Lowry to Truman, 4 March 1952; and Rose A. Conway to Lowry, 7 March 1952; both in BGCA, CN 74, 1–11 (originals in HTPL).

37. *Columbia* (S.C.) *Record*, 4 March 1950, in BGCA, CN 360, R1.

38. Graham to Harry Truman, 18 July 1950; and Graham to Truman, 26 June 1950; both in BGCA, CN 74, 1–11 (originals in HTPL).

39. Eric J. Paddon, "Modern Mordecai: Billy Graham in the Political Arena, 1948–1980" (Ph.D. dissertation, Ohio University, 1999), 61.

40. William G. McLoughlin, *Billy Graham: Revivalism in a Secular Age* (New York: Ronald Press, 1960), 112.

41. Frank Boykin to Graham, 27 February 1953; and Boykin to Sherman Adams, 27 February 1953. Copies in possession of Sam Hodges, *Dallas Morning News* (originals in Alabama Department of Archives and History).

42. For background on Luce, see Robert E. Herzstein, *Henry R. Luce,* Time, *and the American Crusade in Asia* (New York: Cambridge University Press, 2005). On Judd, see Lee Edwards, *Missionary for Freedom: The Life and Times of Walter Judd* (New York: Paragon House, 1990). See contents of Albert C. Wedemeyer Papers, 39–3; and Alfred Kohlberg Papers, 74-"Graham, Billy"; both in Hoover Institution Archives. On Kohlberg, see Joseph Keeley, *The China Lobby Man: The Story of Alfred Kohlberg* (New Rochelle, N.Y.: Arlington House, 1969). On Wedemeyer, see Albert C. Wedemeyer, *Wedemeyer Reports!* (New York: Henry Holt, 1958).

43. See correspondence in BGCA, CN 318, 18–15. Bell to Hollington K. Tong, 7 June 1956, BGCA, CN 318, 52–17. Pollock, *Foreign Devil,* 230.

44. Quoted in Mark G. Toulouse, "*Christianity Today* and American Public Life: A Case Study," *Journal of Church and State* 35, no. 2 (Spring 1993): 269.

45. On Southern Baptist missionaries and race, see Mark Newman, *Getting Right with God: Southern Baptists and Desegregation, 1945–1995* (Tuscaloosa: University of Alabama Press, 2001), 129–149; and Alan Scott Willis, *All According to God's Plan: Southern Baptist Missions and Race, 1945–1970* (Lexington: University Press of Kentucky, 2005).

46. Unidentified clippings (likely from Augusta, Georgia, newspaper), 10 October 1950, in BGCA, CN 360, R1.

47. Mary L. Dudziak, *Cold War Civil Rights: Race and the Image of American Democracy* (Princeton, N.J.: Princeton University Press, 2000), 3–17 (quoted on 12).

48. Jeff Woods, *Black Struggle, Red Scare: Segregation and Anti-Communism in the South, 1948–1968* (Baton Rouge: Louisiana State University Press, 2003), 1–11 (quoted on 2).

49. Graham, "No Color Line in Heaven," *Ebony,* September 1957, 102.

50. The understanding of racial moderation employed here refers specifically to a southern context and draws influence from historian William H. Chafe's description of white moderates/progressives ("who welcomed an atmosphere of tolerance but did not initiate or endorse change in the racial status quo") and especially from Charles Eagles's description of Raleigh, North Carolina, newspaper editor Jonathan Daniels (who "advocated [a] cautious, compromising, prudent approach to change" and who "counsel[ed] obedience to the law and gradual progress in racial matters"). See Chafe, *Civilities and Civil Rights: Greensboro, North Carolina, and the Black Struggle for Freedom* (New York: Oxford University Press, 1980), 57; and Eagles, *Jonathan Daniels and Race Relations: The Evolution of a Southern Liberal* (Knoxville: University of Tennessee Press, 1982), 235.

51. *Columbia* (S.C.) *State,* 26 February 1950, in BGCA, CN 360, R1. See also UP article, 28 February 1950, in BGCA, CN 1, 1–1.

52. Arthur W. Hepner, "Sin and Salvation on the Sawdust Trail," *Everybody's Digest,* July 1950, 26, in BGCA, CN 360, R61.

53. Quoted in Bill Adler, ed., *The Wit and Wisdom of Billy Graham* (New York: Random House, 1967), 141.

54. *Memphis Commercial Appeal*, 18 May 1952.

55. "Sewanee Says No, Billy Graham Says Yes," *Christian Century*, 13 August 1952, 934. On the tumultuous desegregation of the University of the South's School of Theology, see Donald Smith Armentrout, *The Quest for the Informed Priest: A History of the School of Theology* (Sewanee, Tenn.: School of Theology, University of the South, 1979), 279–312.

56. Graham to Ralph McGill, 31 October 1953, Emory University Special Collections, Ralph McGill Papers, 5–9. *Atlanta Constitution*, 24, 25, and 31 May 1954; all in BGCA, CN 360, R24. On McGill, see Harold H. Martin, *Ralph McGill, Reporter* (Boston: Little, Brown, 1973), 132–133, 152, 302–303. On the transformation of post–World War II southern liberalism, see Julia Anne McDonough, "Men and Women of Goodwill: A History of the Commission on Interracial Cooperation and the Southern Regional Council, 1919–1954" (Ph.D. dissertation, University of Virginia, 1994).

57. Online chronology of BGEA events, http://www.wheaton.edu/bgc/archives/bgeachro/bgeachron02.htm (accessed 20 February 2006). Chappell, *Stone of Hope*, 141.

58. William McLoughlin, *Billy Graham: Revivalist in a Secular Age* (New York: Ronald Press, 1960), 163; John Pollock, *Billy Graham: The Authorized Biography* (London: Hodder & Stoughton, 1966), 98; and *America's Hour of Decision* (Wheaton, Ill.: Van Kampen Press, 1951), 57.

59. "The Whiskey Rebellion," *Time*, 20 February 1950, 18. Journalist Robert Sherill attributed to Graham the decision of U.S. Senator Herman Talmaldge (D-Ga.) to give up alcohol. Robert Sherill, *Gothic Politics in the Deep South: Stars of the New Confederacy* (New York: Grossman, 1968), 54.

60. Haymaker to Pollock, 20 May 1965, BGCA, CN 1, 1–5.

61. Herbert Jenkins interview, 8 March 1977, BGCA, CN 141, 4–41. BGCA, CN 74, photograph folders, "BGEA: Atlanta Crusade, 1950: Billy Graham—Atlanta, Ga; Oct. 29–Dec. 3, 1950"; and "BGEA: Columbia Crusade, 1950; Billy Graham—Columbia, South Carolina; Feb–Mar, 1950." Pollock, *Billy Graham*, 104.

62. See, for example, *Jackson* (Miss.) *Clarion-Ledger*, 10 July 1952. *Jackson* (Miss.) *Daily News*, 28 June 1952 and 17 June 1952. See also *Jackson* (Miss.) *Daily News* clipping, 9 July 1952, in BGCA, CN 7, 2–8.

63. *Jackson* (Miss.) *Daily News* (UP), 9 July 1952.

64. *Jackson* (Miss.) *Daily News* clipping, 9 July 1952, in BGCA, CN 7, 2–8.

65. Gerald S. Strober, *Graham: A Day in Billy's Life* (Garden City, N.Y.: Doubleday, 1976), 55. *Jackson* (Miss.) *Clarion-Ledger,* 10 July 1952. Graham to Dr. G. Merrill Lenox, 12 July 1952, BGCA, CN 1, 1–18. *Jackson* (Miss.) *Daily News*, 13 July 1952.

66. Several authors and Graham associates have suggested that the 1952 Jackson crusade was desegregated and/or that the Chattanooga ropes incident actually occurred in Jackson. See Strober, *A Day in Billy's Life*, 55; John Pollock, *To All the Nations: The Billy Graham Story* (San Francisco: Harper & Row, 1985), 105; Russ Busby, *Billy Graham: God's Ambassador* (Alexandria, Va.: Time-Life, Minneapolis: BGEA, and Del Mar, Calif.: Tehabi Books), 212; and *Billy Graham: God's Ambassador* (Nashville, Tenn.: Gaither Films,

2006). Then and during the years immediately following the crusade, however, Graham stated or strongly implied that services there were segregated. For example, see Graham, "Billy Graham Makes Plea for an End to Intolerance," *Life*, 1 October 1956, 144.

67. The Chattanooga account, as treated above and below, is accepted as described by Graham (though likely embellished for narrative effect) in the evangelist's own autobiography. The first reference to the story I have found comes from a 1976 interview with a journalist for the *Augusta* (Ga.) *Chronicle*. "I had to physically take the ropes down in Chattanooga," Graham said. See *Augusta* (Ga.) *Chronicle*, 26 April 1976, in BGCA, CN 360, R26. John Pollock's first authorized biography of Graham, also the first published treatment of the Chattanooga crusade, does not include the ropes story but does note that "Graham told the crusade committee that Negroes must be allowed to sit anywhere." William Martin, who based his description of the Chattanooga crusade in part on conversations with Graham, included the story. See Pollock, *Billy Graham*, 98; and *Crusades: Twenty Years with Billy Graham* (Minneapolis: World Wide Press, 1966), 107–108. Martin, *Prophet*, 169–171, 648.

68. Marshall Frady, *Billy Graham: A Parable of American Righteousness* (Boston: Little, Brown, and Co., 1979), 408.

69. It is possible that a few of Graham's pre-Chattanooga southern services were nonsegregated for the simple reason that the hosting committee did not see fit to establish a separate seating section. See Pollock, *Crusades*, 107–108. Such appears to have been the case with the 1952 Washington, D.C., crusade. Before the start of the crusade, Graham announced that there would be no segregated seating. See Nancy Gibbs and Michael Duffy, *The Preacher and the Presidents: Billy Graham in the White House* (New York: Center Street, 2007), 27. While Washington, D.C., was then in certain respects a southern city, it was also an exceptional one. The city was under federal civil rights jurisdiction and at the time was transitioning away from formalized Jim Crow practices. Holding a segregated crusade in the nation's capital, moreover, might have cost Graham support from congressmen outside the South.

70. *Chattanooga Times* and *Chattanooga News–Free Press*, March–April 1953. Graham, *Just as I Am*, 426.

71. *Billy Graham and the Black Community* (Minneapolis: World Wide Publications, 1973), 10. Susan E. Tiffet and Alex S. Jones, *The Trust: The Private and Powerful Family Behind* The New York Times (Boston: Little, Brown, 1999), 275–276, 329, 407, passim. Frady, *Parable*, 408–409. Pollock, *Billy Graham*, 98.

72. See Haymaker to Harold G. Sanders, 11 November 1960, BGCA, CN 1, 4–18.

73. See "The Greater Dallas Evangelistic Crusade with Billy Graham: *Instructions for Ushers*," undated [1953], BGCA, CN 1, 1–16. See also Pollock, *Billy Graham*, 98. Graham's Asheville crusade, held later in 1953, might have been segregated, as well. See Hopkins, "Race Problem," 51–52.

74. Gibbs and Duffy, *Preacher and the Presidents*, 47.

75. In 1955, Graham informed a Presbyterian seminary professor in Richmond that "due to the racial situation I do not think it would be wise to accept any crusades in the

deep South." Graham to James Appleby, 26 August 1955, BGCA, CN 1, 1–32. Graham received an invitation from a group of Montgomery ministers in 1954. Alfred L. Bixler to Graham, 25 November 1954, BGCA, CN 1, 6–8. In 1954, Graham turned down an invitation to travel to Phenix City, Alabama, a city racked by corruption and violence linked with, among other things, an illicit drug market. One correspondent thought the evangelist could "give the people of our section some reassurance and encouragement at this critical time in our State's history." Oakley Melton Jr. to Jerry Beaven, 5 August 1954, BGCA, CN 1, 6–8. See also *New York World-Telegram and Sun* (AP), 25 August 1954, in BGCA, CN 360, R24; and Hopkins, "Race Problem," 60–61. In 1957, Graham reportedly turned down an invitation to lead several services in Birmingham. See *Selma* (Ala.) *Times-Journal* editorial, published in *Piedmont* (Ala.) *Journal*, 28 June 1957, in BGCA, CN 360, R26.

76. Grady Wilson to J. D. Grey, 27 May 1954, BGCA, CN 1, 1–25.

77. Graham to James M. Gregg, 24 July 1954, BGCA, CN 1, 1–24.

78. Graham to James M. Gregg, 24 July 1954, BGCA, CN 1, 1–24. Gregg interview, 27 February 1979, BGCA, CN 141, 11–15. Albert Rose interview, 27 February 1979, BGCA, CN 141, 14–5.

79. Quoted in David Lockard, *The Unheard Billy Graham* (Waco, Tex.: Word Books, 1971), 121. *Nashville Banner*, August–September 1954.

80. Graham to Appleby, 26 August 1955; and Haymaker to Appleby, 2 September 1955; both in BGCA, CN 1, 1–32. *New Orleans Weekly*, 9 October 1954, in BGCA, CN 360, R25. *Richmond Times-Dispatch*, 30 November 1954, in BGCA, CN 1, 1–32.

81. *Richmond Times-Dispatch*, 19 May 1956 and 25 April 1956. *Kansas City* (Mo.) *Call*, 25 March 1955, in BGCA, CN 360, R25. *Richmond News Leader*, 27 April 1956.

82. Graham, "Plea," 138–151. For more on the article, see Chapter 2.

83. *Birmingham World*, 18 March 1955, in BGCA, CN 360, R25.

84. *Louisville Courier-Journal*, 28 September 1956, 30 September 1956, 4 October 1956, and 22 October 1956. Louisville Crusade committee photograph in "BGEA: Louisville Crusade; Sep 30–Oct 28, 1956," BGCA, CN 1.

85. Chappell, *Stone of Hope*, 145–146, 276–277n52. Graham, *Just as I Am*, 51. Paul Harvey, *Freedom's Coming: Religious Culture and the Shaping of the South from the Civil War Through the Civil Rights Era* (Chapel Hill: University of North Carolina Press, 2005), 192–193.

86. David Edwin Harrell, Jr., "The South: Seedbed of Sectarianism," in *Varieties of Southern Evangelicalism*, ed. Harrell (Macon, Ga.: Mercer University Press, 1981), 53. Harrell wrote primarily in reference to revivalists of a sectarian, Pentecostal-Holiness variety. See also Harrell, *White Sects and Black Men in the Recent South* (Nashville: Vanderbilt University Press, 1971), 100–106.

87. Paul Harvey, "God and Negroes and Jesus and Sin and Salvation: Racism, Racial Interchange, and Interracialism in Southern Religious History," in *Religion in the American South: Protestants and Others in History and Culture*, ed. Donald G. Mathews and Beth Barton Schweiger (Chapel Hill: University of North Carolina Press, 2005), 291–307.

88. On New Orleans, see James B. Bennett, "Catholics, Creoles, and the Redefinition of Race in New Orleans," in *Race, Nation, and Religion in the Americas*, ed. Henry Goldschmidt and Elizabeth McAlister (New York: Oxford University Press, 2004), 183–208. A comprehensive 1956 study conducted by the Fund for the Republic listed Louisville and Oklahoma City—early locations for desegregated Graham crusades—as among the few Jim Crow cities that featured at least token desegregation policies at events ranging from hotel conventions to the state fair. David Loth and Harold Fleming, *Integration North and South* (New York: Fund for the Republic, 1956), 100–101, 106.

89. Jerry Beavan to Graham, 23 September 1955, BGCA, CN 1, 1–34.

90. *New Orleans Weekly*, 9 October 1954, in BGCA, CN 360, R25.

91. "Billy Graham Text," 4 July 1956, FCP, TSLA, 17–6 (R4). Graham specifically cited an incident in Oklahoma City.

92. See, for example, Graham, "'God Is My Witness,'" part III, *McCall's*, June 1964, 146; and Pollock, *Billy Graham*, 288.

93. David R. Goldfield, *Black, White, and Southern: Race Relations and Southern Culture, 1940 to the Present* (Baton Rouge: Louisiana University Press, 1990), 45–49. Numan V. Bartley, *The New South, 1945–1980: The Story of the South's Modernization* (Baton Rouge: Louisiana State University Press, 1995), 175. Loth and Fleming, *Integration North and South*, 68, 72, 105–106.

94. Newman, *Getting Right with God*, 23–24; Joel L. Alvis, Jr., *Religion and Race: Southern Presbyterians, 1946–1983* (Tuscaloosa: University of Alabama Press, 1994), 90.

95. Haymaker to Harold G. Sanders, 11 November 1960, BGCA, CN 1, 4–18. Haymaker apparently had the job of explaining the BGEA's desegregation policy to crusade and rally committees. See also Haymaker to Graham, 26 May 1959, BGCA, CN 1, 6–7.

96. Graham, "No Color Line in Heaven," 100.

97. Graham to C. C. Warren, 20 December 1955, BGCA, CN 1, 4–1.

98. *Columbia* (S.C.) *State*, 26 March 1950, in BGCA, CN 360, R1.

99. Martin, *Prophet*, 131–132.

100. W. D. H. to Connelly, 4 December 1951; Graham to Truman, undated [received 23 December 1951]; W. D. H. to Connelly, 28 December 1951; Graham to Truman, 29 January 1952; and "acm" to Connelly, 31 January 1952; all in BGCA, CN 74, 1–11 (originals in HTPL).

101. Graham to Truman, 18 July 1950, BGCA, CN 74, 1–11 (original in HTPL).

102. Graham, *Just as I Am*, 448.

103. Joseph R. Bryson to John McCormick, 25 May 1950; and presidential schedule, 14 July 1950, BGCA, CN 74, 1–11 (originals in HTPL).

104. Martin, *Prophet*, 143.

105. Sam Hodges, "Political Party Man," *Mobile Press-Register*, 20 December 2001, http://www.al.com/news/mobileregister/index.ssf?/specialreport/mobileregister/boykin_07.html (accessed 24 August 2007).

106. Chappell, *Stone of Hope*, 141.

107. Graham, *Just as I Am*, 188.

108. Martin, *Prophet*, 129.

109. *Columbia* (S.C.) *Record*, 4 and 10 March 1950. *Atlanta Journal*, 28 February 1950. Bartley, *The New South*, 274. *Greenville* (S.C.) *Piedmont*, 20 March 1950, in BGCA, CN 360, R1.

110. AP article, unidentified South Carolina newspaper, 20 March 1950, in BGCA, CN 360, R1; and *Portland Oregonian*, 7 August 1950, in BGCA, CN 360, R3. According to Martin, the invitation to run for the Senate (and possibly for the presidency in 1956) came from "a former member of Roosevelt's cabinet." Martin, *Prophet*, 146. Byrnes was the only Graham intimate who then fell into this category. According to Billy Graham's father, he and Frank Porter Graham were not related but grew up within a few miles of each other. See clipping, *Chattanooga News–Free Press*, 30 August 1952, in BGEA Photo Album IV, BGCA, CN 17.

111. Donald E. Hoke, "Knowledge on Fire," *Christian Life*, July 1949, 9, in BGCA, CN 360, R61. In 1958, Graham told *Holiday* magazine that he had received overtures from political conservatives about running in the Democratic Party primary against the incumbent senator of North Carolina, Kerr Scott. See Noel Houston, "Billy Graham— Part II," *Holiday*, March 1958, 114.

112. James T. Robertson to David Lawrence, 10 November 1951, BGCA, CN 544, 1–1.

113. *American Mercury* clipping, undated (likely mid- or late 1950s), in BGCA, CN 360, R54. Graham contributed to, and received additional praise from, the publication. See, for example, Graham, "Our World in Chaos: The Cause and Cure," *American Mercury*, July 1956, 21–27; and front cover, *American Mercury*, June 1957.

114. *Oklahoma City Times*, 13 June 1957; and *Jamaica* (N.Y.) *L. I. Press*, 23 June 1957; both in BGCA, CN 360, R26.

115. *Northwestern Pilot*, January 1948, in BGCA, CN 360, R61. W. A. Criswell, *Standing on the Promises: The Autobiography of W. A. Criswell* (Waco, Tex.: Word, 1990), 186–188. "Graham Fills Cotton Bowl," undated, unidentified newspaper clipping in Dwight D. Eisenhower Presidential Library, Eisenhower, Dwight D.: Records as President. President's Personal Files. 966-"PPF 1052 Graham, Billy." *Boston Globe*, 27 March 1950, in BGCA, CN 360, R1. Edward B. Fiske, "The Closest Thing to a White House Chaplain," *New York Times Magazine*, 8 June 1969, 113.

116. Carol Flake, *Redemptorama: Culture, Politics, and the New Evangelicalism* (Garden City, N.Y.: Anchor, 1984), 52, 126. Martin, *Prophet*, 300, 135, 139–140. *Dallas Daily Times Herald*, 8 June 1953, in BGCA, CN 360, R5.

CHAPTER 2. EVANGELICAL UNIVERSALISM IN THE POST-BROWN SOUTH

Note to epigraphs: *Hour of Decision* sermon, "Solving Our Race Problems Through Love," 25 August 1963, Billy Graham Center Archives (BGCA), Collection 191 (CN 191), Tape 711c. *Knoxville News-Sentinel*, 15 December 1958.

1. *Baptist Bible Tribune*, 5 July 1968 (reprint of Religious News Service, 24 February

1956). Criswell statements also in Michael Phillips, *White Metropolis: Race, Ethnicity, and Religion in Dallas, 1841–2001* (Austin: University of Texas Press, 2006), 134.

2. *Presbyterian Outlook*, 11 April 1955, in BGCA, CN 360, Reel 25 (R25).

3. *Baltimore Sun*, 5 August 1955; both in BGCA, CN 360, R25.

4. Graham address, Southern Baptist Historical Library and Archives (SBHLA), Christian Life Commission—Minutes, 1956, 1–13. Oklahoma City *Black Dispatch*, 1 June 1956, in BGCA, CN 360, R8. Deletion in *The Christian Index*, 7 June 1956, 7, in SBHLA.

5. Billy Graham, "Billy Graham Makes Plea for an End to Intolerance," *Life*, 1 October 1956, 138–151.

6. Graham to Hugh Moffett, 13 September 1956, BGCA, CN 318, 33–17. Moffet noted that Graham is "doubtful about the wisdom of his writing on this subject now." See "Billy Graham Text," 4 July 1956, Frank Goad Clement Papers (FCP), Tennessee State Library and Archives (TSLA), Box 17, Folder 6 (17–6) (R4). Theologian Reinhold Niebuhr's criticism of the evangelist's social ethic may have provided additional motivation to stick with the *Life* piece. See Andrew Finstuen, "Hearts of Darkness: American Protestants and the Doctrine of Original Sin, 1945–1965" (Ph.D. dissertation, Boston College, 2006), 255, 258n102.

7. Graham, "Plea," 138, 140, 143. The Hamitic curse reads: "Cursed be Canaan; a slave of slaves shall he be to his brothers" (Genesis 9:25, Revised Standard Version). According to some apologists for slavery and, later, some supporters for racial segregation, black Africans descended from Canaan and, hence, constituted a biblically sanctioned servant class. See Stephen R. Haynes, *Noah's Curse: The Biblical Justification of American Slavery* (New York: Oxford University Press, 2002).

8. "Billy Graham Text," FCP, TSLA, R4. *Presbyterian Outlook*, 11 April 1955; and *Baltimore Sun*, 5 August 1955; both in BGCA, CN 360, R25.

9. Graham, "Plea," 144, 140, 143, 138, 146, 151. Historian Alan T. Nolan described the accuracy of this popular story about Lee as "highly unlikely." See Nolan, *Lee Considered: General Robert E. Lee and Civil War History* (Chapel Hill: University of North Carolina Press, 1991), 207. "A Round Table Has Debate on Christians' Moral Duty," *Life*, 1 October 1956, 139–140, 143, 145, 146, 151–152, 154, 159–160, 162.

10. Graham, "Plea," 144, 146.

11. Graham, "No Color Line in Heaven," *Ebony*, September 1957, 99, 100, 102. William Martin, *A Prophet with Honor: The Billy Graham Story* (New York: William Morrow, 1991), 221. Jerry Berl Hopkins, "Billy Graham and the Race Problem, 1949–1969" (Ph.D. dissertation, University of Kentucky, 1986), 79; and *Amsterdam News*, 20 July 1957, in BGCA, CN 360, R26.

12. Quoted in Graham, "Why Don't Our Churches Practice the Brotherhood They Preach?" *Reader's Digest*, August 1960, 53, 54; and "No Solution to Race Problem 'At the Point of Bayonets,'" *U.S. News and World Report*, 25 April 1960 (originally written for UPI), 94.

13. Theologian Harvey Cox quoted in Lewis V. Baldwin, *The Legacy of Martin Luther King, Jr.: The Boundaries of Law, Politics, and Religion* (South Bend, Ind.: University of Notre Dame Press, 2002), 85.

14. Richard J. Carwardine, *Evangelicals and Politics in Antebellum America* (New Haven: Yale University Press, 1993), 1–49.

15. Grant Wacker, "Searching for Norman Rockwell: Popular Evangelicalism in Contemporary America," in *The Evangelical Tradition in America*, ed. Leonard I. Sweet (Macon, Ga.: Mercer University Press, 1984), 295, 311–312.

16. Contrary to historiographical assumptions, this dynamic was present among white Christian leaders in the antebellum South. See Beth Barton Schweiger, *The Gospel Working Up: Progress and the Pulpit in Nineteenth-Century Virginia* (New York: Oxford University Press, 2000).

17. Robert T. Handy, *A Christian America: Protestant Hopes and Historical Realities*, 2nd ed. (New York: Oxford University Press, 1984), 159–184, 194. See also Phillip E. Hammond, *The Protestant Presence in Twentieth-Century America* (Albany: State University of New York Press, 1992), 27–54.

18. Charles E. Hambrick-Stowe, *Charles G. Finney and the Spirit of American Evangelicalism* (Grand Rapids, Mich.: Eerdmans, 1996), 142, 173–174, 267, passim.

19. James F. Findlay, Jr., *Dwight L. Moody: American Evangelist, 1837–1899* (Chicago: University of Chicago Press, 1969), 274–284 (quoted on 283).

20. See David O. Moberg, *The Great Reversal: Evangelism Versus Social Concern* (Philadelphia: J. B. Lippincott, 1972), 28–45.

21. Robert F. Martin, *Hero of the Heartland: Billy Sunday and the Transformation of American Society, 1862–1935* (Bloomington: Indiana University Press, 2002), 101–119, 132–134. See also Lyle W. Dorsett, *Billy Sunday and the Redemption of Urban America* (Grand Rapids, Mich.: Eerdmans, 1991), 153, passim.

22. Hopkins, "Race Problem," 23–24.

23. Sunday quoted in David S. Gutterman, *Prophetic Politics: Christian Social Movements and American Democracy* (Ithaca, N.Y.: Cornell University Press, 2005), 67. Finstuen, "Hearts of Darkness."

24. Bruce Schulman, *Lyndon Johnson and American Liberalism* (Boston: Bedford St. Martin's, 1995), 83.

25. Graham address, SBHLA, Christian Life Commission—Minutes, 1956, Box 1, Folder 13 (1–13).

26. Quoted in David Lockard, *The Unheard Billy Graham* (Waco, Tex.: Word Books, 1971).

27. Derek Chang, "'Marked in Body, Mind, and Spirit': Home Missionaries and the Remaking of Race and Nation," in *Race, Nation, and Religion in the Americas*, ed. Henry Goldschmidt and Elizabeth McAlister (New York: Oxford University Press, 2004), 135.

28. Quoted in Lockard, *Unheard*, 95.

29. "Solving Our Race Problems," BGCA 191, T711e.

30. "LIFE Meeting" address, 19 May 1964, BGCA, CN 1, 6–9.

31. Graham, "A Christian America," *American Mercury*, March 1955, 72, in BGCA, CN 360, R64.

32. Timo Pokki, *America's Preacher and His Message: Billy Graham's View of Conversion and Sanctification* (Lanham, Md.: University Press of America, 1999), 92, 135–143 (quoted on 141).

33. Graham, "Stains on the Altar," 4 November 1966 sermon, BGCA, CN 14, T13.

34. Carl F. H. Henry, *Aspects of Christian Social Ethics* (Grand Rapids, Mich.: Baker Book House, 1964), 16, 25–26. Henry edited *Christianity Today* during the 1950s and 1960s.

35. D. G. Hart, *That Old-Time Religion in Modern America: Evangelical Protestantism in the Twentieth Century* (Chicago: Ivan R. Dee, 2002), 146. The discussion of evangelical social ethics in this chapter and elsewhere is indebted to Dennis P. Hollinger, *Individualism and Social Ethics: An Evangelical Syncretism* (Lanham, Md.: University Press of America, 1982), 40, 111–112, and passim.

36. Henry, *Aspects*, 79.

37. Henry stressed that the "Christian view of society does not require forcing the fruits of regeneration upon unregenerate men. Rather, the Christian view seeks public recognition, in theory and life, of those principles of justice necessary to national stability. With this distinction in mind, Christian believers will know that their primary task is to win individuals to Jesus Christ as Redeemer and Lord, a task not to be confused with misguided attempts to Christianize the world order." See Henry, *Aspects*, 120.

38. Atlanta press conference, 29 December 1967, BGCA, CN 24, T12.

39. Billy Graham service, "God and the Nations," *Hour of Decision* sermon pamphlet (Minneapolis: BGEA, 1964).

40. Anthony Lake Newberry, "Without Urgency or Ardor: The South's Middle-of-the-Road Liberals and Civil Rights, 1945–1960" (Ph.D. dissertation, Ohio University, 1982), 16, passim.

41. On southern moderates, see Calvin Trillin, "Remembrance of Moderates Past," *New Yorker*, 21 March 1977, 86, 85. The classic work on civility among white southern moderates is William H. Chafe, *Civilities and Civil Rights: Greensboro, North Carolina, and the Black Struggle for Freedom* (New York: Oxford University Press, 1980), 6–8, passim. A recent essay views civility as a desperate, largely ineffectual strategy to retain white political supremacy. See Joseph Crespino, "Civilities and Civil Rights in Mississippi," in *Manners in Southern History*, ed. Ted Ownby (Jackson: University Press of Mississippi, 2007), 114–136.

42. Newberry, "Without Urgency or Ardor," 431, 186.

43. For more on the overtly political side of the Graham-Eisenhower relationship, see Chapter 3.

44. Frank Boykin to Eisenhower, 19 March 1956, Dwight D. Eisenhower Presidential Library (EPL), Eisenhower, Dwight D.: Records as President (RP), President's Personal Files (PPF), 966-"PPF 1052 Graham, Billy."

45. Billy Graham Evangelistic Team news release, 22 March 1956, BGCA, CN 1, 6–9. Diary, 20 March 1956; and diary notes, 21 March 1956; both in EPL, Eisenhower, Dwight D.: Papers as President (PP), Ann Whitman Diary Series (AWDS), 8-"March '56 Diary."

46. See Newberry, "Middle-of-the-Road," 323.

47. After hearing a sermon promoting civil rights legislation, Eisenhower told the chaplain of the Navy, "You can't legislate morality." On Eisenhower's response to *Brown*, see Taylor Branch, *Parting the Waters: America in the King Years, 1954–1963* (New York: Touchstone, 1988), 180, 191 (quoted on 213).

48. Eisenhower to Graham, 22 March 1956; and Graham to Eisenhower, 27 March 1956; both in EPL, RP, PPF, 966-"PPF 1052 Graham, Billy."

49. Graham to Eisenhower, 27 March 1956; and Graham to Eisenhower, 4 June 1956; both in EPL, RP, PPF, 966-"PPF 1052 Graham, Billy."

50. Graham to Nixon, 4 June 1956, National Archives and Records Administration, Pacific Region, Laguna Niguel, Richard M. Nixon Pre-Presidential Papers, Series 320, 299-"Graham, Billy." Graham to Eisenhower, 4 June 1956, EPL, RP, 966-"PPF 1052 Graham, Billy."

51. Graham, *Just as I Am: The Autobiography of Billy Graham* (New York: Harper-Collins, 1997), 201. Martin, *Prophet*, 247. "South's Churchmen: Integration and Religion," *Newsweek*, 7 October 1957, 34, 37, in BGCA, CN 360, R67.

52. "South's Churchmen," in BGCA, CN 360, R67. See also "Love and Little Rock," *Hour of Decision* sermon, 29 September 1957, BGCA, CN 191, T403g. *Huntington* (W.Va.) *Advertiser* (AP), 26 September 1957; *Durham* (N.C.) *Sun* (UPI), 26 September 1957; and *Carthage* (Md.) *Evening Press* (AP), 24 September 1957; all in BGCA, CN 360, R26.

53. Quoted in Frye Gaillard, *The Dream Long Deferred* (Chapel Hill: University of North Carolina Press, 1988), 9–10.

54. *Charlotte News*, 24 April 1958, in BGCA, CN 360, R26. Unsigned letter [Willis Haymaker or Jerry Beavan] to Graham, 8 February 1958; and (Miss) "Jackie" Edwards to Haymaker, 6 May 1958; both in BGCA, CN 1, 3–13.

55. *Columbia* (S.C.) *State*, 7 and 12 October 1958. Soldiers in Andrew H. Myers, *Black, White, and Olive Drab: Racial Integration at Fort Jackson, South Carolina, and the Civil Rights Movement* (Charlottesville: University of Virginia Press, 2006), 152–153.

56. See *Birmingham News*, 12 May 1957; *Jackson* (Miss.) *State Times*, 23 June 1957; and *Magee* (Miss.) *Courier*, 4 July 1957; all in BGCA, CN 360, R26.

57. *Atlanta Constitution* (AP), 16 October 1958, in BGCA, CN 360, R26.

58. *Columbia* (S.C.) *State*, 23 October 1958. Myers, *Black, White, and Olive Drab*, 153. On segregationists and church-state separation, see David L. Chappell, *A Stone of Hope: Prophetic Religion and the Death of Jim Crow* (Chapel Hill: University of North Carolina Press, 2004), 139–140. James E. Towns, ed., *The Social Conscience of W. A. Criswell* (Dallas, Tex.: Crescendo, 1977), 226.

59. *Columbia* (S.C.) *State*, 27 and 28 October 1958. *Charlotte Observer*, 27 October 1958, in BGCA, CN 360, R12.

60. The Birmingham address very likely was segregated (it drew advance press as such), yet technically would not have violated Graham's stated policy against holding segregated evangelistic services. See *Oakland Tribune* (UPI), 10 June 1958; *Mobile* (Ala.)

Press (UPI), 17 November 1958; and *Bowling Green* (Ky.) *News* (AP), 21 November 1958; all in BGCA, CN 360, R26.

61. Numan V. Bartley, *The New South, 1945–1980: The Story of the South's Modernization* (Baton Rouge: Louisiana State University Press, 1995), 196, 223–230.

62. Graham, *Just as I Am*, 201–202. Drew Pearson, *Diaries: 1949–1959* (New York: Holt, 1974), 487–488.

63. *Knoxville News-Sentinel*, 15 December 1958.

64. *Knoxville News-Sentinel*, 15 December 1958. Graham, *Just as I Am*, 202. *Nashville Tennessean*, 15 December 1958.

65. Ernest Q. Campbell and Thomas F. Pettigrew, *Christians in Racial Crisis: A Study of Little Rock's Ministry* (Washington, D.C.: Public Affairs Press, 1959), 55–56, 182. See also Graham, *Just as I Am*, 201–202.

66. *El Paso Herald-Post*, 27 September 1957, in BGCA, CN 360, R26. Brooks Hays, *Politics Is My Parish* (Baton Rouge: Louisiana State University Press, 1981), 195.

67. *Columbia* (S.C.) *State*, 16 October 1958.

68. *Arkansas Gazette*, 23 December 1958, in BGCA, CN 360, R26. *Arkansas Gazette*, 6, 9, 10, 12, and 13 September 1959. Campbell and Pettigrew, *Christians in Racial Crisis*, 102.

69. *Arkansas Gazette*, 13 and 14 September 1959. Undated Little Rock rally report [1959], BGCA, CN 19, 5–48. *Arkansas Democrat*, 12 and 14 September 1959.

70. *Arkansas Democrat*, 9 September 1959.

71. On Karam, see Roy Reed, *Faubus: The Life and Times of an American Prodigal* (Fayetteville: University of Arkansas Press, 1997), 190, 226–227. "Filmed Testimony of Jimmy Karam, ca. 1960," BGCA, CN 74, F8. The filmed testimony contradicts Graham's later claim that Karam converted at the New York City crusade. See Graham, *Just as I Am*, 321. *Arkansas Gazette*, 14 September 1959.

72. "Little Rock's Convert," *Time*, 28 September 1959, 42. In 1962, while appearing on "The Today Show," Graham apparently suggested that *Ebony* magazine publish an article on the "new Jimmy Karam." Graham's suggestion rendered both *Ebony* and Arkansas Council on Human Relations nonplussed. Jimmy Karam to Lillian S. Calhoun, 13 December 1962, BGCA, CN 544, 11–1. Unidentified letter to Graham, 27 June 1962, University of Arkansas Special Collections, Arkansas Council on Human Relations Records, 8–82.

73. *Arkansas Democrat*, 10 September 1959. *Arkansas Gazette*, 14 September 1959. *Arkansas Gazette*, 20 September 1959, in BGCA, CN 360, R27.

74. On law and order, see, for example, *Arkansas Gazette*, 28 September 1958, in *Crisis in the South: The Little Rock Story: A Selection of Editorials from the* Arkansas Gazette (Little Rock: *Arkansas Gazette*, 1959), 54. *Arkansas Democrat*, 11 September 1959.

75. Elizabeth Jacoway, "Taken by Surprise: Little Rock Business Leaders and Desegregation," in *Southern Businessmen and Desegregation*, ed. Jacoway and David R. Colburn (Baton Rouge: Louisiana State University Press, 1982), 15–41. David L. Chappell, *Inside Agitators: White Southerners in the Civil Rights Movement* (Baltimore: Johns Hopkins Uni-

versity Press, 1994), 107–118. Chappell focused specifically on law and order, while Jacoway emphasized concerns over the city's image.

76. "A Fifth Column of Decency," *Life*, 30 September 1957. "The Eagle and the Rock," *Life*, 7 October 1957, 48. On the later usage of "law and order," see Michael W. Flamm, *Law and Order: Street Crime, Civil Unrest, and the Crisis of Liberalism in the 1960s* (New York: Columbia University Press, 2005).

77. Graham made the "flag waving" remark in an address to the student body of Asheville High School. See *Alabama Baptist*, 24 September 1959. *Arkansas Gazette*, 14 September 1959.

78. See Frank Boykin to Graham, 2 April 1960. Copy in possession of Sam Hodges, *Dallas Morning News* (original in Alabama Department of Archives and History).

79. Klan in Noel Houston, "Billy Graham—Part II," *Holiday*, March 1958, 114; *Rock Hill* (S.C.) *Herald*, 24 June 1957, in BGCA, CN 360, R26; and *Martinsville* (Va.) *Bulletin*, 9 December 1957, in BGCA, CN 360, R26. Hopkins, "Race Problem," 88–89; and Martin, *Prophet*, 234.

80. "Nation Eyes Dixie Christians," *Christian Life*, June 1956, 13, in BGCA, CN 360, R65. The 1956 flap was not the first time Graham had faced inquiries about First Baptist Church and, by extension, about Criswell. One year earlier, in response to a relatively innocent question from an interviewer who was likely unfamiliar with Criswell, Graham said he doubted that First Baptist would turn nonwhites away from services. See *Presbyterian Outlook*, 11 April 1955, in BGCA, CN 360, R25.

81. *Southern School News*, July 1957, 4. *Biblical Recorder*, 12 March 1966, 11, in BGCA, CN 360, R88.

82. Undated Daniel letter to *Dallas News* [October 1956], enclosed in Tyler W. Payton to Bell, 16 October 1956, BGCA, CN 318, 41–10.

83. *Miami Herald* (AP), 26 August 1962, in BGCA, CN 360, R29.

84. *Albany* (Ga.) *Herald*, 21 July 1957; *Selma* (Ala.) *Times-Journal* editorial, published in *Piedmont* (Ala.) *Journal*, 28 June 1957; and *Miami Life*, 19 October 1957; all in BGCA, CN 360, R26.

85. Quoted in Robert Sherill, *Gothic Politics in the Deep South: Stars of the New Confederacy* (New York: Grossman, 1968), 231.

86. William C. McIntire to L. Nelson Bell, 12 January 1959, BGCA, CN 318, 15–15. Howard Chatham to Graham, 27 September 1957, University of North Carolina at Chapel Hill, Southern Historical Collection, Luther Hodges Papers, Series 5, Subseries 5.3. Margaret Pope to Bell, 24 June 1964 [enclosed in Pope to Ruth Graham, 25 June 1964], BGCA, CN 318, 42–15.

87. *Camden* (S.C.) *Chronicle*, 15 April 1960, in BGCA, CN 360, R27.

88. On Bell, see Chappell, *A Stone of Hope*, 140–141, 117–121; and Michael D. Hammond, "Conscience in Conflict: Neo-Evangelicals and Race in the 1950s" (M.A. thesis, Wheaton College, 2002), 48–83. Tyler W. Payton to Bell, 16 October 1956, BGCA, CN 318, 41–10. Bell to R. D. Littleton, 11 September 1965, BGCA, CN 318, 43–12. Bell to Edward Jones, 21 October 1958, BGCA, CN 318, 15–15. See also Bell to John F. Frierson, 22 July 1957, BGCA, CN 318, 24–25.

89. Towns, ed., *The Social Conscience of W. A. Criswell*, 162–171.

90. The relationship between faith and segregation has garnered no small amount of scholarly back-and-forth. This debate has occurred in the shadow of scholar Samuel S. Hill, who emphasized the extent to which white southern Christianity offered an implicit sanctification of Jim Crow. Samuel S. Hill, *Southern Churches in Crisis Revisited* (Tuscaloosa: University of Alabama Press, 1999). Some scholars have identified more specific, if relatively unsophisticated, forms of theologized racism, which operated most powerfully in the realms of folk sensibility and sexual purity. Paul Harvey, *Freedom's Coming: Religious Culture and the Shaping of the South from the Civil War Through the Civil Rights Era* (Chapel Hill: University of North Carolina Press, 2005), 229–245; and "God and Negroes and Jesus and Sin and Salvation: Racism, Racial Interchange, and Interracialism in Southern Religious History," in *Religion in the American South: Protestants and Others in History and Culture*, ed. Donald G. Mathews and Beth Barton Schweiger (Chapel Hill: University of North Carolina Press, 2004), 287, 285–291 passim. Jane Dailey, "Sex, Segregation, and the Sacred after *Brown*," *Journal of American History* 91, no. 1 (June 2004): 120, 122; 119–144 passim. For an argument on behalf of a more overt form of theological racism, see Bill J. Leonard, "A Theology for Racism: Southern Fundamentalists and the Civil Rights Movement," in *Southern Landscapes*, ed. Tony Badger et al. (Tübingen, Germany: Stauffenburg Verlag, 1996), 165–181. On the other hand, historian David L. Chappell has stressed the general unwillingness of most white southern Christian leaders to risk their theological capital in defense of segregation. Chappell, *Stone of Hope*, 107, 150, 122. Harvey notes a similar phenomenon, yet places its emergence in the 1960s. Harvey, "God and Negroes," 284. A Vanderbilt theologian writing in the early 1960s identified segregationism as fundamentally a "religious issue," yet stressed its "dying spirit" and declining "authentic folk quality." See James Sellers, *The South and Christian Ethics* (New York: Association Press, 1962), 118–128.

91. *Durham Times*, 19 March 1955, in BGCA, CN 360, R25. See, for example, Howard Thurman, *Jesus and the Disinherited* (Boston: Beacon Press, 1976 [1949]).

92. Lewis W. Gillenson, "Billy Graham: Can He Save the World from Sin?" *McCall's*, November 1954, 98, in BGCA, CN 360, R64.

CHAPTER 3. THE POLITICS OF DECENCY

Note to epigraphs: Tom McMahan, *Safari for Souls: With Billy Graham in Africa* (Columbia, S.C.: State-Record Company, 1960), 57. John Stennis to Billy Graham, 4 March 1955, Congressional and Political Research Center, Mississippi State University Libraries, John C. Stennis Collection, Series Yellows-Outgoing Correspondence Copies, 1952–1953.

1. *Salem* [Ore.] *Capitol Journal*, 3 March 1956, in Billy Graham Center Archives (BGCA), Collection 360 (CN 360), Reel 25 (R25).

2. *Durham Times*, 19 March 1955, in BGCA, CN 360, R25. *New York Post* (AP), 21 May 1957, in BGCA, CN 360, R9.

3. Martin Luther King, Jr., to Graham, 31 August 1957, in Clayborne Carson et al., eds., *The Papers of Martin Luther King, Jr.*, volume 4, *Symbol of the Movement, January 1957–December 1958* (Berkeley: University of California Press, 2000), http://www.stan ford.edu/group/King/publications/papers/vol4/contents.htm (accessed 10 January 2007).

4. On Graham and King, see Edward L. Moore, "Billy Graham and Martin Luther King, Jr.: An Inquiry into White and Black Revivalistic Traditions" (Ph.D. dissertation, Vanderbilt University, 1979), 4, 453–468 and passim. Taylor Branch, *Parting the Waters: America in the King Years, 1954–63* (New York: Simon and Schuster, 1988), 219.

Eisenhower may have recommended that Graham contact King in the first place. Tantalizingly vague Eisenhower White House notes allude to a recommended "note to Billy Graham about a Negro Bishop—Dr. Martin Luther King?" King, who was actually a Baptist pastor, was then emerging as the spokesperson for a Montgomery bus boycott. See "Notes dictated by the President after long telephone conversation with Mrs. Oveta Culp Hobby," 21 March 1956, Eisenhower Presidential Library (EPL), Eisenhower, Dwight D.: Papers as President (PP), Ann Whitman Diary Series, Box 8, Folder "March '56 Diary" (8-"March '56 Diary").

5. "As Billy Graham Sees His Role," *New York Times Magazine*, 21 April 1957, 19. "Invocation Delivered at Billy Graham Evangelistic Association Crusade," 18 July 1957, http://www.stanford.edu/group/King/publications/papers/vol4/contents.htm (accessed 10 January 2007).

6. Branch, *Parting*, 227–228.

7. On King's correspondence with southerners, see Lewis V. Baldwin, *The Legacy of Martin Luther King, Jr.: The Boundaries of Law, Politics, and Religion* (South Bend, Ind.: University of Notre Dame Press, 2002), 57–58n48. King to Graham, 31 August 1957, http://www.stanford.edu/group/King/publications/papers/vol4/contents.htm.

8. *New York Times*, 12 March 1956. Prominent segregationist minister Carey Daniel, a Citizens' Council leader from Dallas (and a critic of Graham), was a cousin of the governor. Tyler W. Payton to L. Nelson Bell, 16 October 1956, BGCA, CN 318, 41–10).

9. Graham to Price Daniel, 23 March 1956, Texas State Library and Archives Commission (TSLAC), Sam Houston Regional Library and Research Center (SHRL), U.S. Senator Price Daniel Papers, 104-"Billy Graham."

10. Dan Murph, *Texas Giant: The Life of Price Daniel* (Austin, Tex.: Eakin Press, 2002), 170. James Reston, Jr., *The Lone Star: The Life of John Connally* (New York: Harper and Row, 1989), 464–465.

11. *San Antonio Light*, 5 July 1958, in BGCA, CN 360, R26. King to Graham, 23 July 1958, http://www.stanford.edu/group/King/publications/papers/vol4/contents.htm. (accessed 30 June 2008).

12. Grady Wilson to King, 28 July 1958, BGCA, CN 544, 37–3.

13. UPI, undated [26 July 1958]; *San Antonio Express*, 26 July 1958; *Dallas Times-Herald* (AP), 18 July 1958; all in BGCA, CN 360, R26. Press release, W. Lee O'Daniel, 30 June 1958, TSLAC, SHRL, Texas Governor Price Daniel Campaign Files, 225-"Press Releases, File Copies."

14. Murph, *Texas Giant*, 220.

15. Reinhold Niebuhr, "Literalism, Individualism, and Billy Graham," *Christian Century*, 23 May 1956, 641; and "Proposal to Billy Graham," *Christian Century*, 8 August 1956, 921–922; both in BGCA, CN 360, R65. For a comprehensive treatment of Niebuhr's critique of Graham, see Andrew Finstuen, "Hearts of Darkness: American Protestants and the Doctrine of Original Sin, 1945–1965" (Ph.D. dissertation, Boston College, 2006), 246–263.

16. William Martin, *Prophet with Honor: The Billy Graham Story* (New York: William Morrow, 1991), 228–229.

17. Niebuhr, "A theologian says evangelist is oversimplifying the issues of life," *Life*, 1 July 1957, 92, in BGCA, CN 360, R66. For Niebuhr's views on civil rights, see, for example, Niebuhr, "The Race Problem in America," *Christianity and Crisis*, 26 December 1955, 169–170; "School, Church, and the Ordeals of Integration," *Christianity and Crisis*, 1 October 1956, 121–122; "A Theologian's Comments on the Negro in America," *Reporter*, 29 November 1956, 24–25; "The Effect of the Supreme Court Decision," *Christianity and Crisis*, 4 February 1956, 3; and "The States' Rights Crisis," *New Leader*, 29 September 1958, 6–7. Later, however, Niebuhr came to recognize the fundamental legitimacy of the civil rights movement to an extent Graham never did. See Niebuhr, "Revolution in an Open Society," *New Leader*, 27 May 1963, 7–8. Dr. Peter Kuryla generously shared the above articles with me.

18. On the strikingly moderate and cautious response of many American intellectuals to the early civil rights movement, see Carol Polsgrove, *Divided Minds: Intellectuals and the Civil Rights Movement* (New York: Norton, 2001).

19. James McBride Dabbs, "The Man Across the Table from Billy Graham," *Christian Century*, 16 January 1957, 75–76.

20. Francis Pickens Miller, *Man from the Valley: Memoirs of a 20th-Century Virginian* (Chapel Hill: University of North Carolina Press, 1971), 218–219.

21. Graham to Truman, received 23 December 1951; Graham to John Steelman, 26 December 1951; W. D. H. to Connelly, 28 December 1951; Graham to Matthew J. Connelly, 9 January 1952; Jerry Beavan to Truman, 28 January 1952; Graham to Truman, 29 January 1952; and "acm" to Connelly, 31 January 1952; all in BGCA, CN 74, 1–11 (original in Harry S. Truman Presidential Library).

22. Geoffrey Perret, *Eisenhower* (New York: Random House, 1999), 395–402. Stephen E. Ambrose, *Eisenhower*, volume 1: *Soldier General of the Army President-Elect, 1890–1952* (New York: Simon and Schuster, 1983), 515–549. Lee Edwards, *Missionary for Freedom: The Life and Times of Walter Judd* (New York: Paragon House, 1990), 185–187.

23. Martin, *Prophet*, 147–148. Graham, *Just as I Am: The Autobiography of Billy Graham* (New York: HarperCollins, 1997), 189–192. Eisenhower to Graham, 8 November 1951; Graham to Eisenhower, 3 December 1951; and Graham to Eisenhower, 14 February 1952; all in BGCA, CN 74, 1–12 (original in EPL).

24. Martin, *Prophet*, 147.

25. *Greensboro Daily News*, 17 October 1951, in BGCA, CN 360, R4. Clipping, 17 October 1951, in BGCA, CN 74, 1–12 (original in EPL).

26. Graham, *Just as I Am*, 191–192. Graham to Walter Judd, 22 July 1952, Hoover Institution Archives (HIA), Walter Judd Papers (WJP), 30–6. Graham to Arthur B. Langlie, 9 June 1952, University of Washington Libraries Special Collections (UWSC), Arthur B. Langlie Papers, 12–41. Eisenhower to Arthur B. Langlie, 11 August 1952, EPL, Eisenhower, Dwight D.: Records as President (RP), President's Personal Files (PPF), 966-"PPF 1052 Graham, Billy."

27. Graham to Walter Judd, 22 July 1952, HIA, WJP, 30–6. Spencer in *Jackson* (Miss.) *Daily News* clipping, 17 June 1952, in BGCA, CN 7, 2–8; and Joseph Crespino, *In Search of Another Country: Mississippi and the Conservative Counterrevolution* (Princeton, N.J.: Princeton University Press, 2007), 84. *Jackson* (Miss.) *Clarion-Ledger* clipping, 26 June 1952; and *Jackson* (Miss.) *Daily News* clipping, 16 June 1952; both in BGCA, CN 7, 2–8.

28. Robertson to Graham 5 May 1952; Graham to Robertson, undated [9 May 1952]; Robertson to Graham, 12 May 1952; Graham to Leslie L. Biffle, 19 June 1952; Graham to Robertson, 19 June 1952; and Robertson to Graham, 21 June 1952, A. Willis Robertson Papers, College of William and Mary Special Collections, 121/131.

29. Just before the 1956 election, Nelson Bell wrote to Eisenhower with the results of a *Christianity Today* poll showing overwhelming support for the president among Protestant ministers. Bell to Eisenhower, 25 October 1956, BGCA, CN 8, 1–28.

30. Earl and Merle Black, *The Rise of Southern Republicans* (Cambridge, Mass.: Harvard University Press, 2002), 61, 207–209. Ambrose, *Eisenhower*, 550.

31. In documenting the rise of urban Republicanism, historians Hugh D. Graham and Numan Bartley argued that the 1952 presidential election "clearly established the G.O.P. as the respectable party of the urban and suburban affluent whites in the South's large and small cities." Graham and Bartley, *Southern Politics and the Second Reconstruction* (Baltimore: Johns Hopkins University Press, 1975), 81–110 passim (quoted on 86). It should be emphasized that Eisenhower's outreach to the South differed from Nixon's more famous "southern strategy" of 1968–1972. For example, Eisenhower was able to attract votes from African Americans in the South in both 1952 and 1956.

32. Graham to Eisenhower, 24 August 1956, EPL, PP, Name Series (NS), 16-"Graham, Billy."

33. Grady Wilson to Mendel Rivers, 21 November 1952, BGCA, CN 544, 1–2. Ambrose, *Eisenhower*, 567.

34. Richard V. Pierard and Robert D. Linder, *Civil Religion and the Presidency* (Grand Rapids, Mich.: Zondervan, 1988), 201, 203.

35. Charles T. Cook, *"One Thing I Do": The Billy Graham Story* (Wheaton, Ill.: Van Kampen Press, 1954), 122.

36. "Capitol Move," *Newsweek*, 19 December 1952, 44. In the end, the Washington office did not open until 1955, and it closed less than two years later. "Select Chronology Listing of Events in the History of the Billy Graham Evangelistic Association," http:// www.wheaton.edu/bgc/archives/bgeachro/bgeachro02.htm (accessed 13 December 2006).

37. L. Nelson Bell to Judd, 6 November 1956, BGCA, CN 318, 31–4.

38. Graham to Eisenhower, 27 March 1956; and Graham to Eisenhower, 4 June 1956; both in EPL, RP, PPF, 966-"PPF 1052 Graham, Billy." Eisenhower to Graham, 21 June 1956, EPL, PP, NS, 16-"Graham, Billy." Leonard W. Hall to Eisenhower, 3 September 1956, EPL, PP, NS, 16-"Graham, Billy." On the 1956 election, see Branch, *Parting*, 192, 220.

39. Graham to Eisenhower, 8 February 1954, EPL, RP, PPF, 966-"PPF 1052 Graham, Billy."

40. Graham, *Just as I Am*, 441. Graham address at Hannah Milhous Nixon memorial service, 3 October 1967, Richard Nixon Library (RNL), Post Presidential Correspondence, Special People A-K, Graham, Billy and Ruth (PPSP), 1–5. A recent work, based in part on interviews with Graham, places the Graham-Nixon meeting in 1952. See Nancy Gibbs and Michael Duffy, *The Preacher and the Presidents: Billy Graham in the White House* (New York: Center Street, 2007), 55.

41. Charles P. Henderson Jr., *The Nixon Theology* (New York: Harper and Row, 1972), 8–11, 109 (quoted on 51). Nixon's adult theological inclinations overlapped with evangelicalism mostly in the area of personal morality. His personal views probably held more in common with the theologically safe, self-help-oriented perspective of Norman Vincent Peale. See Eric J. Paddon, "Modern Mordecai: Billy Graham in the Political Arena, 1948–1980" (Ph.D. dissertation, Ohio University, 1999), 156–159.

42. Graham to Judd, 22 July 1952, HIA, WJP, 30–6. Edwards, *Missionary for Freedom*, 195.

43. Leonard Lurie, *The Running of Richard Nixon* (New York: Coward, McCann, Geoghegan, 1972), 222.

44. Graham to Nixon, 7 January 1956 and 25 June 1956; and Graham to *New York Herald Tribune* reporter, 29 September 1958; all in National Archives and Records Administration (NARA), Pacific Region, Laguna Niguel (PRLN), Richard M. Nixon Pre-Presidential Papers (RNPP), Series 320 (S320), 299-"Graham, Billy" (299-G).

45. Graham to Nixon, 24 August 1956, NARA, PRLN, RNPP, S320, 299-G. Ghost writing allegations in Gibbs and Duffy, *Preacher and the Presidents*, 70, 364n. Graham to Langlie, 14 July 1956, UWSC, Langlie Papers, 57–17. Graham to Frank Clement, undated [summer 1956]. After the convention, Graham wrote a cordial letter to Clement, but added that "I am sure that you would not expect me to agree with all that you had to say. In fact, I seriously doubt if you agree with all you said. . . . You certainly presented the views of the modern day Democrats." See Graham to Clement, 20 August 1956. Both in Frank Goad Clement Papers (FCP), Tennessee State Library and Archives (TSLA), 17–6 (R4). On Clement, see Charles Reagan Wilson, *Judgment and Grace in Dixie: Southern Faiths from Faulkner to Elvis* (Athens: University of Georgia Press, 1995), 3–4; and Jack Bass and Walter DeVries, *The Transformation of Southern Politics: Social Change and Political Consequence Since 1945* (New York: Basic Books, 1976), 289.

46. Graham to Nixon, 24 August 1956, 10 November 1956, 2 December 1957, and 7 January 1956; Raymond A. Hare to Nixon, 11 May 1959; and unnamed author to Nixon, 18 December 1957; all in NARA, PRLN, RNPP, S320, 299-G.

47. Graham, *Just as I Am*, 201. Graham to Nixon, undated [fall 1957]; and Graham to Nixon, 22 September 1958; both in NARA, RNPP, S320, 299-G.

48. Graham to Nixon, 4 June 1956, 13 September 1955, and 14 July 1956; all in NARA, PRLN, RNPP, S320, 299-G. *Charlotte Observer*, undated [6 August 1956], in BGCA, CN 360, R25.

49. See contents of NARA, PRLN, RNPP, Series 207, 67-"7/20/1957—Billy Graham Meeting—New York City."

50. Graham to Nixon, 10 November 1956, 28 March 1957, 2 December 1957, and 27 August 1958; and Nixon to Graham, 16 August 1956; all in NARA, PRLN, RNPP, S320, 299-G.

51. Contents of NARA, PRLN, RNPP, S207, 299-G.

52. Unlabeled clipping, 23 June 1960, in NARA, PRLN, RNPP, S207, 139-G. Graham introduced Nixon as "a golfing partner who usually beats me."

53. Graham to Eisenhower, 4 August 1960; and Eisenhower to Graham, 10 August 1960; both in BGCA, CN 74, 1-12 (originals in EPL).

54. Graham to Nixon, 22 August 1960, 27 March 1960, 23 August 1960; and Nixon to Graham, 29 August 1960; all in NARA, PRLN, RNPP, S320, 299-G.

55. Graham to Nixon, 21 June 1960, NARA, PRLN, RNPP, S320, 299-G.

56. Following the 1960 election, a distraught Nelson Bell wrote to Nixon expressing fears of "a slow, completely integrated and planned attempt to take over our nation for the Roman Catholic Church. *Many* Roman Catholics are good friends of mine and many of them are completely unaware of what is taking place." Mr. and Mrs. Bell to Nixon, 11 November 1960, BGCA, CN 318, 39-15. Thomas J. Carty, *A Catholic in the White House? Religion, Politics, and John F. Kennedy's Presidential Campaign* (New York: Palgrave MacMillan, 2004), 44-45. Carol V. R. George, *God's Salesman: Norman Vincent Peale and the Power of Positive Thinking* (New York: Oxford University Press, 1993), vii-x.

57. Walker Percy, *The Last Gentleman* (New York: Farrar, Straus, and Giroux, 1966), 203.

58. Curtis Mitchell, *Billy Graham: The Making of a Crusader* (Philadelphia: Chilton Books, 1966), 91. Graham to Nixon, 27 May 1960; and *Chicago Tribune*, 20 May 1960; both in NARA, PRLN, RNPP, S320, 299-G.

59. Graham to Nixon, 21 June 1960, NARA, PRLN, RNPP, S320, 299-G. Graham to Judd, 21 June 1960, HIA, WJP, 30-6. Stephen Ambrose, *Nixon: The Education of a Politician, 1913-1962* (New York: Simon and Schuster, 1987), 553.

60. Appointment sheet, 23 June 1960; unnamed to "Don," 24 June 1960; both in NARA, PRLN, RNPP, S320, 299-G. Nixon, Graham, Judd, and other guests dined together on 25 June 1960. Graham to Judd, 21 June 1960, HIA, WJP, 30-6.

61. Graham to Nixon, 22 July 1960, NARA, PRLN, RNPP, S320, 299-G. Bell to Judd, 9 July 1960; 14 July 1960; Bell to Pew, 9 July 1960; J. Howard Pew to Bell, 11 July 1960; all in BGCA, CN 318, 31-4.

62. Carty, *A Catholic in the White House?*, 54.

63. Bell to Maxey Jarman, 2 September 1960; BGCA, CN 318, 30–16.

64. Graham to Johnson, 8 August 1960; and Johnson to Graham, 16 August 1960; both in Lyndon Johnson Presidential Library and Archives (LJPA), Lyndon Baines Johnson Archives, 4-"G."

65. My description of the Montreux conference is based primarily on Graham to Nixon, 22 and 23 August 1960; both in NARA, PRLN, RNPP, S320, 299-G; and L. Nelson Bell to J. Howard Pew, 1 September 1960, BGCA, CN 318, 41–17. Background on the role of religion in the 1960 campaign (including the Montreux meeting and its fallout) comes from Carty, *A Catholic in the White House?*, 49–66; and George, *Salesman*, 201–210.

66. George, *Salesman*, 200–210. Encouragement of Peale in Graham, *Just as I Am*, 391.

67. Nixon to Graham, 29 August 1960, in NARA, PRLN, RNPP, S320, 299-G. Bell to Nixon, 9 September 1960, BGCA, CN 318, 39–15.

68. Graham to *Time*, 28 August 1960; statement to *Newsweek*, undated [August 1960]; and Graham to Nixon, 1 September 1960; all in NARA, PRLN, RNPP, S320, 299-G. "The Religion Issue (Cont.)," *Time*, 29 August 1960, 14; and letter to the editor, *Time*, 19 September 1960, 6.

69. Bell to Jarman, 2 September 1960, BGCA, CN 318, 30–16. Bell to Nixon, 2 September 1960, BGCA, CN 318, 39–15.

70. Graham to Nixon, 1 September 1960, 24 September 1960, 17 October 1960, and 2 November 1960; all in NARA, PRLN, RNPP, S320, 299-G.

71. Graham to Nixon, 17 November 1959; Len Hall to Nixon, 23 May 1960; Graham to Nixon, 27 May 1960; unsigned handwritten note, undated [June 1960?] containing text, "Billy Graham—Come out for RN Before Democratic National Convention"; all in NARA, PRLN, RNPP, S320, 299-G.

72. Graham to Nixon, 22 August 1960; and Nixon to Mrs. W. Frank Graham (and related note), 22 October 1960; both in NARA, PRLN, RNPP, S320, 299-G. *Charlotte News*, 11 September 1968, in BGCA, CN 360, R31.

73. Gibbs and Duffy, *Preacher and the Presidents*, 103.

74. Graham to Nixon, 24 September 1960; Graham to Nixon, 1 September 1960; and AP, 30 October 1960; all in NARA, PRLN, RNPP, S320, 299-G.

75. This recounting of the *Life* narrative relies on two letters from Graham to Nixon, dated 12 June 1961 and 17 July 1961; and "Billy Graham's story LIFE magazine did not use," undated [October 1960]; all in NARA, PRLN, RNPP, S320, 299-G. *Boston Globe* leak in Gibbs and Duffy, *Preacher and the Presidents*, 101.

76. Graham to Nixon, 12 June and 17 July 1961; both in NARA, PRLN, RNPP, S320, 299-G. Ralph McGill to Graham, 28 October 1960, Emory University Special Collections, Ralph McGill Papers, 10–3. Graham, "'We Are Electing a President of the World,'" *Life*, 7 November 1960, 109–110. Bell to Pew, 29 October 1960, BGCA, CN 318, 41–17.

77. Nixon, *Six Crises* (Garden City, N.Y.: Doubleday, 1962), 365. In subsequent

works, Nixon emphasized that he always advised Graham not to risk his ministry by endorsing him. See, for example, Nixon, *In the Arena: A Memoir of Victory, Defeat, and Renewal* (New York: Simon and Schuster, 1990), 90–91.

78. Bell to Pew, 29 October 1960, BGCA, CN 318, 41–17. *Greenville* (S.C.) *Piedmont*, 4 November 1960; and *Cleveland Press-News* (UPI), 3 November 1960; both in BGCA, CN 360, R27. Lowell S. Streiker and Gerald S. Strober, *Religion and the New Majority: Billy Graham, Middle America, and the Politics of the 70s* (New York: Association Press, 1972), 61.

79. Nixon to Graham, 15 January 1961 and 17 August 1961; and Graham to Nixon, 12 June 1961; all in NARA, PRLN, RNPP, S320, 299-G. Nixon to John Pollock, 30 December 1985, RNL, PPSP, 1–4.

80. Graham to Daniel, 13 January 1956; and Stuart Symington to Frank Carlson, Price Daniel, Alton Lennon, and John Stennis, 25 March 1954; both in TSLAC, SHRL, Daniel Papers, 104-"Billy Graham." Graham to Judd, 13 January 1956, HIA, WJP, 30–6. "Interview with Billy Graham," undated [1957 or 1958] film, Records of the United States Information Agency records (USIA), NARA, video copy of USIA film 306.2143.

81. Mitchell, *Making*, 22.

82. Graham, "No Color Line in Heaven," *Ebony*, September 1957, 102.

83. "Confidential Report on African Tour from Jerry Beavan and Charlie Riggs," 21 December 1959, BGCA, CN 1, 4–13. AP article, undated [1960]; and "3,000 see crusade launched," undated [February 1960]; both in BGCA, CN 360, R14. "So. Africa Bias Is Hit by Graham," undated [1960], in BGCA, CN 360, R54. *New York Times*, 17 Feb. 1960, in BGCA, CN 1, 4–13. Graham finally held desegregated meetings in South Africa in 1973.

84. McMahan, *Safari*, 51.

85. Graham, "No Color Line," 100.

86. Quoted in Graham, "Why Don't Our Churches Practice the Brotherhood They Preach?" *Reader's Digest*, August 1960, 52; and "No Solution to Race Problem 'At the Point of Bayonets,'" *U.S. News and World Report*, 25 April 1960 (originally written for UPI), 94.

87. Mark Newman, *Getting Right with God: Southern Baptists and Desegregation, 1945–1995* (Tuscaloosa: University of Alabama Press, 2001), 129–149. Alan Scot Willis, *All According to God's Plan: Southern Baptist Missions and Race, 1945–1970* (Lexington: University of Kentucky Press, 2005).

88. McMahan, *Safari*, 35.

89. "Safari for Souls" brochure, February 1960, HIA, WJP, 30–6.

90. McMahan, *Safari*, 99, 80, 16.

91. *AME Church Review* 78.205 (July–September 1960): 52. "Confidential Report," 21 December 1959, BGCA, CN 1, 4–13. Letter, Dr. Dennis C. Dickerson to Steven P. Miller, 15 December 2006 (in possession of author).

92. "JDH" to "rmw," 15 March 1960; and UPI clipping, 31 March 1960, in NARA, PRLN, RNPP, S320, 299-G. McMahan, *Safari*, 34.

93. McMahan, *Safari*, 57.

CHAPTER 4. "ANOTHER KIND OF MARCH"

Note to epigraphs: *Birmingham News*, 26 April 1965. *Florida Sentinel-Bulletin*, 24 April 1965, in Billy Graham Center Archives (BGCA), Collection 360 (CN 360), Reel 30 (R30).

1. Billy Graham, *Just as I Am: The Autobiography of Billy Graham* (New York: HarperCollins, 1997), 360, 426.

2. On King in the late 1950s and early 1960s, see Taylor Branch, *Parting the Waters: America in the King Years, 1954–1963* (New York: Touchstone, 1988), 200–450 passim.

3. See *Charlotte News* (AP), [late June 1962]; and AP story, 26 July 1962; both in BGCA, CN 360, R29. Likewise, Graham initially endorsed a subsequent constitutional amendment that would have reversed the ruling, but he quickly distanced himself from the effort. See "AC Highlights Few, but Foreign Missions One of Them," *Biblical Recorder*, 30 May 1964, 2, in BGCA, CN 360, R84.

4. Edward Gilbreath, "Billy Graham Had a Dream," *Christian History* 47 (1995): 44–46. Gilbreath attributed to Graham the aphorism, often cited by King, that eleven o'clock is "the most segregated hour" in the nation (44). The claim is doubtful. While Graham did use such language in a 1960 *Reader's Digest* article, he prefaced his words with a qualifying clause ("it has become a byword that"), suggesting derivation from other sources. See Graham, "Why Don't Our Churches Practice the Brotherhood They Preach?" *Reader's Digest*, August 1960, 53. See also Russ Busby, *Billy Graham: God's Ambassador* (Alexandria, Va.: Time-Life, Minneapolis: Billy Graham Evangelistic Association [BGEA], and Del Mar, Calif.: Tehabi Books, 1999), 212–217.

5. On the "limited Civil Rights Movement," see Peter A. Kuryla, "The Integration of the American Mind: Intellectuals and the Creation of the Civil Rights Movement, 1944–1983" (Ph.D. dissertation, Vanderbilt University, 2006), 174–211. "King and Graham as Ghetto-Mates," *Christian Century*, 10 August 1966, 976–977. The Graham-King revision has sought to counter criticisms of Graham by black public figures, such as Jesse Jackson, who told *Christianity Today* that the evangelist "would have preached to the slaves in Egypt . . . then he'd have gone and played golf with Pharaoh." King, in contrast, would have "taken them to Canaan." See "You Can Pray If You Want To," *Christianity Today*, 12 August 1977, 15.

6. Quoted in John Pollock, *Billy Graham: Evangelist to the World: An Authorized Biography of the Decisive Years* (New York: Harper and Row, 1979), 127. Graham, *Just as I Am*, 426.

7. For a theologically centered analysis along these lines, see Michael G. Long, *Billy Graham and the Beloved Community* (New York: Palgrave Macmillan, 2006). Long, though, goes much too far when he describes Graham as "the major Protestant obstructionist to the beloved community that Martin Luther King, Jr. dreamed of for America" (224). This argument does not account for the fact that King (retrospective eulogizing of him aside) had few consistent allies among even liberal whites.

8. Branch, *Parting*, 227–228, 594–595. "There was a time that [Graham] would even

preach before segregated audiences," King told the Canadian viewers. "But now he refuses to preach to any audience that is segregated, which, I think is a marvelous step." *Front Page Challenge* interview, 28 April 1959, in Clayborne Carson et al., eds., *The Papers of Martin Luther King, Jr.*, volume 5, *Threshold of a New Decade, January 1959–December 1960* (Berkeley: University of California Press, 2005), 193.

9. Graham to Nixon, 23 August 1960, National Archives and Records Administration, Pacific Region, Laguna Niguel, Richard M. Nixon Pre-Presidential Papers, Series 320, Box 299, Folder "Graham, Billy" (299-"Graham, Billy.")

10. Branch, *Parting*, 314. Graham, *Just as I Am*, 360, 426.

11. Marshall Frady, *Billy Graham: A Parable of American Righteousness* (Boston: Little, Brown, 1979), 416. A similar line appears in Pollock, *Evangelist to the World*, 127.

12. William Martin, *A Prophet with Honor: The Billy Graham Story* (New York: William Morrow, 1991), 235.

13. "Billy Graham and Race," undated [1965], BGCA, CN, 345, 44–1. A similar comment appears in Pollock, *Evangelist to the World*, 127.

14. *Columbia* (Tenn.) *Herald* (UPI), 30 November 1960, in BGCA, CN 360, R27. Graham declined to take a position on the sit-ins in his hometown of Charlotte but expressed support for a biracial committee formed to address the demonstrations. See *Charlotte Observer*, 2 April 1960, in BGCA, CN 360, R27.

15. Graham, "Billy Graham's Own Story: 'God Is My Witness,'" part III, *McCall's*, June 1964, 146. See Branch, *Parting*, 594–595, 602.

16. Following the Miami-to-Chicago flight, King directed two aides to consult with BGEA staffers about public relations matters. See Branch, *Parting*, 594–595. *Chicago Tribune*, 29 May 1962, in BGCA, CN 360, R28. See also *Chicago Sun-Times*, 29 May 1962, in BGCA, CN 360, R28. The photograph has often been misidentified as a product of the 1957 New York City crusade. See Gilbreath, "Dream," 44; and David L. Chappell, *A Stone of Hope: Prophetic Religion and the Death of Jim Crow* (Chapel Hill: University of North Carolina Press, 2004), 142. See also photograph, "King, Martin Luther, Jr.," BGCA, CN 17.

17. Knoxville press conference transcript, 21 May 1970, BGCA, CN 24, 1–23.

18. *New York Times*, 18 May 1961, in BGCA, CN 360, R27.

19. Greenville, S.C., address, March 1965, CN 26, BGCA, T89. *Montgomery Advertiser*, 27 April 1965.

20. Frady, *Parable*, 416. Quoted in Graham, "Racial Prejudice: The Answer," *Report*, December 1965, 9–11, in BGCA, CN 345, 44–1.

21. *New York Times*, 18 April 1963; and *Minneapolis Tribune* (New York Times Service), 18 April 1963, in BGCA, CN 360, R29.

22. S. Jonathan Bass, *Blessed Are the Peacemakers: Martin Luther King, Jr., Eight White Religious Leaders, and the "Letter from Birmingham Jail"* (Baton Rouge: Louisiana State University Press, 2001), 104–105.

23. *Chicago Defender*, 25 May 1960; and *Norfolk Journal and Guide*, 19 March 1960; both in BGCA, CN 360, R27.

24. See *Hattiesburg* (Miss.) *American*, 25 April 1963; *Petersburg* (Va.) *Progress-Index*, 22 April 1963; *Minneapolis* Spokesman, 25 April 1963; and *Chicago Defender*, 11 May 1963; all in BGCA, CN 360, R29.

25. *Tupelo* (Miss.) *Journal* (UPI), 2 May 1963; and *Westerly* (R.I.) *Sun*, 6 May 1963; both in BGCA, CN 360, R29. Andrew Michael Manis, *A Fire You Can't Put Out: The Civil Rights Life of Birmingham's Reverend Fred Shuttlesworth* (Tuscaloosa: University of Alabama Press, 1999), 362.

26. "The Crowded Stadium," *Christianity Today*, 27 September 1963, 37, in BGCA, CN 360, R81.

27. Martin Luther King, Jr., "Letter from Birmingham City Jail," in *A Testament: The Essential Writings and Speeches of Martin Luther King, Jr.*, ed. James M. Washington (San Francisco: HarperCollins, 1991), 295.

28. *Cumberland Presbyterian*, 22 October 1963, in BGCA, CN 360, R81.

29. "Solving Our Race Problems Through Love," 25 August 1963, BGCA, CN 191, T711c.

30. *Los Angeles Times*, 29 August 1963; and UPI story, 29 August 1963; both in BGCA, CN 360, R29.

31. *Atlanta Constitution*, 15 January 1964.

32. Kenneth L. Woodward, "The Preaching and the Power," *Newsweek*, 20 July 1970, 52. This is the earliest citation of this oft-referenced quote that I could locate.

33. *Honolulu Star Bulletin*, 2 February 1965, in BGCA, CN 360, R30. "Graham Says Atlanta Crusade 'Must Be Integrated,'" *The Standard*, 2 March 1964, in BGCA, CN 360, R82.

34. AP, 16 August 1965, in BGCA, CN 360, R30; *Camden Courier-Post*, 25 April 1967, in BGCA, CN 360, R31; and *Milton* (Pa.) *Standard* (UPI), 25 April 1967, in BGCA, CN 360, R31.

35. Statement quoted in *Memphis Press-Scimitar*, 6 April 1968, in BGCA, CN 360, R31. "Billy Graham: Person to Person," *Light of Life Magazine*, June 1968, 14, BGCA, CN 360, R96. Prayer and sermon quoted in Long, *Beloved Community*, 2–3, 222.

36. Graham, *Just as I Am*, 403–418. Martin, *Prophet*, 299.

37. Graham to Nixon, 21 October 1963 and 20 December 1963; both in Richard Nixon Presidential Library (RNL), Wilderness Years, Correspondence Files (WYCF), 1963–1965, 13-"Graham, Billy." "An Evening at the White House," *Christianity Today*, 3 January 1964, 36.

38. Quoted in Frady, *Parable*, 260–262.

39. On the southern metropolitan vote and the GOP, see Matthew D. Lassiter, *The Silent Majority: Suburban Politics in the Sunbelt South* (Princeton, N.J.: Princeton University Press, 2006), 229–231. See also Hugh D. Graham and Numan V. Bartley, *Southern Politics and the Second Reconstruction* (Baltimore: Johns Hopkins University Press, 1975), 107.

40. Graham quickly, if politely, ended the 1960 draft effort. See *Americus* (Ga.) *Times-Reader*, 11 June 1960; and *Miami Daily News*, 25 August 1960; both in BGCA, CN 360, R27.

41. Quoted in Long, *Beloved Community*, 55, 242n107.

42. In 1964, Graham supporters George Champion, J. Howard Pew, Arthur Langlie, and Roger Hull participated in the founding of the Presbyterian Laymen's Committee, designed to oppose liberal currents within the United Presbyterian Church (northern Presbyterian). See James A. Gittings, "What Sort of Man Is Roger Hull?" *Presbyterian Life*, 1 August 1969, 11–13, 31–33, in BGCA, CN 360, R98.

43. Bela Kornitzer to John Bolten, 8 January 1962; and Kornitzer to Bolten, 16 January 1962; both in Drew University Special Collections, Bela Kornitzer Collection, 21–2. For background on Bolten, see Martin, *Prophet*, 187–188. On Conlan, see *Arizona Republic*, 5 April 1976, in BGCA, CN 360, R26.

44. John Conlan to Willis Haymaker, 20 December 1961; undated brochure [1962] titled "Freedom or Slavery: A Message of Urgent Importance"; Grady Wilson to Conlan, 18 January 1962; all in BGCA, CN 544, 11–1.

45. Conlan to Wilson, 7 March 1962; and Wilson to Conlan, 27 March 1962; all in BGCA, CN 544, 11–1. On Christian Citizen, see *New York Times*, 1 February 1962; and John G. Turner, *Bill Bright and Campus Crusade for Christ: The Renewal of Evangelicalism in Postwar America* (Chapel Hill: University of North Carolina Press, 2008), 109–110. Turner cites Conlan as a supporter of Christian Citizen. Conlan may have been less than forthcoming about his actual relationship to von Frellick.

46. Conlan to Wilson, 7 March 1962, BGCA, CN 544, 11–1.

47. *Washington Post*, 30 November 1974. Stanley H. Brown, *H. L. Hunt* (Chicago: Playboy Press, 1976), 185, 187, 201–202. Artis Burst, *The Three Families of H. L. Hunt* (New York: Weidenfeld and Nicolson, 1988).

48. Wayne Poucher to Loren F. Bridges (copied to Conlan), 27 August 1962; Bridges to Conlan, 5 September 1962; and John W. Curington to Bridges, 11 March 1964; all in BGCA, CN 45, 3–55. See also T. W. Wilson to Grady Wilson, 14 December 1963, BGCA, CN 544, 14–4. Conlan maintained ties to the BGEA, helping to organize the 1964 Graham crusade in Phoenix. See Conlan to Bob Root, 20 November 1963; and Conlan to Root, 28 November 1963; both in BGCA, CN, 8–1.

49. The meeting, although not the content thereof, is referred to in *Houston Post*, 19 October 1963, in BGCA, CN 360, R29.

50. H. L. Hunt to Grady Wilson, 11 May 1963, BGCA, CN 544, 12–16. "Between Election Campaigns," undated, no author, BGCA, CN 544, 12–16. *Houston Post*, 19 October 1963; and *Dallas Times-Herald*, 1 May 1963; UPI and AP stories, 2 May 1963; and *Lakeland* (Fla.) *Ledger*, 2 May 1963; all in BGCA, CN 360, R29. "New Face in Politics? Graham Attracts Interest," *U.S. News and World Report*, 13 May 1963, 19.

51. Nancy Gibbs and Michael Duffy, *The Preacher and the Presidents: Billy Graham in the White House* (New York: Center Street, 2007), 126.

52. *Houston Press*, 31 January 1964, in BGCA, CN 360, R29. Graham to Nixon, 21 October 1963, RNL, WYCF, 1963–1965, 13-"Graham, Billy."

53. *Houston Press*, 31 January 1964, in BGCA, CN 360, R29. Martin, *Prophet*, 300–301, 675. Maxey Jarman interview, 26 February 1979, BGCA, CN 141, 40–15. "H. E. Butt,

Jr., Biography," http://www.hebuttfdn.org/AboutFoundation/biography.asp (accessed 26 January 2007). Wilson to Howard Butt, 11 February 1964, BGCA, CN 544, 14–2.

54. *Houston Press*, 1 February 1964; UPI story, 2 February 1964; and *Lakeland* (Fla.) *Ledger* (AP), 2 February 1964; all in BGCA, CN 360, R29.

55. *New York World Telegram and Sun*, 1 February 1964, in BGCA, CN 360, R29.

56. "Billy Won't Run for President," *Christian Century*, 12 February 1964, in BGCA, CN 360, R82.

57. Message "Re Billy Graham Call," 7 February 1964, RNL, WYCF, 1963–1965, 13-"Graham, Billy." Nixon to Graham, 13 May 1964, RNL, WYCF, 1966–1968, 3-"Graham, Dr. Billy."

58. Wilson to Dan Liu, 11 February 1964, BGCA, CN 544, 15–8.

59. Johnson and Steve Smith, 11 May 1964, Lyndon Johnson Presidential Library and Archives (LJPA), White House Conversation Recordings (WHCR), 3381. See also Michael R. Beschloss, ed., *Taking Charge: The Johnson White House Tapes, 1963–1964* (New York: Simon and Schuster, 1997), 344. *Florence* (S.C.) *News* (AP), 18 May 1964, in BGCA, CN 360, R29.

60. *Houston Chronicle*, 23 February 1964; and *San Francisco News-Call Bulletin*, 11 July 1964; both in BGCA, CN 360, R29.

61. Earle B. Mayfield to Johnson, 21 July 1966, LJPA, White House Central Files (WHCF), Name File (NF), 227a-"WHCF Name."

62. "President Hears Billy Graham at Disciples Church," *California Covenanter* clipping, 22 October 1964, in BGCA, CN 360, R85.

63. Graham, *Just as I Am*, 411. A Johnson supporter called Graham's August 1964 visit to the White House "a great day, far greater in so many ways than the Press reported." See George Harris to Moyers, 9 September 1964, BGCA, CN 74, 3–6 (original in LJPA).

64. Moyers to Ross Coggins, 21 October 1964; and Moyers to Coggins, 29 October 1964; both in LJPA, WHCF, NF, 227a-"WHCF Name." "Close" in Eric J. Paddon, "Modern Mordecai: Billy Graham in the Political Arena, 1948–1980" (Ph.D. dissertation, Ohio University, 1999), 208. Goldwater reference in Gibbs and Duffy, *Preacher and the Presidents*, 131. Johnson and Graham, 20 October 1964, LJPA, WHCR, 5926; and Beschloss, ed., *Reaching for Glory: Lyndon Johnson's Secret White House Tapes, 1964–1965* (New York: Simon and Schuster, 2001), 88.

65. Paddon, "Modern Mordecai," 208. Several weeks before the October visit, Jenkins was arrested for engaging in a homosexual act. Johnson was paranoid that the Goldwater campaign would use the incident for political advantage. In accepting Johnson's invitation, Graham (who likely knew the meaning of "morals charge") passed along his "love and sympathy" for "dear Walter." Johnson and Graham, 20 October 1964; and Beschloss, *Reaching for Glory*, 88. See also Branch, *Pillar of Fire: America in the King Years, 1963–65* (New York: Simon and Schuster, 1998), 513–514, 517–518.

66. Notes from Nixon-Graham telephone conversation, 22 October 1964, RNL, WYCF, 1963–1965, 13-"Graham, Billy."

67. Johnson and Graham, 5 November 1964.

68. Graham to Nixon, 21 October 1963, RNL, WYCF, 1963–1965, 13-"Graham, Billy."

69. Nelson Bell to J. Howard Pew, 2 November 1964, BGCA, CN 318, 41–18. Grady Wilson to Mr. and Mrs. Dick Bourell, 27 November 1964, BGCA, CN 544, 14–2. Anne Graham quoted in Curtis Mitchell, *Billy Graham: Saint or Sinner* (Old Tappan, N.J.: Fleming H. Revell, 1979), 230. *Raleigh News and Observer* (AP), 2 November 1964, in BGCA, CN 360, R30.

70. *New York Times* (AP), 3 November 1964. AP article, 23 December 1964, in BGCA, CN 360, R30. Johnson and Graham, 5 November 1964, LJPA, WHCR, 6227.

71. Johnson and Graham, 5 November 1964. Graham to Johnson, 10 November 1964, LJPA, WHCF, NF, 227a-"WHCF Name."

72. "The Gospel at the President's Inaugural," *Herald of Holiness*, 24 February 1965, 11, in BGCA, CN 360, R86.

73. Moyers identified Graham's primary constituency as "respectable, churchgoing, decent middle-class people." Quoted in Frady, *Parable*, 264–265.

74. *Greenville* (S.C.) *News*, 10 March 1966.

75. Gibbs and Duffy, *Preacher and the Presidents*, 112.

76. *Charter Oak* (Iowa) *Times*, 27 August 1964, in BGCA, CN 360, R30. See also *Durham Herald*, 31 March 1964, in BGCA, CN 360, R29.

77. Graham, *World Aflame* (New York: Doubleday, 1965), 7.

78. *Greensboro News*, 14 March 1965, in BGCA, CN 360, R30.

79. *Los Angeles Times* (AP), 16 March 1965, in BGCA, CN 360, R30. *New York Times*, 17 April 1965.

80. For an overview of the CRS, see Chappell, *Inside Agitators: White Southerners in the Civil Rights Movement* (Baltimore: Johns Hopkins University Press, 1994), 208–210. George E. Reedy to Johnson, 2 October 1965, LJPA, WHCF, Central Files (CF), Confidential File (CoF), 56-"HU 2 Equality of Races [first folder]."

81. *Charleston* (S.C.) *News and Courier*, 20 April 1964, in BGCA, CN 360, R29.

82. Graham credited the activists for their courage, yet questioned their "method of dealing with racial attitudes. He spoke at a press conference held in New York City. There, liberal Republican senator Jacob Javits presented him with the George Washington Carver Institute Award for his "indefatigable quest for moral justice." (The Carver Institute was established to honor the centennial of the birth of its namesake.) See *Amsterdam News*, 4 July 1964, in BGCA, CN 360, R29; and *United Evangelical Action* clipping, August 1964, 21, in BGCA, CN 360, R84.

83. John Stennis to Graham, 27 June 1964; Stennis to Wanda Ann Mercer, 30 June 1964; Stennis to Graham, 30 June 1964; Graham to Stennis, 4 July 1964; and *Congressional Record* clipping, 30 June 1964; all in Congressional and Political Research Center, Mississippi State University Libraries, John C. Stennis Collection, Series 46-Personal, Folder 241. On Stennis and the Civil Rights Act, see Joseph Crespino, *In Search of Another Country: Mississippi and the Conservative Counterrevolution* (Princeton, N.J.: Princeton University Press, 2007), 99.

84. LeRoy Collins to Marvin Watson, 2 June 1965, LJPA, WHCF, EX FG 155–18, 228-"Community Relations Service 11/23/63–8/23/63."

85. Branch, *Pillar*, 266. Graham reference in "Civil Rights and Demonstrative Religion," *Christianity Today* clipping, 10 April 1964, in BGCA, CN 360, R83.

86. Johnson to prospective members of the Citizens Committee, 1 July 1964, LJPA, WHCF, EX FG 155–18, 228-"Community Relations Service 11/23/63–7/5/64"; telegram list, 1 July 1964, in LJPJ, WHCF, NF, 227a-"WHCF Name." Graham, *Just as I Am*, 413. Johnson and Luther Hodges, 2 July 1964, LJPA, WHCR, 4123. Arthur Dean, a New York lawyer and statesman, accepted the chairmanship.

87. Graham to Johnson, 6 July 1964, LJPA, WHCF, EX FG 155–18, 228-"Community Relations Service 7/6/64–7/22/64." During the summer of 1964, the Minneapolis Presbytery of the United Presbyterian Church passed a resolution calling on Graham to "consider prayerfully the possibility that Mississippi in the summer of 1964 needs your ministry of the Gospel of Reconciliation more than any other place in the world." See "Dr. Graham Asked to Help in Mississippi," *Challenge*, 29 August 1964, 12, in BGCA, CN 360, R84. Graham responded, rather unconvincingly, that he had few ties with church leaders in Mississippi. See *Minneapolis Star*, 2 September 1964, in BGCA, CN 360, R30.

88. "Prayer Versus Prejudice," *Christianity Today* clipping, 28 August 1964, in BGCA, CN 360, R84.

89. UPI article, 23 December 1964, in BGCA, CN 360, R30.

90. Graham, *Just as I Am*, 405–406. Graham to Nixon, 11 October 1965, RNL, WYCF, 1963–1965, 13-"Graham, Billy."

91. Marvin Watson to Johnson, 1 March 1967; and John W. Macy, Jr., to Johnson, 21 December 1966; both in LJPA, Office Files of John Macy, 222-"Graham, Billy." "Beyond These Hills," film and brochure, 1967, BGCA, CN 74, F16 and 3–3. "The Crowded Stadium," *Christianity Today*, 27 September 1963, 37, in BGCA, CN 360, R81. Baptist Press (BP) story, 15 June 1967, CN 345, 44–13. Shriver to Johnson, 12 July 1967; Robert E. Kintner to Shriver, 19 June 1967; and Shriver to George Christian, 9 May 1967; all in LJPA, WHCF, NF, 227a-"WHCF Name." Desired delay and calls in Gibbs and Duffy, *Preacher and the Presidents*, 145. Letters in *Baptist Standard*, 23 August 1967; and *Christian Index*, 31 August 1967; both in BGCA, CN 360, R94.

92. Martin, *Prophet*, 344–345, 347.

93. See, for example, Luther Holcomb to Douglas Nobles, 14 December 1966, LJPA, WHCF, NF, 227a-"WHCF Name"; and Los Angeles press conference, 13 August 1963, BGCA, CN 24, T3.

94. *Baptist Standard* clipping, 2 December 1964, in BGCA, CN 360, R85.

95. *Memphis Commercial Appeal*, 27 August 1962, in BGCA, CN 360, R29. The lack of publicity concerning the desegregated nature of the rally was likely intentional on the part of Alabama newspapers.

96. BGEA mass mailing, Graham to "Friend," July 1963, CN 74, 1–6.

97. *Atlanta Constitution*, 14 January 1964.

98. Atlanta press conference transcript, 5 November 1964, BGCA, CN 24, 4–15.

99. *Knoxville News-Sentinel* (UPI), 9 May 1963; and *Columbia* (S.C.) *State* (AP), 26 May 1963; both in BGCA, CN 360, R29.

100. Raymond D. Hurlbert to Graham, 13 September 1963, BGCA, CN 1, 6–8. See also *Birmingham News*, 19 September 1963, in BGCA, CN 360, R29.

101. Pearson in Gibbs and Duffy, *Preacher and the Presidents*, 112. Bass, *Peacemakers*, 186, 287n36. AP, 25 September 1963, in BGCA, CN 360, R29.

102. *Cumberland Presbyterian* (Religious News Service), 22 October 1963, in BGCA, CN 360, R81.

103. Quoted in Long, *Beloved Community*, 114, 247n19.

104. For background on Turner, see J. Mills Thornton III, *Dividing Lines: Municipal Politics and the Struggle for Civil Rights in Montgomery, Birmingham, and Selma* (Tuscaloosa: University of Alabama Press, 2002), 350. Haymaker to John C. Turner, 4 August 1950, BGCA, CN 1, 9–3. Turner to Graham, 29 September 1963; Haymaker to Turner, 1 November 1963; and Gilbert L. Guffin to Graham, 8 November 1963; all in BGCA, CN 1, 6–8. *Birmingham News*, 16 January 1963, in BGCA, CN 360, R29. Around the time of the Birmingham rally, Graham considered holding a service in Warrenton, N.C., located in the racially tense eastern part of the state. However, the proposed rally did not garner adequate support from the town's ministers. See Haymaker to Smyth, 21 April 1964, BGCA, CN 1, 6–11.

105. Notes on "*Controversial Calls*," 19 February 1964, BGCA, CN 17, 4–45. Hurlbert to Haymaker, 22 November 1963, BGCA, CN 1, 6–8.

106. Minutes, Greater Birmingham Crusade Executive Committee, 3 April 1964, BGCA, CN 17, 4–39.

107. Executive committee list, undated, BGCA, CN 17, 4–19. See also *Shades Valley* (Ala.) *Sun*, 26 March 1964, in BGCA, CN 17, 4–54; *Bulletin News*, 19 February 1964, BGCA, CN 17, 4–11; and news release, 14 February 1964, BGCA, CN 17, 4–14. For background on Drew, see Branch, *Parting*, 690. *Katzenbach v. McClung*, 379 U.S. 294 (1964).

108. *New York Times*, 30 March 1964. Minutes, meeting between city and rally leaders, 2 May 1964, Birmingham Public Library Archives (BPLA), Albert Burton Boutwell Papers (ABBP), 264.10.34. Greater Birmingham Crusade Executive Committee, 3 April 1964, BGCA, CN 17, 4–39.

109. *New York Times*, *Birmingham News*, and *Birmingham Post-Herald*, 30 March 1964. *Gadsen* (Ala.) *Times*; and UPI story; both in BGCA, CN 360, R29. Photographs, "BGEA: Birmingham Easter Rally; March 29, 1964," BGCA, CN 17. Sherwood Wirt, *Billy: A Personal Look at the World's Best-Loved Evangelist* (Wheaton, Ill.: Crossway Books, 1997), 131–134. For background on Ware, see Branch, *Parting*, 703; Manis, *A Fire*, 184–187; Thornton, *Dividing Lines*, 172; and Bass, *Peacemakers*, 106.

110. *Birmingham Post-Herald*, 25 March 1964. Greater Birmingham Crusade Executive Committee, 3 April 1964, BGCA, CN 17, 4–39. John Drew to Cook, 4 March 1964, BGCA, CN 17, 4–31. *Birmingham World*, 4 April 1964.

111. *Atlanta Constitution*, 27 March 1964, in BGCA, CN 360, R29.

112. P. Boyd Mather, "National Association of Evangelicals," *Christian Century*, 13 May 1964, 653–654, in BGCA, CN 360, R84.

113. Wirt, "New Day in Birmingham," *British Weekly and Christian World*, 9 April 1964, in BGCA, CN 360, R83. Birmingham *Post-Herald*, 30 March 1964; and Billy Graham service, "The Risen Christ—Adequate for the World's Greatest Problem," *Hour of Decision* sermon, 29 March 1964, BGCA, CN 191, T742c.

114. *Birmingham News*, 5 April 1964. AP articles, 31 [or 30] March 1964, in BGCA, CN 360, R29.

115. *Pittsburgh Courier*, 18 April 1964.

116. *Raleigh News and Observer*, 2 April 1964. "Debate in the Senate; A Meeting in Birmingham," *Time* clipping, undated [April 1964], in BGCA, CN 360, R83.

117. *Birmingham News*, 31 December 1964, in BGCA, CN 360, R30. Cook to Boutwell, 4 April 1964, BPLA, ABBP, 264.10.34. Invitations, 24 March 1964, BGCA, CN 17, 5–1. Cook to Melvin Bailey, 4 April 1964, BGCA, CN 17, 4–17. Ministerial Association of Birmingham petition, 4 May 1964, BPLA, Protestant Pastors' Union Papers, 911.2.30.

118. *Greensboro News*, 14 March 1965, in BGCA, CN 360, R30. Curtis Mitchell, *Billy Graham: The Making of a Crusader* (Philadelphia: Chilton Books, 1966), 14–18.

119. Notes from conversation, Mooneyham and Root, undated [1965], BGCA, CN 345, 44–1; John [surname illegible] to Mooneyham, 3 April 1965; Paul M. Grist to Smyth and Mooneyham, 23 May 1965; and Smyth to Grist, 8 June 1965; all in BGCA, CN 17, 7–7.

120. Mitchell, *Making*, 27–29. *Atlanta Constitution*, 23 April 1965.

121. Johnson to Graham, 13 April 1965, LJPA, WHCF, NF, 227a-"WHCF Name."

122. AP article, 26 April 1965, in BGCA, CN 360, R30; transcript, *Billy Graham in Alabama*, 1965, BGCA, CN 214, 1–27; and Graham to "Friend," 15 April 1965, LJPJ, WHCF, NF, 227a-"WHCF Name." See also *Birmingham News*, 6 April 1965; and *Montgomery Advertiser* (UPI), 11 April 1965. Graham acknowledged Johnson's request in a 1967 address. See "The Quiet Revolution," 29 December 1967, BGCA, CN 345, 43–3.

123. *Florida Sentinel-Bulletin*, 24 April 1965, in BGCA, CN 360, R30.

124. Los Angeles press conference, 13 August 1963, BGCA, CN 24, T3. Notes from conversation, Mooneyham and Bob Root, undated [1965], BGCA, CN 345, 44–1.

125. *New York Times*, 17 April 1965; "Billy Heads South," *Time*, 30 April 1965, 88; *Atlanta Constitution* (AP), 23 April 1965; *New York Times*, 26 April 1965; and *Birmingham News*, 26 April 1965.

126. Ministerial Association Special Committee to Smyth, 8 April 1965, BGCA, CN 17, 7–7.

127. Memo, Eva Prior to Walter Smyth, 2 April 1965, BGCA, CN 17, 99–18. During the anniversary of the Easter rally, Graham team member Grady Wilson led a multiday revival held at the church of Earl Stallings, a member of the Birmingham Eight. Stallings's church had a desegregated seating policy. Stallings to John Dillon, 27 January 1965, BGCA, CN 13, 25–2.

128. Allan R. Watson to Graham, 7 February 1965, BGCA, CN 17, 7–7.

129. Mitchell, *Making*, 28.

130. *Dothan* (Ala.) *Eagle*, 27 July 1963, in BGCA, CN 360, R29. *New York Times*, 25 and 26 April 1965. *Birmingham News*, 9 May 1965.

131. *Dothan* (Ala.) *Eagle*, 22 April 1965. Resolution, Houston County Board of Revenue and Control, undated [1965], BGCA, CN 17, 7–7. Mitchell, *Making*, 33.

132. Robert S. Denny to Graham, 15 February 1965, BGCA, CN 345, 4–21. *Billy Graham in Alabama*, BGEA film, 1965, BGCA, CN 113, F35. Mitchell, *Making*, 42.

133. *Charlotte Observer* and other newspapers (AP), 25 April 1965; all in BGCA, CN 360, R30. "Taking Advantage of Time," *Hour of Decision* sermon, 25 April 1965, BGCA, CN 191, T798a.

134. Montgomery desegregation in Thornton, *Dividing Lines*, 137. The chair of the Montgomery crusade stressed to an official at the city's athletic stadium that the "integrated" crusade "will not in any way be associated with the political conflicts of our time. They will be strictly a religious meeting [*sic*], the spiritual impact of which should be a great blessing to our community." See J. R. White to Ernest P. O'Connor, 5 April 1965, BGCA, SC 12.

135. Wayne Flynt, *Alabama Baptists: Southern Baptists in the Heart of Dixie* (Tuscaloosa: University of Alabama Press, 1998), 462. Notes on Montgomery crusade, 20 April 1965, BGCA, CN 17, 99–18.

136. Mrs. W. A. Brockway to BGEA, 28 April 1965, BGCA, CN 12, 8–41. Robert H. Person to Haymaker, 8 June 1965, BGCA, CN 1, 5–32. Photograph of mutilated sign, "BGEA Montgomery Crusade," undated [June 1965], BGCA, CN 1; see also Gilbreath, "Dream," 46. Memo, Smyth to Haymaker (or Haymaker to Smyth), 1 June 1965, BGCA, CN 17, 80–8. Edward Thornton to Graham, 30 April 1965 [copied to Wallace]; Ocllo and Frank Boykin to Graham [copied to Wallace], 17 May 1965; and Wallace to Boykin, 10 June 1965; all in Alabama Department of Archives and History (ADAH), George Wallace Administrative Records (GWAR), "Fiscal Year 1965" (SG022387), Folder 022. In a 1960 letter to Graham, Boykin argued that black New York Congressman Adam Clayton Powell was only posing as a black man. Boykin to Graham, 2 April 1960. Copy in possession of Sam Hodges, *Dallas Morning News* (original in ADAH).

137. *Birmingham News*, 13 June 1965. *Alabama Journal*, 7 June 1965.

138. Total crowd size for the eight-day crusade stood at around 100,000. See *Birmingham News*, 21 June 1965; and *Alabama Journal*, 22 June 1965, in BGCA, CN 360, R30. Photographs, "BGEA Montgomery Crowds," BGCA, CN 1; and *Montgomery Advertiser*, 14 June 1965. *Montgomery Advertiser*, 14, 18, and 20 June 1965.

139. Moyers to David Kucharsky, 28 June 1965, LJPA, WHCF, NF, 227a-"WHCF Name." Graham to Johnson, 4 May 1965, CN 74, 3–6 (original in LJPA).

140. "Marching for Christ in Montgomery," *Hour of Decision* sermon, 20 June 1965, BGCA, CN 191, T806j. In an AP statement based on his sermon, Graham disingenuously referred to "marches we have read about in other parts of the country." AP statement, undated [June 1965], BGCA, CN 506, 8–7. *Miami Herald*, 25 June 1965. *Honolulu Star Bulletin*, 4 February 1965, in BGCA, CN 360, R30.

141. *Miami Herald*, 28 June 1965, in BGCA, CN 360, R30. Lady Bird Johnson, *A White House Diary* (New York: Holt, Rinehart, and Winston, 1979), 301.

142. Howard Jones to Graham, 14 May 1965; Jones to Smyth, 14 May 1965; Graham to Jones, 28 May 1965; and Smyth to Jones, 21 May 1965; all in BGCA, CN 17, 80–34.

143. On Ralph Bell, see Bell to Smyth, 30 March 1965, BGCA, CN 17, 75–35 [located in Box 76]; and Barrows to Smyth, 6 May 1965, BGCA, CN 17, 76–26.

144. *Montgomery Advertiser* and *Alabama Journal*, 16 June 1965; both in BGCA, CN 360, R30; "God's Radiance in Alabama," *Decision*, August 1965, 8. BGEA film, "Billy Graham in Alabama," BGCA, CN 113, F35.

145. James H. Owens, "Billy Graham—A Contemporary Micaiah," *Christianity Today*, 30 June 1965, 24, in BGCA, CN 360, R87. Executive committee list, 17 May 1965, BGCA, CN 17, 7–39. For background on Wilson, see Thornton, *Dividing Lines*, 602n86.

146. Flynt, *Alabama Baptists*, 479. "Montgomery Church Turns Down Open Policy" (BP), *Western Recorder*, 6 May 1965, 6, in BGCA, CN 360, R87.

147. Leroy Collins to Johnson, 24 March 1965, LJPA, WHCF, FX FG 155–18, 228–11/23/63–8/22/63.

148. Robert Strong sermon, "Holy Week and the Civil Rights Demonstrators at the Churches," delivered 11 April 1965, BGCA, CN 5, 8–15.

149. J. Edward Thornton to W. H. Martindale [copied to Wallace], 17 May 1965, ADAH, GWAR, "Fiscal Year 1965" (SG022387), Folder 022.

150. *Alabama Journal*, 26 June 1965; and *Presbyterian Outlook*, 25 October 1965, 5–6, in BGCA, CN 506, 8–7. Leighton Ford to *Presbyterian Outlook*, 23 July 1965, BGCA, CN 12, 8–41. Trinity Presbyterian bulletin, 20 June 1965, BGCA, CN 1, 5–32. The Strong flap took an even more complex turn after Calvin Thielman, pastor of the Presbyterian church in Montreat (and a Johnson supporter), met with the black serviceman during a White House–supported visit to Vietnam. Thielman's gesture, which came at the request of Ford, was interpreted by some as an effort to protect the interests of segregationist Presbyterians in Alabama. Thielman soon faced the unfair charge of being a racist. See James Mays to Douglas Cator, 7 October 1965; Bell to Cator, 16 October 1965; and Bell to Mays, 25 October 1965; all in BGCA, CN 318, 52–2. On Ford's emphasis on social ethics, see Richard Quebedeaux, *The Worldly Evangelicals* (New York: Harper and Row, 1978), 55.

151. *Alabama Journal*, 10 June 1965.

152. Executive committee list, 17 May 1965, BGCA, CN 17, 7–39. *Montgomery Advertiser-Journal*, 13 June 1965.

153. "Holy Week and the Civil Rights Demonstrators," BGCA, CN 5, 8–15.

154. *Atlanta Journal*, 19 October 1988. Attachment to James S. Love, Jr., to Johnson, 8 July 1965, LJPA, EX FG 155–18, 228-"11/23/63–7/5/64." Collins to Johnson, 24 March 1965, LJPA, WHCF, FX FG 155–18, 228–11/23/63–8/22/63. Winton M. Blount (with Richard Blodgett), *Doing It My Way* (Lyme, Conn.: Greenwich Publishing Group, 1996), 90–91.

155. Telegram, Cliff Barrows to Walter Smyth, 6 May 1965, BGCA, CN 17, 76–26. Graham schedule, undated [June 1965], BGCA, CN 17, 7–36.

156. Winton Blount interview, 10 July 1974, University of North Carolina at Chapel Hill, Southern Historical Collection, Southern Oral History Program, #4007, A-4 (Blount). Blount, *My Way*, 76, 79.

157. On the "complicated move toward moderation" in mid-1960s Mississippi, see Crespino, *In Search of Another Country*, 108–143, 161 (quote from 109).

158. Robert Sherill, *Gothic Politics in the Deep South: Stars of the New Confederacy* (New York: Grossman, 1968), 321–323.

159. *Birmingham Post-Herald*, 15 April 1965.

160. *Birmingham News*, 7 April 1965, in BGCA, CN 360, R30.

161. "Union" quoted in Sherill, *Gothic Politics*, 322. *Birmingham News*, 25 April 1965 and 2 May 1965. Two years earlier, a Columbus, Ga., columnist had favorably contrasted Graham with Wallace as an ideal spokesperson for the South. See *Columbus* (Ga.) *Ledger*, 15 September 1963, in BGCA, CN 360, R29.

162. The latter expression comes from Dan T. Carter, *The Politics of Rage: George Wallace, the Origins of the New Conservatism and the Transformation of American Politics*, 2nd edition (Baton Rouge: Louisiana State University Press, 2000).

163. Los Angeles press conference, 13 August 1963, BGCA, CN 24, T3. "Churches Had Better Wake Up and Meet Spiritual Hunger of Laymen," *Biblical Recorder* clipping, 30 May 1964, in BGCA, CN 360, R84.

164. Mitchell, *Making*, 29. *Alabama Journal*, 26 April 1965.

165. Roland and Florence Ingram to Wallace, 24 April 1965; see also Paul J. Mason to Wallace, 24 April 1965; both in ADAH, GWAR, "Fiscal Year 1965" (SG022387), Folder 022. See also Chappell, *Stone of Hope*, 141n43.

166. Greater Birmingham Crusade Executive Committee, 2 April 1964, BGCA, CN 17, 4–39.

167. Boykin to Wallace, 1 June 1965, ADAH, GWAR, "Fiscal Year 1965" (SG022387), Folder 022.

168. Flynt, *Alabama Baptists*, 462.

169. *Birmingham Post-Herald* (UPI), 17 June 1965. *Alabama Journal*, 16 June 1965.

170. *Charleston* (S.C.) *News and Courier*, 24 June 1965, BGCA, CN 360, R30.

171. Chamber of Commerce advertisement, undated [June 1965], BGCA, CN 1, 5–32.

172. *Birmingham Post-Herald* (AP), 21 June 1965.

173. *Birmingham News*, 6 April 1965.

174. *New York Times*, 17 April 1965.

175. "Billy Graham in Alabama," 1965, BGCA, CN 113, F35.

176. Mitchell, *Saint or Sinner*, 299. Lewis F. Brabham, *A New Song in the South: The Story of the Billy Graham Greenville, S.C., Crusade* (Grand Rapids, Mich.: Zondervan, 1966), 145. Bob Jones, Jr., "The Position of Bob Jones University in Regard to the Proposed Billy Graham Crusade in Greenville," 8 February 1965, BGCA, CN 12, 13–13.

177. Graham to Ralph McGill, 12 March 1966, Emory University Special Collections, Ralph McGill Papers, 15–7.

178. *New York Times*, 23 April 1965.

179. V. O. Key famously used the phrase "way out" in reference to the politically Solid South. See Key, *Southern Politics in State and Nation* (New York: A. A. Knopf, 1949), 664.

CHAPTER 5. BILLY GRAHAM'S SOUTHERN STRATEGY

Note to epigraphs: "The Quiet Revolution," Great American Award presentation, 29 December 1967, Billy Graham Center Archives (BGCA), Collection 345 (CN 345), Box 43, Folder 3 (43–3). *Charlotte Observer*, 15 October 1971.

1. "The Quiet Revolution," BGCA, CN 345, 43–3. Graham Newsday, Inc., article in *Mattoon* (Ill.) *Journal-Gazette*, 12 January 1968, in BGCA, CN 360, Reel 31 (R31).

2. Quoted in Matthew D. Lassiter, *The Silent Majority: Suburban Politics in the Sunbelt South* (Princeton, N.J.: Princeton University Press, 2006), 236. "Address to the Nation on the War in Vietnam," 3 November 1969, Public Papers of President Nixon (PPPN), http//:www.nixonfoundation.org (accessed 20 February 2006).

3. Telephone messages, 15, 23, and 26 November 1960; and Graham to Nixon, 28 November 1960; all in National Archives and Records Administration (NARA), Pacific Region, Laguna Niguel (PRLN), Richard M. Nixon Pre-Presidential Papers (RNPP), Series 320 (S320), 299-"Graham, Billy" (299-G). The meeting was apparently the idea of Joseph Kennedy, the president-elect's father. Nancy Gibbs and Michael Duffy, *The Preacher and the Presidents: Billy Graham in the White House* (New York: Center Street, 2007), 107. Graham eventually met with Kennedy in January 1961. Through former Arkansas congressman Brooks Hays, Graham later invited Kennedy to attend a service at the 1962 Chicago crusade. The president politely declined. See Hays to Ralph Dungan, 30 March 1962; and Kenneth O'Donnell to Hays, 2 April 1962; both in John Fitzgerald Kennedy Library, White House Central Name Files, 1035-"Graham, B."

4. Graham to Nixon, 17 August 1974, Richard Nixon Presidential Library [RNL], Post Presidential Correspondence, 1974–1979, Billy Graham (PPBG), 1–2.

5. Nixon to Graham 15 January 1961; Graham to Nixon, 2 February 1961; Graham to Nixon, 17 May 1961; and Nixon to Graham, 17 August 1961; all in NARA, PRLN, RNPP, S320, 299-G.

6. Nixon to unnamed, 23 February 1962; Graham to Nixon, 12 March 1962; and Nixon to Graham, 18 June 1962; all in NARA, PRLN, RNPP, S320, 299-G.

7. Nixon, "A Nation's Faith in God," *Decision*, November 1962, 4.

8. Graham, *Just as I Am: The Autobiography of Billy Graham* (New York: HarperCollins, 1997), 443. *Los Angeles Times*, 26 July 1962, in BGCA, CN 360, R29.

9. Graham to Nixon, 11 November 1962, NARA, PRLN, RNPP, S320, 299-G. Nixon did not see this letter until January 1963.

10. *Houston Post* (AP), 14 November 1962, in BGCA, CN 360, R29.

11. Nixon to Graham, 13 September 1963; and Graham to Nixon, 21 October 1963;

both in RNL, Wilderness Years, Correspondence Files, 1963–1965 (WYCF), 1963–1965, 13-"Graham, Billy." See also the other contents of this folder.

12. Graham, "Billy Graham's Own Story: 'God Is My Witness,'" part III, *McCall's*, June 1964, 64. *Houston Press*, 28 October 1963; and *Arkansas Gazette*, 27 May 1964; both in BGCA, CN 360, R29.

13. "Billy's Apostles," *Newsweek*, 23 June 1969, 65. Nixon to Graham, 7 November 1963 and 30 December 1963, RNL, WYCF, 1963–1965, 13-"Graham, Billy."

14. Billy Graham, *Just as I Am*, 427. William Martin, *A Prophet with Honor: The Billy Graham Story* (New York: William Morrow, 1991), 315. On Hill, see Gerald S. Strober, *Graham: A Day in Billy's Life* (Garden City, N.Y.: Doubleday, 1976), 49; John Pollock, *Billy Graham: Evangelist to the World: An Authorized Biography of the Decisive Years* (New York: Harper and Row, 1979), 128; and *Los Angeles Times*, 14 August 1970, in BGCA, CN 360, R33.

15. *Atlanta Constitution* (AP), 16 October 1958.

16. AP, 16 August 1965, in BGCA, CN 360, R30; and *New York Times* (UPI), 16 August 1965. According to Taylor Branch, King used Graham's pronouncements as motivation for his visiting with residents of Watts. Branch, *At Canaan's Edge: America in the King Years, 1965–1968* (New York: Simon and Schuster, 2006), 294–297. Graham's response to Watts portended the popular interpretation of the riots as marking the disintegration of the classic, nonviolent phase of the civil rights movement.

17. *Charlotte News*, 17 August 1965; and *Dothan* (Ala.) *Eagle*, 4 August 1967 (reprinted in *Alabama Baptist*, 14 September 1967).

18. AP, 17 August 1965, in BGCA, CN 360, R30.

19. "The Risen Christ," BGCA, CN 191, Tape 742c (T742c).

20. "Solving Race Problems," *U.S. News and World Report*, 25 April 1966, in BGCA, CN 345, 46–3.

21. Graham, "False Prophets in the Church," *Christianity Today*, 19 January 1968, 3. See also Graham, "Social Injustice," *Hour of Decision* sermon (Minneapolis: BGEA, 1967).

22. *Alabama Baptist* (Religious News Service [RNS]), 12 October 1967, 1.

23. Graham, "Rioting or Righteousness," *Hour of Decision* sermon (Minneapolis: BGEA, 1967).

24. Graham to Johnson, 21 June 1968, Lyndon Johnson Presidential Library and Archives (LJPA), White House Central Files (WHCF), Name File (NF), 227a-"WHCF Name." *Dallas Times-Herald*, 14 January 1963, in BGCA, CN 360, R29. In 1969, Nixon named Warren Burger to replace Warren. Graham backed Connally's Texas gubernatorial candidacy when crusading in El Paso just before the 1962 election and later cited the incident as the only time he had ever endorsed a candidate. See, for example, *Lee Phillips Show* ("Noonbreak"), 15 September 1980, in BGCA, CN 74, Video 31.

25. Graham, "Rioting or Righteousness."

26. Nixon to Graham, 12 September 1966, RNL, WYCF, 1966–1968, 3-"Graham, Dr. Billy."

27. Graham to Nixon, 15 February 1965, RNL, WYCF, 1963–1965, 13-"Graham, Billy."

28. *Atlanta Constitution*, 30 December 1967; see also Atlanta press conference, 29 December 1967, T13.

29. Narrative written by Graham, undated [1976], RNL, PPBG, 1–1. While Graham recalled advising Nixon to run, his recounting does not include the use of providential language. Richard M. Nixon, *RN: The Memoirs of Richard Nixon* (New York: Grosset and Dunlap, 1978), 292–293.

30. *Good Housekeeping* article [1968] cited in undated narrative written by Graham [1976], RNL, PPBG, 1–1. See also Jonathan Aitken, *Nixon: A Life* (Washington, D.C.: Regnery, 1993), 346–347. Bebe Rebozo, perhaps Nixon's closest friend, and T. W. Wilson, Graham's chief aide, were also present at Key Biscayne. On Nixon's precampaigning, see Dan T. Carter, *The Politics of Rage: George Wallace, the Origins of the New Conservatism and the Transformation of American Politics*, 2nd edition (Baton Rouge: Louisiana State University Press, 2000), 325.

31. George Christian to Graham, 15 January 1968, LJPA, WHCF, CF, NF, 146-"GR." Johnson's later announcement that he would not seek reelection did not necessarily surprise Graham, to whom the president had much earlier confessed he might not run again, citing health concerns. See Graham interview, 12 October 1983, LJPA, http://www.lbjlib.utexas.edu/johnson/archives.hom/oralhistory.hom/Graham-B/Graham-B.PDF (accessed 20 February 2006).

32. Narrative written by Graham, undated [1976], RNL, PPBG, 1–1. Graham claimed that, at the time of the Key Biscayne conversation, Johnson had not explicitly told him he would not run.

33. Atlanta press conference transcript, 29 December 1967, BGCA, CN 24, 1–7. *Virginian-Pilot*, 7 May 1972, in BGCA, CN 360, R34. *Arkansas Gazette*, 30 November 1969, in BGCA, CN 360, R31. A 1960 biography of Graham described him as a registered Democrat who nonetheless appeared to favor Republican policies. See William G. McLoughlin, *Billy Graham: Revivalist in a Secular Age* (New York: Ronald Press, 1960), 96–97.

34. James Rowe to Johnson, 31 July 1968, LJPA, WHCF, NF, 227a-"WHCF Name."

35. Harry S. Dent, *The Prodigal South Returns to Power* (New York: John Wiley and Sons, 1978), 269.

36. *Philadelphia Inquirer* column published in *Acworth* (Ga.) *North Cobb News*, 6 June 1968, in BGCA, CN 360, R31.

37. Graham to Ronald Reagan, 10 October 1967, NARA, Ronald Reagan Library, Governor's Papers: Correspondence Unit. "Billy's Political Pitch," *Newsweek*, 10 June 1968, 62–63 (quoted on 63).

38. *Los Angeles Times*, 5 June 1968, in BGCA, CN 345, 45–6; and *Houston Tribune*, 13 June 1968, in BGCA, CN 360, R31.

39. *Biblical Recorder*, 15 June 1968, in BGCA, CN 360, R96.

40. *Nashville Banner* (AP), 27 May 1968, in BGCA, CN 360, R31. Deborah Hart Strober and Gerald S. Strober, *Billy Graham: An Oral and Narrative Biography* (San Francisco: Jossey-Bass, 2006), 88.

41. "Billy's Political Pitch," *Newsweek*, 10 June 1968, 62–63.

42. The term "southern strategy" retains much usefulness, provided that it is *not* (a) viewed as a static phenomenon that had the same meaning in 1968, 1970, 1972, or later; (b) interpreted in isolation from Nixon's many other electoral ambitions; or (c) seen as necessarily a successful enterprise. Nixon targeted the South for a number of evolving and not always complementary reasons, including fear of Reagan's challenge in 1968, concerns about the Wallace runs of 1968 and 1972, memories of lost opportunities during the 1960 election, displeasure with the Democratic Congress in 1970, and dreams about creating a long-term electoral majority.

43. Nadine Cohodas, *Strom Thurmond and the Politics of Southern Change* (New York: Simon and Schuster, 1993), 365; Dent, *Prodigal*, 77–84, 97; and Carter, *Rage*, 329–330.

44. *Charlotte* Observer, 18 August 1968. *Durham Herald* and *Lexington* (N.C.) *Dispatch* (UPI), 2 November 1968; both in BGCA, CN 360, R31. *Miami Herald*, 11 August 1968.

45. A Nixon staffer said that Graham merely wanted to get in touch with friends from Alabama at the convention. See *Arkansas Gazette*, 27 June 1970, in BGCA, CN 360, R33. Dennis Wainstock, *The Turning Point: The 1968 United States Presidential Campaign* (Jefferson, N.C.: McFarland, 1988), 107.

46. Lewis Chester et al., *An American Melodrama: The Presidential Campaign of 1968* (New York: Viking Press, 1969), 486. Jules Witcover, *The Resurrection of Richard Nixon* (New York: G. P. Putnam's Sons, 1970), 353. Graham, "Watergate," *Christianity Today*, 4 January 1974, 12. *Miami News*, 7 August 1968; and *Miami Herald*, 8 and 9 August 1968.

47. Graham, *Just as I Am*, 446.

48. "Religion and the '68 Candidates," *Christianity Today*, 19 July 1968, 47–49.

49. Graham, *Just as I Am*, 446–447. *Seattle Argos*, 23 August 1968, in BGCA, CN 360, R96. Miami *Herald*, 10 August 1968.

50. "Inside the Nixon Camp," *Newsweek*, 19 August 1968, 35; and "Billy: Out of Politics" (RNS story), *Christian Index*, 29 August 1968, 5; both in BGCA, CN 360, R96.

51. Kevin P. Phillips, *The Emerging Republican Majority* (New Rochelle, N.Y.: Arlington House, 1969), 206–207, 250.

52. Lassiter, *Silent Majority*, 232–241.

53. Nixon to Haldeman, 30 November 1970, BGCA, CN 74, 3–7 [original in NARA, Nixon Presidential Materials (NPM)].

54. In the cusp of the 1968 election, Graham said the presence of Wallace on the ballot did not factor into his belatedly announced support for Nixon—and that he had "no comment" on Wallace. See "The Election: Who Was for Whom," *Christianity Today*, 22 November 1968, 43, in BGCA, CN 360, R97. Earl and Merle Black, *The Rise of Southern Republicans* (Cambridge, Mass.: Harvard University Press, 2002), 210.

55. Campaign memos quoted in Joe McGinniss, *The Selling of the President 1968* (New York: Trident Press, 1969), 124, 238. The memo describing Graham as the "second most revered man in the South" did not indicate whether Wallace held first place. William

Safire, *Before the Fall: An Insider's View of the Pre-Watergate White House* (New York: Doubleday, 1975), 55–56. Nixon did allow that a "The Dick Nixon I Know" magazine piece by Graham might be acceptable.

56. *Atlanta Constitution* and *Toledo Blade*, 4 October 1968; both in BGCA, CN 360, R31.

57. *Hastings* (Neb.) *Tribune* (UPI), 4 November 1968; *Dallas News* (UPI), 5 November 1968; and *Anderson* (S.C.) *Daily Mail*, 12 November 1968; all in BGCA, CN 360, R31.

58. Graham, *Just as I Am*, 448.

59. Dan Carter has argued that Nixon was "disingenuous" in not conceding the racial implications of his political strategy. Carter, *Rage*, 327.

60. Hugh D. Graham and Numan V. Bartley, *Southern Politics and the Second Reconstruction* (Baltimore: Johns Hopkins University Press, 1975), 127.

61. Journalist and historian Wayne Greenshaw called Blount one of the "four or five people [who] more or less founded the modern-day Republican Party." See *Atlanta Journal*, 19 October 1988. *Washington Post*, 8 August 1979. William Walton interview, 9 May 1978, BGCA, CN 141, 14–28.

62. Grady Wilson to Mendel Rivers, 21 November 1952; and Wilson to Frank Boykin, 21 October 1952; both in BGCA, CN 544, 1–2. Charles Colson to John Connally, 24 June 1972, BGCA, CN 275, 9–11.

63. Kenneth L. Woodward, "The Preaching and the Power," *Newsweek*, 20 July 1970, 54.

64. Bob Faiss to Jim Jones, 10 September 1968, BGCA, CN 74, 3–6 (original in LJPA). Lyndon B. Johnson, *The Vantage Point: Perspectives of the Presidency, 1963–1969* (New York: Holt, Rhinehart, and Winston, 1971), 555. Robert Dallek, *Flawed Giant: Lyndon Johnson and His Times, 1961–1973* (New York: Oxford University Press, 1998), 578–580.

65. Graham to W. Thomas Johnson, 19 November 1969, LJPA, LBJ Archives, Post-Presidential Name File, 4-"Reverend Billy Graham."

66. Introduction of Richard Nixon, Pittsburgh, PA, 3 September 1968, BGCA, CN 345, 19–10. Lowell S. Streiker and Gerald S. Strober, *Religion and the New Majority: Billy Graham, Middle America, and the Politics of the 70s* (New York: Association Press, 1972), 68.

67. *Columbia* (S.C.) *Record* (AP photograph), 12 September 1968, in BGCA, CN 360, R31. Jane Schmerhorn, "On the Nixon Caravan, It's Bouquets for Pat," *Detroit News* magazine [Fall 1968], 17–18, in BGCA, CN 360, R96.

68. *Raleigh News and Observer*, 7 September 1968, in BGCA, CN 360, R31.

69. Lassiter, *Silent Majority*, 137, 233.

70. *Charlotte News*, 19 September 1968, in University of North Carolina at Charlotte Manuscript Special Collections, A. Grant Whitney Papers, 5–15.

71. Streiker and Strober, *Religion and the New Majority*, 68.

72. *Miami News* (AP), 21 October 1968, in BGCA, CN 360, R31.

73. Leonard Garment, *Crazy Rhythm: My Journey from Brooklyn, Jazz, and Wall Street to Nixon's White House, Watergate and Beyond . . .* (New York: Times Books, 1997), 134–136.

74. *Dallas Herald Times*, 31 October 1968, in BGCA CN 360, R31. Woodward, "The Preaching and the Power," 54. Martin, *Prophet*, 354. Graham also alluded to his vote for the Democratic gubernatorial candidate in North Carolina, Bob Scott. Scott's opponent was the North Carolina delegate who had unexpectedly switched his convention vote from Nixon to Reagan. See *Durham Herald* and *Lexington* (N.C.) *Dispatch* (UPI), 2 November 1968, in BGCA, CN 360, R31.

75. Phil Jane to Graham, 7 November 1968, BGCA, CN 15, 3–1.

76. McGinniss, *Selling*, 163. Nixon to John Pollock, 30 December 1986, RNL, PPSP, 1–4.

77. Johnson to Graham, 23 November 1968, LJPA, WHCF, NF, 227A-"WHCF Name." John Connally, *In History's Shadow: An American Odyssey* (New York: Hyperion, 1993), 231.

78. Graham, *Just as I Am*, 416.

79. "Evangelist Billy Graham's Inaugural Prayer," *Christian Patriot* clipping, March 1969; and letter to the editor, *Christian Century* clipping, 2 April 1969; both in BGCA, CN 360, R98.

80. Inaugural address, 20 January 1969, PPPN.

81. Richard V. Pierard and Robert D. Linder, *Civil Religion and the Presidency* (Grand Rapids, Mich.: Zondervan, 1988), 213.

82. "America's Great Crises," *Hour of Decision* sermon (Minneapolis: BGEA, 1957).

83. Charles P. Henderson Jr., *The Nixon Theology* (New York: Harper and Row, 1972), 12–13. Interview in David Frost, *Billy Graham Talks with David Frost* (Philadelphia: A. J. Holman, 1971), 35.

84. Curt Smith, *Long Time Gone: The Years of Turmoil Remembered* (South Bend, Ind.: Icarus Press, 1982), 41.

85. Reinhold Niebuhr, "The King's Chapel and the King's Court," *Christianity and Crisis*, 4 August 1969, 212.

86. Herschel Hobbs to Graham, 21 January 1969; and Hobbs to Nixon, 22 January and 28 February 1969; all in Southern Baptist Historical Library and Archives, Herschel Harold Hobbs Papers, 27–1.

87. Smith, *Long Time*, 50.

88. H. R. Haldeman, *The Haldeman Diaries: Inside the Nixon White House* [CD-ROM] (Santa Monica, Calif.: Sony Imagesoft, 1994), 31 January 1972.

89. *Alexander v. Holmes County* (Miss.) *Board of Education*, 396 U.S. 1218 (1969). Dent, *Prodigal*, 153–154; Garment, *Rhythm*, 215; Nixon, *Memoirs*, 443; and *Minneapolis Star*, 5 September 1970, in BGCA, CN 360, R33. Thomas Cookerly to Grady Wilson, 28 August 1970; Wilson to Cookerly, 16 October 1970; and Cookerly to G. David Gentling, 26 October 1970; all in BGCA, CN 544, 26–5. On Crutchfield, see Brian Ward, *Radio and the Struggle for Civil Rights in the South* (Gainesville: University Press of Florida, 2004), 222–234. Crutchfield recruited other celebrities, both black and white, to make similar spot announcements (349). "Graham Urges All to Obey School Integration Laws," *Covenant Companion*, undated clipping [Fall 1970], in BGCA, CN 360, R101. Wallace Henley, *The White House Mystique* (Old Tappan, N.J.: Fleming H. Revell, 1976), 25, 18.

90. Spots 1 and 2, "Interview & Short Spots w/ Billy Graham" [dated 10 September 1970, but recorded earlier in the month], NARA, NPM, White House Communications Agency Videotape Collection, VTR #3839. Nixon quoted in Nixon to Pollock, 30 December 1986, RNL, PPSP, 1–4.

91. *Orlando Star*, 12 September 1970, in BGCA, CN 360, R33. On Charlotte, see Lassiter, "The Suburban Origins of 'Color-Blind' Conservatism: Middle-Class Consciousness in the Charlotte Busing Crisis," *Journal of Urban History* 30 no. 4 (May 2004): 573.

92. Letter, Graham to Johnson, 3 January 1969, LJPA, WHCF, NF, 227A-"WHCF Name."

93. "Confidential Missionary Plan for Ending the Vietnam War" (submitted by Graham to Nixon), 15 April 1969; and letter (with enclosure), Graham to Kissinger, 28 December 1970; both in BGCA, CN 74, 3–7 (originals in NARA, NPM).

94. Graham, "A Clarification," *Christianity Today*, 19 January 1973, 36. White House conversation 1–14, 7 April 1971, NARA, NPM. See *New York Times*, 9 April 1971.

95. *Dick Cavett Show*, 5 May 1970, NARA, NPM, WHCA, VTR #3704.

96. Sermon text, 20 May 1972, BGCA, CN 17, 25–15.

97. White House conversation 24–33, 8 May 1972, NARA, NPM. See UPI, 22 May 1964, in BGCA, CN 360, R27; and RNS story, *The Christian* clipping, 12 June 1964, in BGCA, CN 360, R84.

98. Dwight Chapin to Haldeman 8 January 1973, BGCA, CN 74, 3–7 (original in NARA, NPM). In his foreign travels, Graham helped to communicate Nixon's policies to foreign leaders. For example, he took notes for Nixon on his meeting with Indian President Indira Gandhi and, in a striking performance as a proxy diplomat, explained Nixon's China policy to a concerned Generalissimo and Madame Chiang Kai-shek, who had asked Graham to visit them. Graham also accompanied Pat Nixon on an official visit to Liberia. Graham to Nixon, undated [1972], NARA, NPM, National Security Council Files (NSCF), NF, 816-"Dr. Billy Grahamm" [*sic*]. Haldeman to Kissinger, 11 and 19 November 1971 [with attached talking points], BGCA, CN 74, 3–7 (original in NARA, NPM). White House conversation 16–124, 10 December 1971, NARA, NPM.

99. Calvin Trillin, "Waiting for the Roses," *New Yorker*, 16 January 1971, 85–89. Haldeman, *Diaries*, 15 May 1971. The *Dick Cavett Show* had initially asked the White House for "a high Administration official" but was told that Graham was available. See Saul Braun, "Nearer, Silent Majority, to Thee," *Playboy*, February 1971, 199, in BGCA, CN 360, R102.

100. Robert Mason, *Richard Nixon and the Quest for a New Majority* (Chapel Hill: University of North Carolina Press, 2004), 77.

101. On Nixon's shifting political strategy, see Mason, *New Majority*, 88, 37–76; and Carter, *Rage*, 387.

102. Dent to Haldeman, 16 March 1970, NARA, NPM, White House Special Files (WHSF), Staff Member and Office Files (SMOF), Harry S. Dent (Dent), 8-"1970 Middle America [2 of 2]." Nixon to Haldeman, 9 February 1970, in Bruce Oudes, ed., *From: The*

President: Richard Nixon's Secret Files (New York: Harper and Row, 1989), 95. *Tennessean*, 1 February 1971, in BGCA, CN 318, 39–9. Graham recited Bible verses in a Cash song, titled "The Preacher Said, 'Jesus Said,'" in *Man in Black* (Columbia Records, House of Cash, 1971), in BGCA, CN 74.

103. For a Durkheimian interpretation of the Knoxville crusade, see Donald Clelland et al., "Conversion in a Billy Graham Crusade: Spontaneous Event or Ritual Performance?" *Sociological Quarterly* 16 (Spring 1975): 162–170. For an overview of Nixon's appearance in Knoxville, see Randall E. King, "When Worlds Collide: Politics, Religion, and Media at the 1970 East Tennessee Billy Graham Crusade," *Journal of Church and State* 39, no. 2 (Spring 1997): 273–295.

104. *Knoxville Journal*, 28 May 1970. Haldeman, *Diaries*, 25 May 1970. Graham quoted in *Knoxville Journal*, 22 May 1970.

105. *Knoxville News-Sentinel*, 29 May 1970; *New York Times*, 29 May 1970; Graham remarks, 28 May 1970, BGCA, CN 345, 28–12; and *Knoxville Journal*, 29 May 1970. Commentary in *Knoxville Journal*, 30 May 1970; and *Knoxville News-Sentinel*, 2 and 5 June 1970; both in BGCA, CN 360, R30. "Presidential I.O.U.," *Texas Methodist* clipping, 12 June 1970, in BGCA, CN 360, R101.

106. Garry Wills, "How Nixon Used the Media, Billy Graham, and the Good Lord to Rap with Students at Tennessee U," *Esquire*, September 1970, 119–122, 179–180.

107. CBS News, 28 May 1970, in BGCA, CN 74, V1. Undated phone message note [1970], BGCA, CN 17, 126–10.

108. *Nashville Banner*, 14 April 1970, in BGCA, CN 318, 30–16.

109. *Knoxville News-Sentinel*, 29 May 1970. See also Hall Gulliver and Reg Murphy, *The Southern Strategy* (New York: Scribner's, 1971), 122. Wesley Pippert, "Billy Graham: Prophet or Politician?" *Christian Life*, May 1971, 29, 54, in BGCA, CN 360, R102.

110. Baton Rouge press conference transcript, 19 October 1970, BGCA, CN 24, 1–27. Black Mountain, N.C., press conference transcript, 13 October 1970, CN 24, 1–26.

111. *Knoxville Journal*, 28 October 1970, in BGCA, CN 360, R33.

112. Lassiter, *Silent Majority*, 251–275; and Mason, "'I Was Going to Build a New Republican Majority and a New Majority': Richard Nixon as Party Leader, 1969–73," *Journal of American Studies* 39, no. 3 (2005): 473.

113. *New York Times*, 5 July 1970. Haldeman, *Diaries*, 12 May and 26 June 1970. On Hill, see Woodward, "The Preaching and the Power," 55; and Haldeman to Garment, 22 October 1969, NARA, NPM, WHCF, SF, RM, 20-"RM-3 . . . [69/70]."

114. John Osborne, "The Reverend Billy's Day," *New Republic* clipping, 30 October 1971, in BGCA, CN 360, R103. Handwritten notes, June 1971, in BGCA, CN 74, 3–5 (original in NARA, NPM).

115. *Charlotte Observer*, 1 November 1971, in BGCA, CN 360, R33.

116. *Charlotte Observer*, 15 and 16 October 1971. Charlotte *News*, 16 October 1971. *Charlotte Observer*, 8 June 1974, in BGCA, CN 360, R35. White House conversations, 11–141 and 11–148, 19 October 1971; and 11–163, 20 October 1971; all in NARA, NPM (quote in 11–163).

117. Staff Secretary to Herbert Klein, 17 July 1969; and Klein to Nixon, 18 July 1969; both in NARA, NPM, WHCF, Subject Files (SF), Religious Matters (RM), 1-"1–69/12–70."

118. Athens (Tenn.) *Post-Athenian* (AP), 2 November 1970, in BGCA, CN 360, R33.

119. Nixon and Haldeman conversation, 13 September 1971, in Stanley Kutler, ed., *Abuse of Power: The New Nixon Tapes* (New York: Free Press, 1997), 31–32.

120. White House conversation 16–124, 10 December 1971, NARA, NPM.

121. White House conversation 662–4, 1 February 1972, NARA, NPM. "Magazines in Jeopardy," *Time*, 10 January 1972, 43, in BGCA, CN 360, R104. Graham and Nixon continued to criticize *Time* in their postpresidential correspondence. Graham to Nixon, 18 August 1986; and Nixon to Graham, 2 September 1986; both in RNL, PPSP, 1–5.

122. On Meir, see Graham to Nixon, 20 September 1969, BGCA, CN 74, 3–7 (original in NARA, NPM). Arthur Gilbert, "Conversation with Billy Graham," *ADL Bulletin*, December 1967, 1–2, 8, in BGCA, CN 345, 45–1. Strober and Strober, *Billy Graham*, 91. Graham was especially close to Rabbi Marc Tanenbaum, director of interreligious affairs for the American Jewish Committee. See "Apostle to the Gentiles," *Newsweek*, 9 November 1970, 53, in BGCA, CN 360, R101.

123. White House conversation 662–4, 1 February 1972, NARA, NPM. Haldeman, *Diaries*, 4 December 1970, and 1 February 1972. See also Mason, *New Majority*, 130, 162.

124. White House conversation 662–4, 1 February 1972. Memo by Alexander Butterfield, 7 August 1972, RNL, Donated Nixon Documents, http://www.nixonlibrary.gov/virtuallibrary/documents/donated/080772_butterfield.pdf (accessed 25 July 2007). Haldeman, *Diaries*, 1 February 1972.

125. Nixon to Haldeman, 14 March 1972, in Oudes, *From*, 388.

126. Philadelphia press conference transcript, 7 June 1972, BGCA, CN 345, 62–1.

127. Talking papers, 15 February and 26 April 1972; both in BGCA, CN 74, 3–7 (original in NARA, NPM).

128. See Mason, *New Majority*.

129. Haldeman, *Diaries*, 14, 17, and 22 August 1972. Graham, *Just as I Am*, 417. White House conversation 22–160, 16 April 1972, NARA, NPM. Memo, L. Higby to Haldeman, 28 August 1972, RNL, Donated Nixon Documents, http://www.nixonlibrary.gov/virtuallibrary/documents/donated/082872_higby.pdf (accessed 25 July 2007). Memo by Alexander Butterfield, 7 August 1972, RNL, Donated Nixon Documents, http://www.nixonlibrary.gov/virtuallibrary/documents/donated/080772_butterfield.pdf (accessed 25 July 2007).

130. Nixon to Haldeman, 8 February 1971, in Oudes, *From*, 213.

131. Notes, undated [1971?], BGCA, CN 74, 3–7 (original in NARA, NPM).

132. Dent to Haldeman and John Ehrlichman, 3 February 1969, NARA, NPM, WHSF, SMOF, Dent, 8-"Southern GOP [3 of 3]." Phillips to Dent, 12 March 1970, NARA, NPM, WHSF, SMOF, Dent, 4-"1970s Memos to the President March–Dec." Poll data and "watch" in Carter, *Rage*, 369, 379.

133. Haldeman, *Diaries*, 19 June 1972.

134. Stephen Lesher, *George Wallace: American Populist* (Reading, Mass.: Addison-Wesley, 1994), 462.

135. *Birmingham News*, 22 May 1972. Haldeman, *Diaries*, 14 July 1972.

136. Haldeman, *Diaries*, 20 July 1972.

137. Carter, *Rage*, 449. Haldeman, *Diaries*, 26 September 1972.

138. Vernon McLellan, ed., *Billy Graham: A Tribute from Friends* (New York: Warner Books, 2002), 99–100. Helms to Bell; and Helms to Nat Cavalluzzi, 9 April 1968; both in BGCA, CN 318, 29–3.

139. Mason, *New Majority*, 161–191. Winton Blount interview, 10 July 1974, University of North Carolina at Chapel Hill, Southern Historical Collection, Southern Oral History Program, #4007, A-4 (Blount). "Remarks at Greensboro, North Carolina," 4 November 1972, PPPN.

140. *Greensboro Daily News*, 5 November 1972.

141. Marshall Frady, *Billy Graham: A Parable of American Righteousness* (Boston: Little, Brown, 1979), 266. Photographs of Jesse Helms visit [dated 1972], BGCA, CN 17.

142. *Winston-Salem* (N.C.) *Journal*, 3 October 1972, in BGCA, CN 360, R34.

143. Ernest B. Furgurson, *Hard Right: The Rise of Jesse Helms* (New York: Norton, 1986), 92–102.

144. In a 1988 letter to Nixon, Graham noted that he did not "always agree" with Helms. Still, he considered the senator to be intelligent and a good Christian. Graham to Nixon, 30 December 1988, RNL, Post Presidential Correspondence, Special People A–K, Graham, Billy and Ruth (PPSP), 1–4.

145. Haldeman, *Diaries*, 16 September 1972.

146. Nixon to Haldeman, 30 November 1970, BGCA, CN 74, 3–7 (original in NARA, NPM). The contents of this memo contradict the recent argument by Robert Mason that, for the 1972 campaign, the "consolidation and expansion of . . . Protestant support was not an element of the search for a new majority." However, Mason does note the role of Graham as Nixon's leading contact with Protestants. See Mason, *New Majority*, 151.

147. Haldeman, *Diaries*, 27 June 1972. Graham to Nixon, 4 August 1972; and enclosed *Los Angeles Times* review of *Religion and the New Majority*, undated; both in RNL, Donated Nixon Materials, http://www.nixonlibrary.gov/virtuallibrary/documents/donated/080472_graham.pdf (accessed on 25 July 2007).

148. James A. McIntosh to Dwight Chapin, 18 February 1969, NARA, NPM, WHCF, SF, RM, 1-"RM . . . 2-28-69."

149. Charles B. Wilkinson to Graham, 24 January 1969; and "Confidential and Private List of Suggested Protestant Clergymen to Be Invited for White House Services," 25 January 1969; both in BGCA, CN 74, 3–7 (original in NARA, NPM).

150. San Francisco press conference transcript, 7 September 1972, BGCA, CN 345, 62–1.

151. See, for example, Joan Hall to Charles Colson, 7 June 1972, NARA, NPM, WHSF, SMOF, Charles W. Colson, 113-"Southern Baptist Convention."

152. Neil Yates to Dwight Chapin, 29 July 1970, NARA, NPM, WHCF, SF, RM, 20-"RM-3 . . . [69/70]."

153. Attendance list, 15 March 1970, BGCA, CN 345, 47–3; and Garment to Graham, 4 May 1970, NARA, NPM, WHCF, SF, RM, 1-"RM . . . 1–69/12–70." Strober, *Graham*, 54. *Los Angeles Times*, 14 August 1970, in BGCA, CN 360, R33. Hill to Graham, 20 December 1969, BGCA, CN 345, 47–1.

154. White House conversation 560–3, 10 August 1971, NARA, NPM. Haldeman to Kissinger, 3 August 1971, BGCA, CN 74, 3–7 (original in NARA, NPM).

155. "Religious Leaders Briefed on Nixon's China Trip," *Biblical Recorder*, 21 August 1971, in BGCA, CN 360, R103.

156. "Washington Meeting, March 29, 1972," in BGCA, CN 74, 3–7 (original in NARA, NPM); Nixon to Haldeman, 14 March 1972, in Oudes, *From*, 388; and Bill Rhatican to Coleman Hicks, 29 March 1972, NARA, NPM, NSCF, NF, 816-"Grahamm [*sic*]."

157. Graham to Nixon, 3 April 1988, RNL, PPSP, 1–4; and 18 November 1981, RNL, PPSP, 1–6. Graham also used his influence to ease worries among conservative Protestants about the appointment of Henry Cabot Lodge Jr. as special envoy to the Vatican, recommending that Nixon invite SBC President Carl F. Bates to officiate at a White House church service. See Constance Stuart to George Bell, 23 July 1970, BGCA, CN 74, 3–7 (original in NARA, NPM).

158. Graham, *Just as I Am*, 452.

159. Graham to Garment, 18 May 1970, NARA, NPM, WHCF, SF, RM, 1-"RM . . . 1–69/12–70."

160. Colson hand-written notes, 27 June 1972, NARA, NPM, SMOF, Colson, 16-"Presidential Meeting Notes [1972–1973]."

161. Note [almost certainly Haldeman], 28 June 1972, BGCA, CN 74, 3–5 (original in NARA, NPM). Martin, *Prophet*, 398.

162. Dent to Nixon, 11 August 1972, NARA, NPM, WHCF, SF, RM, 2-"RM . . . 1–1–71/[12–72]."

163. *Shreveport* (La.) *Journal*, 19 February 1972, in BGCA, CN 360, R34; and *The Baptist Messenger*, 2 March 1972, in NARA, NPM, WHSF, SMOF, Colson, 113-"Southern Baptist Convention."

164. Martin, *Prophet*, 394–395; talking paper, 27 June 1972, BGCA, CN 74, 3–7 (original in NARA, NPM); and Haldeman, *Diaries*, 28 June, 11 July, and 24 July 1972. Bright's support for Nixon visit, "Woodstock," Dallas poll, and "silenced" in John G. Turner, *Bill Bright and Campus Crusade for Christ: The Renewal of Evangelicalism in Postwar America* (Chapel Hill: University of North Carolina Press, 2008), 140–144. The gathering was a likely reason for Graham's early assertion that his greatest assistance to Nixon in 1972 would be with the youth vote. See Haldeman, *Diaries*, 7 February 1971.

165. Henley, *White House Mystique*, 64–66. An October 1972 memo states that, while "CREP [more infamously abbreviated as CREEP] does not feel that at this time it is in the interest of the public good to *organize* clergy, by reason of their clerical profession, to participate in partisan political activity," support from individuals was most welcome.

John McClaughlin to Dave Parker, 5 October 1972, NARA, NPM, WHCF, SF, RM, 2-"1-1-71/[12–72]."

166. Haldeman to Ken Rietz, 26 July 1972, BGCA, CN 74, 3–7 (original in NARA, NPM). This memo was written after the meeting between youth leaders and Nixon workers.

167. Graham to Haldeman, 21 October 1972, BGCA, CN 74, 3–7 (original in NARA, NPM). Haldeman to Nixon, 19 August 1972, BGCA, CN 74, 3–5 (original in NARA, NPM).

168. "The Religious Campaign: Backing Their Man," *Christianity Today*, 27 October 1972, 38–39, in BGCA, CN 360, R106. Later, in an interview with the *San Diego Union*, Graham declared that he had cast an absentee ballot for Nixon. See *Greensboro Daily News* (AP), 2 November 1972. White House conversation 31–85, 16 October 1972, NARA, NPM.

169. Haldeman, *Diaries*, 26 February 1973.

CHAPTER 6. CRUSADING FOR THE SUNBELT SOUTH

Note to epigraphs: Dale S. Russakoff, "Billy Graham: He Walks, He Talks, He Sells Salvation," *Harvard Crimson*, 12 December 1973, http://www.thecrimson.com/printer-friendly.aspx?ref=107729 (accessed 5 March 2007). Pat Watters, "The South and the Nation," *New South*, Fall 1969, 28.

1. "Special Section: The South Today," *Time*, 27 September 1976, 30, 45, 55, 38, 86, and passim.

2. Marshall Frady, *Billy Graham: A Parable of American Righteousness* (Boston: Little, Brown, 1979), 45, 19, 28. Vernon Patterson interview, Billy Graham Center Archives (BGCA), Collection 141 (CN 141), Box 5, Folder 29 (5–29). Graham quoted in *Atlanta Journal and Constitution Magazine*, 9 October 1977. Frady to Don Bailey, undated [1974], BGCA, CN 345, 52–7. Peter Applebome, *Dixie Rising: How the South Is Shaping American Values, Politics, and Culture* (New York: Random House, 1996), 155.

3. Kevin P. Phillips, *The Emerging Republican Majority* (New Rochelle, N.Y.: Arlington House, 1969), 437–443. Kirkpatrick Sale, *Power Shift: The Rise of the Southern Rim and Its Challenge to the Eastern Establishment* (New York: Random House, 1975), 3–15.

4. James C. Cobb, *The Selling of the South: The Southern Crusade for Industrial Development, 1936–1990*, 2nd edition (Urbana: University of Illinois Press, 1993), 187. For additional scholarly treatments of the Sunbelt South, see Raymond A. Mohl, ed., *Searching for the Sunbelt: Historical Perspectives on a Region* (Knoxville: University of Tennessee Press, 1990); Cobb, *Selling*, 179–208; and especially Bruce J. Schulman, *From Cotton Belt to Sunbelt: Federal Policy, Economic Development, and the Transformation of the South, 1938–1980* (New York: Oxford University Press, 1991). Schulman noted that the Sunbelt concept only represented the most visible, prosperous portion of the South. See also Schulman, *The Seventies: The Great Shift in American Culture, Society, and Politics* (Cambridge, Mass.: Da Capo, 2002), 102–117. For a brief critique of the Sunbelt thesis, see C.

Vann Woodward, *Thinking Back: The Perils of Writing History* (Baton Rouge: Louisiana State University, 1986), 140.

5. Matthew D. Lassiter, *The Silent Majority: Suburban Politics in the Sunbelt South* (Princeton, N.J.: Princeton University Press, 2006), 11.

6. Sale, *Power Shift*, 13–14, 94–95 (quote on 14). Walker Percy interview, *New York Times*, 20 February 1977.

7. See, Lassiter, *Silent Majority*; and Kevin M. Kruse, *White Flight: Atlanta and the Making of Modern Conservatism* (Princeton, N.J.: Princeton University Press, 2005). Interestingly, two notable exceptions are works that apply the Sunbelt heuristic to Southern California. See Darren Dochuk, "From Bible Belt to Sunbelt: Plain Folk Religion and Grassroots Politics in the Conservative Southwest, 1940–1980" (Ph.D. dissertation, Notre Dame University, 2005); and Lisa McGirr, *Suburban Warriors: The Origins of the New American Right* (Princeton, N.J.: Princeton University Press, 2001).

8. AP photograph, 1 March 1962, in BGCA, CN 360, Reel 28 (R28). *Vallejo* (Calif.) *Times-Herald* (UPI), 8 February 1963, in BGCA, CN 360, R29.

9. Barry Farrell, "Billy in the Garden," *Life*, 4 July 1969, 2B. John Corry, "God, Country, and Billy Graham," *Harper's*, February 1969, 38. Reinhold Niebuhr, "The King's Chapel and the King's Court," *Christianity and Crisis*, 4 August 1969, 211.

10. Robert N. Bellah, "Civil Religion in America," *Daedalus* 96, no. 1 (Winter 1967): 1–21. See, for example, Joe E. Barnhart, *The Billy Graham Religion* (Philadelphia: Pilgrim Press, 1972), 14; and Charles P. Henderson Jr., *The Nixon Theology* (New York: Harper and Row, 1972), xi.

11. Eric J. Paddon, "Modern Mordecai: Billy Graham in the Political Arena, 1948–1980" (Ph.D. dissertation, Ohio University, 1999), 241.

12. Philip Roth, *Our Gang (Starring Tricky and His Friends)* (New York: Random House, 1971), 176–183.

13. Lassiter, *Silent Majority*, 225–275.

14. Will D. Campbell and James Y. Holloway, "An Open Letter to Dr. Billy Graham," *Katallagete*, Winter 1971, inside cover–3. For background, see Steven P. Miller, "From Politics to Reconciliation: *Katallagete*, Biblicism, and Southern Liberalism," *Journal of Southern Religion* 7 (2004), http://jsr.fsu.edu/Volume7/Millerarticle.htm (accessed 20 February 2006).

15. *Washington Post* (Religious News Service), 20 March 1971; and *Nashville Tennessean*, undated [March 1971]; both in University of Southern Mississippi Archives (USMA), Will Campbell Papers (WCP), 48–18. Graham to Campbell and Holloway, 6 April 1971, USMA, WCP, 4–1. Frady, *Parable*, 395.

16. *Atlanta Journal*, 29 January 1969. *Charlotte Observer*, 15 October 1971. Similarly, the *Arkansas Gazette*, a liberal newspaper that had treated Graham well in the past, became a persistent editorial critic of the evangelist starting in the late 1960s. See, for example, *Arkansas Gazette*, 17 January 1973, in BGCA, CN 360, R35.

17. *Charlotte News*, 15 October 1971.

18. Graham, "By the Foolishness of Preaching," *Hour of Decision* sermon, 13 June 1965, BGCA, CN 191, Tape 805c.

19. On notions of the New South, see Paul Gaston, *The New South Creed: A Study in Southern Mythmaking* (New York: Knopf, 1970).

20. See BGCA, CN 17, 7–7.

21. *Greenville News*, 11 March 1966.

22. William Martin, *A Prophet with Honor: The Billy Graham Story* (New York: William Morrow, 1991), 372. Wallace E. Johnson to Graham, 3 December 1963; D.W. Colvard to Graham, 15 October 1963; C.C. Humphreys to Graham, 17 October 1963; J. M. Lawson, Jr., to Graham, 13 December 1966; and R. Paul Caudill to Graham, 4 January 1967; all in BGCA, CN 345, 46–13.

23. Baton Rouge press conference transcript, 10 October 1970, BGCA, CN 24, 1–27.

24. Black Mountain, N.C., press conference transcript, 13 October 1970, BGCA, CN 24, 1–26.

25. Graham to Ralph McGill, 12 March 1966, Emory University Special Collections, Ralph McGill Papers, 15–7. "Statement . . . upon death of Ralph McGill," 4 February 1969, BGCA, CN 345, 45–8.

26. A rich historiographical tradition exists for viewing religious revivals not simply as secondary products of larger cultural and economic transformations but rather as active congealers of new social relations. Such a perspective, while not without risks, is useful for the historical setting at hand. In *A Shopkeeper's Millennium*, Paul Johnson analyzed Charles Finney's 1831 revival in what was then emerging as the evangelical heartland of the nation, Rochester, New York, where the revival "created a community of militant evangelicals that would remake society and politics." Their postmillennialist optimism, while at some level utopian, served on a temporal level to strengthen emerging capitalist structures. The initial targets of revival were the masters and manufacturers themselves, who in turn channeled their newfound behavioral restraints into workplace discipline. Johnson, to be sure, wrote about a society in which Christianity possessed a type of prescriptive authority not attainable following the "second disestablishment" of American religion during the interwar years of the twentieth century. Moreover, some reviewers have taken Johnson to task for seemingly reducing the significance of personal faith to social location. Paul E. Johnson, *A Shopkeeper's Millennium: Society and Revivals in Rochester, New York, 1815–1837* (New York: Hill and Wang, 1978), 102, 110, 136–141. For similar, if less class-focused, interpretations of other evangelists, see James F. Findlay, Jr., *Dwight Moody, American Evangelist, 1837–1899* (Chicago: University of Chicago Press, 1969); and Robert F. Martin, *Hero of the Heartland: Billy Sunday and the Transformation of American Society, 1862–1935* (Bloomington: Indiana University Press, 2002). On the "second disestablishment," see Robert T. Handy, *A Christian America: Protestant Hopes and Historical Realities*, 2nd edition (New York: Oxford University Press, 1984), 159–184. For an alternative to Johnson's approach, see Nathan O. Hatch, *The Democratization of American Christianity* (New Haven: Yale University Press, 1989), 220–226. Other historians have linked revivalism with challenges to social norms, such as opposition to slavery and support for gender equality. See Michael J. McClymond, "Issues and Explanations in the Study of North American Revivalism," in *Embodying the Spirit: New Perspectives on North American Revivalism*, ed. McClymond (Baltimore: Johns Hopkins University Press, 2004), 24–27.

27. Hubert F. Lee, "Billy Graham Presented 'Man of the South' Award By Wm. H. Barnhardt in Charlotte as 105,000 Watch," *Dixie Business*, Summer 1975, 8.

28. Charlotte press conference transcript, 14 April 1972, BGCA, CN 24, 1–36. *Charlotte Observer*, 12 September 1955, in BGCA, CN 1, 6–9. In the early 1960s, Graham urged federal and state funding to expand the interstate highway system in western North Carolina, arguing that doing so would enhance tourism. See excerpts, Grandfather Mountain, N.C., address, 5 August 1962, BGCA, CN 1, 6–9.

29. Atlanta press conference transcript, 14 December 1972, BGCA, CN 24, 2–12.

30. "Remarks of the President to Southern Regional Reception . . . ," 12 October 1972, National Archives and Records Administration (NARA), Nixon Presidential Materials (NPM), White House Special Files, Staff Member and Office Files, Patrick J. Buchanan 1969–72, 5-"Dent–1972."

31. For more on the 1964 rally, see Chapter 4. According to the *Birmingham News*, the All-America City award "brought with it the opportunity for a new image which [the city's] leaders have since made the most of." *Birmingham News*, 19 December 1971.

32. Arthur P. Cook to Melvin Bailey, 4 April 1964, BGCA, CN 17, 4–17. Cook to Albert Boutwell, 4 April 1964, Birmingham Public Library Archives (BPL), Albert Burton Boutwell Papers (ABBP), #264.10.34.

33. Invitation, 4 May 1964, BPL, Protestant Pastors' Union Papers, #911.2.30; and Walter Smyth to James S. Cantrell, 7 May 1965, BGCA, CN 17, 128–118.

34. Atlanta press conference transcript, 14 December 1972, BGCA, CN 24, 2–12. *Birmingham News*, 12 May 1972.

35. Stanley Mooneyham to Russ Reid, 12 October 1964; and Gilbert L. Guffin letters; all in BGCA, CN 17, 128–118.

36. Hill Ferguson to Graham, 5 May 1965; Denson N. Franklin to Jim McCormick, 25 May 1970; Grady Wilson to Smyth, 3 May 1968; Franklin to Wilson, 27 November 1967; M. E. Wiggins to Graham, 26 May 1970; Franklin et al. to Smyth, 7 August 1968; and Guffin to Smyth, 4 December 1969; all in BGCA CN 17, 128–118. *Portrait of Birmingham, Alabama* (Birmingham: Birmingham Centennial Corporation, 1971), 17.

37. Hill Ferguson to John Jemison, 4 May 1965, BGCA, CN 17, 128–118.

38. *Birmingham News*, 18 December 1971.

39. *Birmingham News*, 14 May 1972. Birmingham press conference transcript, 11 May 1972, BGEA, CN 24, 1–37. Mayoral proclamation, 14 May 1972, BGCA, CN 17, 128–122. On desegregation in Birmingham, see Glenn T. Eskew, *But for Birmingham: The Local and National Movements in the Civil Rights Struggle* (Chapel Hill: University of North Carolina Press, 1997), 326 and passim.

40. Eskew, *But for Birmingham*, 328; and J. Mills Thornton III, *Dividing Lines: Municipal Politics and the Struggle for Civil Rights in Montgomery, Birmingham, and Selma* (Tuscaloosa: University of Alabama Press, 2002), 514. On Birmingham's tense transition toward biracial politics, see Jimmie Lewis Franklin, *Back to Birmingham: Richard Arrington, Jr., and His Times* (Tuscaloosa: University of Alabama Press, 1989), 60–91.

41. *Birmingham News*, 22 May 1972. *Tuscaloosa News* and *Mobile Register* (AP), 12

May 1972; both in BGCA, CN 360, R34. Birmingham press conference transcript, 19 May 1972, BGCA, CN 24, 1–38. *Birmingham News*, 11 May 1972, in BGCA, CN 360, R34.

42. Survey of *Birmingham World*, April–June 1972.

43. *Birmingham News*, 20 May 1972, in BGCA, CN 360, R34. White House conversation 24–33, 8 May 1972, NARA, NPM. Birmingham press conference transcript, 11 May 1972, BGCA, CN 24, 1–37. Sermon text, 20 May 1972, BGCA, CN 17, 25–15. Graham's affirmation of Nixon's Vietnam policy contradicts biographer William Martin's contention that "Graham dealt with his confusion over Vietnam by refusing to comment on it during 1972." See Martin, *Prophet*, 422.

44. *Birmingham Post-Herald*, 17 May 1972, in BGCA, CN 360, R21. According to the *Post-Herald*, Graham's subsequent suggestion that biblical laws be applied specifically to matters of social justice garnered only "scattered applause."

45. *Gadsen* (Ala.) *Times*, 12 May 1972, in BGCA, CN 360, R34. *Birmingham Post-Herald*, 20 May 1972, in BGCA, CN 360, R34.

46. *Birmingham Post-Herald*, 16 May 1972. *Birmingham News*, 16 and 22 May 1972.

47. H. R. Haldeman, *The Haldeman Diaries: Inside the Nixon White House* [CD-ROM] (Santa Monica, Calif.: Sony Imagesoft, 1994), 19 June and 20 July 1972. On Wallace in the 1972 race, see Chapter 5.

48. *Birmingham Post-Herald*, 22 May 1972.

49. "Reaching Black America," *Decision*, August 1973, 10. A member of the Graham team explained the regional dynamics of crusade attendance: "Up North, the crusades have a higher percentage of persons responding to the invitation. . . . This is because in the South more churches preach evangelistic style sermons and make the altar call available more often." See *Birmingham News*, 23 May 1972, in BGCA, CN 360, R34.

50. Guffin to Smyth, 23 May 1972, BGCA, CN 17, 128–127. Jackson B. Bailey to Graham, 30 May 1972, BGCA, CN 17, 129–36.

51. Graham to George G. Seibels Jr., 20 March 1972, BGCA, CN 17, 128–122.

52. *Birmingham News* (AP), 30 May 1972.

53. *Florence* (S.C.) *News*, undated [late May 1972], in BGCA, CN 360, R34. "Springtime in Dixie," *Decision*, August 1972, 8.

54. *Birmingham Post-Herald*, 30 March 1964, in BGCA, CN 360, R29. *Birmingham News*, 31 December 1972. Donald A. Brown, "The Glow of a New Light," *Birmingham*, May 1972, in BGCA, CN 360, R104. On Birmingham's continued racial injustices, see Eskew, *But for Birmingham*, 325–340.

55. Frederick Allen, *Atlanta Rising: The Invention of an International City, 1946–1996* (Atlanta: Longstreet Press, 1996), 69, 112–138.

56. Atlanta press conference transcript, 5 November 1964, BGCA, CN 24, 4–15. Most observers have overlooked the Atlanta Team Office or not understood its significance. From 1964 to 1976, when the office moved to the BGEA headquarters in Minneapolis, Atlanta was the more important office in terms of Graham's daily work.

57. "Washington Meeting, March 29, 1972," BGCA, CN 74, 3–7 (original in NARA, NPM).

58. Tom Wolfe, *A Man in Full* (New York: Farrar, Straus and Giroux, 1998). *Atlanta Journal and Constitution*, 29 November 1998. Tom Barry, "Georgia's Most Respected CEO of 1995: Thomas G. Cousins," *Georgia Trend* (June 1995), http//:www.proquest.umi-.com (accessed 20 February 2006). *Atlanta Journal-Constitution*, 7 December 2006. See Floyd Hunter, *Community Power Structure: A Study of Decision Makers* (Chapel Hill: University of North Carolina Press, 1953).

59. Rolfe H. McCollister interview, 24 July 1977, BGCA, CN 141, 13–32. George Champion interview, 29 July 1979, BGCA, CN 141, 23–14. Roger Hull interview, 10 December 1970, BGCA, CN 141, 4–37. William B. Walton interview, 9 May 1978, BGCA, CN 141, 14–28.

60. Tom Cousins interview, 4 May 1990, BGCA, CN 141, 47–54.

61. *Atlanta Constitution*, 22 March 1973, in BGCA, CN 360, R35. Minutes, "Preliminary Meeting for Atlanta Crusade," 15 March 1972, BGCA, CN 345, 34–1.

62. Barry, "CEO."

63. Charles Rutheiser, *Imagineering Atlanta: The Politics of Place in the City of Dreams* (London: Verso, 1996), 171.

64. On Atlanta's shaky transition toward black political power, see Allen, *Rising*, 167–190.

65. Bill Schemmel, "Atlanta's 'Power Structure' Faces Life," *New South*, Spring 1972, 62–68.

66. Quoted in Kruse, *White Flight*, 236.

67. Cousins interviews, 4 May 1990, BGCA, CN 141, 47–54; and 25 May 1977, BGCA, CN 141, 3–6.

68. *Atlanta Constitution*, 22 March 1973, in BGCA, CN 360, R35.

69. "Preliminary Meeting," BGCA, CN 345, 34–1.

70. Cousins interview, 4 May 1990, BGCA, CN 141, 47–54.

71. *Atlanta Journal and Constitution Sunday Magazine*, 17 June 1973. Cousins interview, 25 May 1977, BGCA, CN 141, 3–6. Jimmy Carter to Georgia General Assembly, 15 June 1973, BGCA, CN 4, 18–17.

72. *Atlanta Journal and Constitution Sunday Magazine*, 17 June 1973.

73. *Atlanta Constitution*, 25 June 1973.

74. Atlanta press conference transcript, 14 December 1972, BGCA, CN 24, 2–12; and Atlanta press conference transcript, 25 June 1973, BGCA, CN 24, 3–8.

75. *Atlanta Journal*, 20 June 1973.

76. *Atlanta Constitution*, 14, 15, 18, and 20 June 1973.

77. *Atlanta Constitution*, 18 June 1973.

78. *Atlanta Daily World*, 19 June 1973.

79. Cousins interviews, 25 May 1977, BGCA, CN 141, 3–6; and 4 May 1990, BGCA, CN 141, 47–54. Executive board directory, January 1973, BGCA, CN 4, 16–3. No more than three out of the thirteen non-BGEA persons Cousins invited to a preliminary meeting were black. See "Preliminary Meeting for Atlanta Crusade," 15 March 1972, BGCA, CN 345, 34–1. In Birmingham, by comparison, the initial crusade executive committee

contained at least five black members out of a total of 34. See Article of Incorporation, Birmingham crusade, 10 November 1971, BGCA, CN 17, 25–3. Russakoff, "Billy Graham: He Walks, He Talks, He Sells Salvation."

80. Minutes, publicity committee, 28 March 1973, BGCA, CN 4, 18–8.

81. "Black Leaders of Atlanta," undated [1973]; and John H. Cox to black pastors; both in 11 June 1973, in BGCA, CN 4, 17–14.

82. Jimmy Carter to Harry Williams, 11 May 1973, BGCA, CN 4, 15–23.

83. Executive committee minutes, 16 May 1973, BGCA, CN 4, 18–23. Greater black participation was also a major concern at the Charlotte crusade, which preceded the Atlanta crusade by one month. See Norman Sanders to Williams and Larry Turner, 12 November 1971, BGCA, CN 4, 12–28.

84. *Atlanta Constitution*, 26 June 1973.

85. *Atlanta Journal*, 15 and 20 June 1973. Cousins interview, 4 May 1990, BGCA, CN 141, 47–54. *Atlanta Constitution*, 19 June 1973. Religious News Service (RNS), 22 June 1973, in BGCA, CN 345, 34–2. *Atlanta Inquirer*, 23 June 1965.

86. Williams comments in *Atlanta Journal*, 15 June 1973. News release from Citizens Concerned with Social Responsibilities of the Church in Baton Rouge, 19 October 1970, BGCA, CN 345, 29–18; and "A Plea for Peace and Social Justice," leaflet distributed on 25 October 1970, BGCA, CN 345, 29–19. Rose Mary Woods to Nixon, 16 June 1973, BGCA, CN 74, 3–7 (original in NARA, NPM). South African statement in Martin, *Prophet*, 412–413. Atlanta press conference transcript, 24 April 1973, BGCA, CN 24, 3–2. Edward E. Plowman, "Billy and the Blacks: Atlanta and Graham Revisited," *Christianity Today*, 20 July 1973, 40. *Today Show* interview with Barbara Walters, 27 April 1973, BGCA, CN 345, 68–1. *Beaumont* (Tex.) *Enterprise*, 14 March 1973, in BGCA, CN 360, R35.

87. *New York Times*, 6 May 1973. *Atlanta Constitution*, 13 June 1973. For more on Graham and Watergate, see Chapter 7.

88. *Rome* (Ga.) *News-Tribune*, 26 June 1973, in BGCA, CN 360, R35.

89. *Washington Post*, 29 June 1973.

90. *Atlanta Journal*, 25 June 1973. Cousins interview, 25 May 1977, BGCA, CN 141, 3–6.

91. *Dade City* (Fla.) *Banner* (UPI), 14 November 1972, in BGCA, CN 360, R35.

92. *Raleigh Times*, 20 September 1973, in BGCA, CN 360, R35. Martin, *Prophet*, 414.

93. *Grenada* (Miss.) *Sentinel-Star* (UPI), 26 April 1973; and *Asheville* (N.C.) *Times* (AP), 16 June 1973; both in BGCA, CN 360, R35.

94. Atlanta press conference transcript, 15 June 1973, BGCA, CN 24, 3–7.

95. *Atlanta Daily World*, 24 June 1973. *Atlanta Inquirer*, 23 June 1973.

96. *Atlanta Journal*, 19 June 1973. *Atlanta Constitution*, 25 June 1973.

97. *Atlanta Constitution*, 20 June 1973.

98. List of platform guests, 18–24 June 1973, BGCA, CN 4, 18–14. Plowman, "Billy and the Blacks," 40.

99. *Atlanta Journal*, 21 June 1973. Atlanta press conference transcript, 25 June 1973, BGCA, CN 24, 3–8. Cousins interview, 4 May 1990, BGCA, CN 141, 47–54.

100. Plowman, "Billy and the Blacks," 40. The total crusade attendance was 266,000. See "Glory in Georgia," *Decision*, September 1973, 14.

101. *Atlanta Constitution*, 23 June 1973. Atlanta press conference transcript, 25 June 1973, BGCA, CN 24, 3–8.

102. *Billy Graham and the Black Community* (Minneapolis: World Wide Productions, 1973), 36. See also *Raleigh Times*, 20 September 1973, in BGCA, CN 360, R35.

103. Cousins interviews, 25 May 1977, BGCA, CN 141, 3–6; and 4 May 1990, BGCA, CN 141, 44–54. *Atlanta Journal*, 20 June 1973, in BGCA, CN 360, R35.

104. Allen, *Rising*, 167–241.

105. U.S. Newswire, 2 December 2002, http//:www.proquest.umi.com (accessed 23 January 2006).

106. Quoted in Rutheiser, *Imagineering*, 3. Racial unity was a major theme when Graham returned to Atlanta in 1994. Then, as well, several high-profile black clergy did not support the effort. See *Atlanta Constitution*, 25 October 1994.

107. Vernon Patterson interview, May/July 1976, BGCA, CN 141, 5–29.

108. Russell Dilday interview, 5 March 1980, BGCA, CN 141, 11–10.

109. Luebke contrasted modernizers with "traditionalists," who held conservative moral and racial views, while resisting threats to the region's low-wage economy. See Paul Luebke, *Tarheel Politics 2000* (Chapel Hill: University of North Carolina Press, 1998), esp. vii–ix, 19–46.

110. See, for example, "Memphis: Liberty in the Liberty Bowl," *Decision*, September 1978, 7–9. James Gregg interview, 27 February 1979, BGCA, CN 141, 11–15. Rolfe H. McCollister interview, 24 July 1977, BGCA, CN 141, 13–32.

111. John Perkins interview (transcript of BGCA, CN 367, T2), 19 June 1987, http:// www.wheaton.edu/bgc/archives/trans/367t02.htm (accessed 6 March 2007). See also John Perkins, *With Justice for All* (Ventura, Calif.: Regal Books, 1982), 115.

112. *Memphis Commercial Appeal*, 3 March 1978; and *Fayetteville* (N.C.) *Observers* (UPI), 15 May 1978; both in BGCA, CN 360, R37.

113. Wayne Greenshaw, *Watch Out for George Wallace* (Englewood Cliffs, N.J.: Prentice-Hall, 1976), 246. Dan T. Carter, *The Politics of Rage: George Wallace, the Origins of the New Conservatism and the Transformation of American Politics*, 2nd edition (Baton Rouge: Louisiana State University Press, 2000), 462–463. In 1998, Franklin Graham stood in for his father (who was ill) in delivering the eulogy at Wallace's funeral. See *Atlanta Constitution* and *Washington Post*, 17 September 1998.

114. On the fate of the South-as-model theme, see Steven P. Miller, "Whither Southern Liberalism in the Post-Civil Rights Era? The Southern Regional Council and Its Peers, 1965–1972," *Georgia Historical Quarterly* 90, no. 4 (Winter 2006): 547–548.

115. Walker Percy, *The Last Gentleman* (New York: Farrar, Straus and Giroux, 1966), 177.

116. Lassiter writes of "white" or "suburban racial innocence" in *Silent Majority*, 304, 323, and passim.

117. On busing, see Mathew D. Lassiter, "The Suburban Origins of 'Color-blind'

Conservatism: Middle-Class Consciousness in the Charlotte Busing Crisis," *Journal of Urban History* 30, no. 4 (May 2004): 549–582. See also Lassiter, *Silent Majority*. On neo-conservatism and the New Right, see Jacquelyn Dowd Hall, "The Long Civil Rights Movement and the Political Uses of the Past," *Journal of American History* 91, no. 4 (March 2005): 1237–1238. On the *Brown* decision, see Raymond Wolters, *The Burden of Brown: Thirty Years of School Desegregation* (Knoxville: University of Tennessee Press, 1984). On the broader intellectual origins of color blindness, see Peter A. Kuryla, "The Integration of the American Mind: Intellectuals and the Creation of the Civil Rights Movement, 1944–1983" (Ph.D. dissertation, Vanderbilt University, 2006), 174–211. For an impassioned critique of "racial realist" scholarship, see Michael K. Brown et al., *White-washing Race: The Myth of a Color-Blind Society* (Berkeley: University of California Press, 2003), 1–33.

118. Billy Graham (with Kurt Singer), "A Southerner Changes His Mind," *Campus Life*, August/September 1970, 54, in BGCA, CN 360, R101.

119. *Newsweek* declared 1976, the same year as the *Time* special issue on the South, "The Year of the Evangelicals." See "Born Again!" *Newsweek*, 25 October 1976, 68–78.

CHAPTER 7. "BEFORE THE WATER GATE"

Note to epigraph: Richard Pierard, "Can Billy Graham Survive Richard Nixon?" *Reformed Journal*, April 1974, 7–13.

1. *New York Times*, 6 May 1973. William Martin, *A Prophet with Honor: The Billy Graham Story* (New York: William Morrow, 1991), 425. Graham said that his first exposure to the passage from Nehemiah came from a *New York Times* article by Harrison Salisbury. See Dallas press conference transcript, 14 June 1973, Billy Graham Center Archives (BGCA), Collection 24 (CN 24), Box 3, Folder 6 (3–6).

2. Susan Friend Harding, *The Book of Jerry Falwell: Fundamentalist Language and Politics* (Princeton, N.J.: Princeton University Press, 2000), 27–28. In Graham crusades, observed a skeptical journalist, "political slogans are spiritualized and depoliticized." As examples, the journalist cited "moral ecology" and "real peace through God." *Chicago Sun-Times*, 12 June 1971, in BGCA, CN 360, Reel 21 (R21).

3. Religious News Service (RNS), 27 September 1973, in BGCA, CN 345, 68–1; Graham, "The National Crisis," televised *Hour of Decision* sermon delivered on New Year's Eve, 1973 (Minneapolis: Billy Graham Evangelistic Association, 1974); Manhattan, Kan., press conference, 4 March 1974, BGCA, CN 24, T20; *Cleveland Press*, 13 April 1974, in BGCA, CN 360, R35; and *Atlanta Journal*, 14 June 1974, in BGCA, CN 360, R35.

4. This was not the first time Graham had turned a tragedy into a life metaphor that seemed to function as a political diversion. He did the same for the My Lai massacre in South Vietnam. "We have all had our Mylais in one way or another," Graham wrote in a 1971 *New York Times* op-ed, "perhaps not with guns, but we have hurt others with a thoughtless word, an arrogant act or a selfish deed." *New York Times*, 9 April 1971. Also

quoted in Nancy Gibbs and Michael Duffy, *The Preacher and the Presidents: Billy Graham in the White House* (New York: Center Street, 2007), 191.

Alhambra (Calif.) *Post-Advocate*, 2 November 1972, in BGCA, CN 360, R35. The most authoritative scholarly account of the Watergate affair is Stanley I. Kutler, *The Wars of Watergate: The Last Crisis of Richard Nixon* (New York: Knopf, 1990). For a cogent synthesis incorporating recent scholarship, see Keith W. Olson, *Watergate: The Presidential Scandal That Shook America* (Lawrence: University Press of Kansas, 2003).

5. White House Conversation 31–85, 16 October 1972, National Archives and Records Administration (NARA), Nixon Presidential Materials (NPM). Graham to H. R. Haldeman, 21 October 1972, BGCA, CN 74, 3–7 (original in NARA, NPM). Haldeman, *The Haldeman Diaries: Inside the Nixon White House* [CD-ROM] (Santa Monica, Calif.: Sony Imagesoft, 1994), 27 October 1972.

6. *Asheville* (N.C.) *Citizen* (AP), 1 May 1973.

7. Nixon and Ronald Ziegler, 28 April 1973, in Kutler, ed., *Abuse of Power: The New Nixon Tapes* (New York: Free Press, 1997), 353. The term "devotional" is used here in an evangelical Protestant sense (i.e., as a scripted, often anecdotal lesson to ponder and apply, rather than as a ritual to perform).

8. Graham team members were encouraged to seek additional publication of both the *New York Times* op-ed and the May 1 statement. See Arthur Mathews to Team Members, 8 May 1973, BGCA, CN 345, 68–1. *New York Times*, 6 May 1973.

9. *New York Times*, 29 May 1974.

10. *Cleveland Press*, 13 April 1974, in BGCA, CN 360, R35. Matthew 3:3 introduces John the Baptist by quoting Isaiah's prophecy concerning "the voice of one crying in the wilderness" (RSV).

11. "Watergate," *Christianity Today*, 4 January 1974, 14. *New York Times*, 29 May 1974. On "crisis," see *New York Times*, 6 May 1973; and Chapter 5. *Cleveland Press*, 13 April 1974, in BGCA, CN 360, R35. Nixon himself cynically attempted to place Watergate in the context of a lawless counterculture that had ennobled civil disobedience. See *Washington Post*, 16 August 1973.

12. Address to the Southern Newspapers Publishers Association, 16 September 1974, BGCA, CN 26, Tape 55.

13. "Watergate," 14, 9, 13. Martin, *Prophet*, 427. In his Senate testimony, John Mitchell said: "The most important thing to this country was the reelection of Richard Nixon. And I was not about to countenance anything that would stand in the way of that reelection." Quoted in Olson, *Watergate*, 89.

14. RNS, 27 September 1973, in BGCA, CN 345, 68–1.

15. *Atlanta Journal*, 14 June 1974, in BGCA, CN 360, R35.

16. *Raleigh News and Observer* (AP), 15 June 1973, in BGCA, CN 360, R35.

17. Graham to Nixon, 6 April 1973, NARA, NPM, White House Central Files (WHCF), 73-"EX FO8 4/1/73–4/30/73." Graham quoted the Living Bible, a colloquial American paraphrase of scripture. See also telephone conversation, Nixon and Graham, 30 April 1973, in Kutler, ed., *Abuse*, 384.

18. Lawrence M. Higby to Nixon, 2 May 1973, BGCA, CN 74, 3–5 (original in NARA, NPM).

19. Dallas press conference transcript, 14 June 1973, BGCA, CN 24, 3–6.

20. *New York Times*, 29 May 1974. Graham himself did not appear in the initial release of the White House transcripts. Nixon aide Charles Colson recalled his first response to seeing the phrase "expletive deleted" in the transcripts: "[Nixon's] dead in the Bible Belt." See Colson, *Born Again* (Old Tappan, N.J.: Chosen Books, 1976), 213.

21. Martin, *Prophet*, 431.

22. *Torrance* (Calif.) *South Bay Breeze*, 18 September 1974, in BGCA, CN 360, R35.

23. Address to the Southern Newspapers Publishers Association, 16 September 1974, BGCA, CN 26, T55.

24. Dennis P. Hollinger, *Individualism and Social Ethics: An Evangelical Syncretism* (Lanham, Md.: University Press of America, 1982), 109, 108. Hollinger's study is a valuable introduction to the post–World War II synergy between evangelical theology and an individual-centered perspective more commonly associated with the libertarian wing of conservatism.

25. Address to the Southern Newspapers Publishers Association, 16 September 1974, BGCA, CN 26, T55.

26. Many evangelicals less intimate with Nixon were much more critical of him. Likewise, members of the early New Right viewed Nixon as a traitor to the conservative cause, and future Christian Right spokesperson Pat Robertson blasted Nixon for having taken advantage of Graham to enhance his political image. See RNS, 12 August 1974 and 7 May 1974 (both in BGCA, CN 345, 68–1); and Richard A. Viguerie, *The New Right: We're Ready to Lead* (Falls Church, Va.: Viguerie Company, 1981), 50–64. Still, Graham's hesitancy to blame Nixon for Watergate and his equivalent lack of interest in legislative reforms were representative of mainstream evangelicalism. To be sure, a number of non-evangelicals (such as the Reform Jewish leader Rabbi Robert Kahn and even George McGovern) also employed Watergate as a synecdoche for larger social problems. See RNS, 21 September 1974 and 14 August 1974; both in BGCA, CN 345, 68–1. Their calls for national introspection did not, however, parallel Graham's call for a nationwide revival, nor did they focus on personal sins to the same extent as Graham.

27. Within the evangelical community, a small but vibrant group of "young evangelicals" arose during the late 1960s and early 1970s to challenge the type of social ethic described in this chapter. The younger generation often harkened back to the evangelical social activism of the nineteenth century. On the origins of the evangelical left, see Richard Quebedeaux, *The Young Evangelicals: Revolution in Orthodoxy* (New York: Harper and Row, 1974).

28. The classic proof texts for ordained authority are Romans 13:1 ("Let every person be subject to the governing authorities. For there is no authority except from God, and those that exist have been instituted by God" [RSV]) and, to a lesser extent, I Peter 2:13–14 ("Be subject for the Lord's sake to every human institution, whether it be to the emperor as supreme, or to governors as sent by him to punish those who do wrong and to praise those who do right" [RSV]).

29. Graham, "Watergate," 18.

30. *Village Voice*, 5 September 1974, in BGCA, CN 360, R35.

31. *Greenville News*, 10 August 1974, in BGCA, CN 360, R35. See also Barbara Walters interview, *Today Show*, 27 April 1973, in BGCA, CN 345, 68–1. Arthur Schlesinger, Jr., *The Imperial Presidency* (Boston: Houghton Mifflin, 1973).

32. See, for example, Kirkpatrick Sale, *Power Shift: The Rise of the Southern Rim and Its Challenge to the Eastern Establishment* (New York: Random House, 1975), 288–293; and Harry S. Dent, *The Prodigal South Returns to Power* (New York: John Wiley and Sons, 1978), 9.

33. Helms to Nixon, 4 May 1973, NARA, NPM, WHCF, 12-JL.

34. Sale, *Power Shift*, 90.

35. Ed King, Gary Rossington, and Ronnie Van Zant, "Sweet Home Alabama," *Second Helping* (MCA Records, 1974).

36. David Greenberg, *Nixon's Shadow: The History of an Image* (New York: Norton, 2003), 194.

37. Text in Alexander Haig to Nixon, 30 January 1974, NARA, NPM, WHCF, 60-"CF SP 3–162 Prayer Breakfast Remarks." See also Martin, *Prophet*, 429.

38. Graham to Nixon, 2 February 1974, in Bruce Oudes, ed., *From: The President: Richard Nixon's Secret Files* (New York: Harper and Row, 1989), 609–610.

39. RNS, 7 December and 28 April 1976; both in BGCA, CN 345, 68–1. See also Richard Quebedeaux, *The Worldly Evangelicals* (New York: Harper and Row, 1979), 104. *Spartanburg* (S.C.) *Herald*, 25 June 1973, in BGCA, CN 360, R35.

40. Jeb Magruder, *An American Life: One Man's Road to Watergate* (New York: Atheneum, 1974), 318.

41. Colson to Nixon, 21 November 1973, NARA, NPM, WHCF, 60-"CF SP 3–162." Wallace Henley, *The White House Mystique* (Old Tappan, N.J.: Fleming H. Revell, 1976), 38. Tom Phillips had given Colson a book about Lincoln's faith. Colson, *Born Again*, 182–183. Hatfield in Richard Pierard and Robert D. Linder, *Civil Religion and the Presidency* (Grand Rapids, Mich.: Zondervan, 1988), 229.

42. Colson, *Born Again*, 11, 108–117 and passim.

43. "Up at Harry's Place," *Time*, 11 July 1969, 15; and Dent interview, 2 March 1987, BGCA, CN 141, 47–74.

44. Harry S. Dent, *Cover Up: The Watergate in All of Us* (San Bernardino, Calif.: Here's Life, 1986), 44–45, 61, 26–27, 13–14, 105. Also like Graham, Dent cited the "water gate" of the Book of Nehemiah in calling for a "spiritual revival" (15). The Billy Graham Lay Center was founded partly to meet the spiritual needs of high-profile converts, such as Colson. See interview with Graham, *Christianity Today*, 18 November 1988, 23.

45. Another evangelical Watergate memoirist, Southern Baptist minister and former Cabinet Committee on Education press aide Wallace Henley, put more stress on the need for political reform that could peal away the veil from the "White House mystique." Yet his "greatest hope" was that Watergate would inspire in political leaders an "inner revolution—the kind wrought only by Christ." Henley, *White House Mystique*, 35.

46. Leon Friedman and William F. Levantrosser, eds., *Watergate and Afterward: The Legacy of Richard M. Nixon* (Westport, Conn.: Greenwood, 1992), 89. During the presidency of George W. Bush, Colson became an increasingly partisan spokesperson against secularism and judicial liberalism. See *Financial Times*, 17 August 2005; and *Florida Times Union*, 16 November 2005.

47. *Washington Post*, 22 August 1981; and Dent interview, 2 March 1987, BGCA, CN 141, 47–54. Dent's reconsideration of his racial politics preceded his faith recommitment.

48. RNS, 7 December 1976, in BGCA, CN 360, R33.

49. *Tampa Tribune* (UPI), 19 March 1975, in BGCA, CN 360, R35.

50. Colson, *Born Again*, 183.

51. In a 1977 interview, Graham said he did not believe Nixon had "yet been totally proven guilty." See *Charlotte Observer*, 8 February 1977.

52. Graham, *Just as I Am: The Autobiography of Billy Graham* (New York: HarperCollins, 1997), 468. Deborah Hart Strober and Gerald S. Strober, *Billy Graham: An Oral and Narrative Biography* (San Francisco: Jossey-Bass, 2006), 93. *Atlanta Constitution*, 10 August 1974, in BGCA, CN 360, R35. Phone call in Gibbs and Duffy, *Preacher and the Presidents*, 237–238.

53. Statement by Graham, 8 September 1974, BGCA, CN 345, 68–1.

54. Albert Wedemeyer to Graham, 18 April 1975; and Graham to Wedemeyer, 25 April 1975. Hoover Institution Archives, Albert Coady Wedemeyer Papers, 39–3.

55. Graham to Nixon, 3 July 1979, Richard Nixon Library (RNL), Post Presidential Correspondence, 1974–1979 Billy Graham (PPBG), 1–1. Martin, *Prophet*, 434, 696.

56. Graham to Nixon, 17 August 1974 and 15 March 1975; and *Albuquerque Tribune*, 18 March 1975; all in RNL, PPBG, 1–2. Graham to John Pollock, 30 December 1986, RNL, PPSP, 1–4. Graham, *Just as I Am*, 463–465. Ruth Graham, who arguably held more conservative political views than her husband, strongly shared his loyalty to Nixon. She speculated to Nixon that "you signed your political death warrant with the Alger Hiss–Whitaker Chambers case. . . . There are many, many of us who wish you were back in the saddle today." Ruth Graham to Nixon, 3 July 1979, RNL, PPBG, 1–1.

57. Pierard, "Can Billy Graham Survive Richard Nixon?" 7–13.

58. *Norfolk Virginian-Pilot*; and *Port Chester* (N.Y.) *Item*, 8 May 1973; both in BGCA, CN 360, R35.

59. A White House memo indicated that Haldeman relished the possibility of rowdiness and obscene signs among the Billy Graham Day protesters. See *Durham Sun* (AP), 2 August 1973, in BGCA, CN 360, R35. Several protesters filed an unsuccessful lawsuit claiming they had been denied admission to the rally because of their appearance. See *Charlotte News*, 12 September 1975, in BGCA, CN 360, R36. *Atlanta Journal*, 17 July 1974, in BGCA, CN 360, R35. On the origins of the IRS flap, see Chapter 5.

60. *Dallas Times Herald*, 13 June 1973, in BGCA, CN 360, R35.

61. *Albany* (Ga.) *Journal*, 24 May 1974, in BGCA, CN 360, R35.

62. Charles Crutchfield to Graham, 20 November and 7 December 1973; and transcript labeled "For Billy Graham interview 11/21/73"; all in Charles H. Crutchfield Papers,

Southern Historical Collection, University of North Carolina at Chapel Hill, 1-"Graham Papers." Crutchfield passed along the Thanksgiving statement, which was actually intended to bolster support for the president, to the White House. See Rose Mary Woods to unnamed [Nixon], undated [1973] BGCA, CN 74, 3–5 (original in NARA, NPM).

63. Graham to Nixon, 17 August 1974, RNL, PPBG, 1–2. In this letter, Graham enclosed a *Time* article explaining why he "had to be in Europe so long this summer." Graham himself claimed that Nixon did not field his repeated phone calls because the president was "protecting" him. Haldeman and Colson doubted the accuracy of this claim, although (when prompted by an interviewer) Nixon separately confirmed its basic assumption. See *Charlotte Observer*, 18 May 1975; Martin, *Prophet*, 430; and Graham to John Pollock, 30 December 1986, RNL, Post Presidential Correspondence, Special People A-K, Graham, Billy and Ruth (PPSP), 1–4.

64. *Alhambra* (Calif.) *Post-Advocate*, 2 November 1972, in BGCA, CN 360, R35.

65. *Atlanta Constitution*, 10 August 1974, in BGCA, CN 360, R35.

66. Quoted in Martin, *Prophet*, 393.

67. CBS Evening News, 8 August 1976, in BGCA, CN 74, V2.

68. For a somewhat similar take, see Eric J. Paddon, "Modern Mordecai: Billy Graham in the Political Arena, 1948–1980" (Ph.D. dissertation, Ohio University, 1999), 267.

69. "Support" in Graham to Gerald Ford, 17 August 1974, Gerald R. Ford Library (GFL), WHCF/IV, 9-"IV/1974/ST 46." Ford to Graham, 24 August 1974; and Warren S. Rustand to Graham, 25 October 1974; both in GFL, WHCF, NF, 1233-"Graham, Billy." *Charlotte Observer*, 18 May 1975.

70. "Anything" in Graham to Ford, 15 January 1976, GFL, WHCF/PR, 11-"PR 3 1/1/1976–3/31/1976. Jerry H. Jones to Bill Nicholson, 20 April 1976; and Graham to Ford, 10 September 1976; both in GFL, WHCF, NF, 1233-"Graham, Billy." Phone conversation in Gibbs and Duffy, *Preacher and the Presidents*, 250.

71. During the Michigan crusade service, Graham introduced Dole but did not permit him to speak. See *Jackson* (Mich.) *Citizen Patriot*; and *Washington* (D.C.) *Star*, 25 October 1976; both in BGCA, CN 360, R36. *New York Times*, 31 October 1976.

72. *Washington Post*, 23 September 1976. CBS Evening News, 22 September 1976, in BGCA, CN 74, V2. Starting in the summer of 1976, Ford sought to woo southern evangelical voters away from Carter. See Daniel Kenneth Williams, "From the Pews to the Polls: The Formation of a Southern Christian Right" (Ph.D. dissertation, Brown University, 2005), 159–160, 166–168.

73. William G. McLoughlin, *Billy Graham: Revivalist in a Secular Age* (New York: Ronald Press, 1960), 93.

74. Martin described Graham's politics as Republican-leaning, but he did not identify Graham as even a de facto Republican. See Martin, *Prophet*, 462–464 and passim. Paddon drew a similar conclusion. See Paddon, "Mordecai," 80. Martin E. Marty more directly termed Graham "a moderate Republican." See *Pittsburgh Post-Gazette*, 31 May 1993.

75. Martin, *Prophet*, 464–471. *Washington Post*, 8 December 1977. *Missoula* (Mont.)

Missoulian (AP), 9 July 1976, in BGCA, CN 360, R26. During Carter's first year in office, the BGEA also faced a brief, but intense, financial scandal that momentarily damaged Graham's reputation. That summer, the *Charlotte Observer* revealed the existence of a seemingly clandestine (but perfectly legal) nonprofit foundation established in the early 1970s and supported by funds channeled through the BGEA. Graham attributed his previous silence about the foundation, called the World Evangelism and Christian Education Fund (WECEF), to the need to avoid a deluge of public requests for donations. Still, its sizable assets ($22.9 million), along with the connection of relatives and peers of Graham to real estate purchased by the WECEF, raised momentary questions about the financial propriety of an evangelist long esteemed for his impeccable financial record. See Martin, *Prophet*, 464–471; and Graham, "Billy Graham on Financing Evangelism," *Christianity Today*, 26 August 1977, 18–20. The scandal broke during the summer of 1977, however— just *before* Carter's first publicized overtures to Graham.

76. See *Cedar Rapids* (Iowa) *Gazette*, 23 July 1975; and *Coos Bay* (Ore.) *World*, 29 July 1975; both in BGCA, CN 360, R36. Earlier request in 27 August 1973 note, BGCA, CN 17, 92–7.

77. *Pickens* (S.C.) *Sentinel*, 14 July 1976, in BGCA, CN 360, R36.

78. *Lake Wales* (Fla.) *Highlander* (AP), 20 September 1972, in BGCA, CN 360, R34.

79. *Atlanta Constitution*, 10 August 1974, in BGCA, CN 360, R35.

80. Graham, *Just as I Am*, 491.

81. *Menominee* (Mich.) *Herald-Leader* (AP), 9 March 1976, in BGCA, CN 360, R36.

82. "Graham: Undecided," *Christianity Today*, 10 September 1976, 65.

83. "Campaign Countdown: 'Bloc Busters,'" *Christianity Today*, 22 October 1976, 48. In a 1979 interview, Maxey Jarman recalled a conversation during which Graham criticized Carter's theology. See W. Maxey Jarman interview, 26 February 1979, BGCA, CN 141, 40–15. UPI story, 29 September 1976, in GFL, WHCF, NF, 1233-"Graham, Billy."

84. *Washington Post*, 3 October 1976 and 27 September 1976.

85. *Washington Post*, 8 January 1977, 17 September 1977, and 8 December 1977. Joseph L. Powell, Jr., to Christian Chinowith, undated [fall 1977]; Bob Maddox to Jimmy and Rosalynn Carter, 5 September 1979; and Anne Wexler and Maddox to Carter, 26 October 1979; both in Jimmy Carter Library (JCL), WHCF, NF, 1282- "Graham, Bi." Graham, *Just as I Am*, 494. In late 1977, Graham quietly donated $10,000 to Maranatha Baptist Church, which had split off from Carter's home Plains Baptist Church in large part over the latter's racial conservatism. Carter's cousin, Hugh, wrote to request a donation. See *Chattanooga News-Free Press* (UPI), 28 December 1977, in BGCA, CN 360, R26.

86. *Louisville Courier-Journal*, 17 June 1977, in BGCA, CN 544, 37–3.

87. Pierard and Linder, *Civil Religion and the Presidency*, 243.

EPILOGUE. BILLY GRAHAM AND AMERICAN CONSERVATISM

Note to epigraphs: Billy Graham service, "John 3:16," *Hour of Decision* broadcast, 21 November 1965, Billy Graham Center Archives (BGCA), Collection 191 (CN 191), Tape

828c (T828c). The quotation is taken, somewhat inexactly, from Rudyard Kipling's "If." George W. Bush, *A Charge to Keep* (New York: William Morrow, 1999), 136.

1. Genevieve Stuttaford, "PW Interviews: Billy Graham," *Publishers Weekly*, 20 June 1977, 10.

2. I employ the term "Christian Right" instead of the commonly employed "Religious Right" because the former entails a greater degree of sociological specificity and has proven unique and enduring enough not to require the modifier "New." A straightforward definition comes from political scientist Clyde Wilcox, who defines the Christian Right as "a social movement that attempts to mobilize evangelical Protestants and other orthodox Christians into conservative political action." See Clyde Wilcox, *Onward Christian Soldiers? The Religious Right in American Politics*, 3rd edition (Boulder, Colo.: Westview, 2006), 6. Christian Right is used in reference to such efforts from the late 1970s to the present, with due acknowledgment that the broader movement has outgrown its counterestablishment origins and developed into an organized wing of the Republican Party. In the process, aspects of the Christian Right's agenda have become less distinguishable from that of more moderate but politically conservative evangelicals. For other overviews of the origins of the Christian Right, see William Martin, *With God on Our Side: The Rise of the Religious Right in America* (New York: Broadway, 1996); and Ruth Murray Brown, *For a "Christian America": A History of the Religious Right* (Amherst, N.Y.: Prometheus, 2002).

3. Strawberry Saroyan, "Christianity, the Brand," *New York Times Magazine*, 16 April 2006, 48.

4. For the former, see William Martin, *A Prophet with Honor* (New York: William Morrow, 1991), 472; and Eric J. Paddon, "Modern Mordecai: Billy Graham in the Political Arena, 1948–1980" (Ph.D. dissertation, Ohio University, 1999), 279. For the latter, see John Meacham, "God, the Bushes, and Billy Graham," *Newsweek* online article, 11 April 2006, http://www.msnbc.msn.com/id/12271894/site/newsweek (accessed 3 April 2007); and Peter J. Boyer, "The Big Tent: Billy Graham, Franklin Graham, and the Transformation of American Evangelicalism," *New Yorker*, 22 August 2005, 42–55.

5. Daniel Kenneth Williams, "From the Pews to the Polls: The Formation of a Southern Christian Right" (Ph.D. dissertation, Brown University, 2005), 74–85 (quoted on 79).

6. Quoted in Billy Graham, "The Unfinished Dream," *Christianity Today*, 31 July 1970, 20–21, in BGCA, CN 360, Reel 101 (R101). See also *Washington Post*, 5 July 1970.

7. *Greensboro Daily News*, 17 October 1951, in BGCA, CN 360, R4.

8. Mark Toulouse calls this approach to Christian civic involvement "public Christian." See Toulouse, *God in Public: Four Ways American Christianity and Public Life Relate* (Louisville, Ky.: Westminster John Knox Press, 2006), 107–134.

9. Price Daniel, "God and the American Vision," *Christianity Today*, 23 June 1958, 13; also cited in Dennis P. Hollinger, *Individualism and Social Ethics: An Evangelical Syncretism* (Lanham, Md.: University Press of America, 1983), 182.

10. Dan Murph, *Texas Giant: The Life of Price Daniel* (Austin, Tex.: Eakin Press, 2002), 170.

11. Raleigh press conference transcript, 21 September 1973, BGCA, CN 24, 3–22.

12. *Jackson* (Miss.) *Clarion-Ledger*, 16 May 1975. *Richmond Times-Dispatch*, 24 July 1976, in BGCA, CN 360, R26.

13. Williams, "From the Pews to the Polls," 148–153. Rolfe H. McCollister interview, 24 July 1977, BGCA, CN 141, 13–32. Kenneth L. Woodward, "Politics from the Pulpit," *Newsweek*, 6 September 1976, 50–51.

14. *Jackson Daily News*, 12 May 1975. On Conlan's earlier aspirations for Graham, see Chapter 4. John Bolten, who had been involved in discussions about a Graham campaign for the White House in 1964, suggested that Conlan also wanted Graham to run in 1976. See Bolten to Lois Ferm, 4 August 1975, BGCA, CN 141, 9–3.

15. *Arizona Republic*, 5 April 1976, in BGCA, CN 360, R26. See also Jim Wallis and Wes Michaelson, "The Plan to Save America: A Disclosure of an Alarming Initiative by the Evangelical Far Right," *Sojourners*, April 1976, 4–12.

16. *Arizona Republic*, 3 September 1976, in BGCA, CN 360, R26

17. Helms to Grady Wilson, 14 January 1980, BGCA, CN 544, 49–2.

18. Martin, *With God on Our Side*, 198. *Fort Lauderdale News*, 1 February 1974, in BGCA, CN 360, R35. Dedication of Christian Broadcasting Network building, 6 October 1979, BGCA, CN 240, V1.

19. On gender and family concerns as the defining issues for the nascent Christian Right, see Brown, *For a "Christian America."* Jerome L. Himmelstein, *To the Right: The Transformation of American Conservatism* (Berkeley: University of California Press, 1990), 99.

20. On the gender-to-race theme in recent southern political culture, see Marjorie Julian Spruill, "'Women for God, Country, and Family': Religion, Politics, and Antifeminism in 1970s America" (unpublished paper in possession of author); and Paul Harvey, *Freedom's Coming: Religious Culture and the Shaping of the South from the Civil War Through the Civil Rights Era* (Chapel Hill: University of North Carolina Press, 2005), 218–250.

21. *Washington Post*, 24 March 1979. Graham allowed for health and rape exceptions on the matter of abortion, a stance that led an early antiabortion group to protest one of his crusades. See also Philadelphia press conference transcript, 7 June 1972, BGCA, CN 345, 62–1; and "Extra Messages," *Christianity Today* clipping, 17 July 1970, in BGCA, CN 360, R101. *Pittsburgh Post-Gazette*, 31 May 1993. *Charlotte Observer*, 7 February 1977.

22. Graham, "Jesus and the Liberated Woman," *Ladies' Home Journal*, December 1970, 40–44, 115. *Louisville Courier-Journal*, 17 June 1977, in BGCA, CN 544, 37–3. Ruth Graham served as an official sponsor of the Christian Action Council, founded in 1975. Martin, *With God on Our Side*, 156, 193–194. Religious News Service, 31 July 1976, in BGCA, CN 345, 68–8; and *Sherman* (Tex.) *Democrat* (UPI), 27 November 1975, in BGCA, CN 360, R36. In the immediate aftermath of the *Roe v. Wade* decision of 1973, conservative Protestants were relatively slow to mobilize against abortion. See Scott Flipse, "Below-the-Belt Politics: Protestant Evangelicals, Abortion, and the Foundation of the New Religious Right, 1960–75," in *The Conservative Sixties*, ed. David Farber and Jeff Roche (New York: Peter Lang, 2003), 127–141.

23. Address to the Southern Newspaper Publishers Association, 16 September 1974, BGCA, CN 26, T55. Black Mountain, N.C., press conference transcript, 13 October 1970, BGCA, CN 24, 1–26.

24. Martin, *With God on Our Side*, 205–206. Nancy Gibbs and Michael Duffy, *The Preacher and the Presidents: Billy Graham in the White House* (New York: Center Street, 2007), 260–261. According a recent biographer, Bright "convened" the Dallas meeting. See John G. Turner, *Bill Bright and Campus Crusade for Christ: The Renewal of Evangelicalism in Postwar America* (Chapel Hill: University of North Carolina Press, 2008), 189.

25. Carol Flake, *Redemptorama: Culture, Politics, and the New Evangelicalism* (New York: Anchor, 1984), 210.

26. *Washington Post*, 29 January 1981. On the Dallas meeting, see Martin, *With God on Our Side*, 214–218.

27. Woodward, "Politics from the Pulpit," 49. Wallis and Michaelson, "The Plan to Save America," 4–12. "Bright Future," *Christianity Today*, 24 September 1976, 56. Arthur H. Matthews, "Crusade for the White House: Skirmishes in a 'Holy War,'" *Christianity Today*, 19 November 1976, 50.

28. As Jerome Himmelstein has noted, the political impact of the Christian Right was more evident later in the 1980s than in 1980, when evangelical voters were no more likely than other voters to switch from Carter to Reagan. Himmelstein, *To the Right*, 120–124.

29. "Jerry Falwell's Troubles," *Newsweek*, 23 February 1981, 23. Kenneth L. Woodward, "The Split-Up Evangelicals," *Newsweek*, 26 April 1982, 91. See also *Fort Collins* (Colo.) *Coloradoan*, 15 November 1980, in BGCA, CN 360, R37.

30. *Washington Post*, 28 April 1986.

31. Joel Carpenter, ed., *The Early Billy Graham: Sermon and Revival Accounts* (New York: Garland, 1988), 23.

32. Quoted in Martin, *With God on Our Side*, 70.

33. Jerry Falwell, ed., *The Fundamentalist Phenomenon: The Resurgence of Conservative Christianity* (Garden City, N.Y.: Doubleday, 1981), 219, 222–223. According to a writer for *Christianity Today*, Falwell "balk[ed] at inviting Billy Graham to preach in his Lynchburg pulpit . . . because of Graham's association with religious 'liberals.'" See Tim Minnery, "The Man Behind the Mask: Bandit or Crusader?" *Christianity Today*, 4 September 1981, 28.

34. Woodward, "The Split-Up Evangelicals," 89, 91.

35. James Michael Beam, "'I Can't Play God Anymore,'" *McCall's*, January 1978, 154.

36. CBS Evening News, 29 March 1979, in BGCA, CN 74, V1. *Washington Post*, 29 June 1979.

37. Transcript of *Hour of Decision* sermon, 21 November 1965, BGCA, CN 345, 42–14. See *Lamont v. Postmaster General*, 381 U.S. 301 (1965).

38. Richard V. Pierard, "Billy Graham and Vietnam: From Cold Warrior to Peacemaker," *Christian Scholar's Review* 10 (1980): 38.

39. See, for example, Graham address, John F. Kennedy, Jr., Forum, 20 April 1982, http://ksgaccman.harvard.edu/iop/events_forum_video.asp?ID=770 (accessed 16 October 2006). Reagan to Graham, 5 October 1981, Ronald Reagan Library (RRL), WHORM: Subject File (WHORM: SF), ME001–03, ID #042394. "Press Statement by Dr. Billy Graham," 19 May 1982, Richard Nixon Library (RNL), Post Presidential Correspondence (PPC), 1–6. *Raleigh News and Observer*, 19 October 1979, in BGCA, CN 360, R37.

40. *Washington Post*, 29 June 1979. Frye Gaillard, "The Conversion of Billy Graham: How the Presidents' Preacher Learned to Start Worrying and Loathe the Bomb," *Progressive*, August 1982, 26–30.

41. *New York Times*, 3 January 1985.

42. Richard Nixon, *In the Arena: A Memoir of Victory, Defeat, and Renewal* (New York: Simon and Schuster, 1990), 90–91; and Graham, *Just as I Am: The Autobiography of Billy Graham* (New York: HarperCollins, 1997), 453. George H. W. Bush, *All the Best, George Bush: My Life in Letters and Other Writings* (New York: Scribner, 1999), 320.

43. *Washington Post*, 7 December 1980. George Harsch IV, "'Puff Graham': American Media, American Culture and the Creation of Billy Graham, 1949–1953" (Ph.D. dissertation, University of Southern Mississippi, 2005), 34.

44. Richard V. Pierard and Robert D. Linder, *Civil Religion and the Presidency* (Grand Rapids, Mich.: Zondervan, 1988), 271. Helene Von Damm, *Sincerely, Ronald Reagan* (New York: Berkley, 1980 [1976]), 89.

45. *Washington Post*, 29 January 1981.

46. Graham, *Just As I Am*, 529–530. ABC Evening News, 4 May 1980, in BGCA, CN 345, V9. WNBC newscast, 4 May 1980, in BGCA, CN 345, V10. Carter rally in *Anderson* (Ind.) *Herald*, 30 April 1980, in BGCA, CN 360, R37.

47. *Washington Post*, 4 August 1980. Graham received an invitation to pray at the 1980 Democratic convention but said that a scheduling conflict with a crusade in Alberta prevented his doing so. *Washington Post*, 1 August 1980.

48. Deborah Hart Strober and Gerald S. Strober, *Billy Graham: An Oral and Narrative Biography* (San Francisco: Jossey-Bass, 2006), 99.

49. See Graham to Reagan, 23 July 1981, RRL, WHORM: SF, ME001–03, ID #042394; Graham to Nancy Reagan, 20 August 1982, RRL, WHORM: SF, CO125, ID #097558; Graham to Reagan, 26 December 1983, RRL, WHORM: SF, CO034–02, ID #193966SS; Graham to Reagan, 17 December 1987, RRL, WHORM: SF, SO002, ID #537376; and Graham to Reagan, 8 February 1988, RRL, WHORM: SF, REo10, ID #563448.

50. *Washington Post*, 29 January 1981.

51. Graham to Nixon, 15 December 1980; RNL, PPC, "Special People," A–K, Graham Billy and Ruth [1990], 1–6.

52. Graham to Ed Meese, 23 February 1985, RRL, WHORM: SF, FG006–01, ID #297854.

53. Reagan to François Mitterand, 7 July 1986, RRL, WHORM: SF, TR163, ID #430849.

54. Reagan to Graham, 17 February 1981, RRL, WHORM: SF, FG001–03, ID #004680. Frederick J. Ryan to Faith Whittlesey and Ed Rollins, 27 June 1983, RRL, WHORM: SF, IV083, ID #139625. Ryan to Linda Chavez, 2 July 1985; and Ann Brock to Fred Ryan, 28 June 1985; both in RRL, WHORM: SF, IV085, ID #304533.

55. In 1988, Graham asked Reagan to sign the Williamsburg Charter, an interfaith and bipartisan statement affirming the First Amendment. The White House counsel feared that supporters of the charter might use it to attack the Christian Right. Correspondence tracking worksheet, undated [July 1988]; and Arthur B. Culvahouse, Jr., to Howard H. Barker, Jr., 7 March 1988; both in RRL, WHORM: SF, IV088, ID #557788CU.

56. Graham to Nixon, 15 December 1980, RNL, PPC, 1–6. Graham soon called to wish Haig well in office. See Alexander M. Haig, Jr., *Caveat: Realism, Reagan, and Foreign Policy* (New York: Macmillan, 1984), 69.

57. Graham to William Clark, 25 April 1983, RRL, Executive Secretariat, National Security Council: Records, System File, System II NSC casefile 8391492.

58. Strober and Strober, *Billy Graham*, 98.

59. Reagan to Graham, 5 October 1981, RRL, WHORM: SF, ME001–03, ID #042394.

60. William L. Stearman to William P. Clark, 10 February 1982, RRL, WHORM: SF, FO008, ID #048718SS.

61. James W. Nance to Reagan, 4 February 1982, RRL, WHORM: SF, FO008, ID #048718SS.

62. Note dated 16 February 1982, RRL, WHORM: SF, FO008, ID #048718SS. Correspondence tracking paper, 24 March 1982, RRL, WHORM: SF, FO008, ID #071277. Bush to Ambassador Arthur Hartman [April 1983], RRL, WHORM: SF, FO008, ID #075190. Martin, *Prophet*, 496–513.

63. *Washington Post*, 13 May 1982.

64. Martin, *Prophet*, 496–513. Reagan letter in Gibbs and Duffy, *Preacher and the Presidents*, 272.

65. Strober and Strober, *Billy Graham*, 97.

66. Graham to Reagan, 23 November 1987, RRL, WHORM: SF, CO165, ID #601483. On the disarmament treaty, see James T. Patterson, *Restless Giant: The United States from Watergate to* Bush v. Gore (New York: Oxford, 2005), 215.

67. Paul Kengor, *God and Ronald Reagan: A Spiritual Life* (New York: HarperCollins, 2004), 291–292.

68. *Washington Post*, 29 January 1981.

69. *Washington Post*, 7 December 1980.

70. Gibbs and Duffy, *Preacher and the Presidents*, 285–288, 293–296.

71. George Bush (with Doug Wead), *Man of Integrity* (Eugene, Ore.: Harvest House, 1988), 44–45.

72. Kim A. Lawson, "Republicans or Reaganites?" *Christianity Today*, 16 September 1988, 38–39.

73. Graham, *Just as I Am*, 584–587. Jim McGrath, ed., *Heartbeat: George Bush in His*

Own Words (New York: Scribner, 2001), 134–135. Graham to Nixon, 21 December 1989, NPL, PPC, 1–4.

74. "Graham's Inaugural Role Opposed," *Christian Century*, 20 January 1993, 48–49. Gibbs and Duffy, *Preacher and the Presidents*, 304.

75. "Graham's Inaugural Role Opposed," 49.

76. "Billy Graham to Lead Prayer at National Prayer Service for 55th Presidential Inauguration," PR Newswire Association, 19 January 2005 (accessed on Lexis-Nexis database, 13 January 2007).

77. Gibbs and Duffy, *Preacher and the Presidents*, 309. During the Clinton presidency, Graham conveyed to North Korean leader Kim Il Sung (who admired Graham) a goodwill message from the White House—something the evangelist had also done for President George H. W. Bush. Gibbs and Duffy, *Preacher and the Presidents*, 311–313.

78. *Buffalo News*, 11 March 1998. *New York Daily News*, 7 March 1998.

79. *New York Times*, 17 March 1998.

80. *Sun* (London), 9 September 1998. Gibbs and Duffy, *Preacher and the Presidents*, 321.

81. Graham to Nixon, 18 August 1986, RNL, PPSP, 1–5.

82. George H. W. Bush, *Man of Integrity*, 45–46. Bill Minutaglio, *First Son: George W. Bush and the Bush Family Dynasty* (New York: Times Books, 1999), 220.

83. George W. Bush, *A Charge to Keep*, 136.

84. Gibbs and Duffy, *Preacher and the Presidents*, 330.

85. Minutaglio, *First Son*, 219.

86. *Ottawa Citizen*, 20 June 1998. Richards actually attempted to turn an anecdote involving Graham against her challenger. Once, during the first Bush presidency, George W. Bush had asserted to his mother that only avowed Christians could go to heaven. The skeptical first lady promptly phoned Graham, who affirmed her son's basic perspective, yet cautioned them both against trying to "play God." Richards used the published story in an appeal to potential Jewish donors. See Minutaglio, *First Son*, 288–289. Molly Ivins and Lou Dubose, *Shrub: The Short but Happy Political Life of George W. Bush* (New York: Vintage, 2000), 58–59.

87. Kevin Phillips makes a similar observation in *American Dynasty: Aristocracy, Fortune, and the Politics of Deceit in the House of Bush* (New York: Viking, 2004), 88.

88. Quoted in Fred Barnes, "The Gospel According to Billy Graham," *Weekly Standard*, 22 March 1999 (accessed on Lexis-Nexis database, 11 October 2006). See also *Houston Chronicle*, 7 March 1999.

89. See Marvin N. Olasky, *Compassionate Conservatism: What It Is, What It Does, and How It Can Transform America* (New York: Free Press, 2000).

90. Elizabeth Mitchell, *W: Revenge of the Bush Dynasty* (New York: Hyperion, 2000), 331.

91. *New York Times*, 21 February 2000.

92. *New York Times*, 23 January 2000.

93. Gibbs and Duffy, *Preacher and the Presidents*, 335–336.

94. Prayer breakfast in *Atlanta Constitution*, 6 November 2000; *Florida Time-Union*, 6 November 2000; and *Boston Herald*, 6 November 2000. Background details in *Florida Times-Union*, 3, 4, and 5 November 2000; *The Observer*, 5 November 2000; *St. Petersburg Times*, 6 November 2005.

95. "Statement by the Rev. Billy Graham Supporting George W. Bush," 6 November 2000, http://www.cnsnews.com/Politics/Archive/200011/POL20001106c.html (accessed 7 July 2008).

96. Paul Kengor, *God and George W. Bush: A Spiritual Life* (New York: ReganBooks, 2004), 78–79.

97. "Billy Graham to Lead Prayer," PR Newswire Association, 19 January 2005 (accessed on Lexis-Nexis database, 13 January 2007). "Billy Graham's Message, National Day of Prayer and Remembrance, National Cathedral, Washington, D. C., Friday, September 14, 2001," http://www.cathedral.org/cathedral/worship/bg010914.html (accessed 25 September 2006).

98. *New York Times*, 30 June 2008.

99. Flake, *Redemptorama*, 273. Graham address, John F. Kennedy, Jr., Forum, 20 April 1982.

100. Boyer, "The Big Tent," passim. *New York Times*, 16 April 2006.

101. Franklin Graham, who drew criticism for his post-9/11 description of Islam as "a very evil and wicked religion," later blasted the "attempt by the secularists to take Jesus Christ and take God out of every aspect of our society." See *New York Times*, 20 November 2001; and *Chicago Sun-Times*, 26 August 2005.

102. *Jeopardy!* 5 January 2006, show 4909, game 22064.

103. *Mobile Register* (AP), 1 June 2007; *Raleigh News and Observer*, 1 June 2007; and *Washington Post*, 15 June 2007 (all accessed in Lexis-Nexis database, 25 July 2007). *New York Times*, 10 November 2007.

ARCHIVAL AND MANUSCRIPT SOURCES

Alabama Department of Archives and History. Montgomery, Ala.
   George Wallace Administrative Records
University of Arkansas Special Collections. Fayetteville, Ark.
   Arkansas Council on Human Relations Records
Auburn University Special Collections. Auburn, Ala.
   Alabama Republican Party Records
Billy Graham Center Archives. Wheaton College. Wheaton, Ill.
Birmingham Public Library Archives. Birmingham, Ala.
   Albert Burton Boutwell Papers
   Protestant Pastors' Union Papers
College of Charleston Special Collections. Charleston, S.C.
   Mendel Rivers Papers
Congressional and Political Research Center. Mississippi State University Libraries
   John C. Stennis Collection
Drew University Special Collections. Madison, N.J.
   Bela Kornitzer Collection
Dwight D. Eisenhower Library. Abilene, Kans.
   Eisenhower Presidential Materials
Emory University Special Collections. Atlanta, Ga.
   Ralph McGill Papers
Gerald R. Ford Library. Ann Arbor, Mich.
Hoover Institution Archives. Stanford University. Stanford, Calif.
   Albert Wedemeyer Papers
   Alfred Kohlberg Papers
   Walter Judd Papers
Jimmy Carter Library. Atlanta, Ga.
John Fitzgerald Kennedy Library. Boston, Mass.
Lyndon Baines Johnson Library. Austin, Tex.
National Archives and Records Administration II. College Park, Md.
   Richard Nixon Presidential Materials
   United States Information Agency Records

National Archives and Records Administration, Pacific Region. Laguna Niguel, Calif.
    Richard M. Nixon Pre-Presidential Papers
University of North Carolina at Charlotte Manuscript Special Collections. Charlotte,
    N.C.
    A. Grant Whitney Papers
Richard Nixon Library. Yorba Linda, Calif.
Ronald Reagan Library. Simi Valley, Calif.
Sam Houston Regional Library and Research Center. Liberty, Tex.
    U.S. Senator Price Daniel Papers
Southern Baptist Historical Library and Archives. Nashville, Tenn.
    Fred Burnett Rhodes Papers
    Christian Life Commission Minutes and Reports
    H. H. Hobbs Papers
Southern Historical Collection. University of North Carolina at Chapel Hill
    Charles H. Crutchfield Papers
    Luther Hodges Collection
    Southern Oral History Program interviews
    Taylor Branch Papers
University of Southern Mississippi Archives. Hattiesburg, Miss.
    Will D. Campbell Papers
Tennessee State Library and Archives. Nashville, Tenn.
    Frank Goad Clement Papers
University of Washington Libraries Special Collections. Seattle, Wash.
    Arthur B. Langlie Papers
College of William and Mary Special Collections. Williamsburg, Va.
    A. Willis Robertson Papers

INDEX

ACKNOWLEDGMENTS

I START BY THANKING Joseph Crespino and Grant Wacker, both of whom read a late draft of the manuscript. Their feedback, delivered in a spirit of incisiveness and openness, helped me to sharpen my arguments and better appreciate their significance (along with, of course, their limits). Other persons who at some point in the process read all or portions of the manuscript, or who offered words of encouragement, include David Chappell, Devin Fergus, Kathleen Flake, Rebecca Gaff, Paul Harvey, Kevin Kruse, Matt Lassiter, Michael Long, Lisa McGirr, Mark Noll, Marjorie Spruill, John Turner, and Stephen Whitfield. I have greatly valued my conversations with many fellow historians of the American South, American religion, or both. Among them are Debi Back, Nicholas Beasley, Tim Boyd, Darren Dochuk, Bob Hutton, Patrick Jackson, Richard King, Miles Mullin, LeeAnn Reynolds, Dan Williams, Ben Wise, and Ann Ziker. Several mentors and colleagues from my time at Vanderbilt deserve specific mention. Don Doyle was always very supportive, and I fondly recall Dennis Dickerson's seminar on religion and the civil rights movement. David Carlton's casual reference to a Graham crusade in Greenville, S.C., sparked my initial interest in the evangelist. Peter Kuryla is a tremendous intellectual companion and a stellar close reader. I may have unintentionally slighted other scholars. If you think this is the case, flag me down at a conference, and I will gladly buy you a coffee or a cold one.

Archivists and librarians are a historian's lifelines. The good folks at the Billy Graham Center Archives were very helpful from the start. Essential assistance also came from staffers at the Nixon Presidential Materials, Nixon Library, Reagan Library, Eisenhower Presidential Library, Southern Historical Collection, College of William and Mary Special Collections, Drew University Special Collections, Mississippi State University Libraries, Sam Houston Regional Library and Research Center, Hoover Institution Archives, and other collections too numerous to name. Several archivists (notably, Linda Whitaker at the Arizona Historical Foundation) very nobly traced inquiries that must have seemed tangential, to say the least. Sam Hodges at the *Dallas Morning News* graciously passed along materials he had compiled about the ever-interesting Frank Boykin. The interlibrary loan staffs at Webster and Vanderbilt universities tracked down the most obscure of requests.

A portion of the epilogue appeared in the following publication and is used by permission of Westminster John Knox Press: "Above Politics? Graham After Watergate," in *The Legacy of Billy Graham: Critical Reflections on America's Greatest Evangelist*, ed. Michael G. Long (Louisville: Westminster John Knox Press, 2008), 179–194. Brief portions of the manuscript also appeared in "Billy Graham, Civil Rights, and the Changing Postwar South," in *Politics and Religion in the White South*, ed. Glenn Feldman (Lexington: University Press of Kentucky, 2005), 157–186; and " 'Another Kind of March': Billy Graham in Civil Rights-Era Alabama," *Alabama Heritage*, Winter 2007, 41–48.

The University of Pennsylvania Press has been a wonderful place to publish my first book. My series editor, Michael Kazin, has an uncanny knack for sizing up the merits and vulnerabilities of the claims we historians are fond of making. I gladly join the chorus of Penn Press authors singing the praises of history editor Robert Lockhart, who probably spent more time on this project than he ever imagined possible. My writing, grasp of the publishing process, and general scholarly maturity are all the better for him.

I am blessed with a loving and supportive family. My parents, Richard and Fannie Miller, have always endorsed my scholarly pursuits. I could not ask for better in-laws than Doug and Rebecca Gaff. This book is dedicated to Clarissa P. Gaff, my wife, friend, conscience, and endless source of love, support, and joy.